Shojo Beat

# Natsume's BOOK of FRIENDS

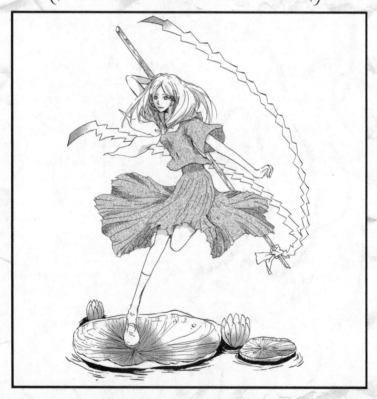

STORY and ART by
**Yuki Midorikawa**

VOLUME **9**

# Natsume's BOOK of FRIENDS

## VOLUME 9 CONTENTS

chapter 32 —— 5

chapter 33 —— 39

chapter 34 —— 71

chapter 35 —— 103

chapter 36 —— 135

Special Episode 9
Natsume Observation Log,
Part 5
————— 167

Afterword —— 183

End Notes —— 189

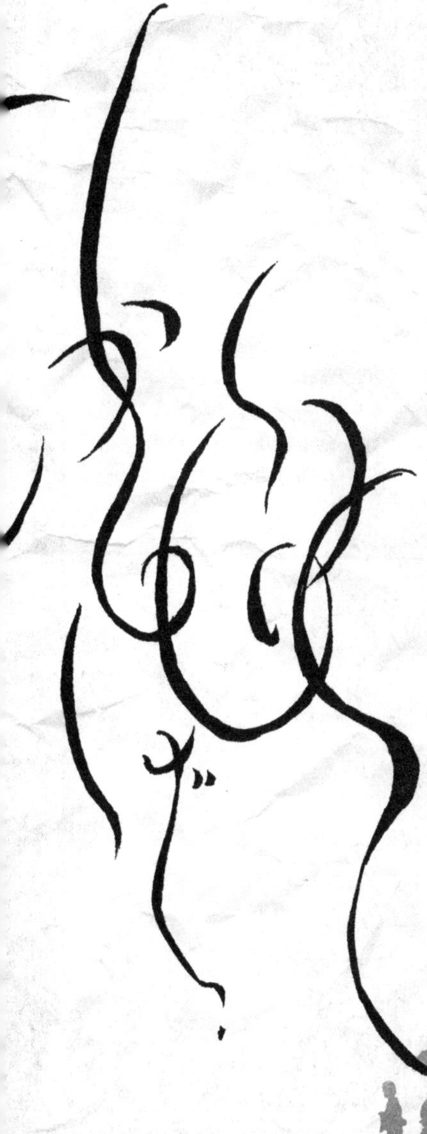

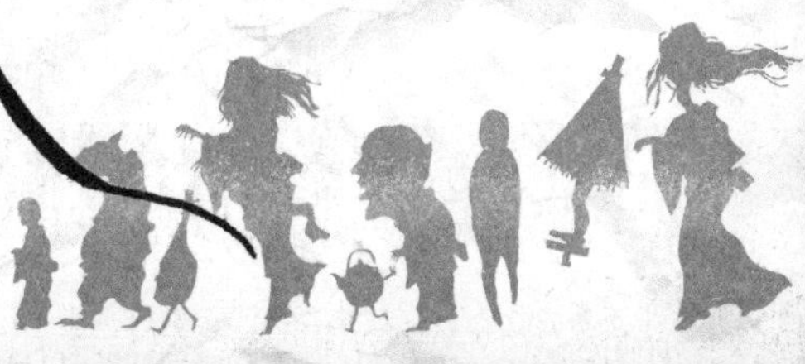

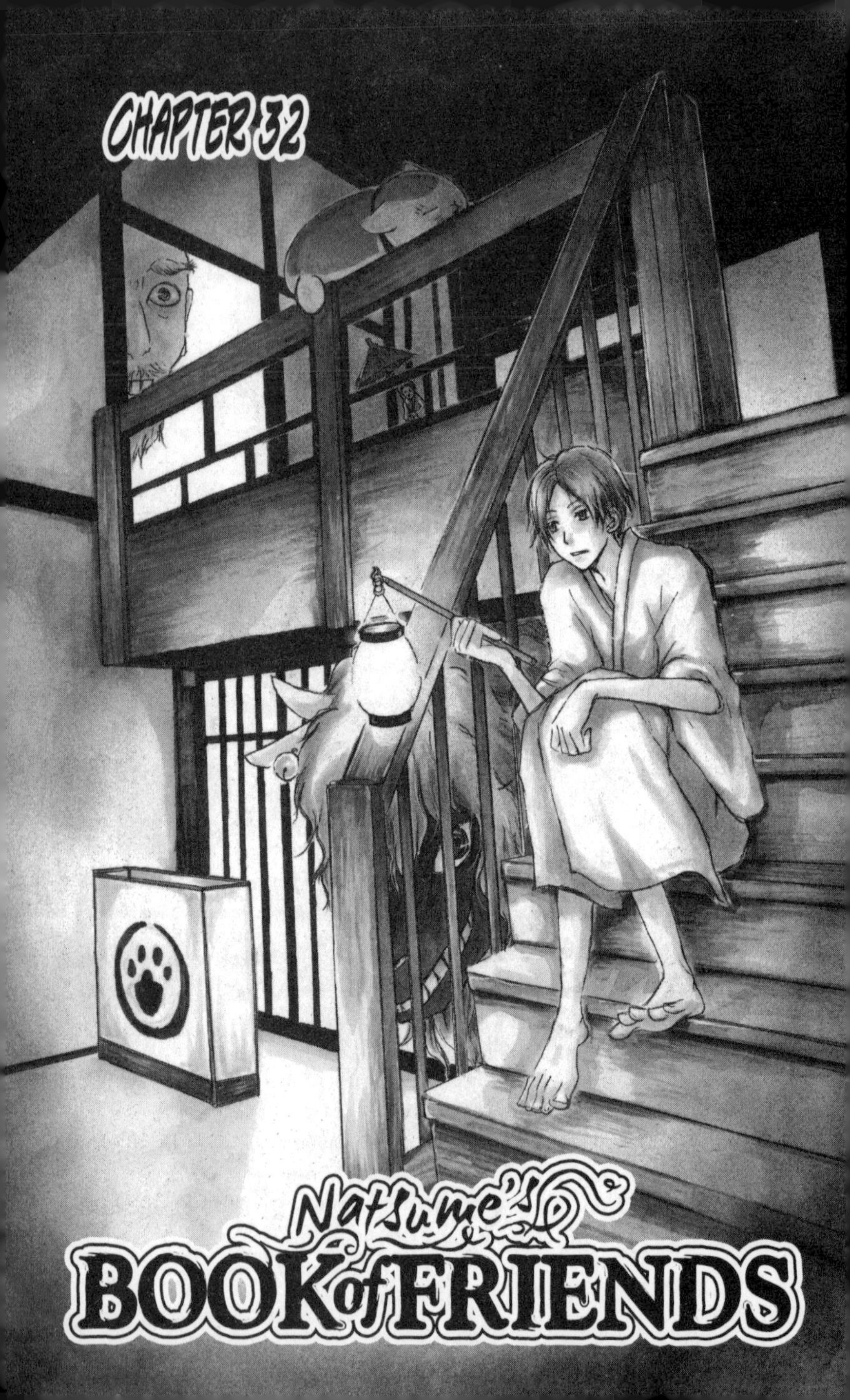
CHAPTER 32
Natsume's
BOOK of FRIENDS

# Natsume's BOOK of FRIENDS
## CHARACTER GUIDE

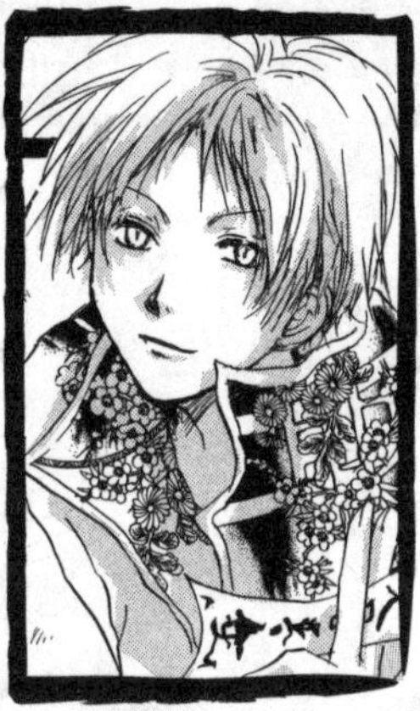

### Takashi Natsume

A lonely orphan with the ability to see the supernatural. He inherited the *Book of Friends* from his grandmother and currently lives with the Fujiwaras, to whom he is distantly related. Like his grandmother, he's powerful enough to subdue yokai with a single punch.

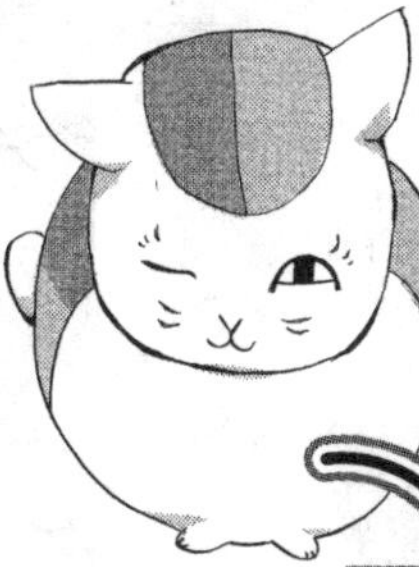

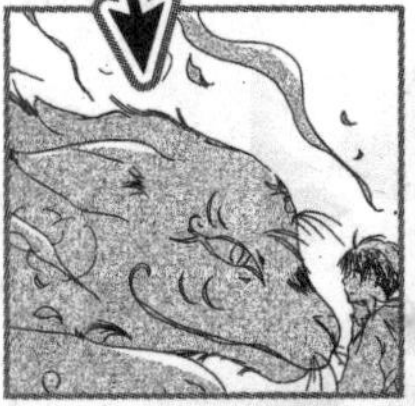

(TRUE FORM)

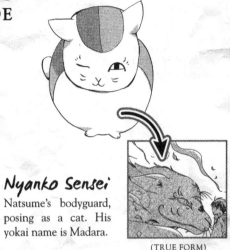

### Nyanko Sensei

Natsume's bodyguard, posing as a cat. His yokai name is Madara.

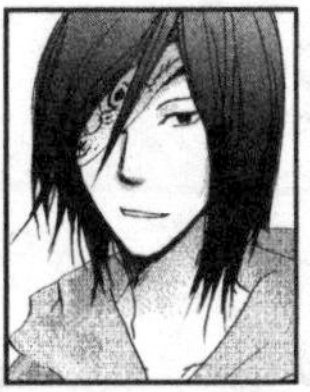

### Seiji Matoba

The powerful leader of a leading family of exorcists, he harbors a grudge against yokai…

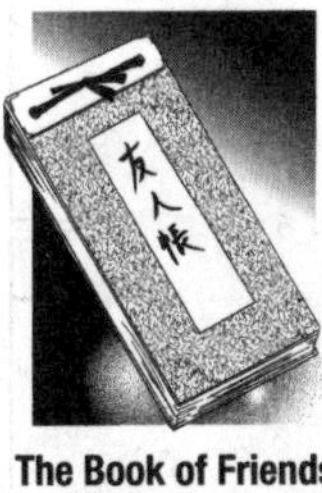

**The Book of Friends**
A collection of contracts put together by Reiko, Takashi's grandmother, that grants her mastery over the yokai who sign.

## THE STORY

Takashi Natsume has a secret sixth sense—he can see supernatural creatures called yokai. And ever since he inherited the *Book of Friends* from his grandmother, the local yokai have been coming after him. Takashi frees Nyanko Sensei from imprisonment and promises he will get the *Book* when Takashi dies. With his new bodyguard, Takashi leads a busy life returning names to yokai.

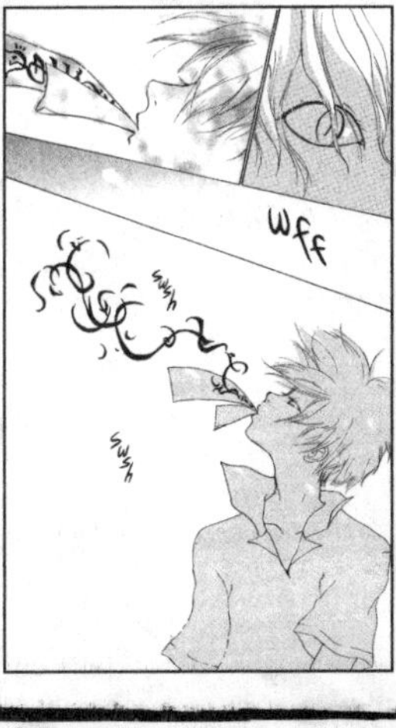
WFF
SWSH
SWSH

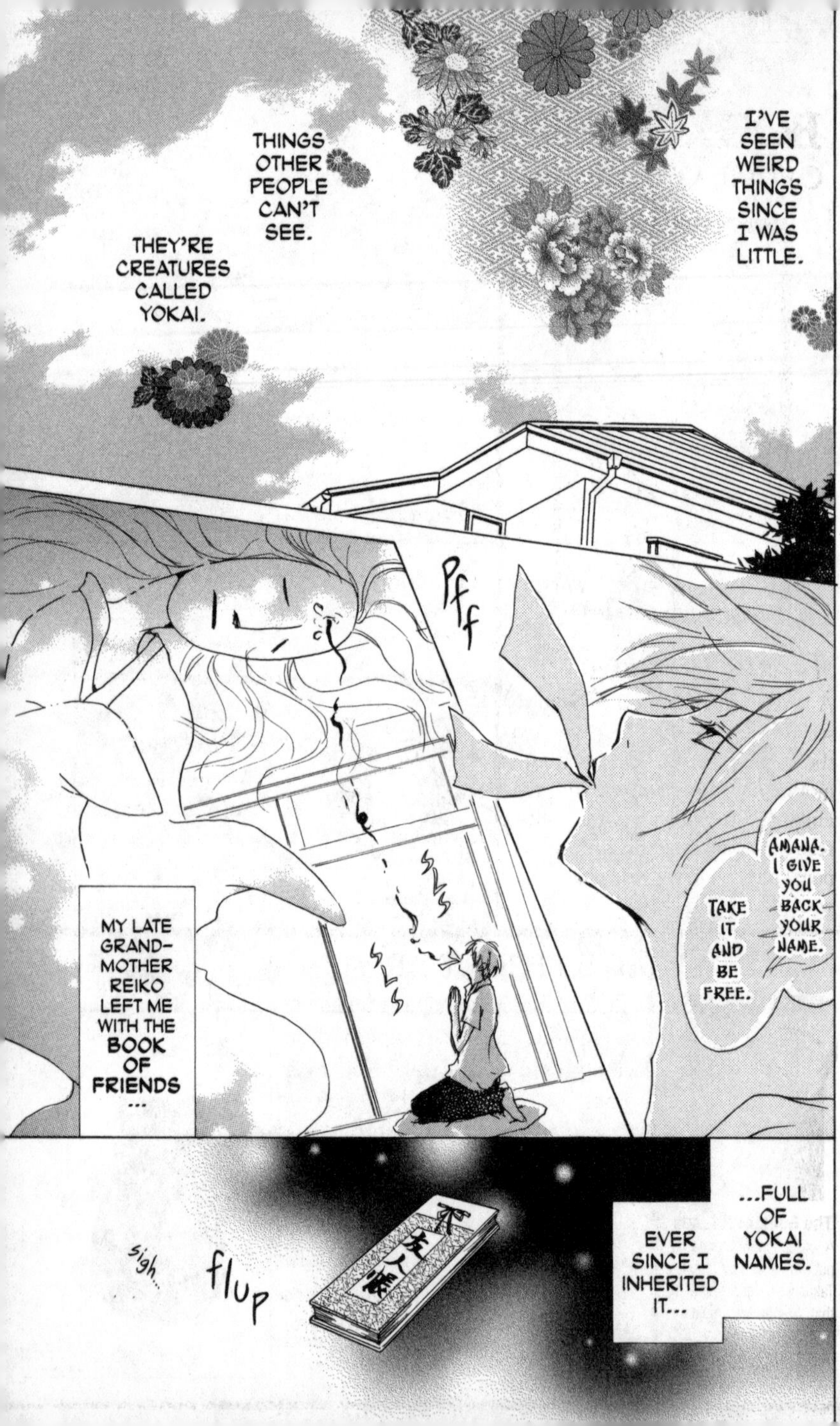

I'VE SEEN WEIRD THINGS SINCE I WAS LITTLE.
THINGS OTHER PEOPLE CAN'T SEE.
THEY'RE CREATURES CALLED YOKAI.
AMANA. I GIVE YOU BACK YOUR NAME.
TAKE IT AND BE FREE.
Pff
MY LATE GRANDMOTHER REIKO LEFT ME WITH THE BOOK OF FRIENDS...
...FULL OF YOKAI NAMES.
EVER SINCE I INHERITED IT...
友人帳
flup
sigh...

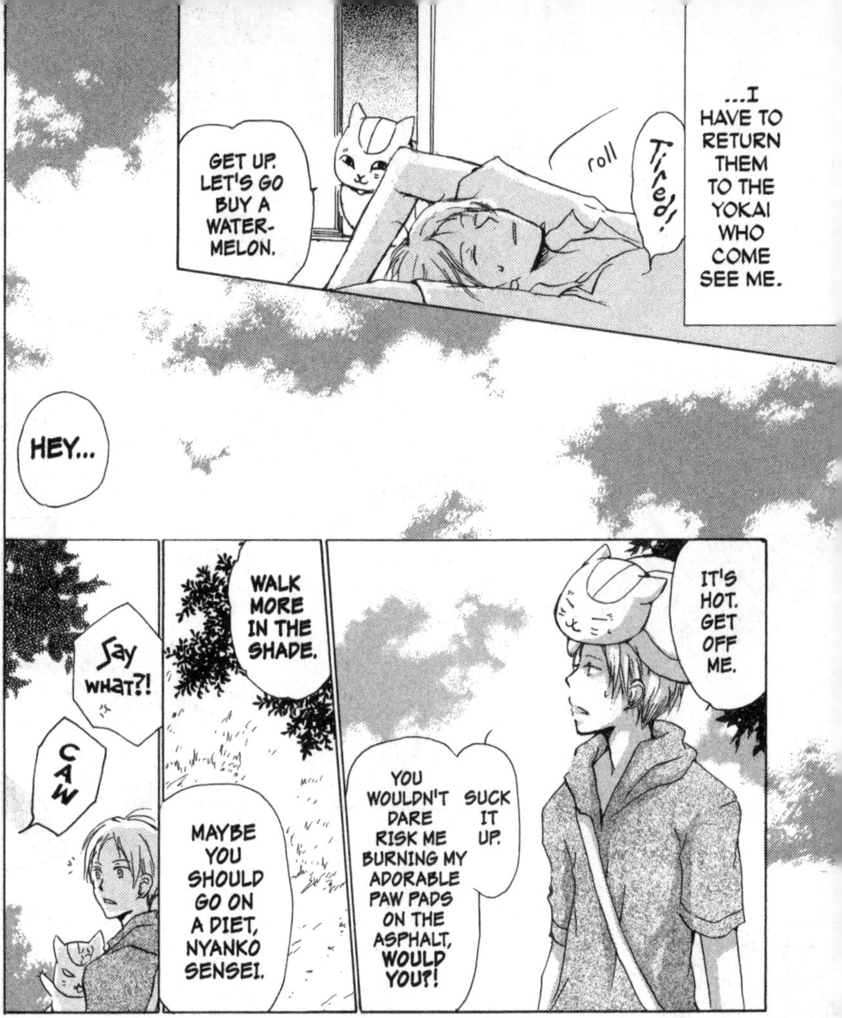
...I HAVE TO RETURN THEM TO THE YOKAI WHO COME SEE ME.
Tired!
roll
GET UP. LET'S GO BUY A WATER-MELON.
HEY...
IT'S HOT. GET OFF ME.
SUCK IT UP.
YOU WOULDN'T DARE RISK ME BURNING MY ADORABLE PAW PADS ON THE ASPHALT, WOULD YOU?!
WALK MORE IN THE SHADE.
MAYBE YOU SHOULD GO ON A DIET, NYANKO SENSEI.
Say what?!
CAW

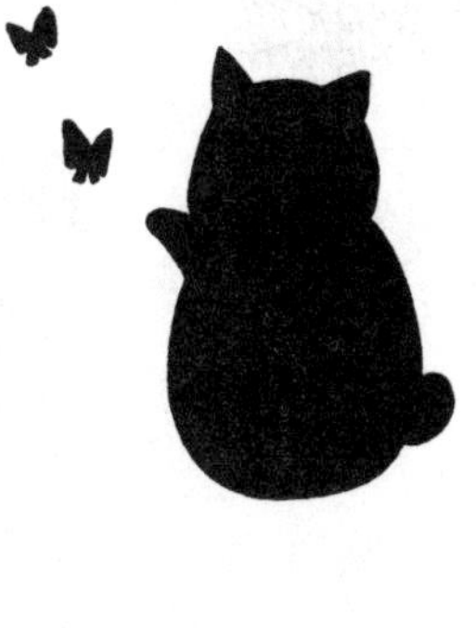

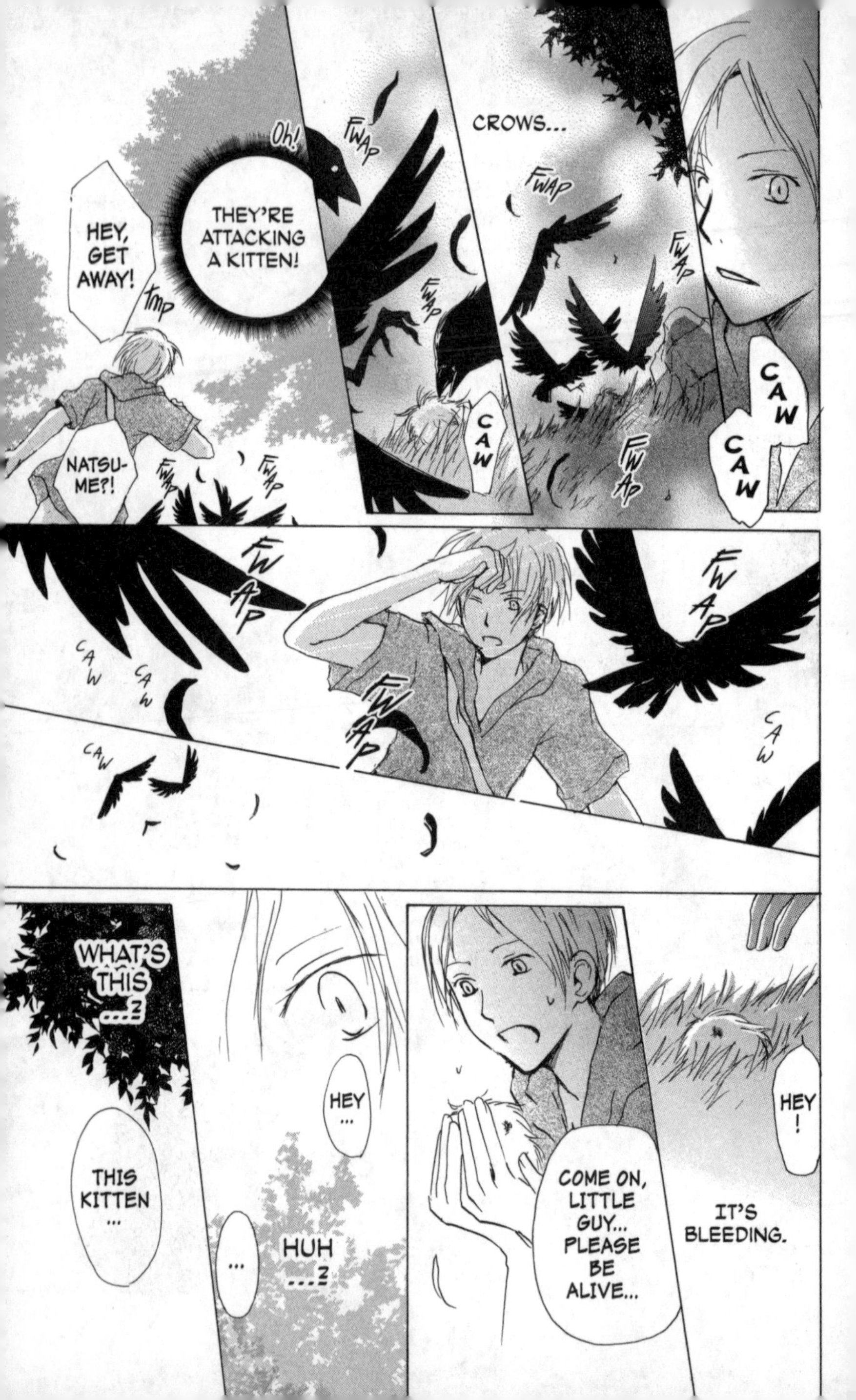
CAW
CAW
CAW
CROWS...
FWAP
FWAP
FWAP
FWAP
CAW
Oh!
THEY'RE ATTACKING A KITTEN!
HEY, GET AWAY!
tmp
NATSU-ME?!
FWAP
FWAP
FWAP
FWAP
FWAP
CAW
CAW
CAW
CAW
HEY!
IT'S BLEEDING.
COME ON, LITTLE GUY... PLEASE BE ALIVE...
HEY...
HUH...?
...
WHAT'S THIS...?
THIS KITTEN...

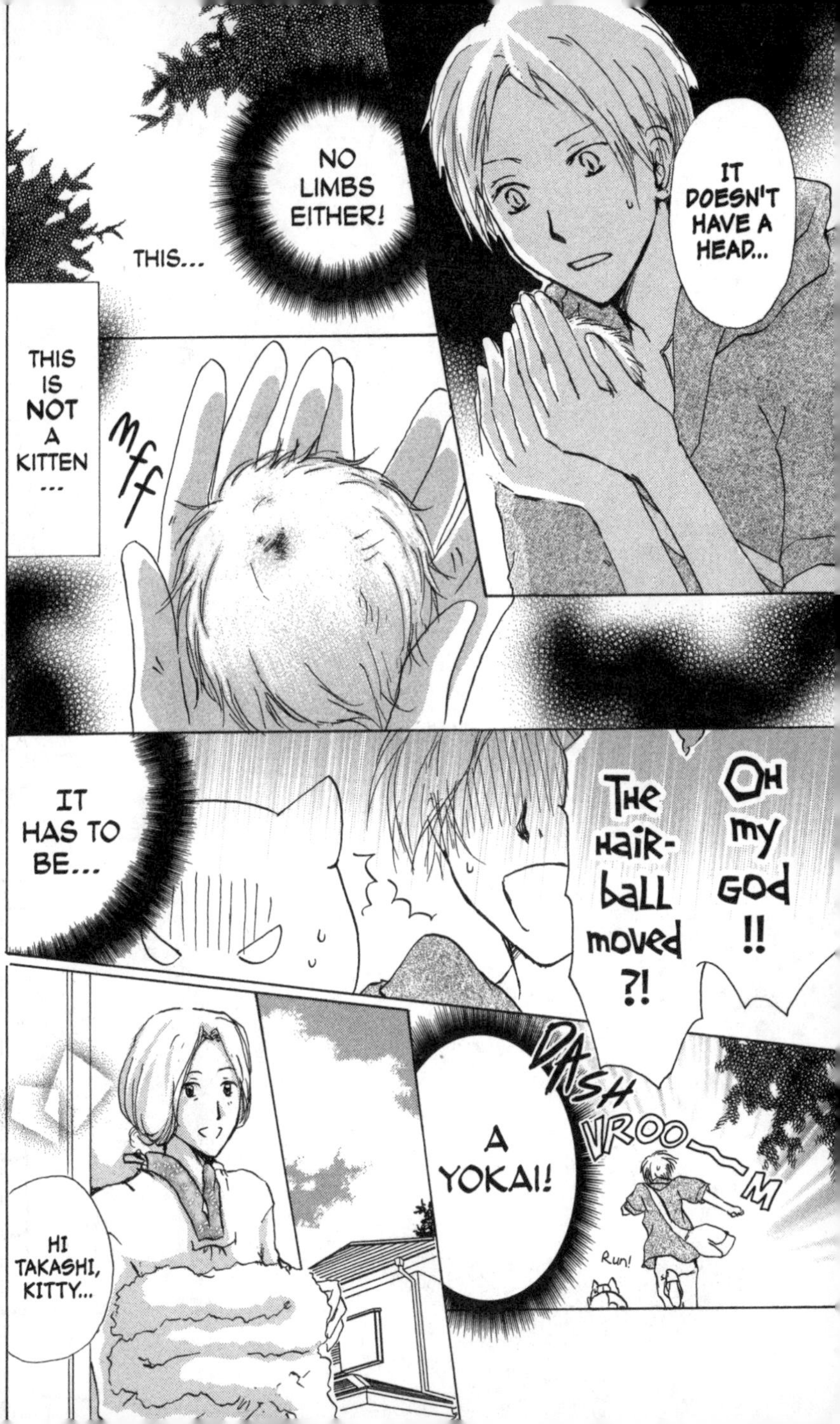
IT DOESN'T HAVE A HEAD...
NO LIMBS EITHER!
THIS...
THIS IS NOT A KITTEN ...
mff
OH my GOD !!
The hair-ball moved ?!
IT HAS TO BE...
DASH
VROO—M
A YOKAI!
Run!
HI TAKASHI, KITTY...

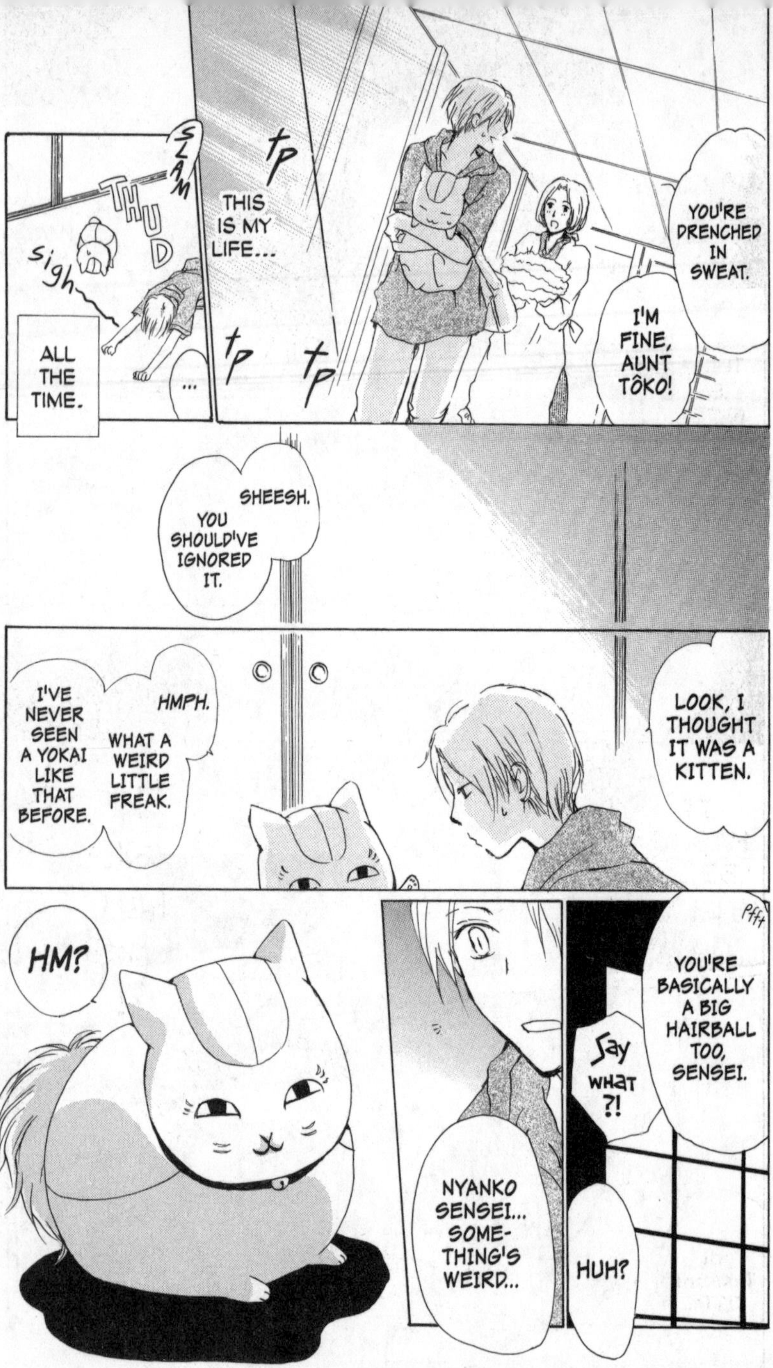
YOU'RE DRENCHED IN SWEAT.
I'M FINE, AUNT TÔKO!
tp
tp
tp
THIS IS MY LIFE...
SLAM
THUD
sigh
...
ALL THE TIME.
SHEESH.
YOU SHOULD'VE IGNORED IT.
LOOK, I THOUGHT IT WAS A KITTEN.
HMPH.
WHAT A WEIRD LITTLE FREAK.
I'VE NEVER SEEN A YOKAI LIKE THAT BEFORE.
Pfft
YOU'RE BASICALLY A BIG HAIRBALL TOO, SENSEI.
Say what?!
HUH?
NYANKO SENSEI... SOME-THING'S WEIRD...
HM?

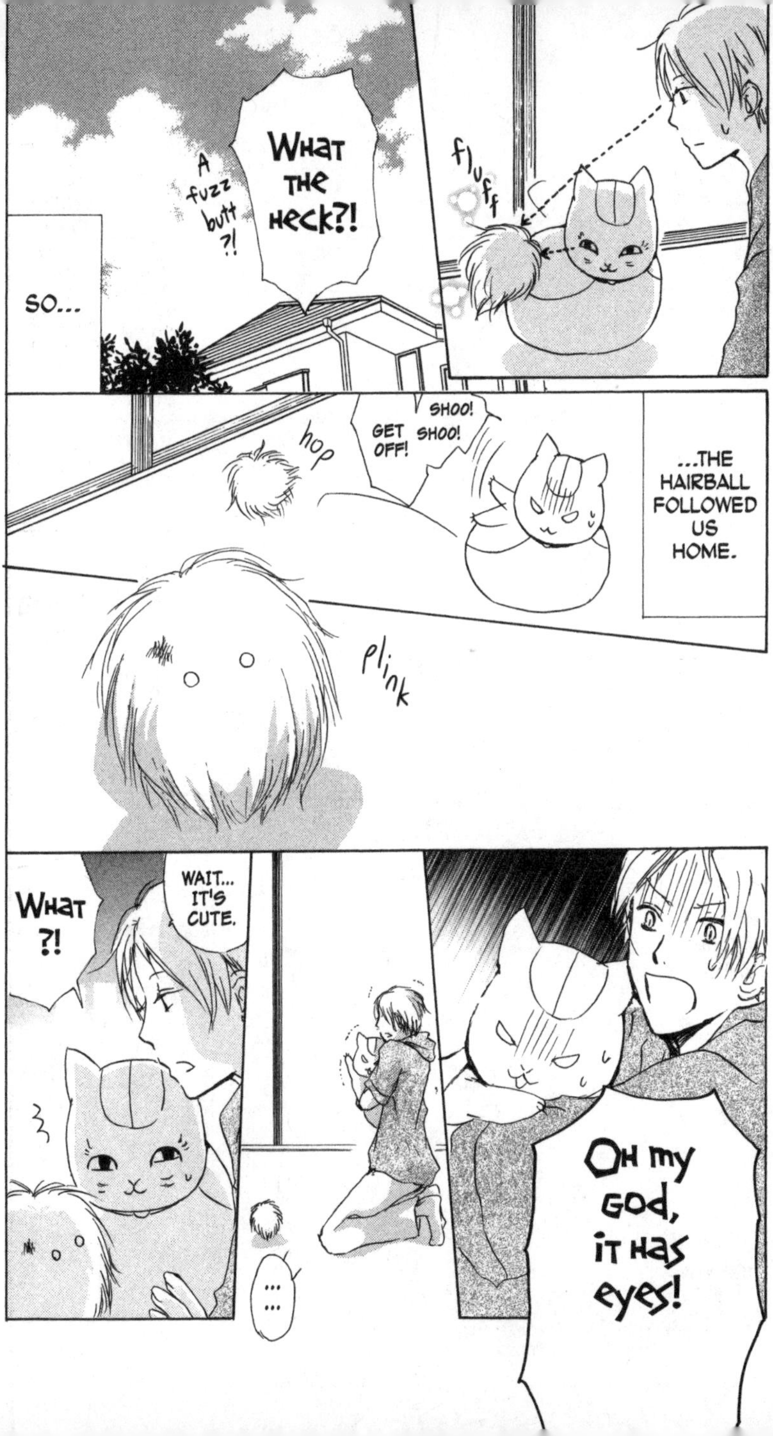
fluff
WHAT THE HECK?!
A fuzz butt ?!
SO...
...THE HAIRBALL FOLLOWED US HOME.
SHOO! SHOO!
GET OFF!
hop
plink
OH my GOD, it HAS eyes!
......
WAIT... IT'S CUTE.
WHAT ?!

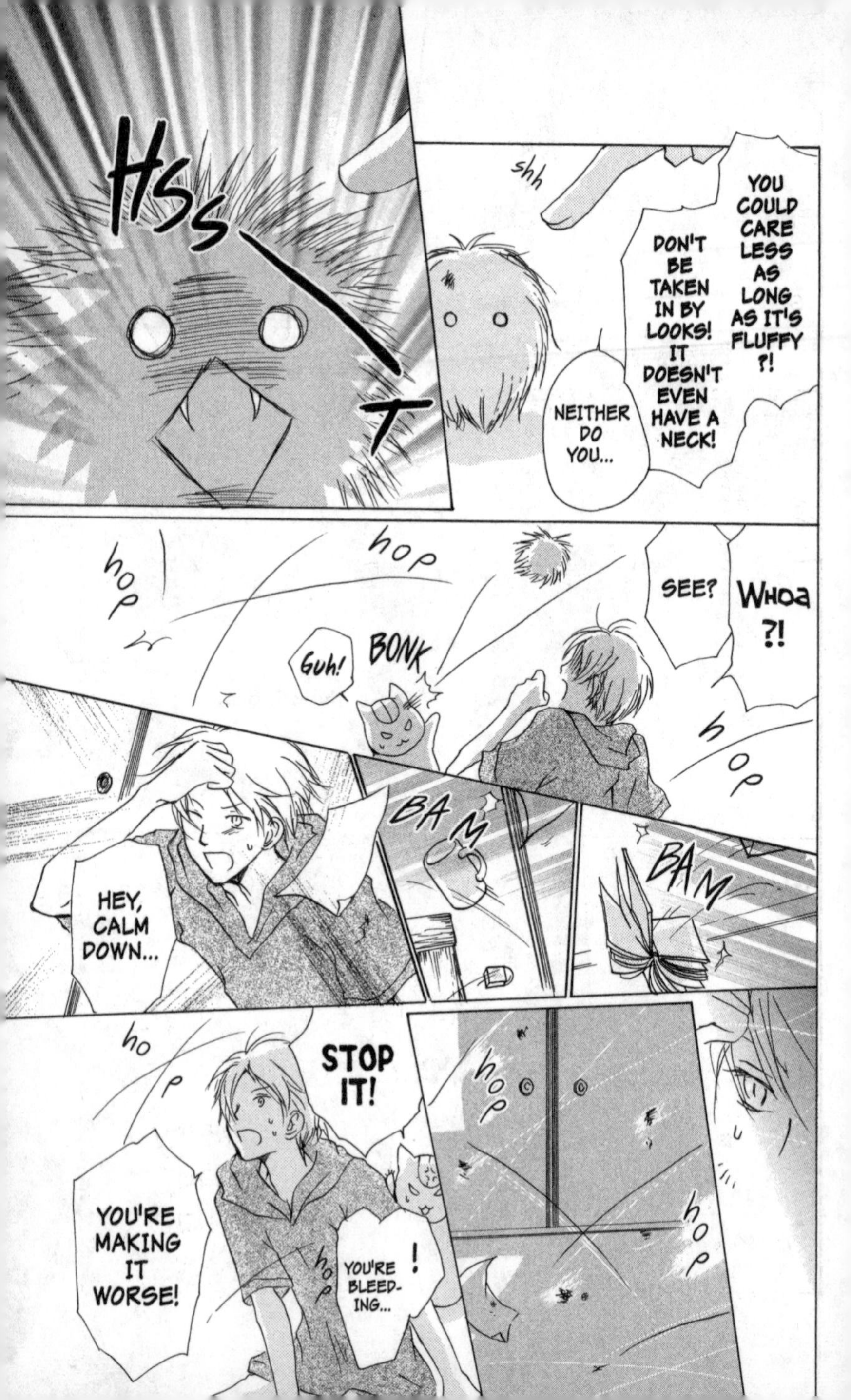

YOU COULD CARE LESS AS LONG AS IT'S FLUFFY?!
DON'T BE TAKEN IN BY LOOKS! IT DOESN'T EVEN HAVE A NECK!
shh
NEITHER DO YOU...
HSS—T
Whoa?!
SEE?
hop
hop
BONK
Guh!
hop
hop
BAM
BAM
HEY, CALM DOWN...
hop
hop
STOP IT!
hop
YOU'RE MAKING IT WORSE!
!
YOU'RE BLEEDING...
hop

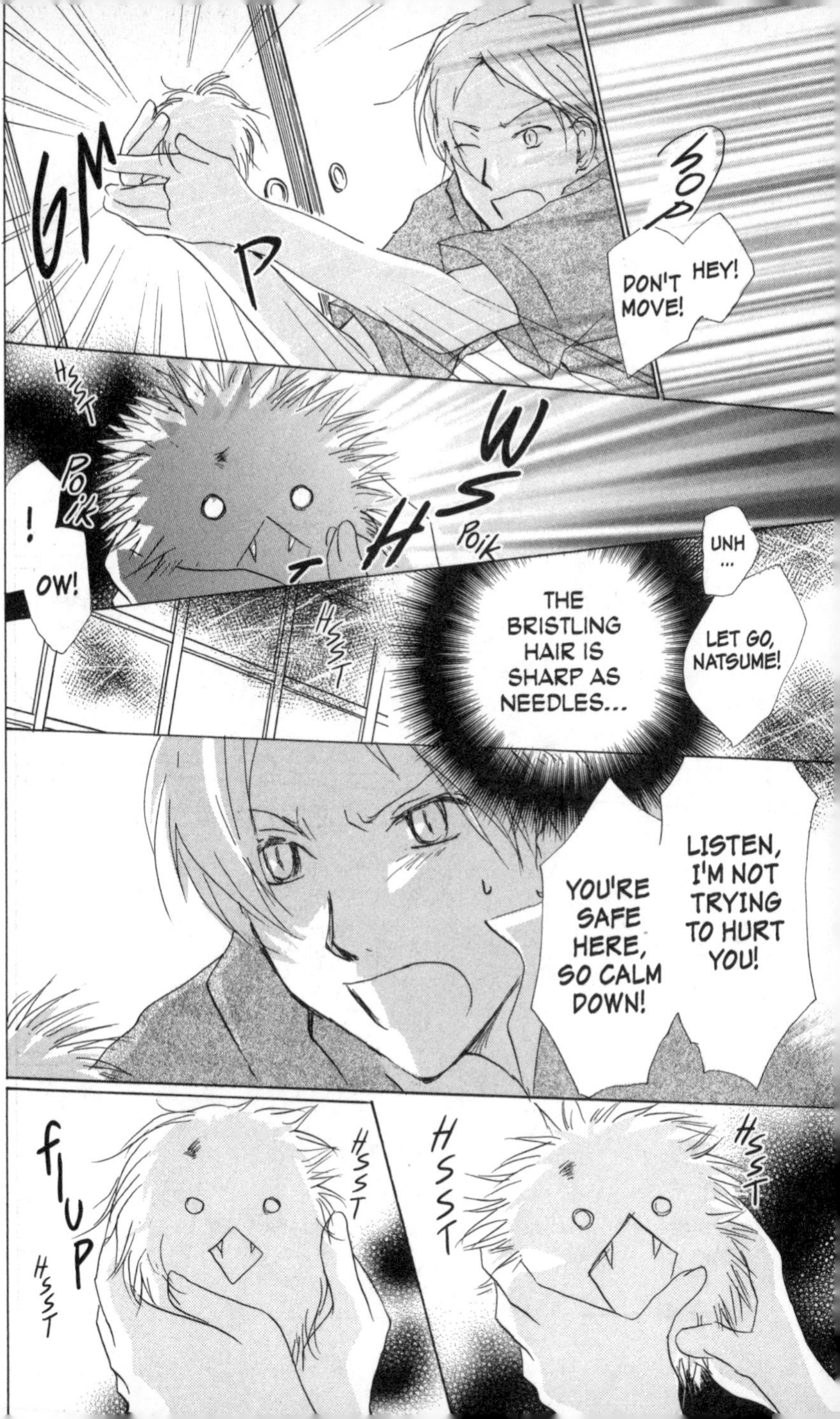
WOP
HEY!
DON'T MOVE!
GM
P
WSH
POIK
POIK
HSSK
!
OW!
UNH ...
LET GO, NATSUME!
THE BRISTLING HAIR IS SHARP AS NEEDLES...
HSST
LISTEN, I'M NOT TRYING TO HURT YOU!
YOU'RE SAFE HERE, SO CALM DOWN!
HSST
HSST
HSST
FLUP
HSST

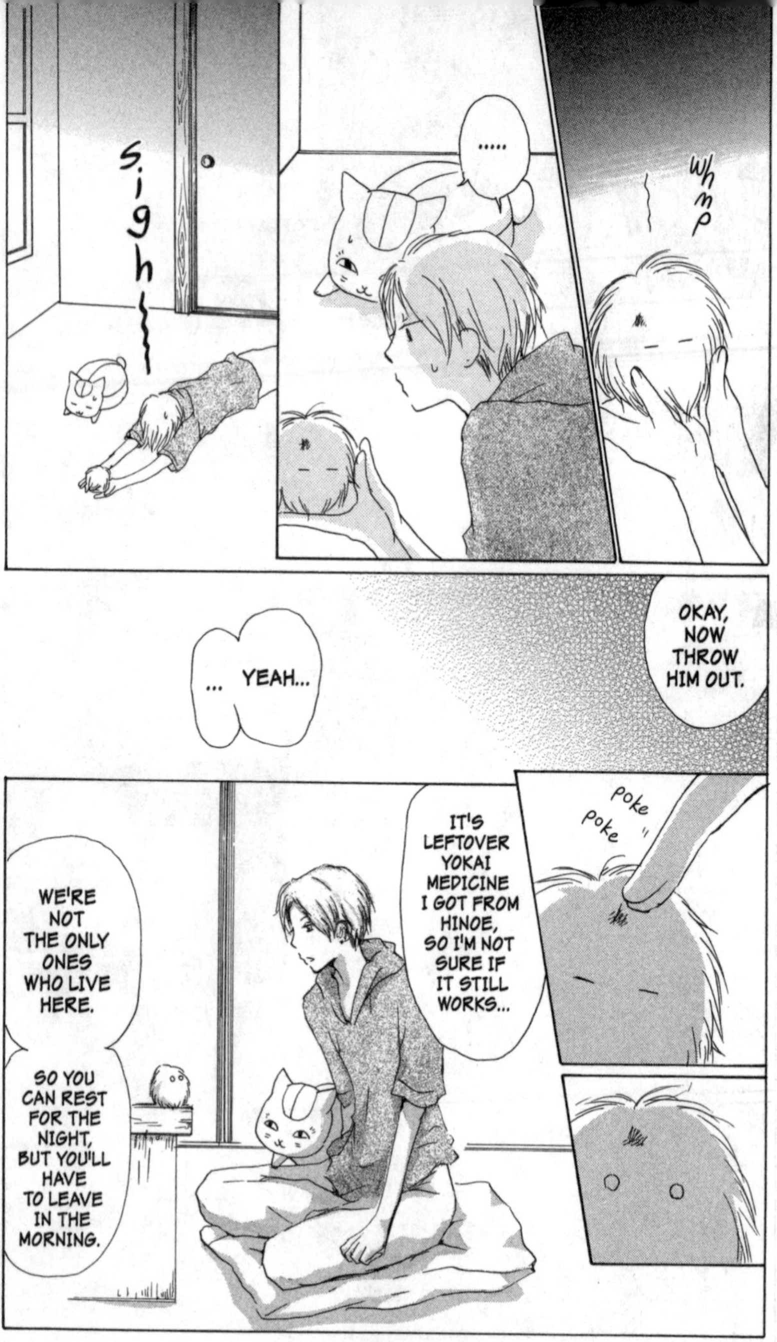
whmp
.....
Sigh~
OKAY, NOW THROW HIM OUT.
... YEAH...
poke poke
IT'S LEFTOVER YOKAI MEDICINE I GOT FROM HINOE, SO I'M NOT SURE IF IT STILL WORKS...
WE'RE NOT THE ONLY ONES WHO LIVE HERE.
SO YOU CAN REST FOR THE NIGHT, BUT YOU'LL HAVE TO LEAVE IN THE MORNING.

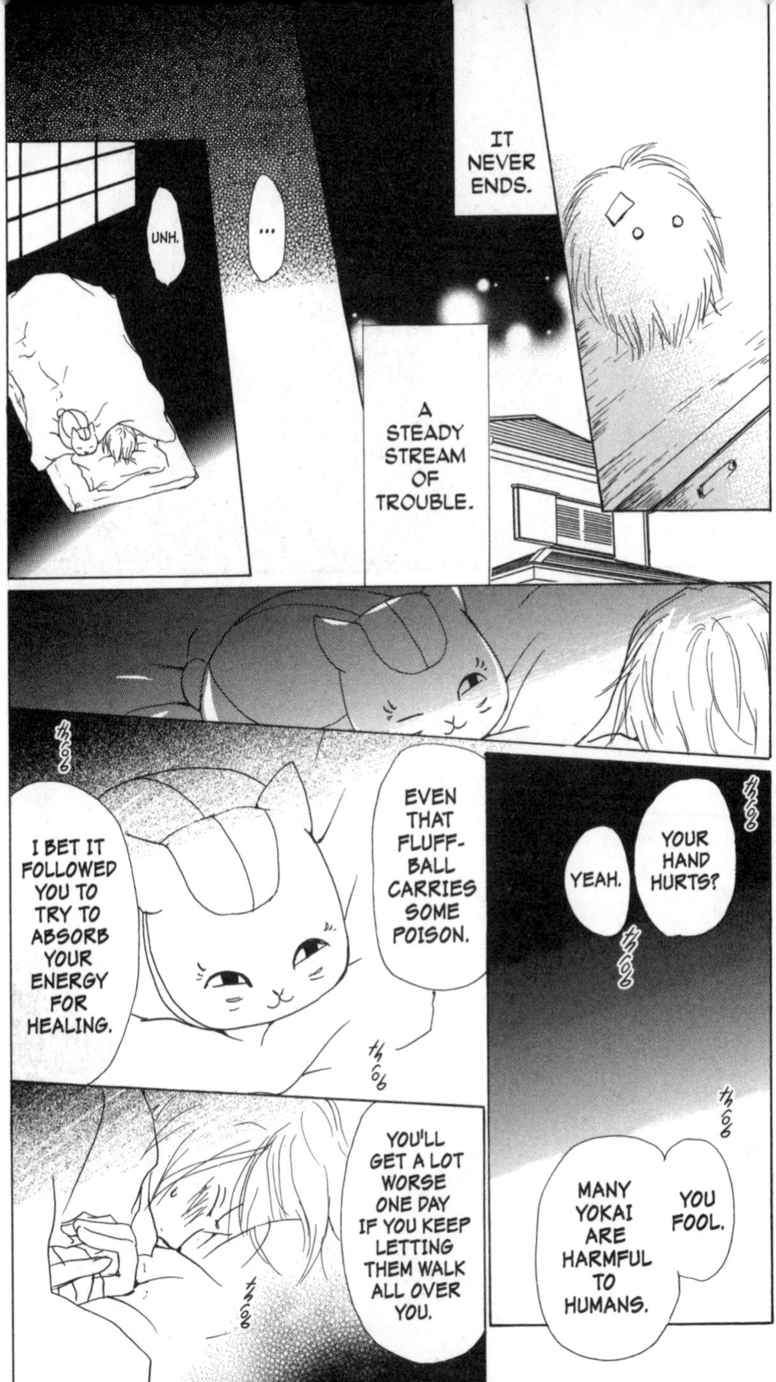

IT NEVER ENDS.
A STEADY STREAM OF TROUBLE.
...
UNH.
YOUR HAND HURTS?
YEAH.
EVEN THAT FLUFF-BALL CARRIES SOME POISON.
I BET IT FOLLOWED YOU TO TRY TO ABSORB YOUR ENERGY FOR HEALING.
YOU FOOL.
MANY YOKAI ARE HARMFUL TO HUMANS.
YOU'LL GET A LOT WORSE ONE DAY IF YOU KEEP LETTING THEM WALK ALL OVER YOU.

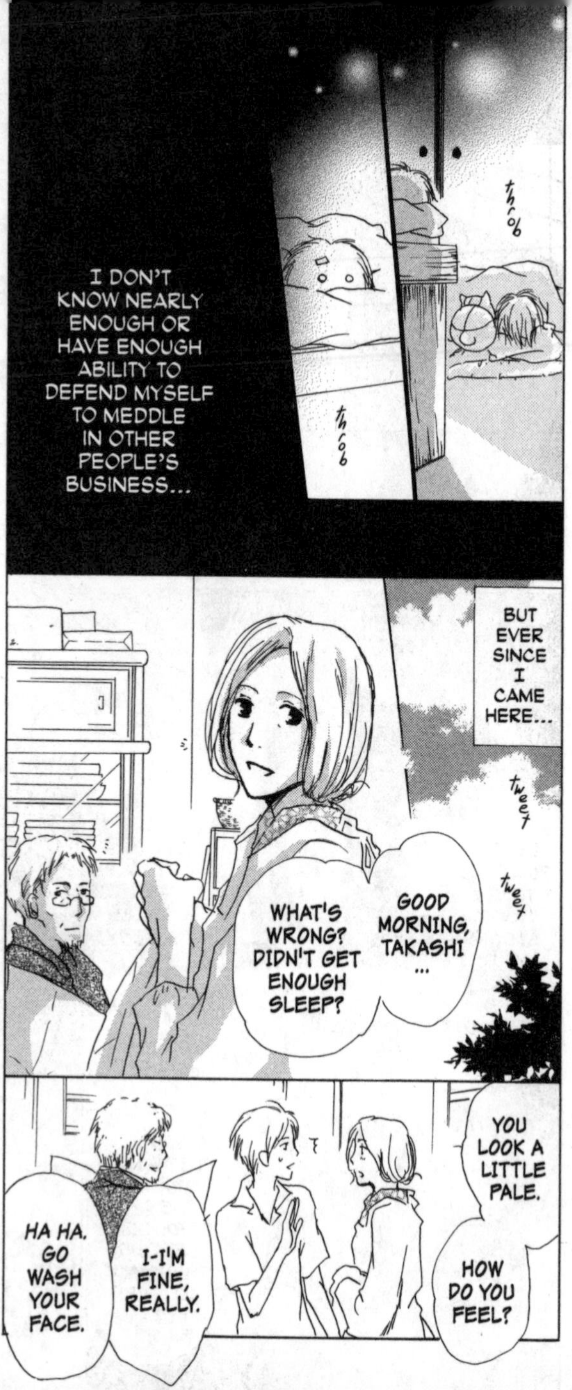
throb
throb
I DON'T KNOW NEARLY ENOUGH OR HAVE ENOUGH ABILITY TO DEFEND MYSELF TO MEDDLE IN OTHER PEOPLE'S BUSINESS...
BUT EVER SINCE I CAME HERE...
tweet
tweet
GOOD MORNING, TAKASHI ...
WHAT'S WRONG? DIDN'T GET ENOUGH SLEEP?
YOU LOOK A LITTLE PALE.
HOW DO YOU FEEL?
I-I'M FINE, REALLY.
HA HA. GO WASH YOUR FACE.

01

Hello, I'm Midorikawa. This is my 17th total graphic novel, and the ninth for Natsume.

I get so excited, embarrassed and happy when I see my books lined up at the bookstore. I'd like to thank the readers who decided to pick this up, and the editors who have patiently stuck with me the whole way.

I'll keep putting everything I have into my work, so please continue with your support.

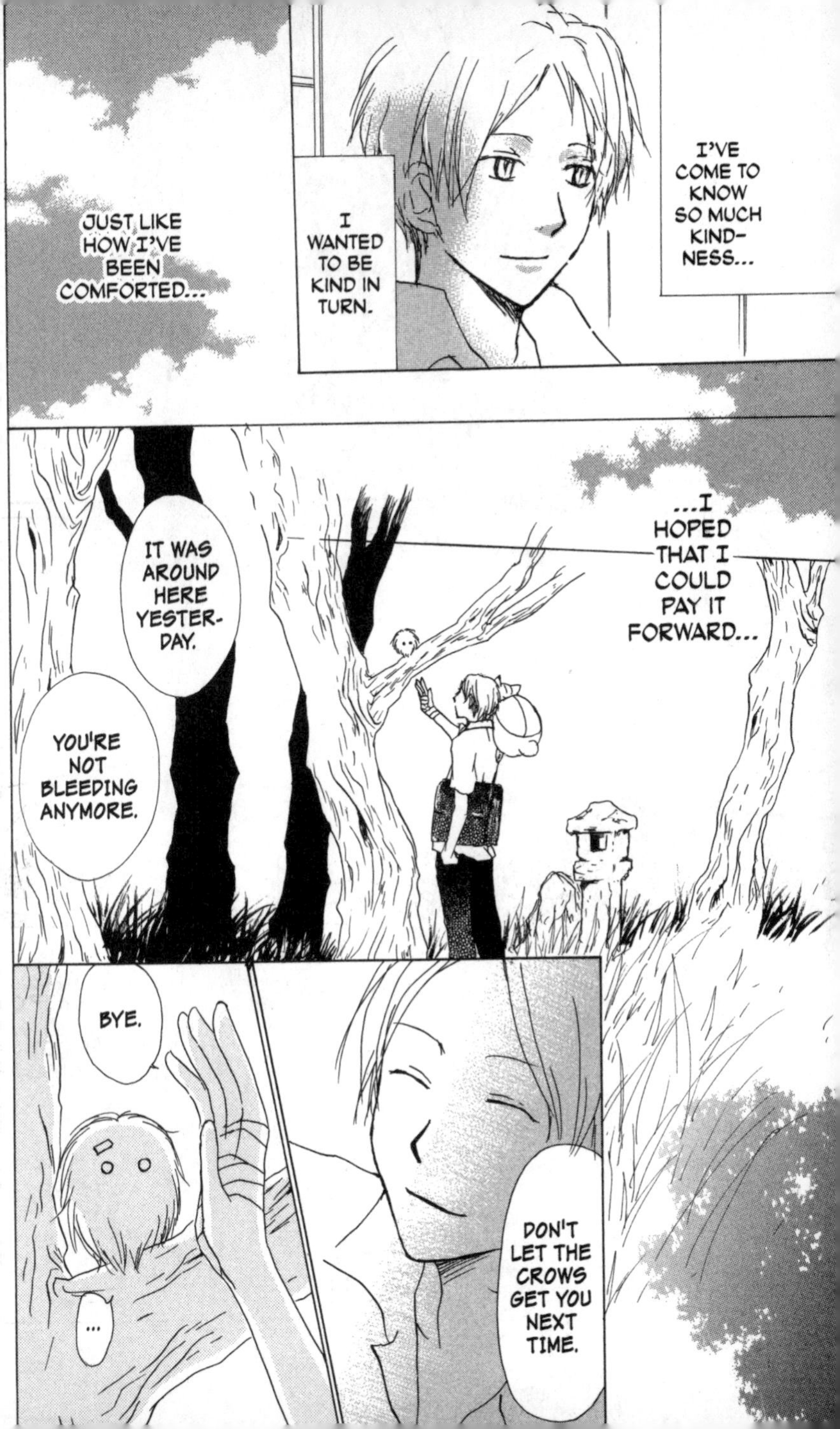
I'VE COME TO KNOW SO MUCH KINDNESS...
I WANTED TO BE KIND IN TURN.
JUST LIKE HOW I'VE BEEN COMFORTED...
...I HOPED THAT I COULD PAY IT FORWARD...
IT WAS AROUND HERE YESTERDAY.
YOU'RE NOT BLEEDING ANYMORE.
DON'T LET THE CROWS GET YOU NEXT TIME.
BYE.
...

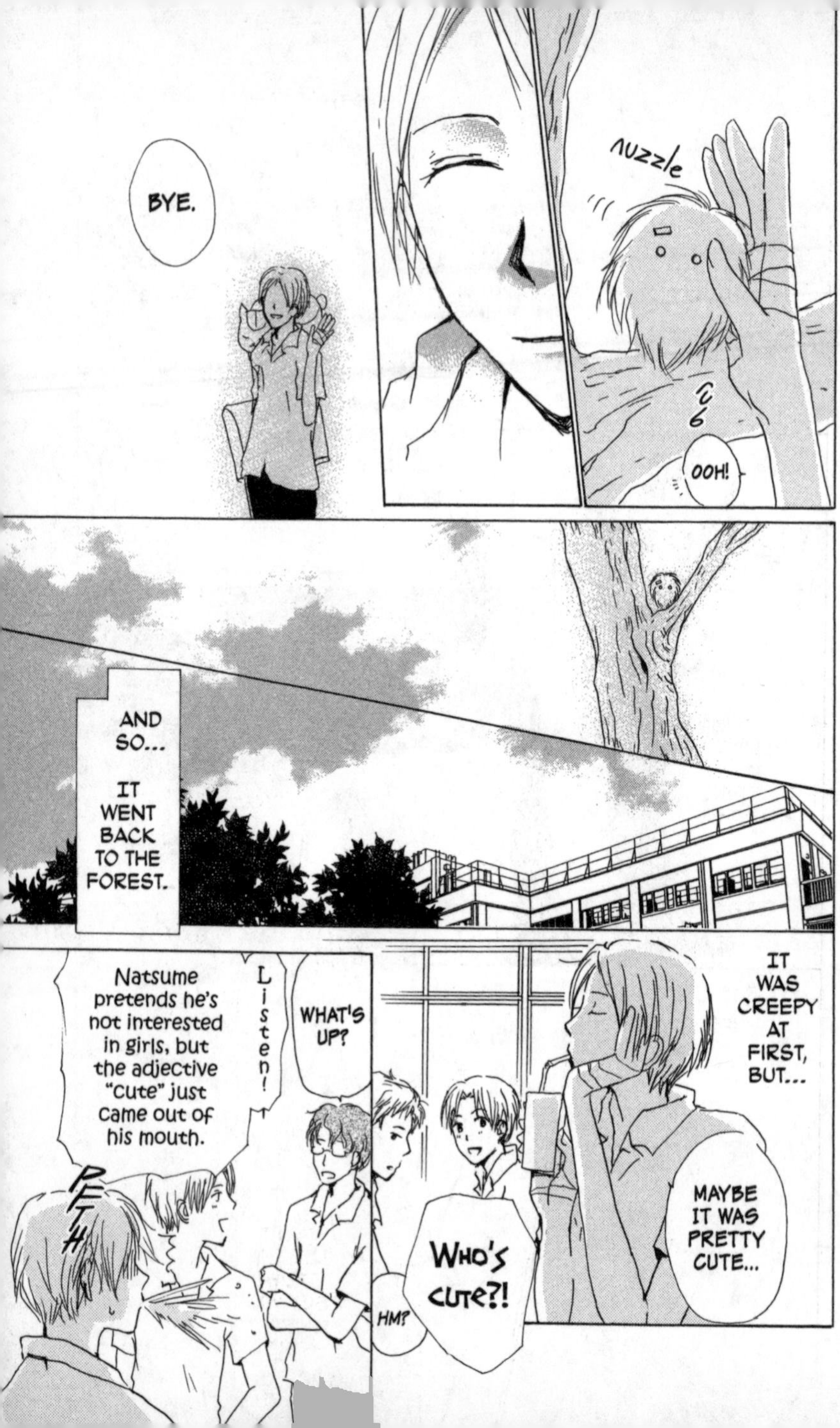
nuzzle
OOH!
BYE.
AND SO...
IT WENT BACK TO THE FOREST.
IT WAS CREEPY AT FIRST, BUT...
MAYBE IT WAS PRETTY CUTE...
WHO'S CUTE?!
HM?
WHAT'S UP?
Listen!
Natsume pretends he's not interested in girls, but the adjective "cute" just came out of his mouth.

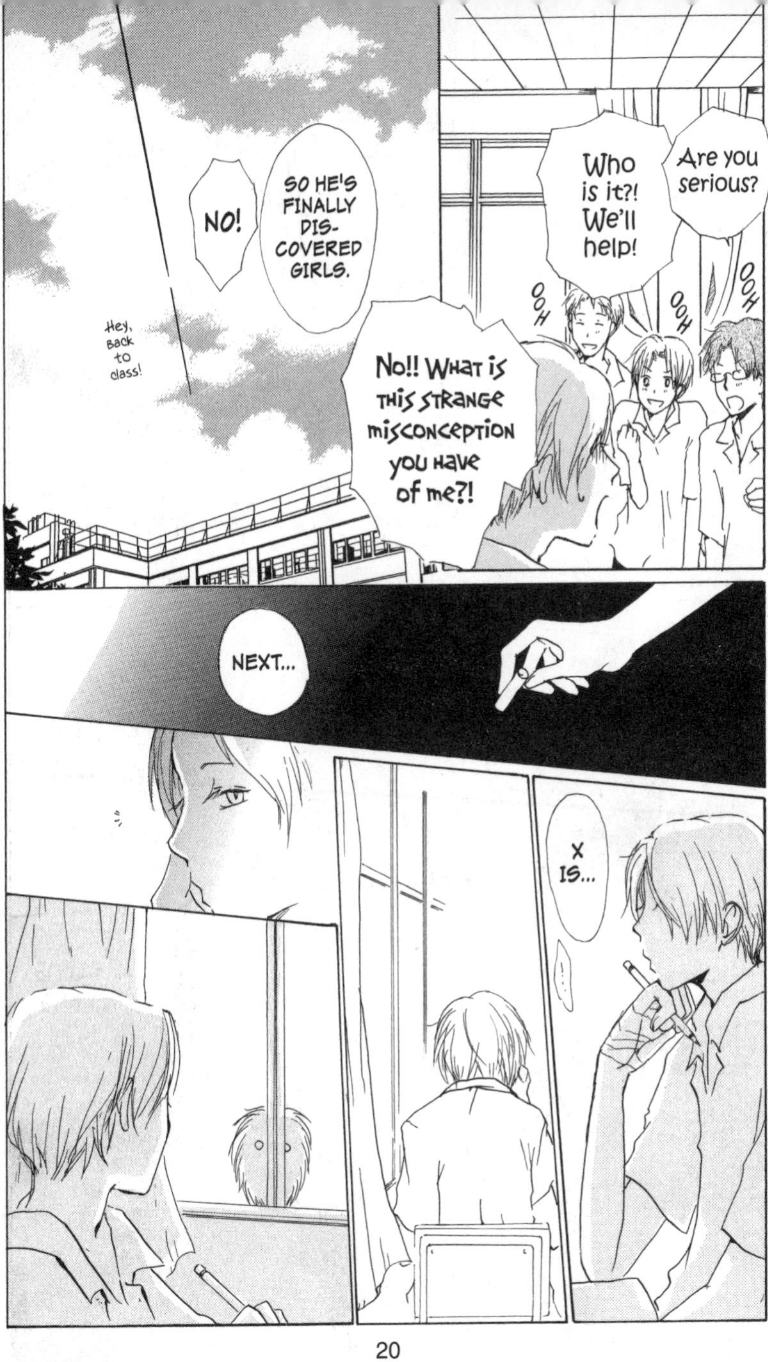
Are you serious?
Who is it?! We'll help!
OOH
OOH
OOH
No!! What is this strange misconception you have of me?!
SO HE'S FINALLY DIS-COVERED GIRLS.
NO!
Hey, back to class!
NEXT...
X IS...
!...

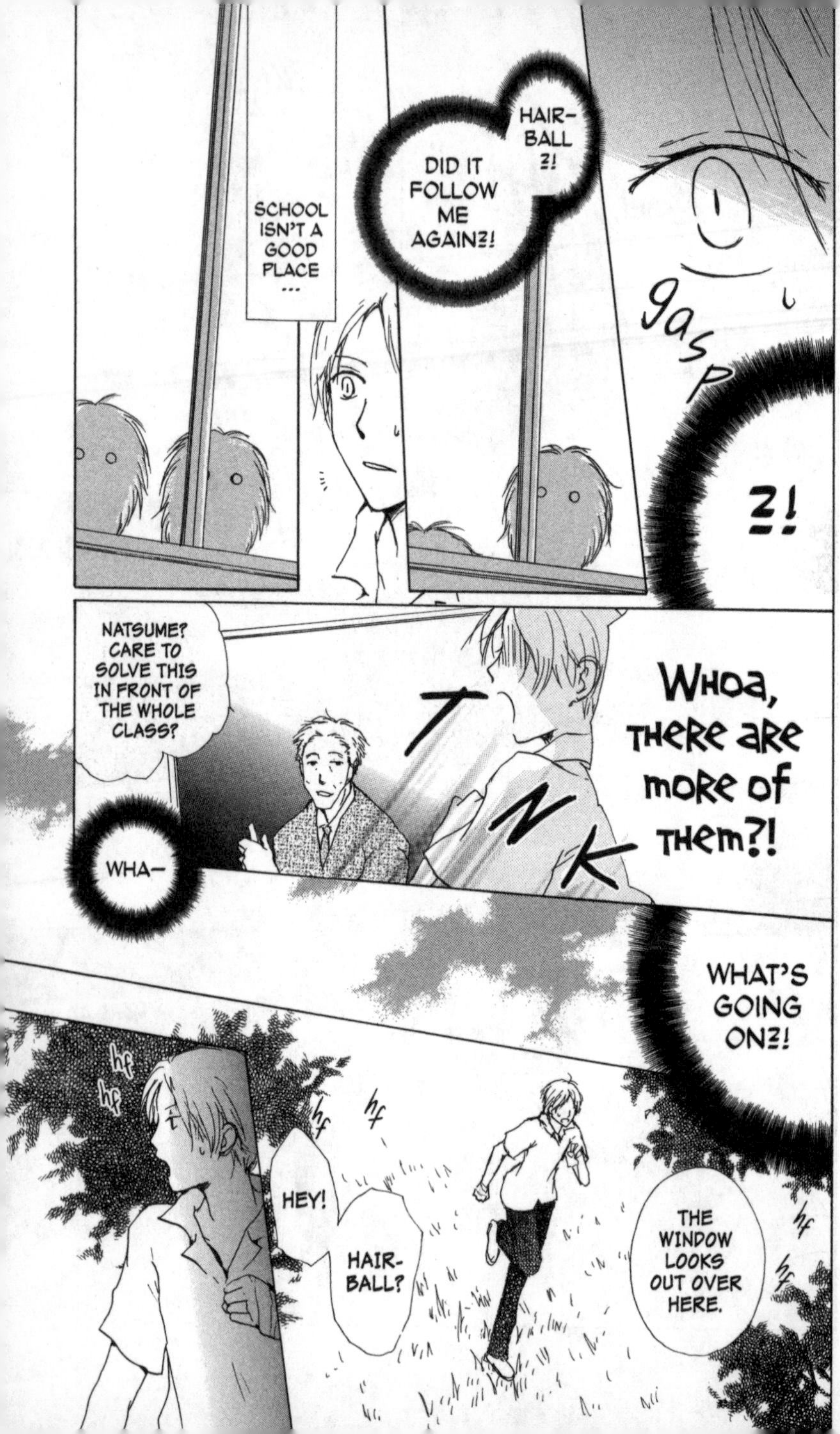
gasp
?!
HAIR-BALL?!
DID IT FOLLOW ME AGAIN?!
SCHOOL ISN'T A GOOD PLACE...
WHOA, THERE ARE MORE OF THEM?!
TNK
NATSUME? CARE TO SOLVE THIS IN FRONT OF THE WHOLE CLASS?
WHA-
WHAT'S GOING ON?!
hf
hf
THE WINDOW LOOKS OUT OVER HERE.
hf
hf
HAIR-BALL?
HEY!
hf
hf

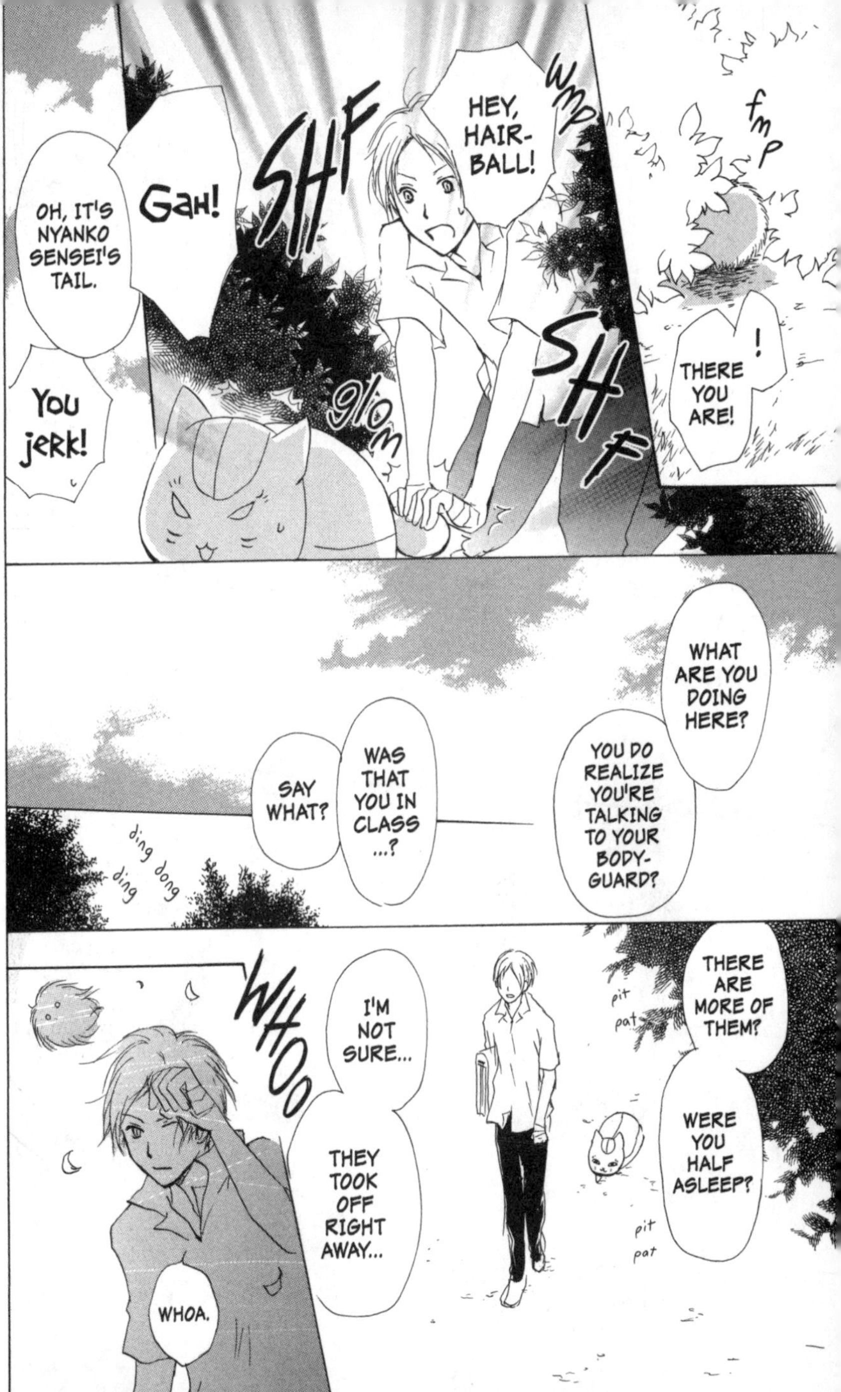
fmp
!
THERE YOU ARE!
wmp
HEY, HAIR-BALL!
SHF
SHF
glom
Gah!
OH, IT'S NYANKO SENSEI'S TAIL.
You jerk!
WHAT ARE YOU DOING HERE?
YOU DO REALIZE YOU'RE TALKING TO YOUR BODY-GUARD?
WAS THAT YOU IN CLASS ...?
SAY WHAT?
ding dong ding
THERE ARE MORE OF THEM?
pit pat
WERE YOU HALF ASLEEP?
pit pat
I'M NOT SURE...
THEY TOOK OFF RIGHT AWAY...
WHOO
WHOA.

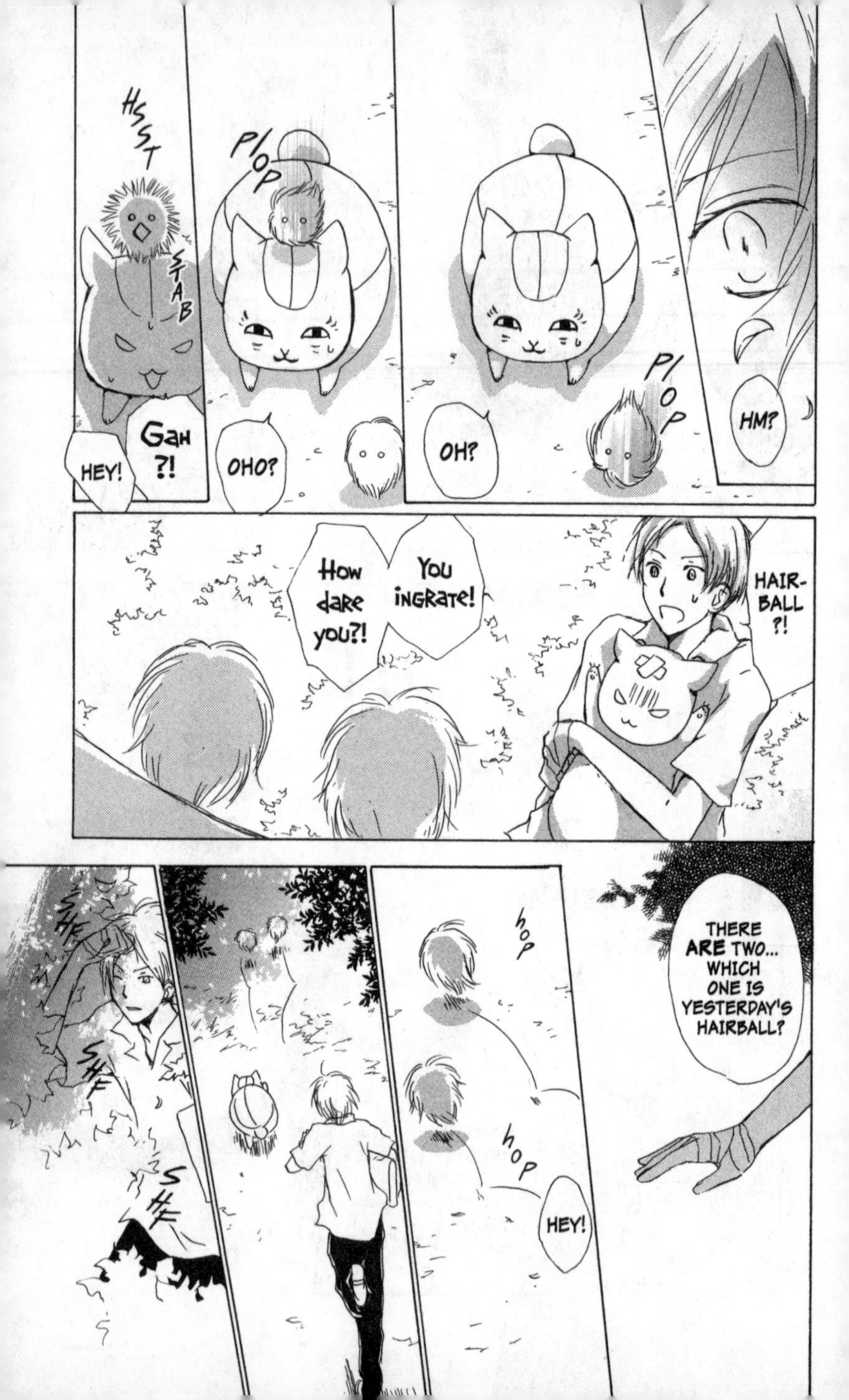
HM?
PLOP
OH?
PLOP
OHO?
HSST
STAB
GAH?!
HEY!
HAIR-BALL?!
You ingrate!
How dare you?!
THERE ARE TWO... WHICH ONE IS YESTERDAY'S HAIRBALL?
hop
hop
HEY!
SHF
SHF
SHF

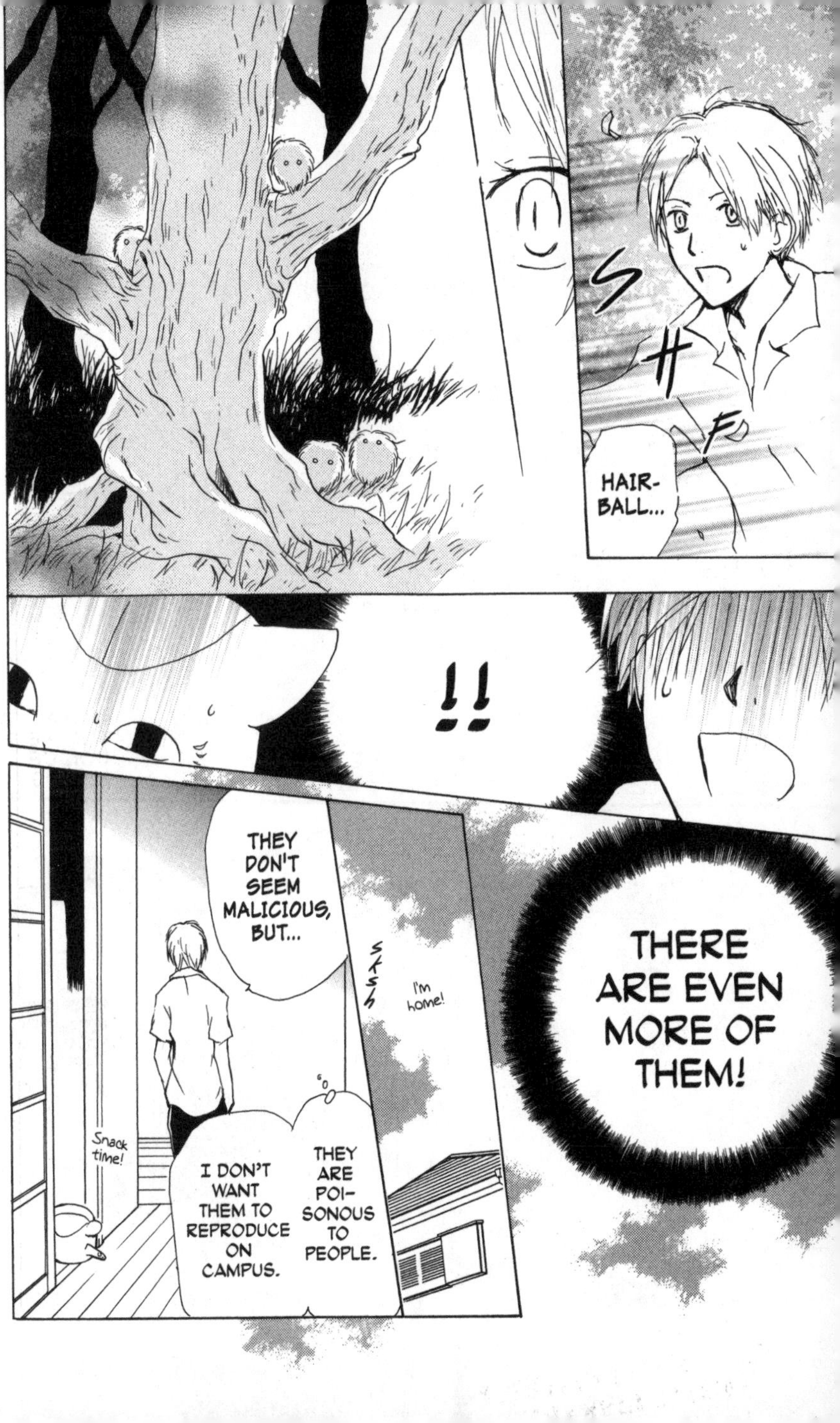
SHF
HAIR-BALL...
!!
THERE ARE EVEN MORE OF THEM!
THEY DON'T SEEM MALICIOUS, BUT...
SKSH
I'm home!
THEY ARE POI-SONOUS TO PEOPLE.
I DON'T WANT THEM TO REPRODUCE ON CAMPUS.
Snack time!

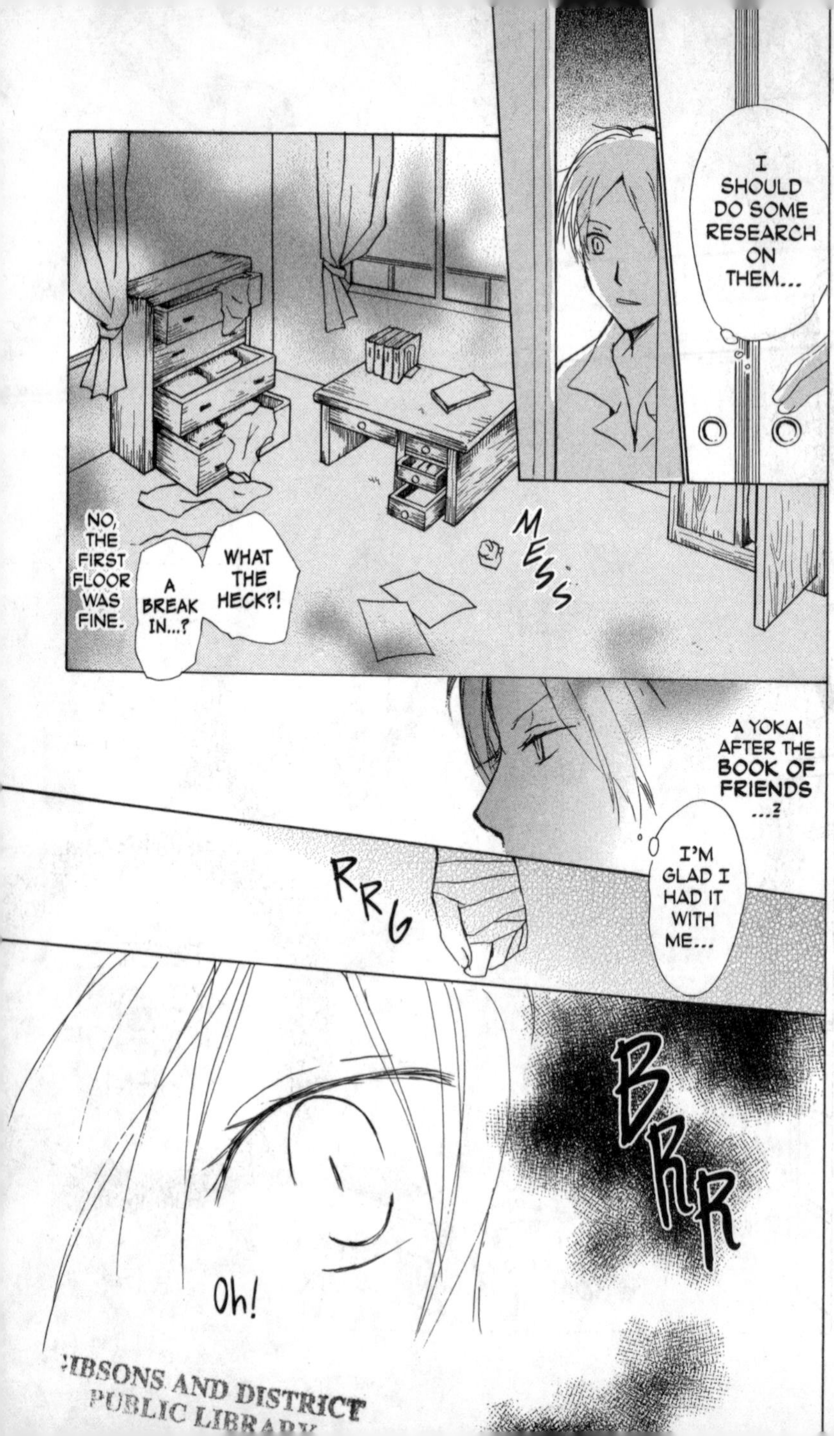
I SHOULD DO SOME RESEARCH ON THEM...
MESS
WHAT THE HECK?!
A BREAK IN...?
NO, THE FIRST FLOOR WAS FINE.
A YOKAI AFTER THE BOOK OF FRIENDS ...?
I'M GLAD I HAD IT WITH ME...
RRG
BRRR
Oh!

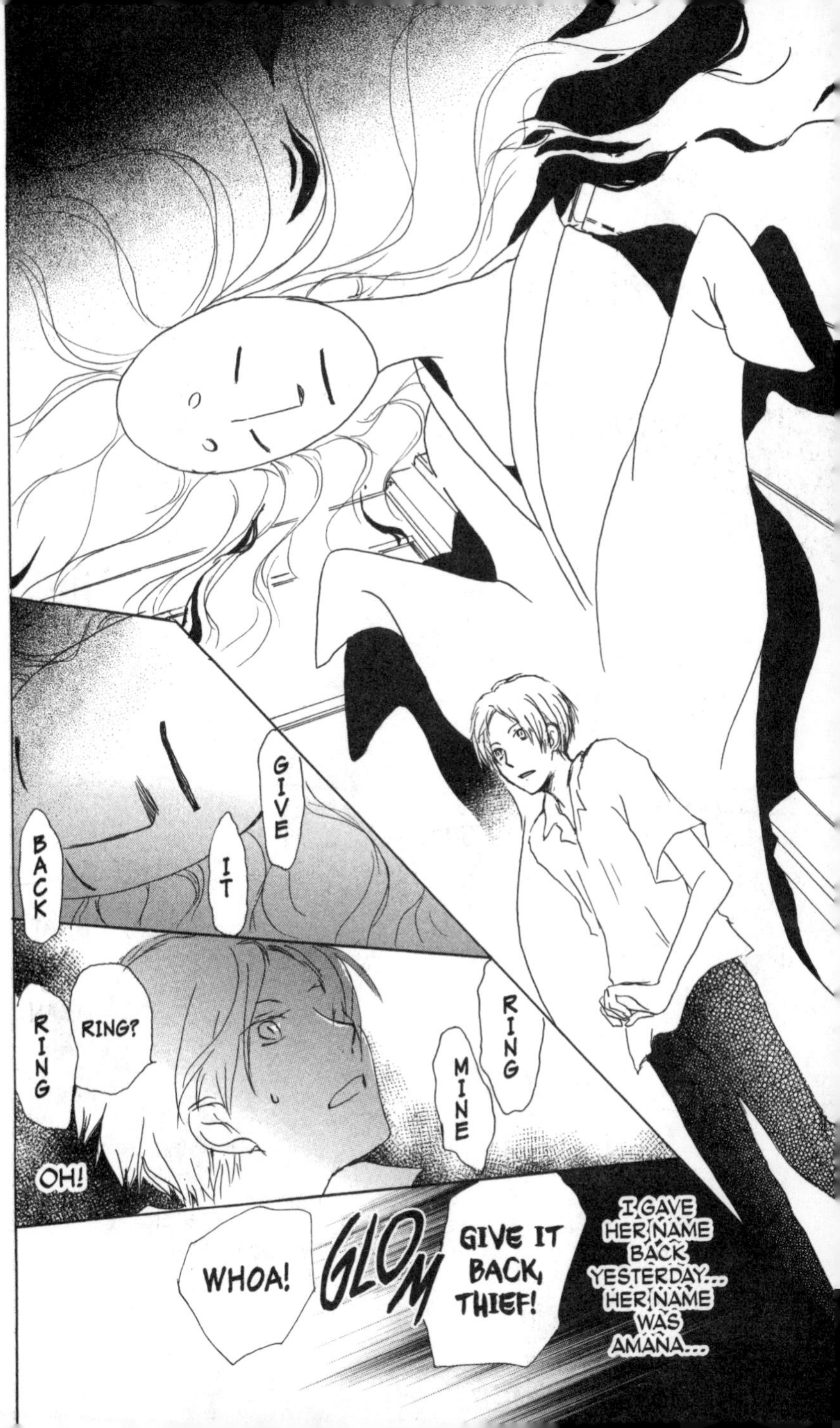
GIVE
IT
BACK
RING
MINE
RING?
RING
OH!
I GAVE HER NAME BACK YESTERDAY... HER NAME WAS AMANA...
GIVE IT BACK, THIEF!
GLOM
WHOA!

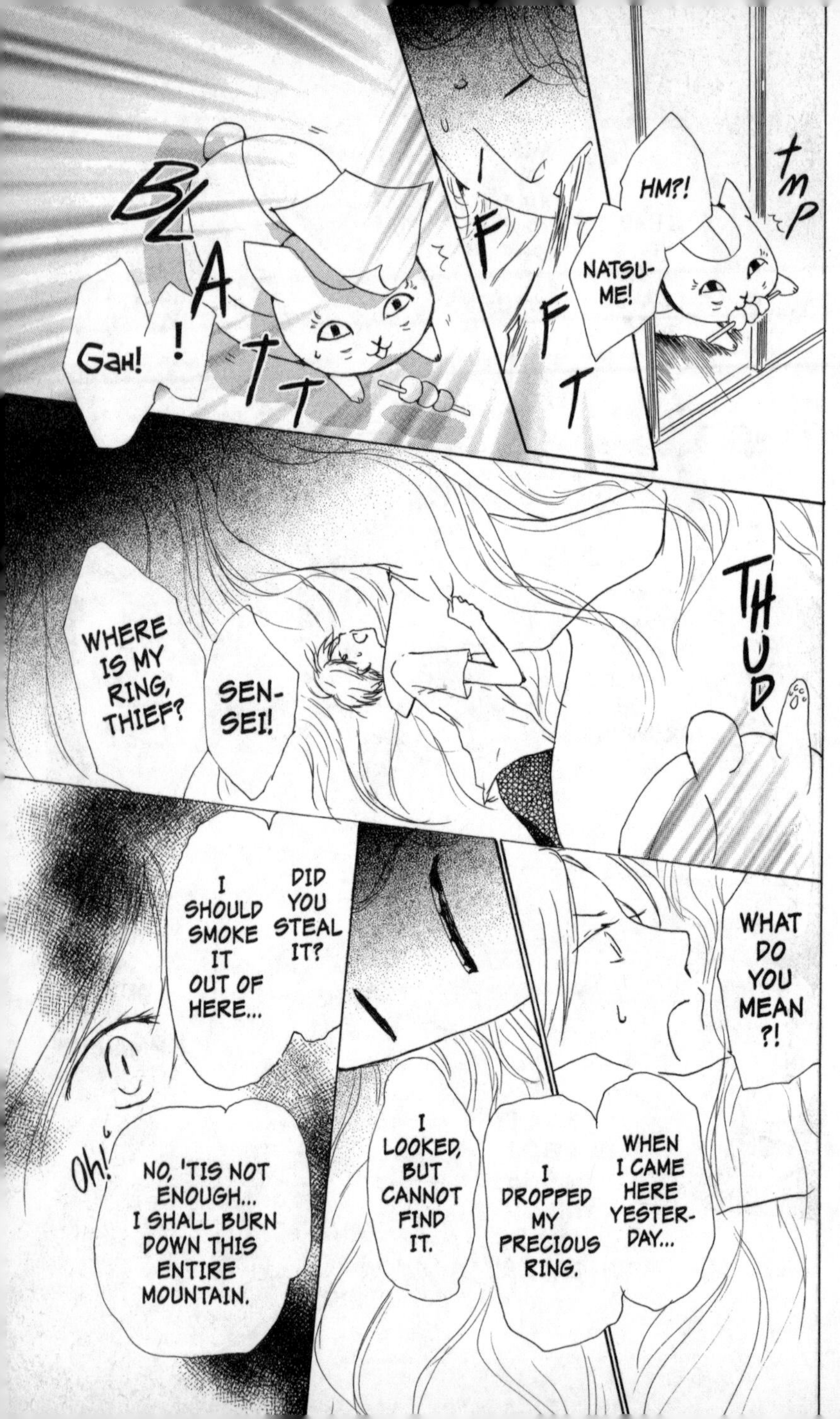
tmp
HM?!
NATSU-ME!
FFFT
BLATTT
!
Gah!
THUD
SEN-SEI!
WHERE IS MY RING, THIEF?
WHAT DO YOU MEAN ?!
WHEN I CAME HERE YESTER-DAY...
I DROPPED MY PRECIOUS RING.
I LOOKED, BUT CANNOT FIND IT.
DID YOU STEAL IT?
I SHOULD SMOKE IT OUT OF HERE...
Oh!
NO, 'TIS NOT ENOUGH... I SHALL BURN DOWN THIS ENTIRE MOUNTAIN.

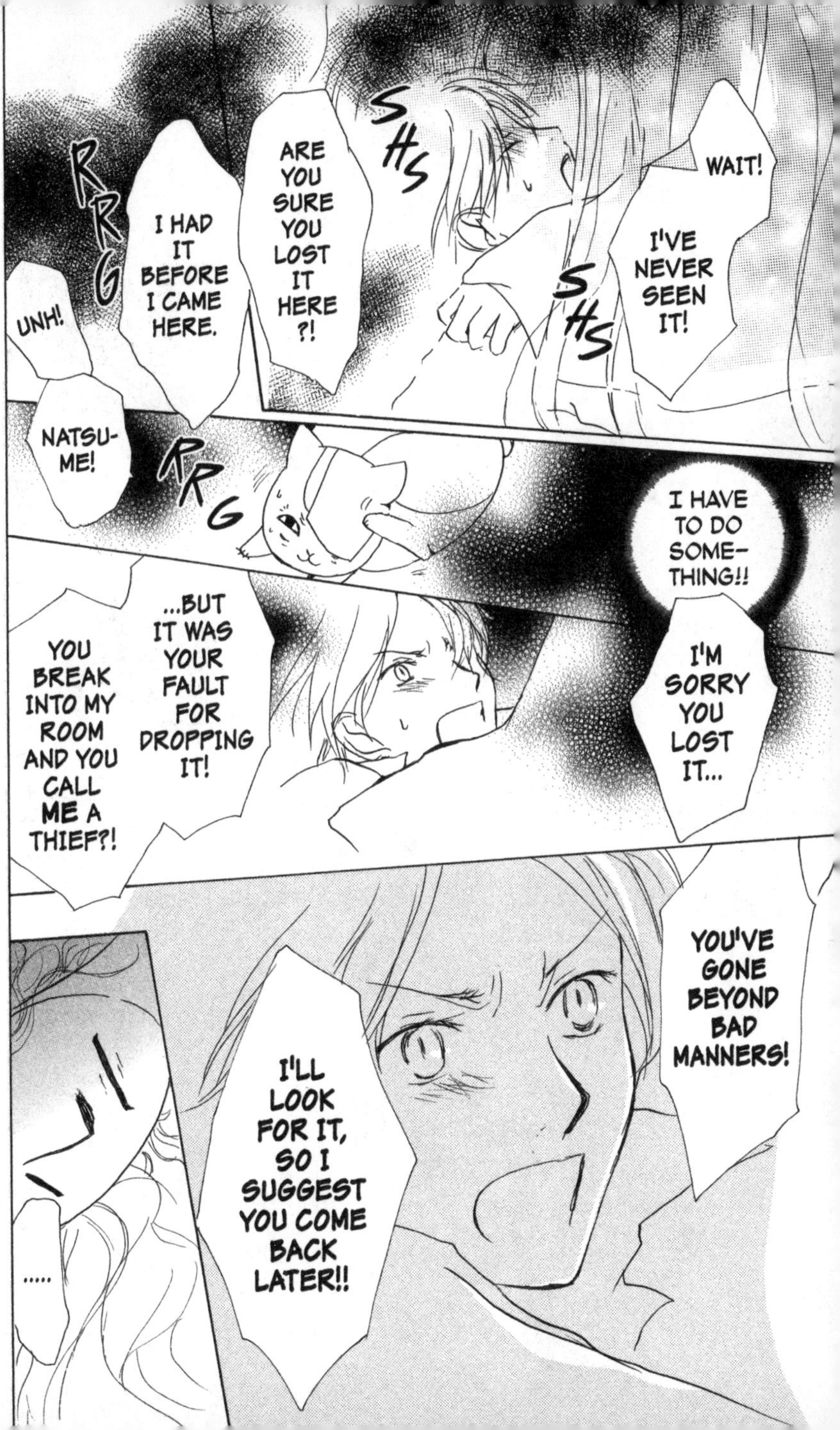
WAIT!
I'VE NEVER SEEN IT!
SHS
SHS
ARE YOU SURE YOU LOST IT HERE?!
RRG
I HAD IT BEFORE I CAME HERE.
UNH!
I HAVE TO DO SOMETHING!!
NATSUME!
RRG
I'M SORRY YOU LOST IT...
...BUT IT WAS YOUR FAULT FOR DROPPING IT!
YOU BREAK INTO MY ROOM AND YOU CALL ME A THIEF?!
YOU'VE GONE BEYOND BAD MANNERS!
I'LL LOOK FOR IT, SO I SUGGEST YOU COME BACK LATER!!
.....

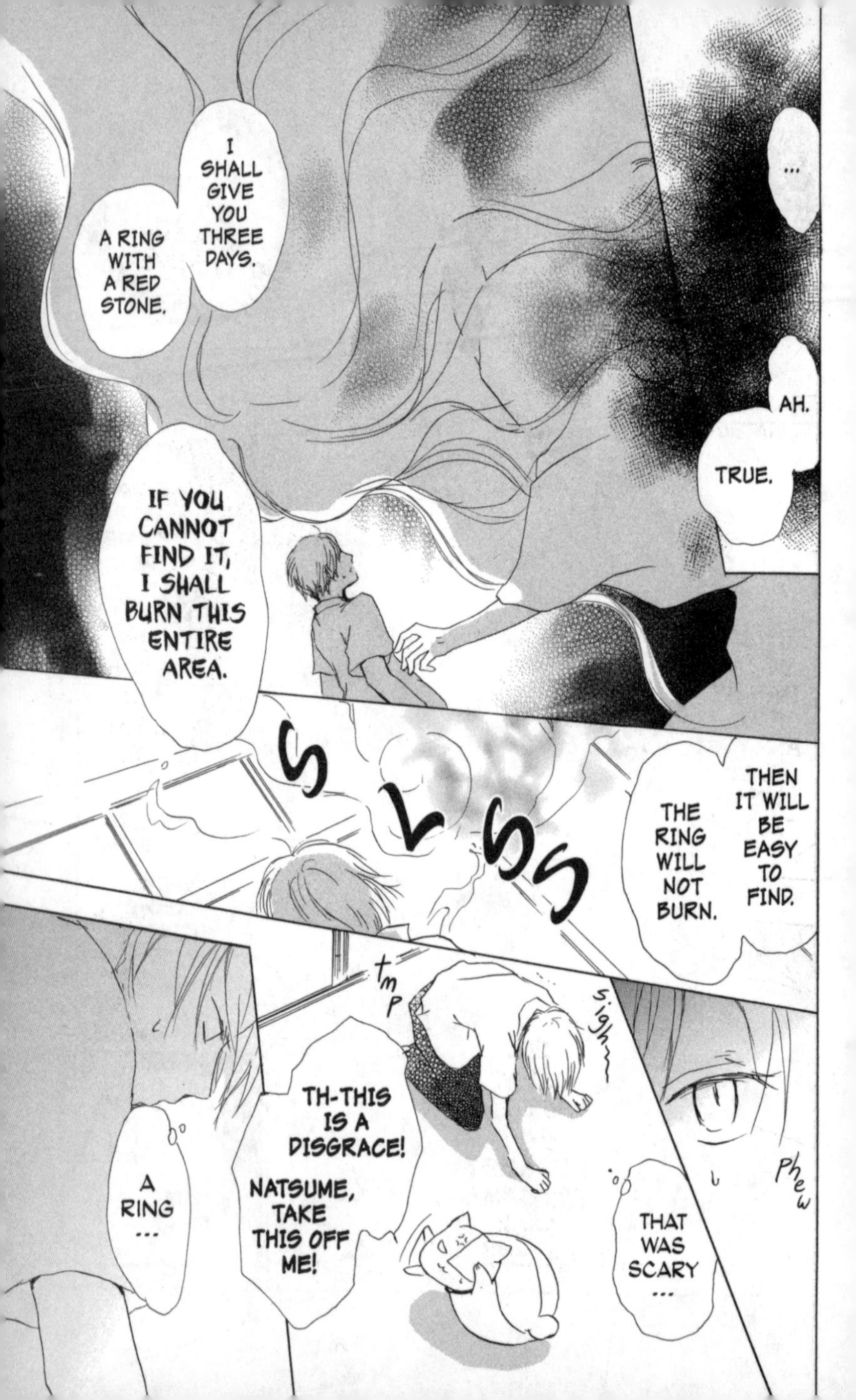
...
AH.
TRUE.
I SHALL GIVE YOU THREE DAYS.
A RING WITH A RED STONE.
IF YOU CANNOT FIND IT, I SHALL BURN THIS ENTIRE AREA.
SLSS
THEN IT WILL BE EASY TO FIND.
THE RING WILL NOT BURN.
Phew
THAT WAS SCARY...
sigh
tmp
TH-THIS IS A DISGRACE!
NATSUME, TAKE THIS OFF ME!
A RING...

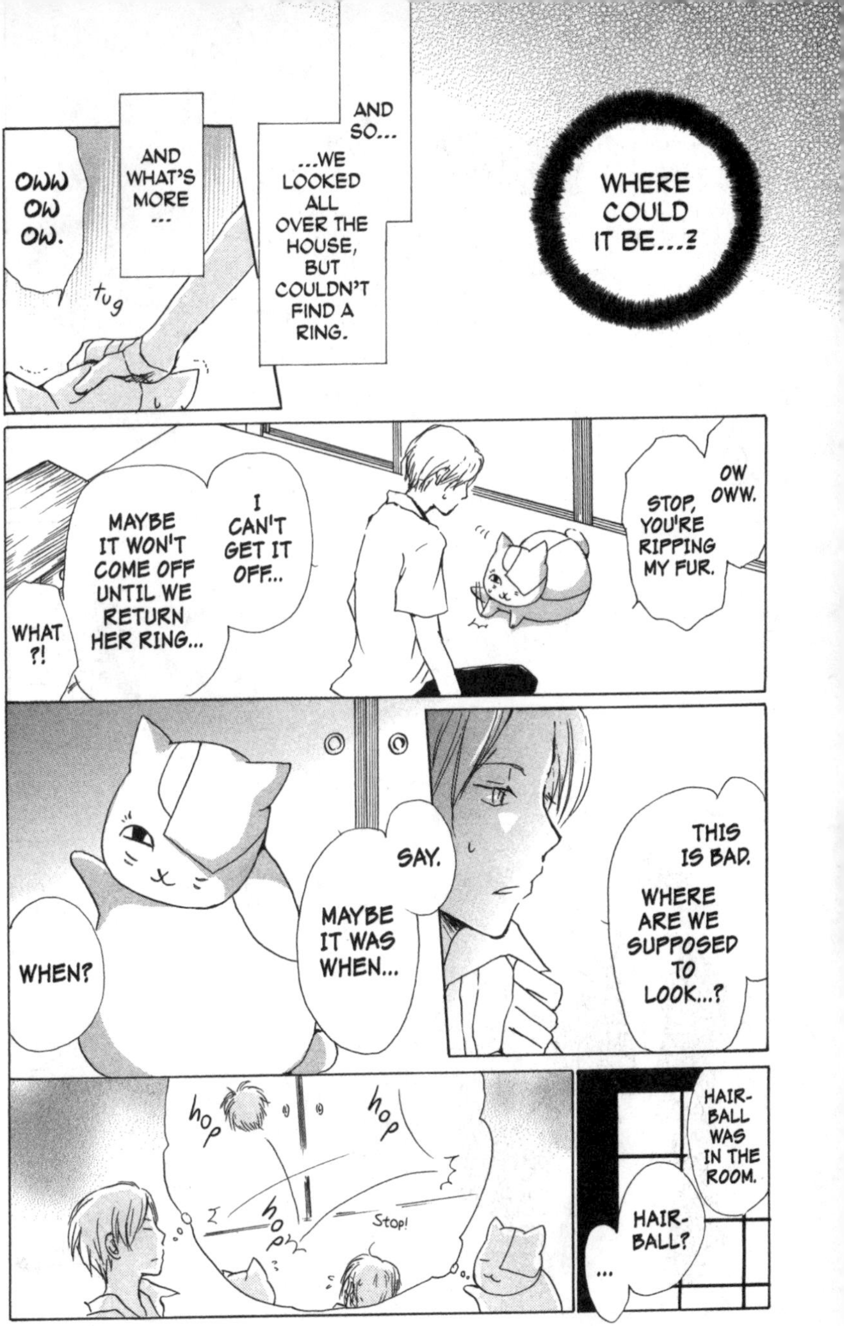
WHERE COULD IT BE...?
AND SO...
...WE LOOKED ALL OVER THE HOUSE, BUT COULDN'T FIND A RING.
AND WHAT'S MORE...
OWW OW OW.
tug
OW OWW.
STOP, YOU'RE RIPPING MY FUR.
I CAN'T GET IT OFF...
MAYBE IT WON'T COME OFF UNTIL WE RETURN HER RING...
WHAT?!
THIS IS BAD.
WHERE ARE WE SUPPOSED TO LOOK...?
SAY.
MAYBE IT WAS WHEN...
WHEN?
HAIR-BALL WAS IN THE ROOM.
HAIR-BALL?
...
hop
hop
hop
Stop!

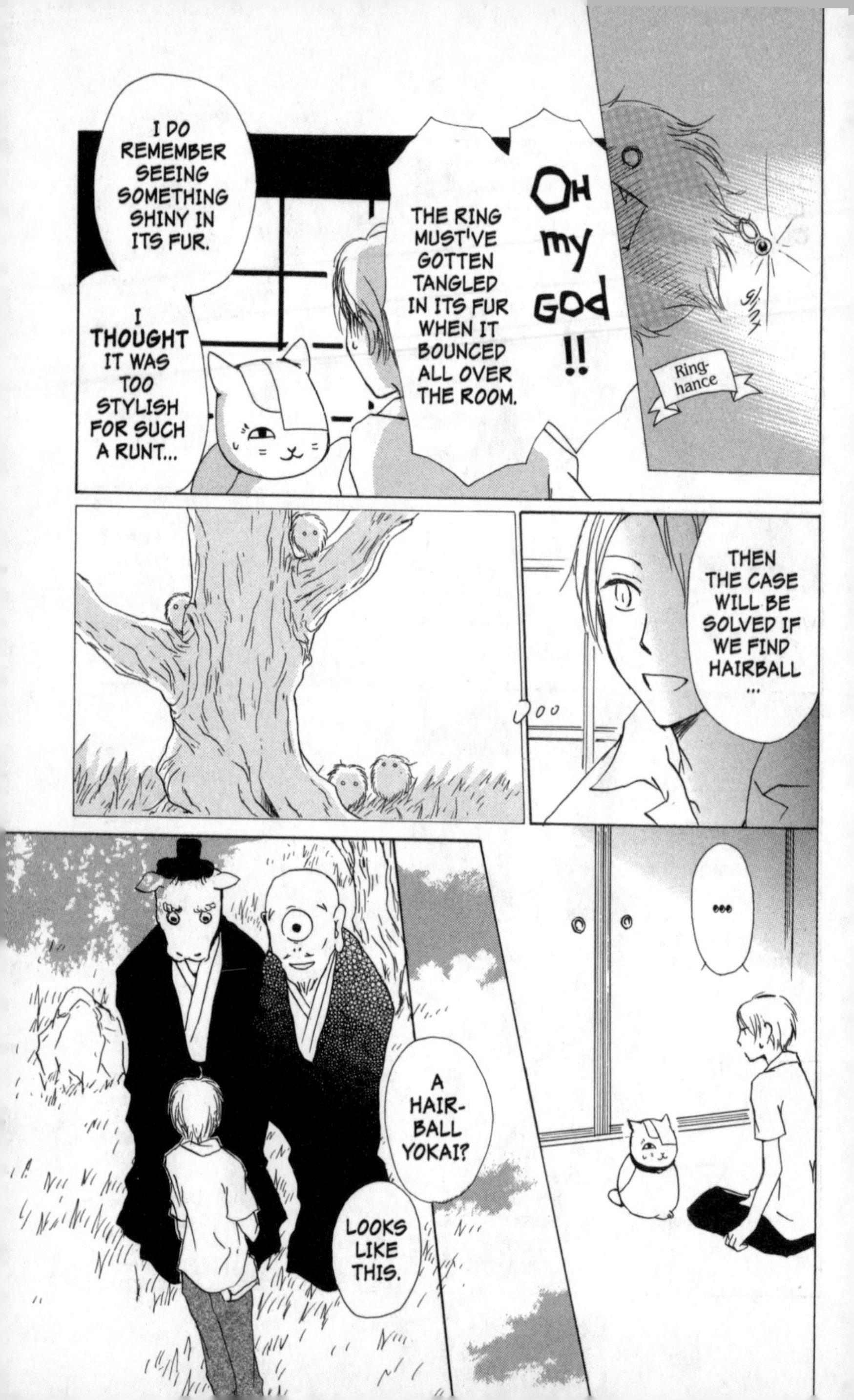
OH my GOD!!
glint
Ring-hance
THE RING MUST'VE GOTTEN TANGLED IN ITS FUR WHEN IT BOUNCED ALL OVER THE ROOM.
I DO REMEMBER SEEING SOMETHING SHINY IN ITS FUR.
I THOUGHT IT WAS TOO STYLISH FOR SUCH A RUNT...
THEN THE CASE WILL BE SOLVED IF WE FIND HAIRBALL...
...
A HAIR-BALL YOKAI?
LOOKS LIKE THIS.

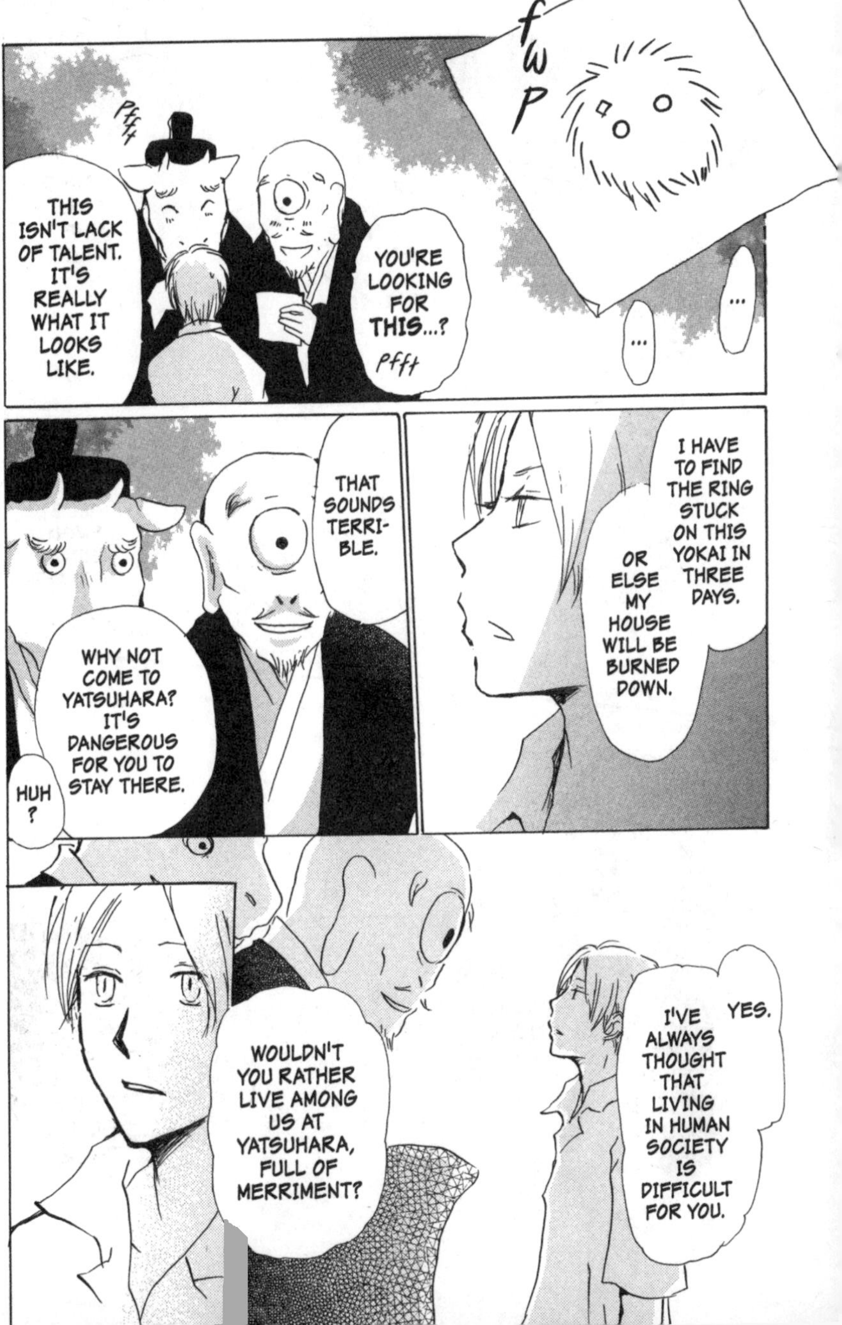
fwp
...
...
pfft
YOU'RE LOOKING FOR THIS...?
pfft
THIS ISN'T LACK OF TALENT. IT'S REALLY WHAT IT LOOKS LIKE.
I HAVE TO FIND THE RING STUCK ON THIS YOKAI IN THREE DAYS.
OR ELSE MY HOUSE WILL BE BURNED DOWN.
THAT SOUNDS TERRIBLE.
WHY NOT COME TO YATSUHARA? IT'S DANGEROUS FOR YOU TO STAY THERE.
HUH?
YES.
I'VE ALWAYS THOUGHT THAT LIVING IN HUMAN SOCIETY IS DIFFICULT FOR YOU.
WOULDN'T YOU RATHER LIVE AMONG US AT YATSUHARA, FULL OF MERRIMENT?

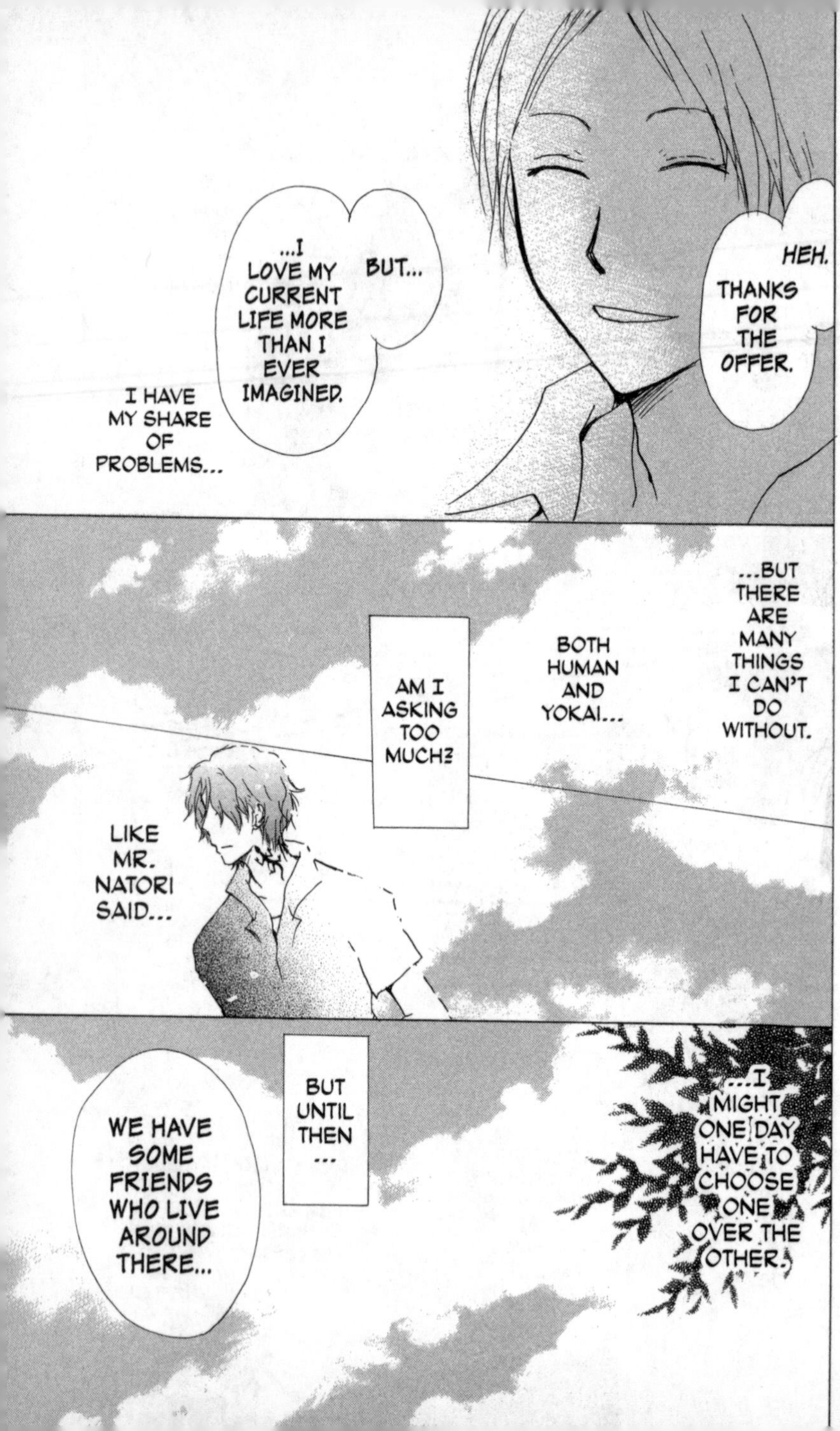
HEH. THANKS FOR THE OFFER.
BUT...
...I LOVE MY CURRENT LIFE MORE THAN I EVER IMAGINED.
I HAVE MY SHARE OF PROBLEMS...
...BUT THERE ARE MANY THINGS I CAN'T DO WITHOUT.
BOTH HUMAN AND YOKAI...
AM I ASKING TOO MUCH?
LIKE MR. NATORI SAID...
...I MIGHT ONE DAY HAVE TO CHOOSE ONE OVER THE OTHER.
BUT UNTIL THEN...
WE HAVE SOME FRIENDS WHO LIVE AROUND THERE...

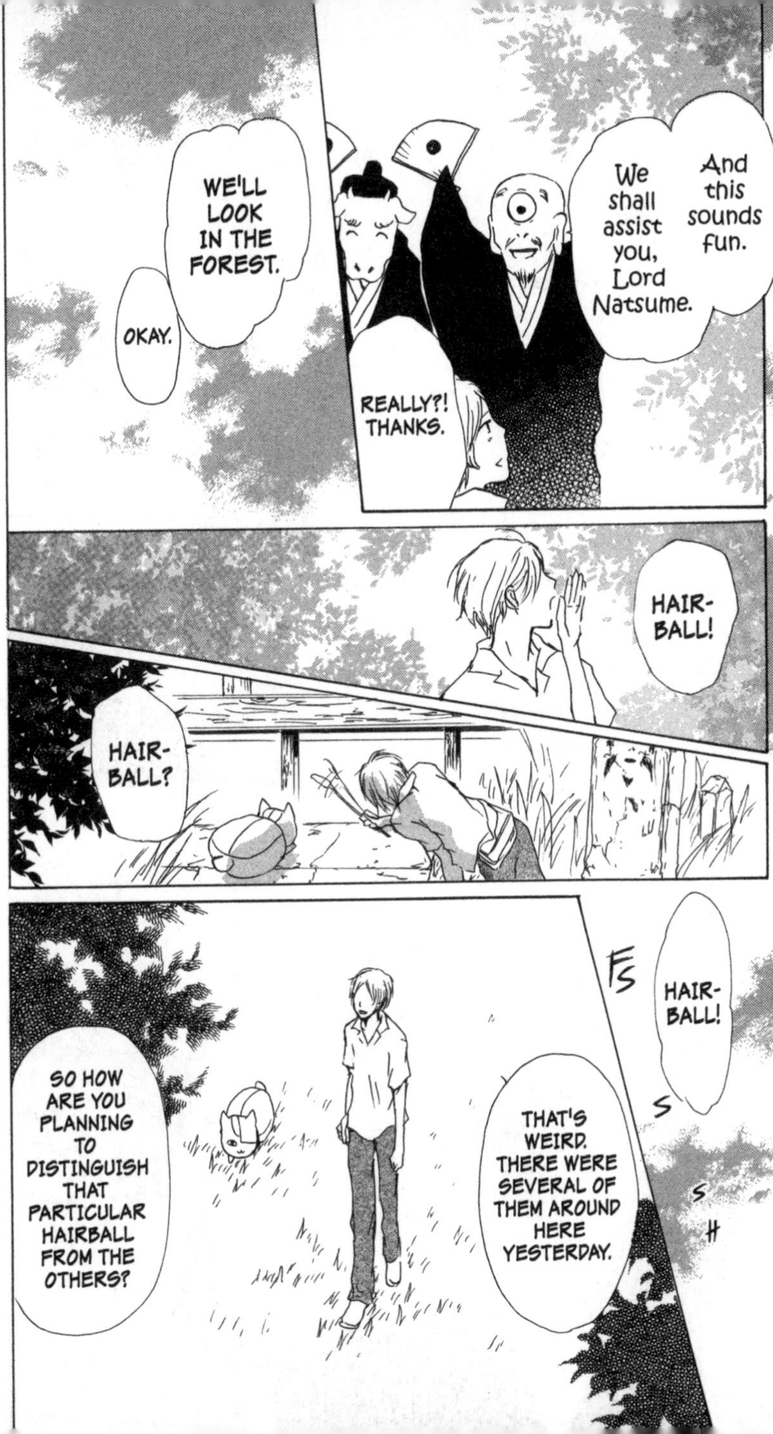

We shall assist you, Lord Natsume.
And this sounds fun.
REALLY?! THANKS.
WE'LL LOOK IN THE FOREST.
OKAY.
HAIR-BALL!
HAIR-BALL?
HAIR-BALL!
FS
THAT'S WEIRD. THERE WERE SEVERAL OF THEM AROUND HERE YESTERDAY.
S
S H
SO HOW ARE YOU PLANNING TO DISTINGUISH THAT PARTICULAR HAIRBALL FROM THE OTHERS?

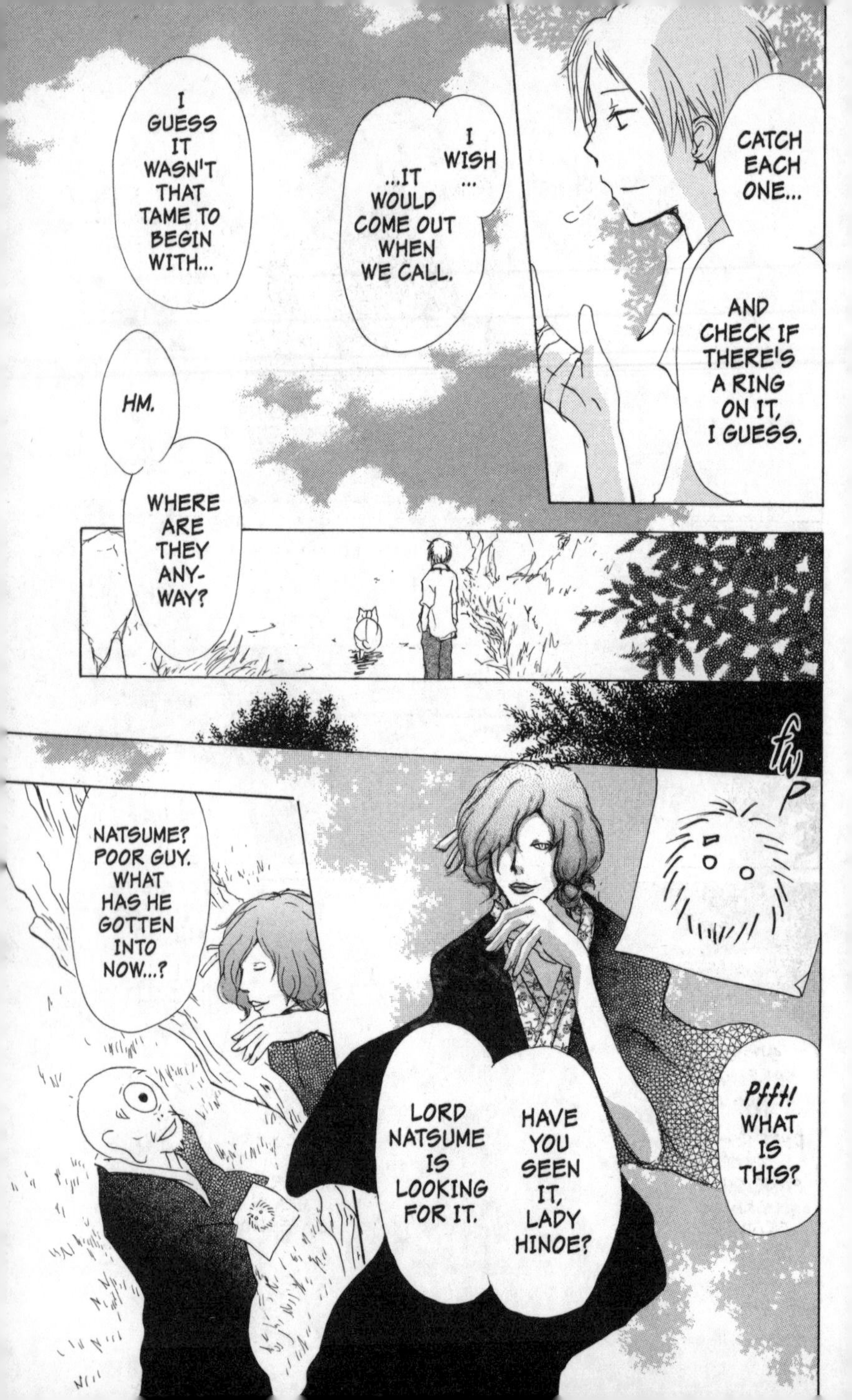
CATCH EACH ONE...
AND CHECK IF THERE'S A RING ON IT, I GUESS.
I WISH ...
...IT WOULD COME OUT WHEN WE CALL.
I GUESS IT WASN'T THAT TAME TO BEGIN WITH...
HM.
WHERE ARE THEY ANY-WAY?
fwp
Pfft! WHAT IS THIS?
HAVE YOU SEEN IT, LADY HINOE?
LORD NATSUME IS LOOKING FOR IT.
NATSUME? POOR GUY. WHAT HAS HE GOTTEN INTO NOW...?

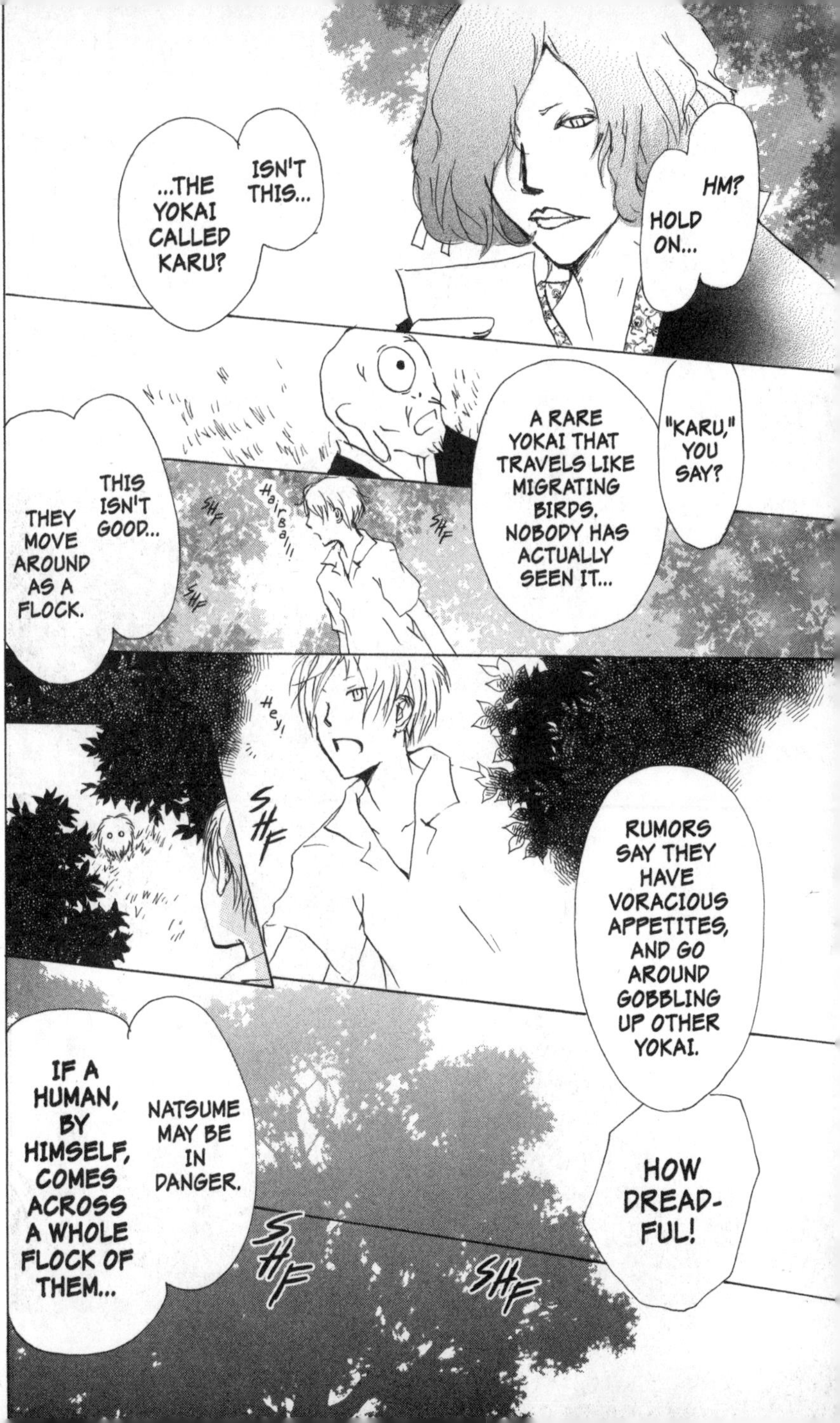
HM? HOLD ON...
ISN'T THIS...
...THE YOKAI CALLED KARU?
"KARU," YOU SAY?
A RARE YOKAI THAT TRAVELS LIKE MIGRATING BIRDS. NOBODY HAS ACTUALLY SEEN IT...
SHF
Hairball!
SHF
THIS ISN'T GOOD...
THEY MOVE AROUND AS A FLOCK.
SHF
RUMORS SAY THEY HAVE VORACIOUS APPETITES, AND GO AROUND GOBBLING UP OTHER YOKAI.
Hey!
SHF
HOW DREAD-FUL!
SHF
SHF
NATSUME MAY BE IN DANGER.
IF A HUMAN, BY HIMSELF, COMES ACROSS A WHOLE FLOCK OF THEM...

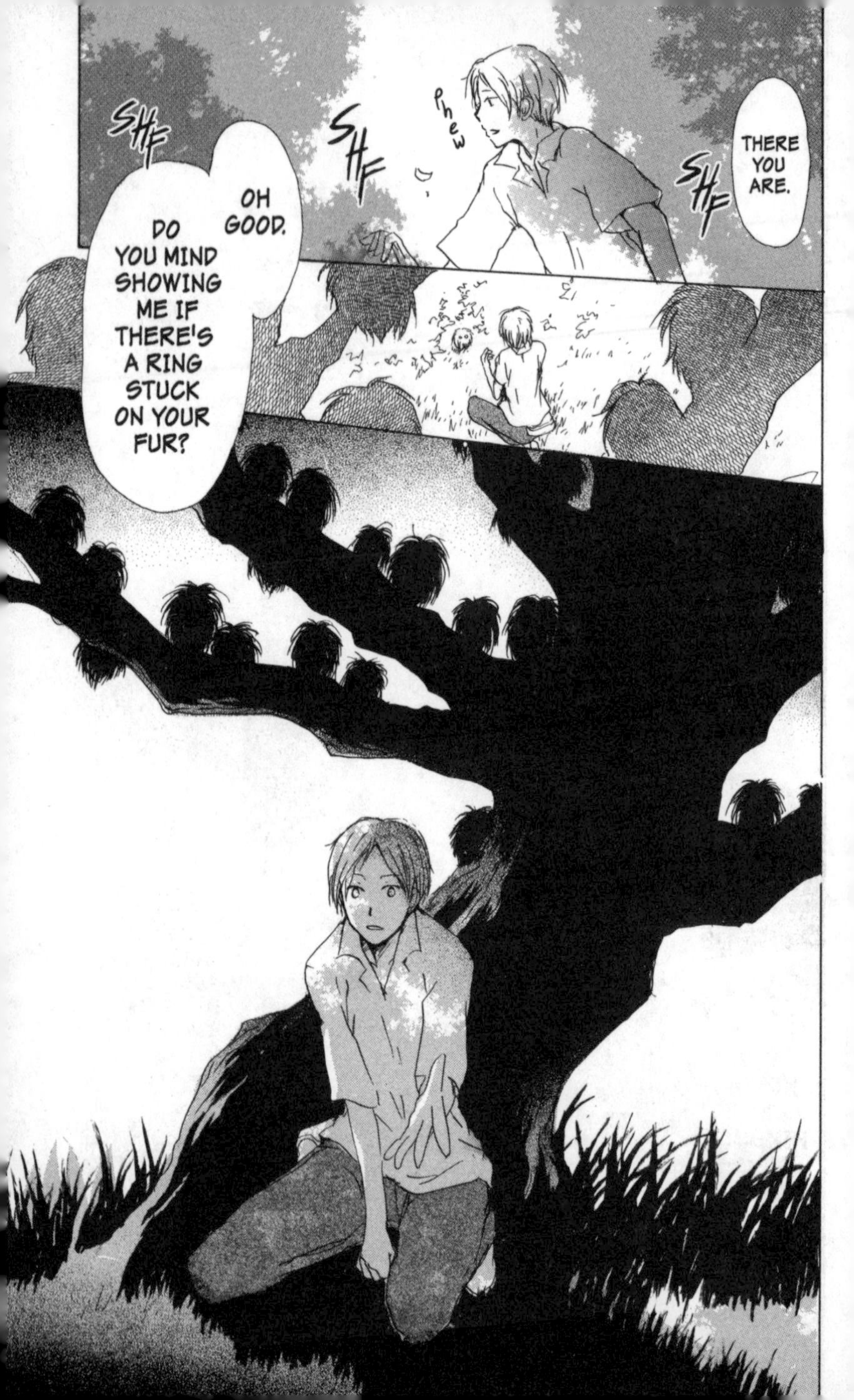
SHF
THERE YOU ARE.
Phew
SHF
SHF
OH GOOD.
DO YOU MIND SHOWING ME IF THERE'S A RING STUCK ON YOUR FUR?

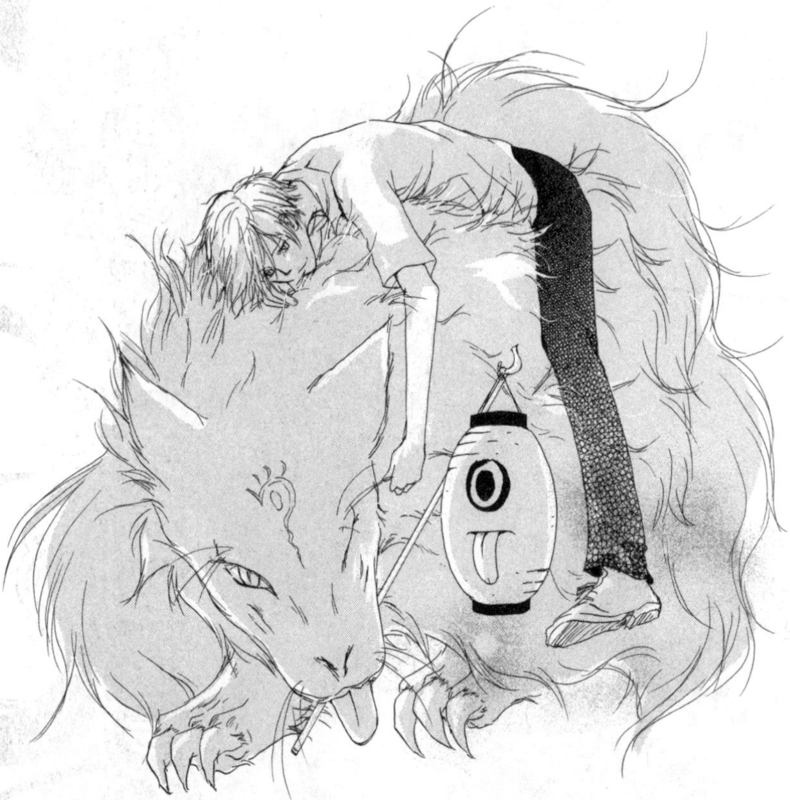

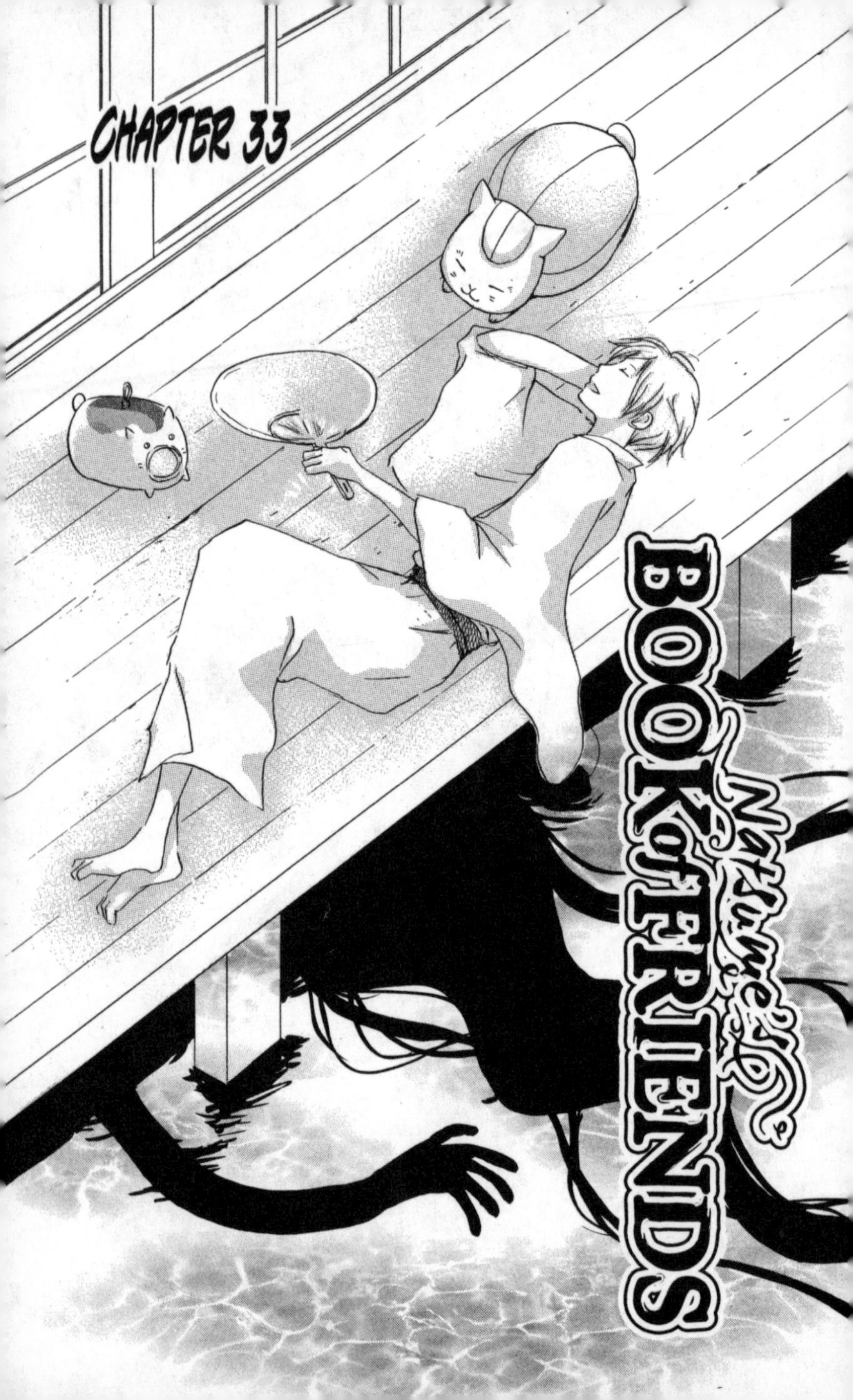
CHAPTER 33
Natsume's
BOOK of FRIENDS

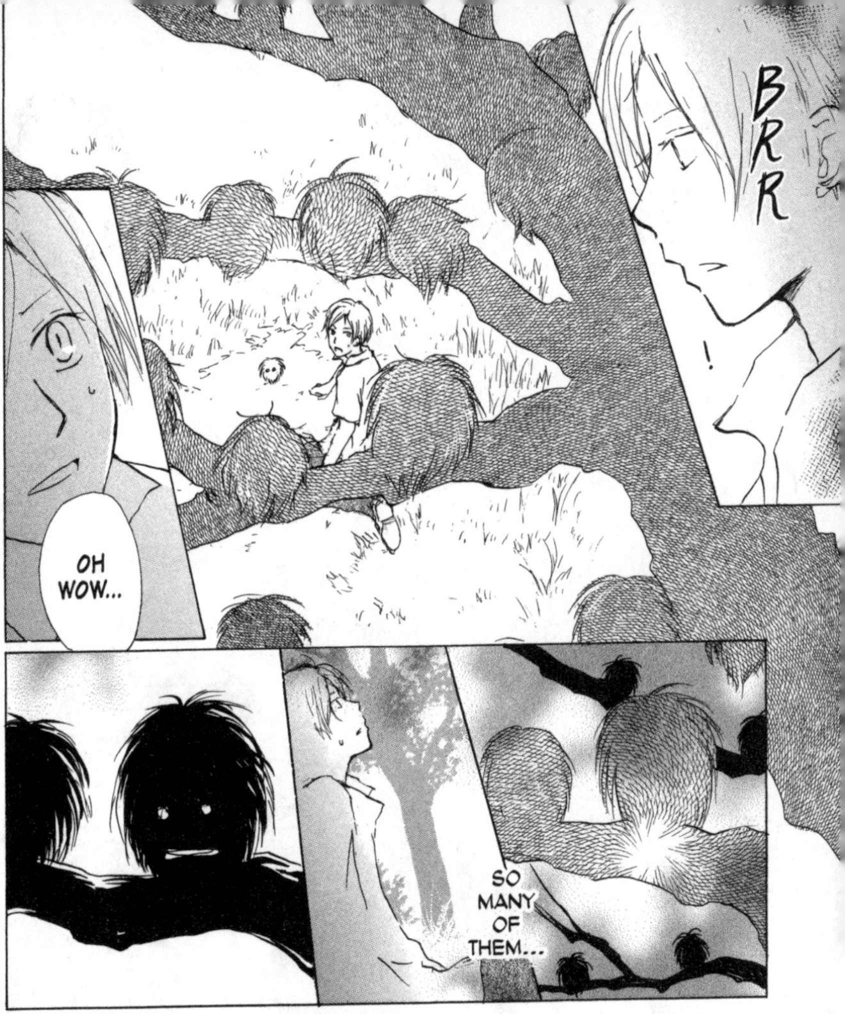
BRR
!
OH WOW...
SO MANY OF THEM...

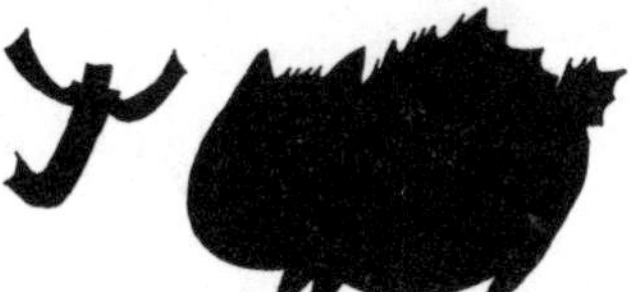

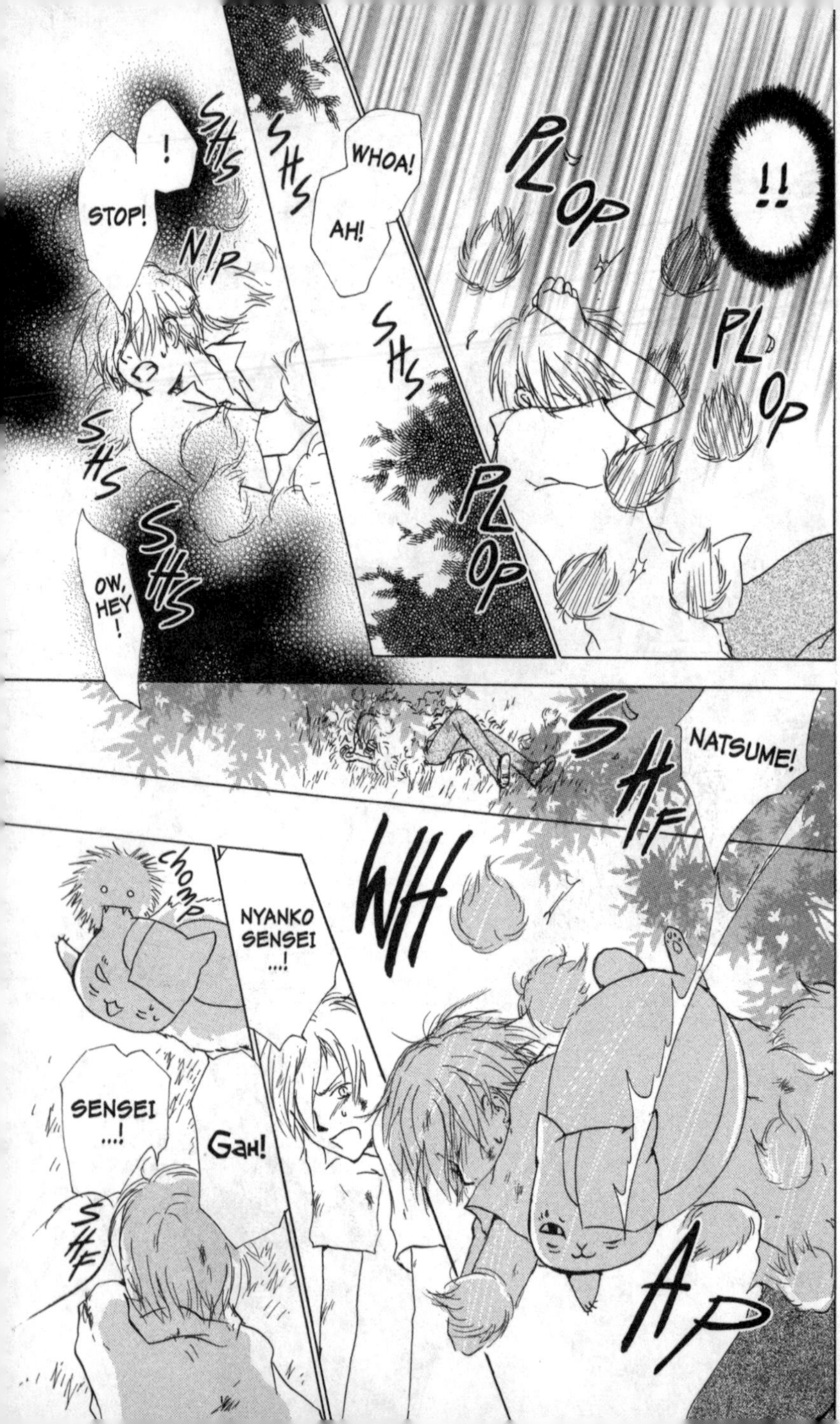

!!
PLOP
PLOP
PLOP
WHOA!
AH!
SHS
SHS
!
STOP!
SHS
NIP
SHS
SHS
OW, HEY!
NATSUME!
SHF
WHAP
NYANKO SENSEI ...!
chomp
SENSEI ...!
Gah!
SHF

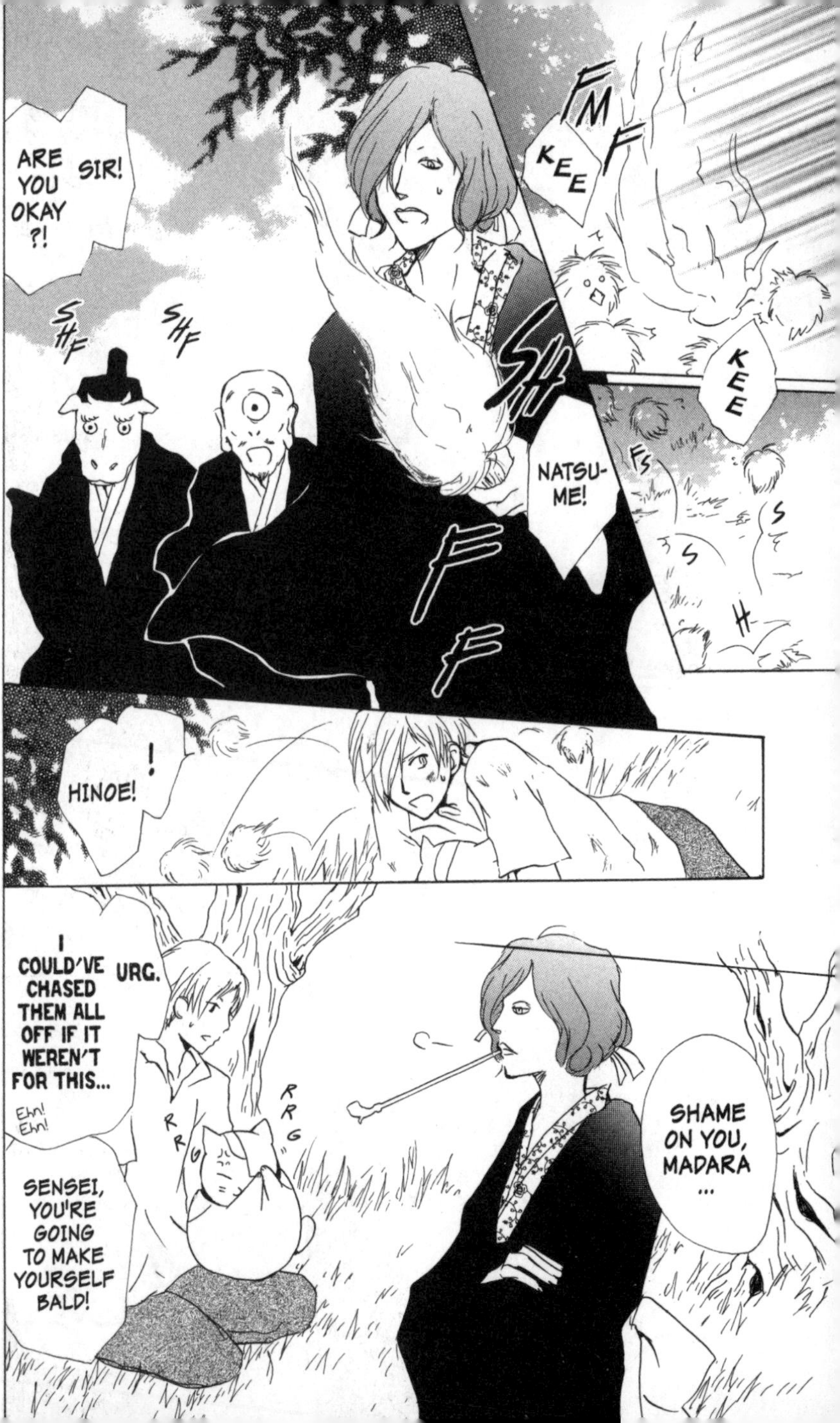
FMF
KEE
KEE
FS
SSH
SIR!
ARE YOU OKAY?!
SHF
SHF
SH
NATSU-ME!
FF
!
HINOE!
SHAME ON YOU, MADARA...
RRG
RRG
URG.
I COULD'VE CHASED THEM ALL OFF IF IT WEREN'T FOR THIS...
Ehn! Ehn!
SENSEI, YOU'RE GOING TO MAKE YOURSELF BALD!

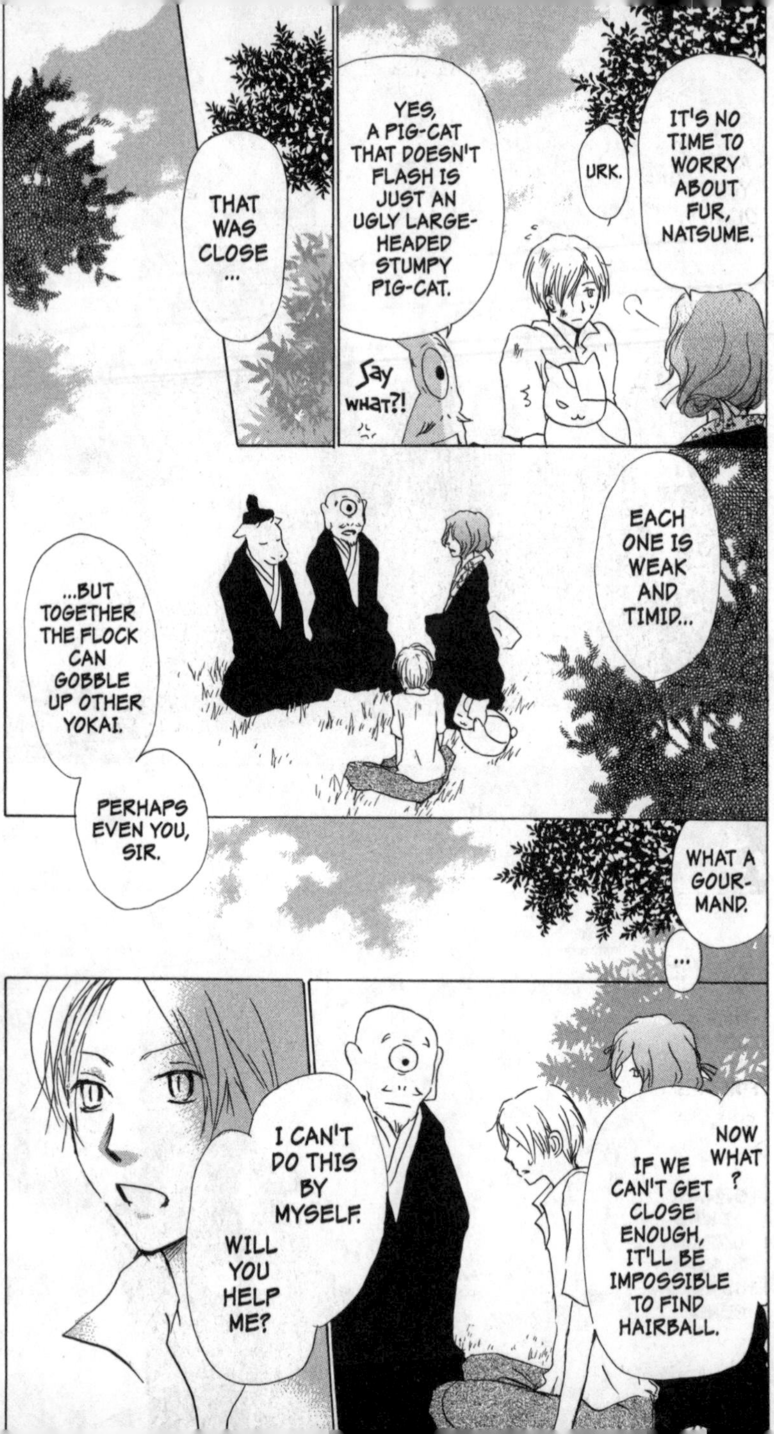
IT'S NO TIME TO WORRY ABOUT FUR, NATSUME.
URK.
YES, A PIG-CAT THAT DOESN'T FLASH IS JUST AN UGLY LARGE-HEADED STUMPY PIG-CAT.
SAY WHAT?!
THAT WAS CLOSE ...
EACH ONE IS WEAK AND TIMID...
...BUT TOGETHER THE FLOCK CAN GOBBLE UP OTHER YOKAI.
PERHAPS EVEN YOU, SIR.
WHAT A GOUR-MAND.
...
NOW WHAT?
IF WE CAN'T GET CLOSE ENOUGH, IT'LL BE IMPOSSIBLE TO FIND HAIRBALL.
I CAN'T DO THIS BY MYSELF.
WILL YOU HELP ME?

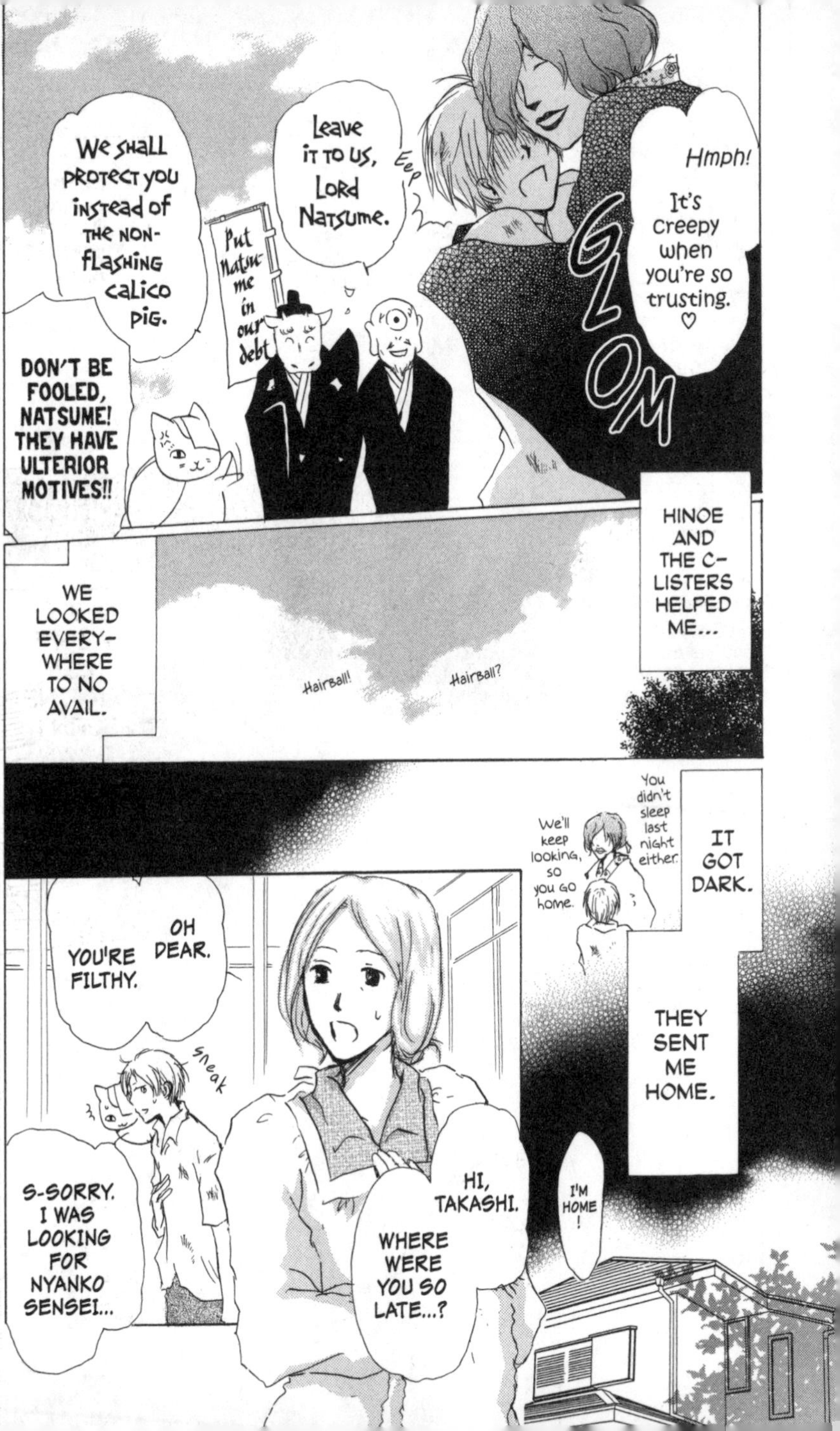
Hmph!
It's creepy when you're so trusting. ♡
GLOM
Eep
Leave it to us, Lord Natsume.
Put Natsume in our debt
We shall protect you instead of the non-flashing calico pig.
DON'T BE FOOLED, NATSUME! THEY HAVE ULTERIOR MOTIVES!!
HINOE AND THE C-LISTERS HELPED ME...
Hairball?
Hairball!
WE LOOKED EVERYWHERE TO NO AVAIL.
IT GOT DARK.
You didn't sleep last night either.
We'll keep looking, so you go home.
THEY SENT ME HOME.
I'M HOME!
HI, TAKASHI.
WHERE WERE YOU SO LATE...?
OH DEAR.
YOU'RE FILTHY.
sneak
S-SORRY. I WAS LOOKING FOR NYANKO SENSEI...

## 02

### ❋ $\frac{1}{4}$ columns

I'm talking about this space here in the graphic novels. Now in my 17th volume total, I wonder what more I could write about. I wish there were some interesting incidents, but my life is really simple and casual. If you have any requests, any topics you want to know about, please send me a note.

### ❋ C-listers

I totally missed the window in which I could have given them names. I hope I can sneak in a situation where they can introduce themselves.

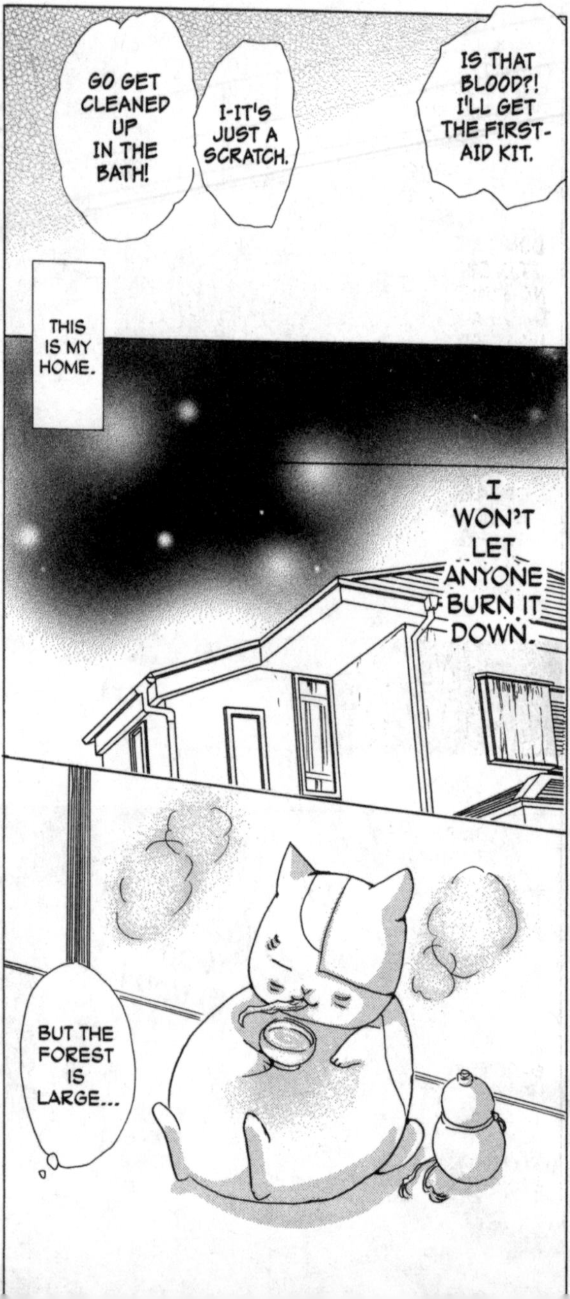
IS THAT BLOOD?! I'LL GET THE FIRST-AID KIT.
I-IT'S JUST A SCRATCH.
GO GET CLEANED UP IN THE BATH!
THIS IS MY HOME.
I WON'T LET ANYONE BURN IT DOWN.
BUT THE FOREST IS LARGE...

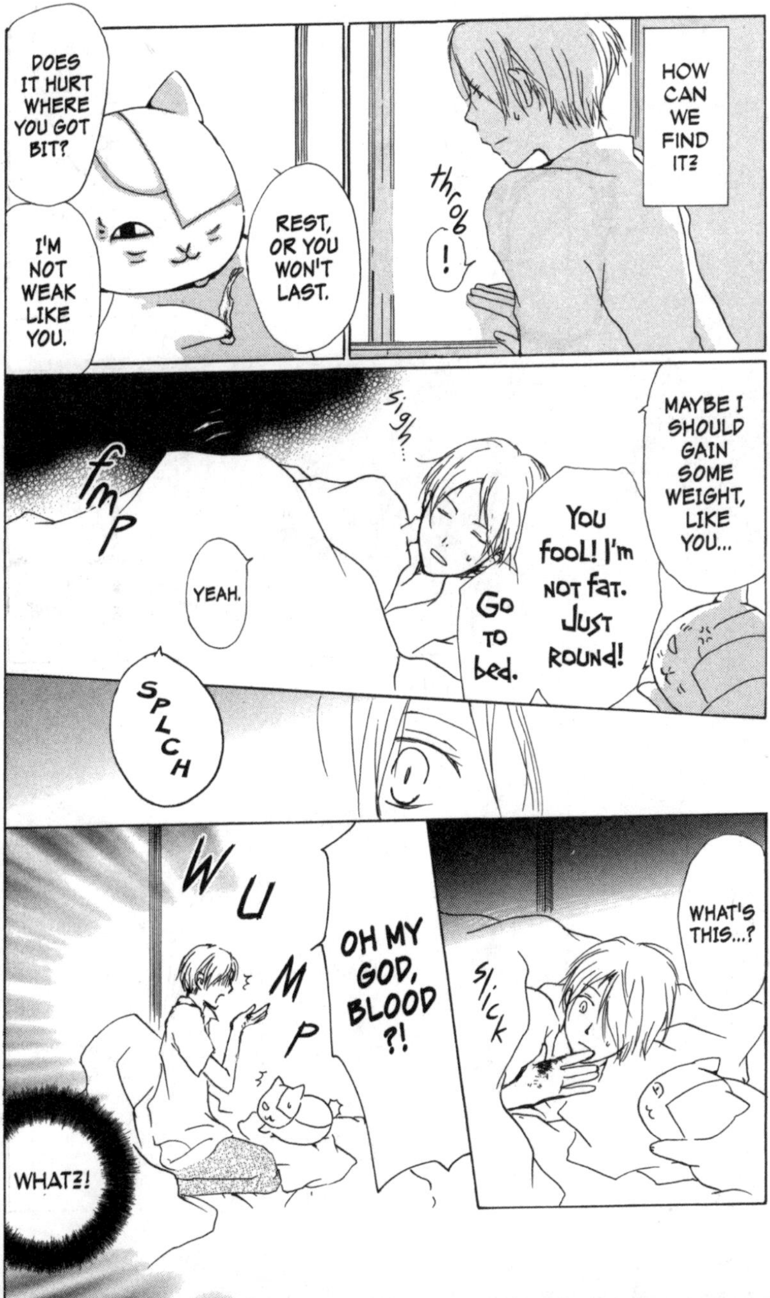
HOW CAN WE FIND IT?
throb
!
DOES IT HURT WHERE YOU GOT BIT?
REST, OR YOU WON'T LAST.
I'M NOT WEAK LIKE YOU.
MAYBE I SHOULD GAIN SOME WEIGHT, LIKE YOU...
You fool! I'm not fat. Just round!
Go to bed.
sigh...
YEAH.
fmp
SPLCH
WHAT'S THIS...?
slick
OH MY GOD, BLOOD?!
WUMP
WHAT?!

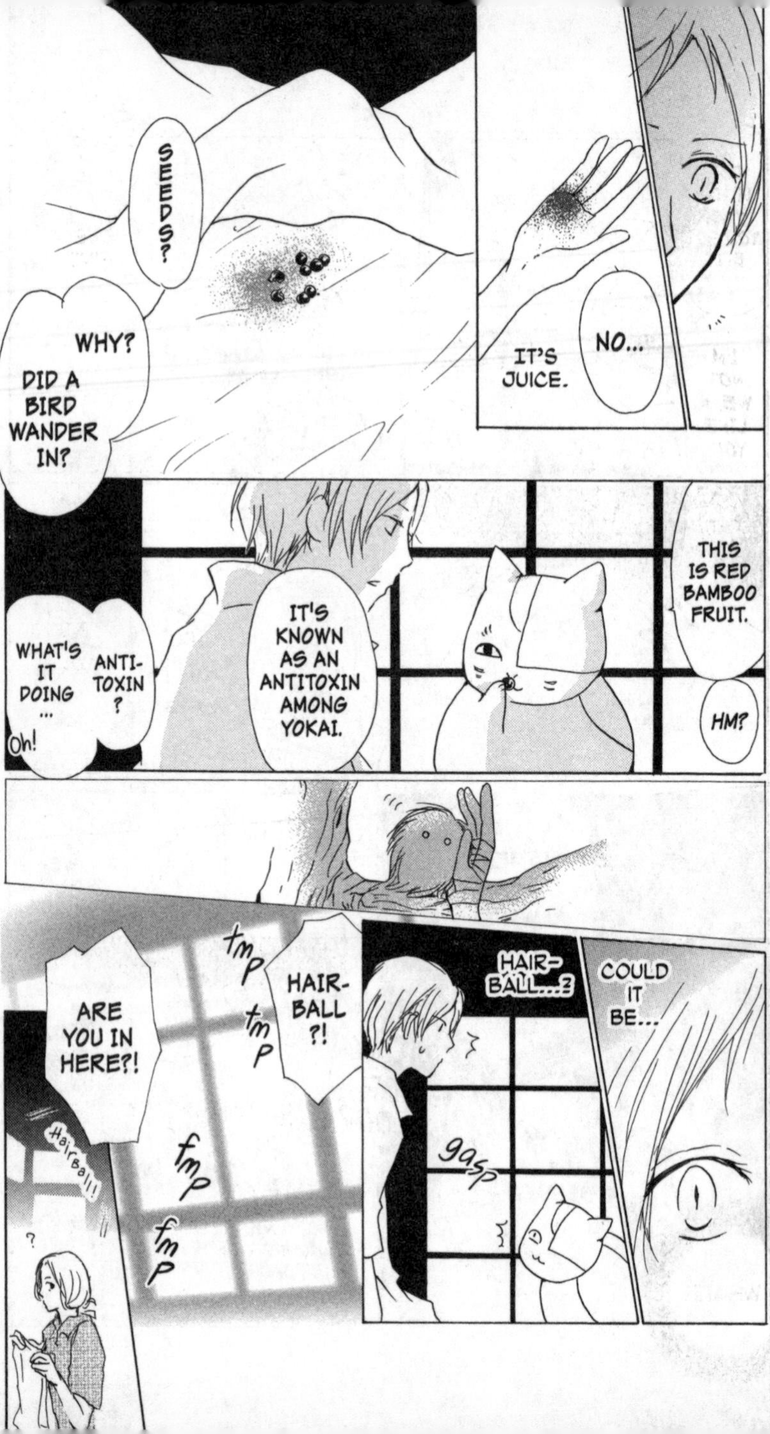
SEEDS?
NO...
IT'S JUICE.
WHY?
DID A BIRD WANDER IN?
THIS IS RED BAMBOO FRUIT.
HM?
IT'S KNOWN AS AN ANTITOXIN AMONG YOKAI.
ANTI-TOXIN?
WHAT'S IT DOING ...
Oh!
COULD IT BE...
HAIR-BALL...?
gasp
HAIR-BALL?!
tmp tmp
ARE YOU IN HERE?!
fmp fmp
Hairball!
?

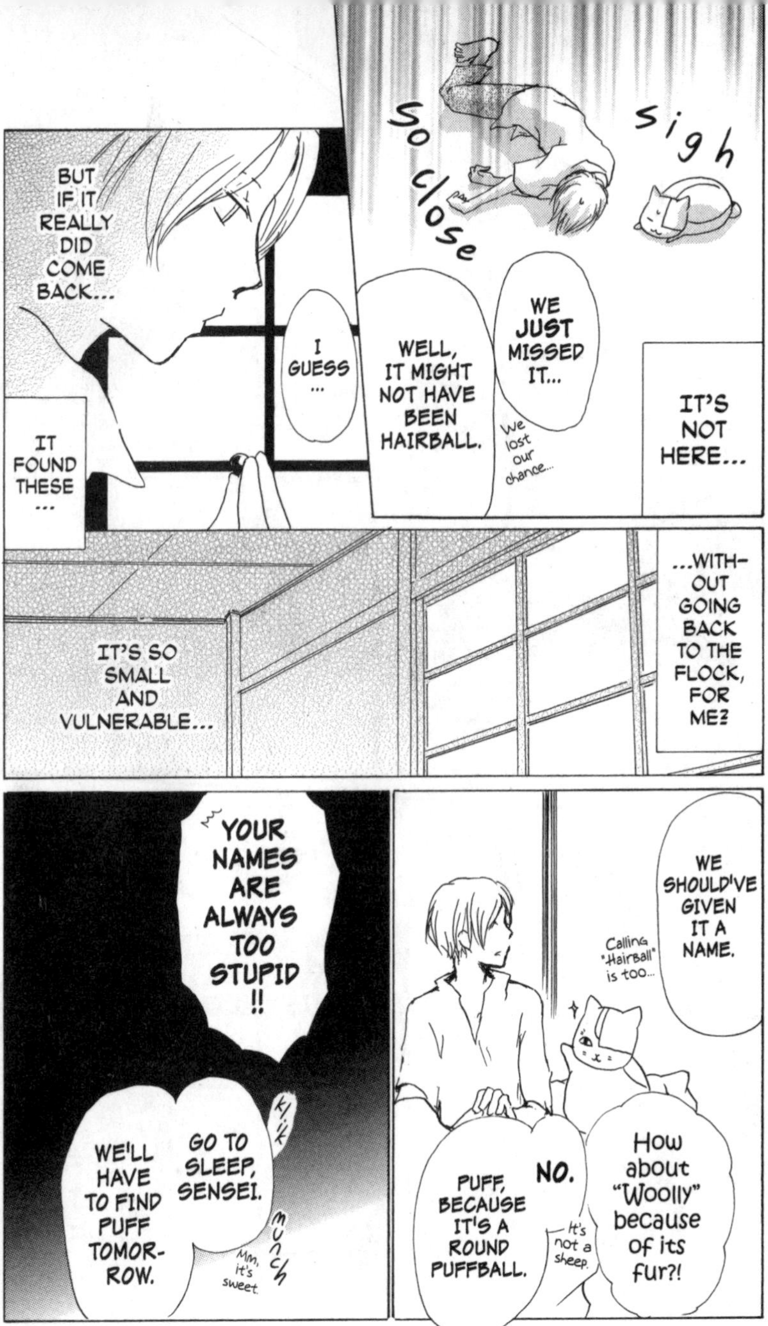
sigh
So close
IT'S NOT HERE...
WE JUST MISSED IT...
We lost our chance...
WELL, IT MIGHT NOT HAVE BEEN HAIRBALL.
I GUESS...
BUT IF IT REALLY DID COME BACK...
IT FOUND THESE...
...WITHOUT GOING BACK TO THE FLOCK, FOR ME?
IT'S SO SMALL AND VULNERABLE...
WE SHOULD'VE GIVEN IT A NAME.
Calling "Hairball" is too...
How about "Woolly" because of its fur?!
It's not a sheep.
NO.
PUFF, BECAUSE IT'S A ROUND PUFFBALL.
YOUR NAMES ARE ALWAYS TOO STUPID!!
klik
GO TO SLEEP, SENSEI.
munch
Mm, it's sweet.
WE'LL HAVE TO FIND PUFF TOMORROW.

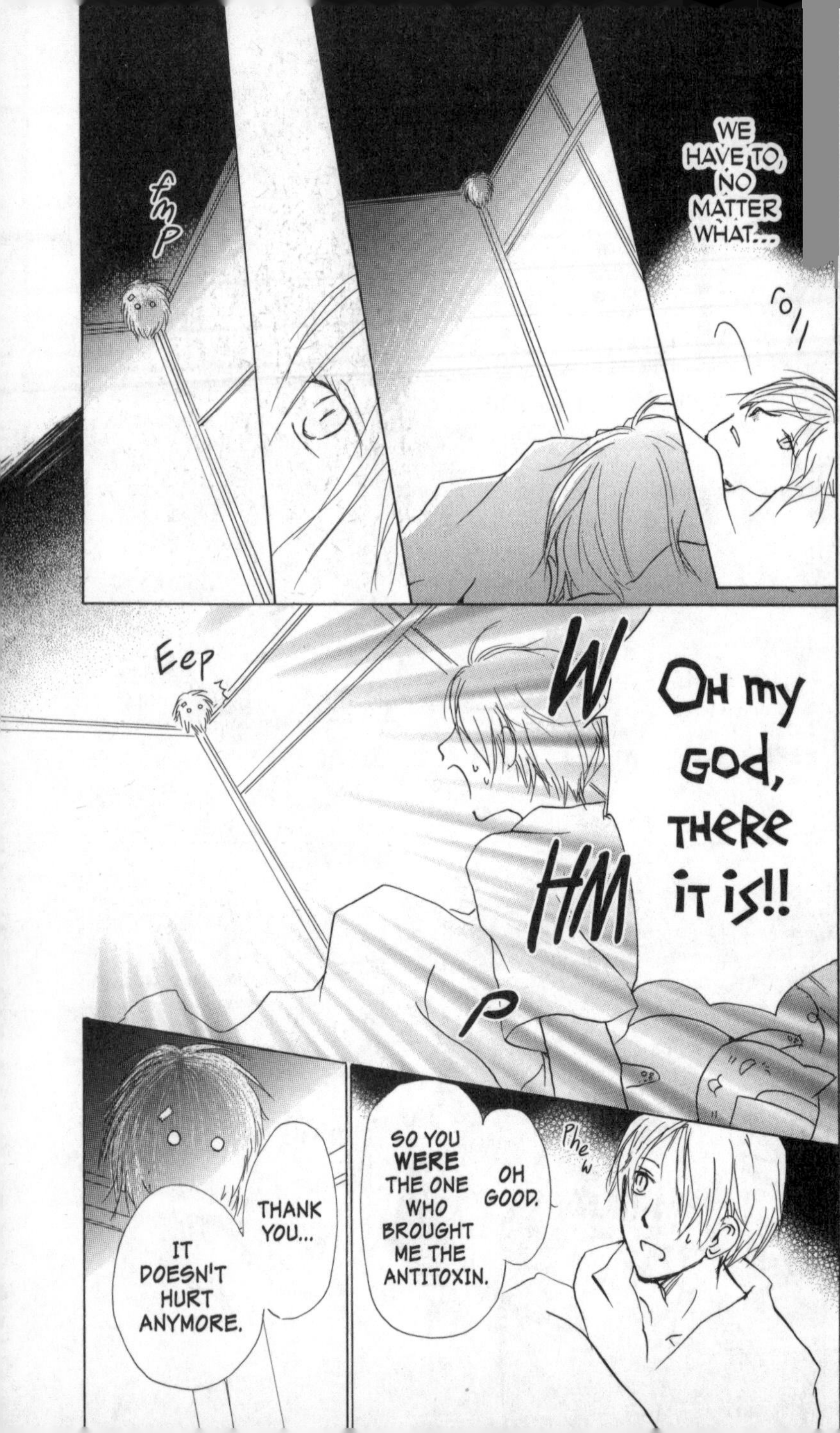
WE HAVE TO, NO MATTER WHAT...
roll
fmp
Oh my god, there it is!!
WHMP
Eep
Phew
OH GOOD.
SO YOU WERE THE ONE WHO BROUGHT ME THE ANTITOXIN.
THANK YOU...
IT DOESN'T HURT ANYMORE.

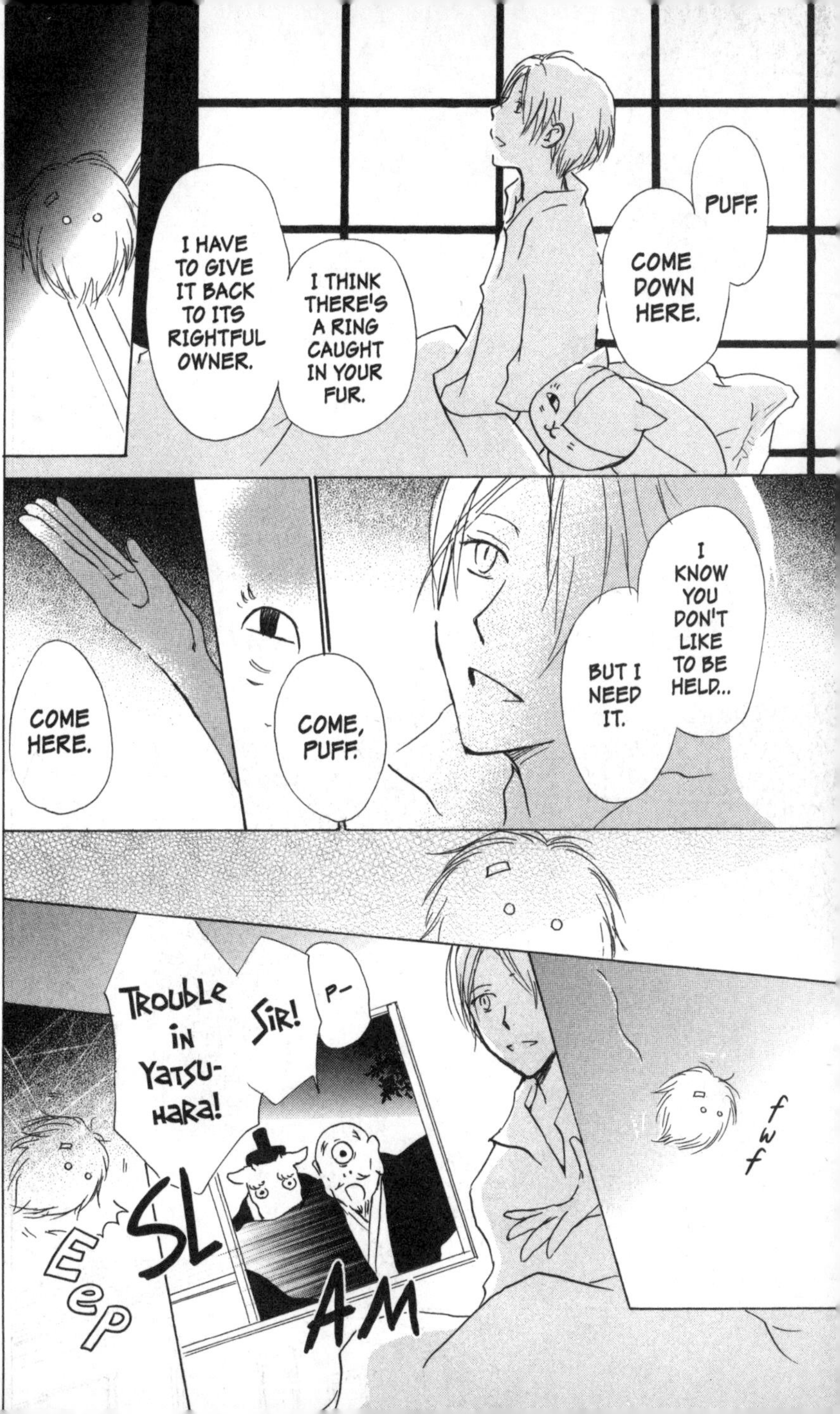
PUFF.
COME DOWN HERE.
I THINK THERE'S A RING CAUGHT IN YOUR FUR.
I HAVE TO GIVE IT BACK TO ITS RIGHTFUL OWNER.
I KNOW YOU DON'T LIKE TO BE HELD...
BUT I NEED IT.
COME, PUFF.
COME HERE.
fwf
P-
SIR!
Trouble in Yatsu-hara!
SLAM
Eeep

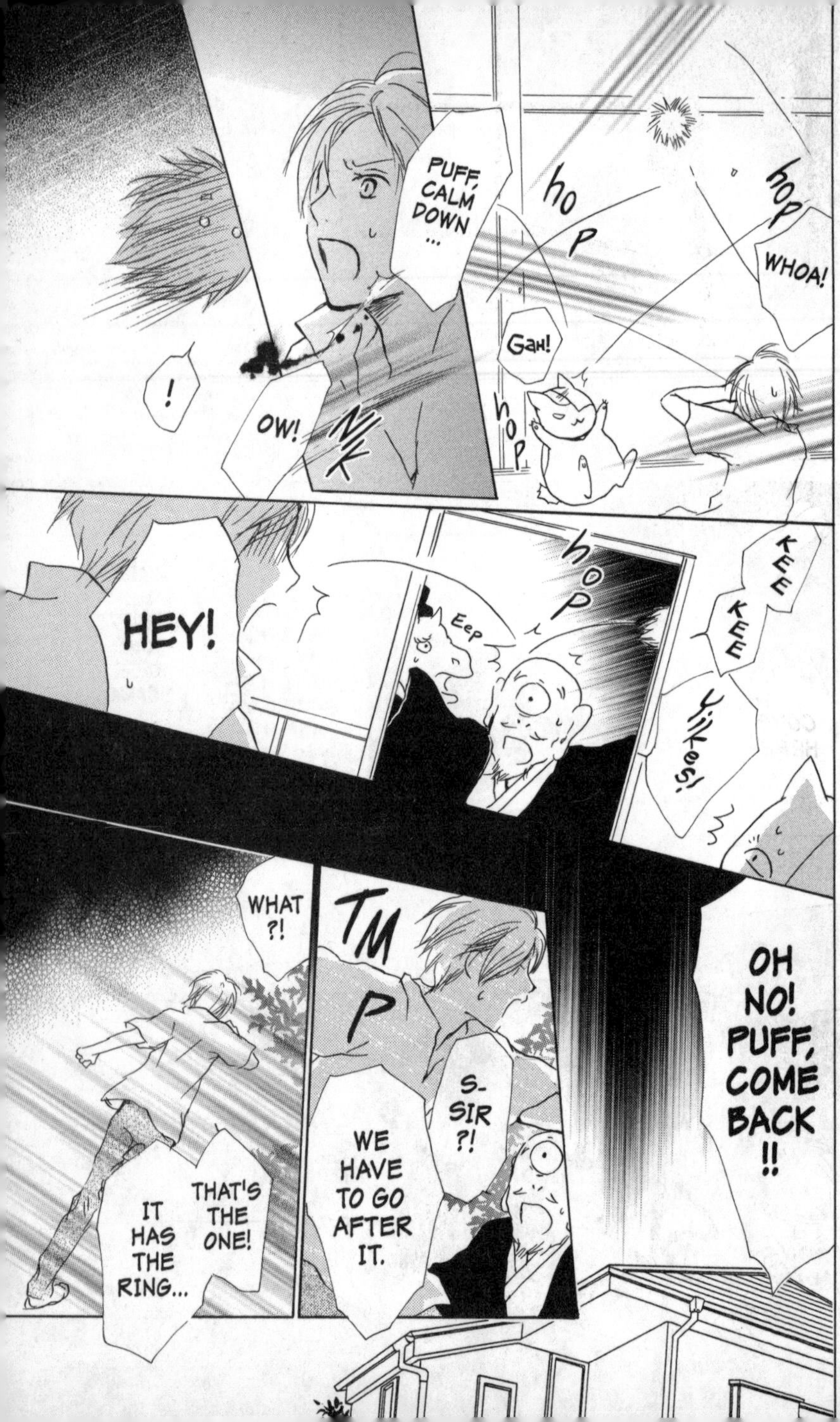
hop
WHOA!
hop
Gah!
hop
PUFF, CALM DOWN...
NIK
OW!
!
KEE KEE
Yikes!
hop
Eep
HEY!
OH NO! PUFF, COME BACK!!
TMP
S-SIR?!
WE HAVE TO GO AFTER IT.
WHAT?!
THAT'S THE ONE!
IT HAS THE RING...

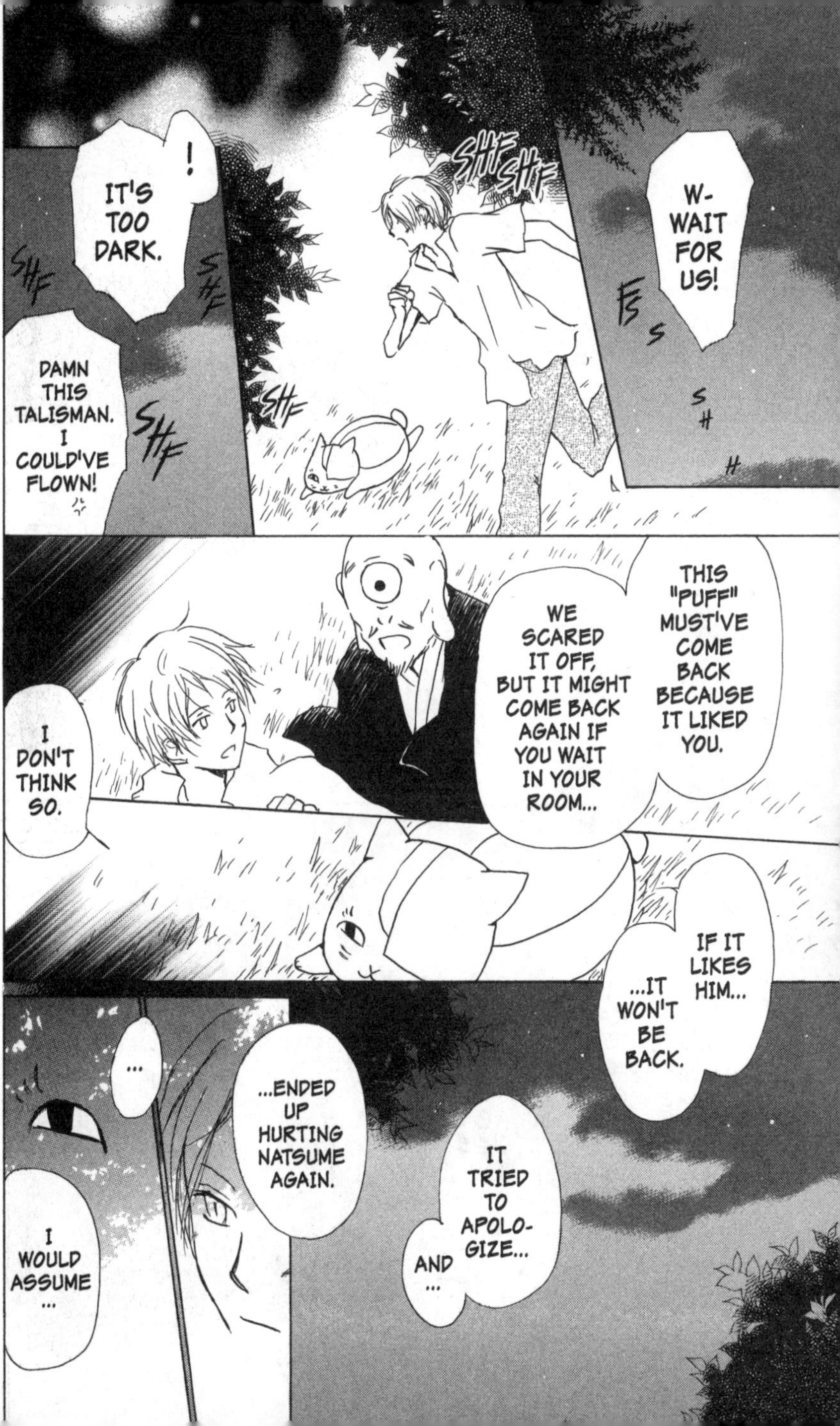
W-WAIT FOR US!
SHF SHF
SS
SHH
SHF
!
IT'S TOO DARK.
SHF
SHF
DAMN THIS TALISMAN. I COULD'VE FLOWN!
SHF
THIS "PUFF" MUST'VE COME BACK BECAUSE IT LIKED YOU.
WE SCARED IT OFF, BUT IT MIGHT COME BACK AGAIN IF YOU WAIT IN YOUR ROOM...
I DON'T THINK SO.
IF IT LIKES HIM...
...IT WON'T BE BACK.
IT TRIED TO APOLOGIZE...
AND ...
...ENDED UP HURTING NATSUME AGAIN.
...
I WOULD ASSUME ...

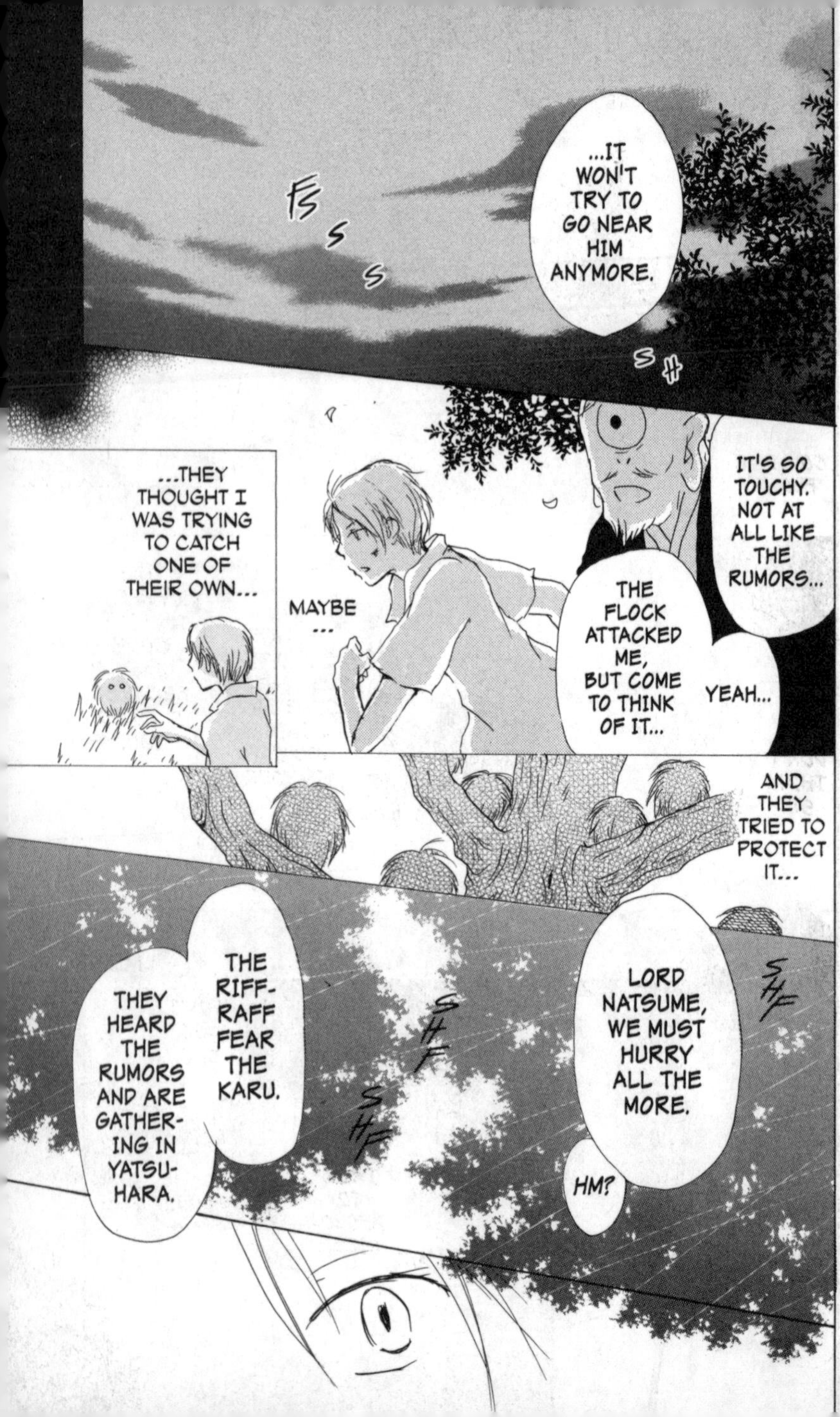
FSSS
...IT WON'T TRY TO GO NEAR HIM ANYMORE.
SH
IT'S SO TOUCHY. NOT AT ALL LIKE THE RUMORS...
YEAH...
THE FLOCK ATTACKED ME, BUT COME TO THINK OF IT...
MAYBE...
...THEY THOUGHT I WAS TRYING TO CATCH ONE OF THEIR OWN...
AND THEY TRIED TO PROTECT IT...
SHF
LORD NATSUME, WE MUST HURRY ALL THE MORE.
HM?
SHF
THE RIFF-RAFF FEAR THE KARU.
THEY HEARD THE RUMORS AND ARE GATHERING IN YATSU-HARA.
SHF

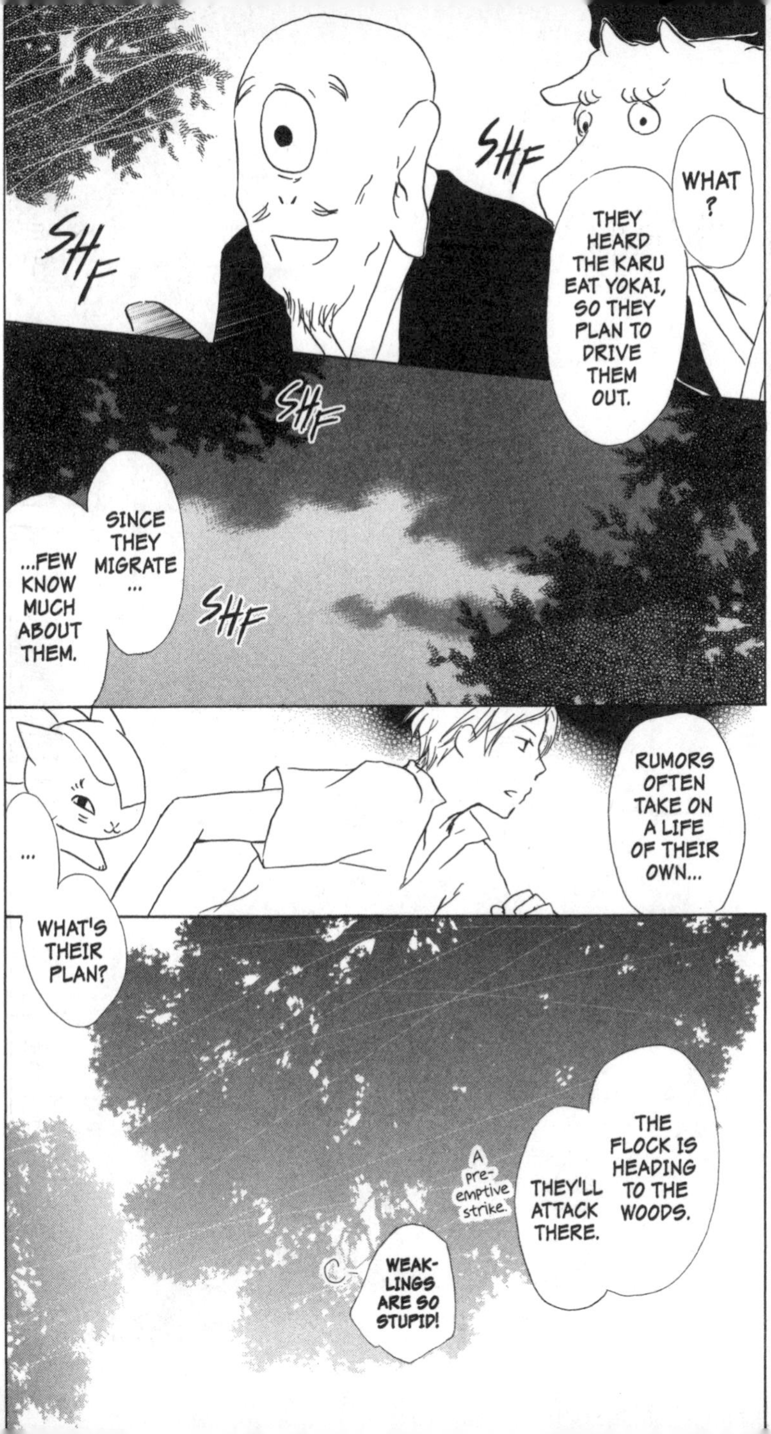
WHAT?
THEY HEARD THE KARU EAT YOKAI, SO THEY PLAN TO DRIVE THEM OUT.
SHF
SHF
SHF
SINCE THEY MIGRATE...
...FEW KNOW MUCH ABOUT THEM.
SHF
RUMORS OFTEN TAKE ON A LIFE OF THEIR OWN...
...
WHAT'S THEIR PLAN?
THE FLOCK IS HEADING TO THE WOODS.
THEY'LL ATTACK THERE.
A pre-emptive strike.
WEAK-LINGS ARE SO STUPID!

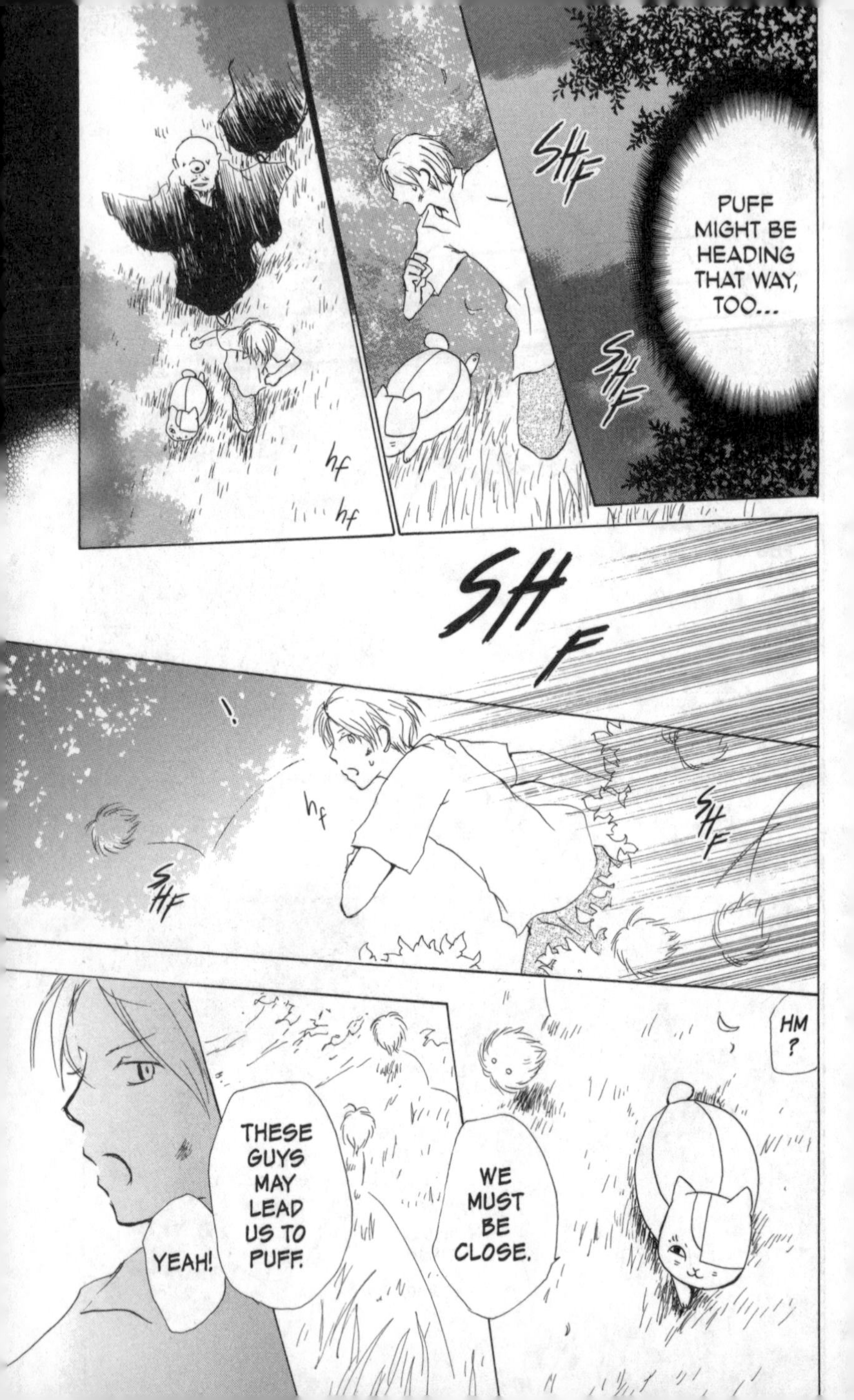
SHF
PUFF MIGHT BE HEADING THAT WAY, TOO...
SHF
hf
hf
SHF
SHF
!
hf
SHF
HM?
WE MUST BE CLOSE.
THESE GUYS MAY LEAD US TO PUFF.
YEAH!

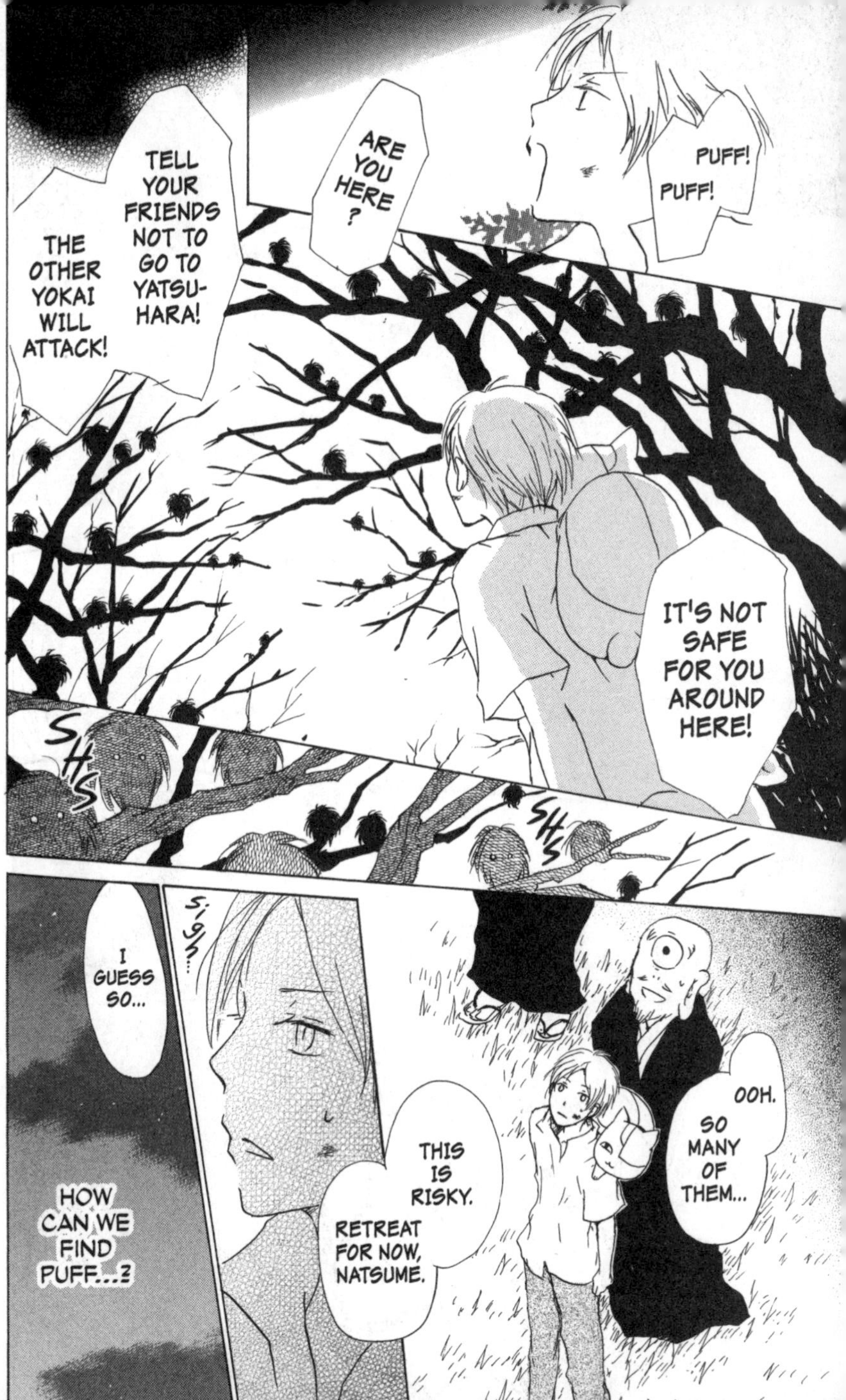

PUFF!
PUFF!
ARE YOU HERE?
TELL YOUR FRIENDS NOT TO GO TO YATSU-HARA!
THE OTHER YOKAI WILL ATTACK!
IT'S NOT SAFE FOR YOU AROUND HERE!
SHS
SHS
OOH. SO MANY OF THEM...
THIS IS RISKY.
RETREAT FOR NOW, NATSUME.
sigh...
I GUESS SO...
HOW CAN WE FIND PUFF...?

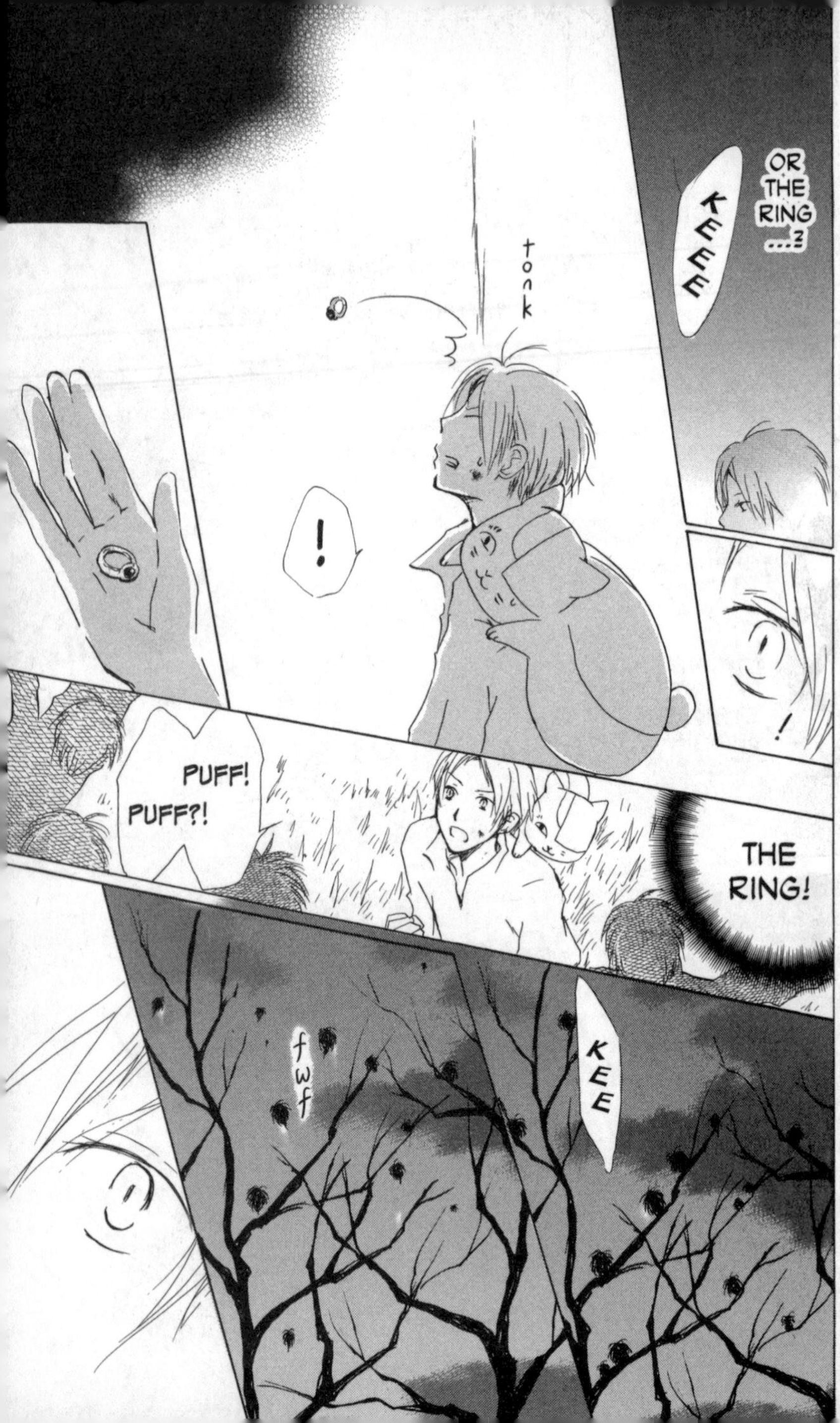
OR THE RING ...?
KEEE
tonk
!
!
THE RING!
PUFF! PUFF?!
KEE
fwf

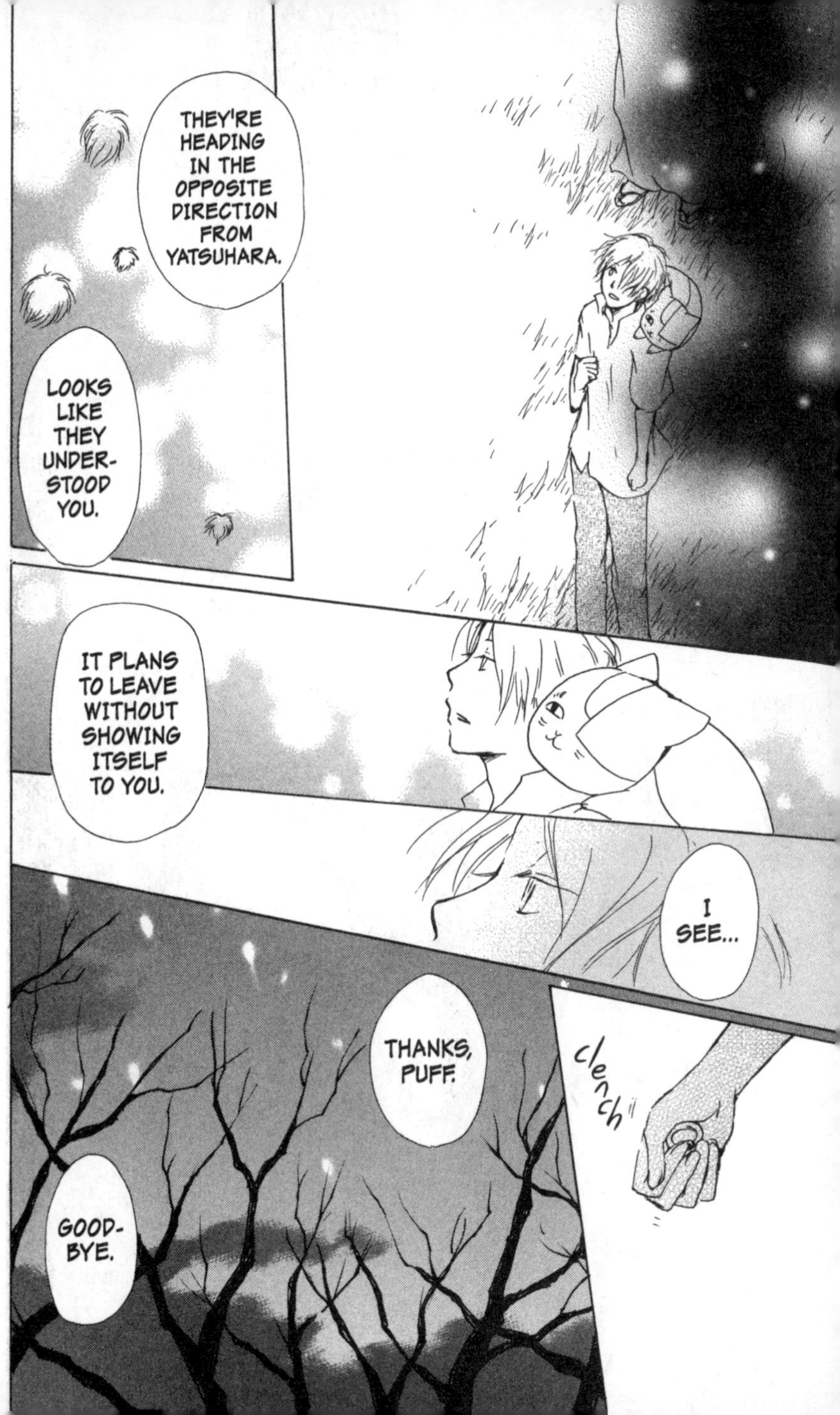
THEY'RE HEADING IN THE OPPOSITE DIRECTION FROM YATSUHARA.
LOOKS LIKE THEY UNDER-STOOD YOU.
IT PLANS TO LEAVE WITHOUT SHOWING ITSELF TO YOU.
I SEE...
clench
THANKS, PUFF.
GOOD-BYE.

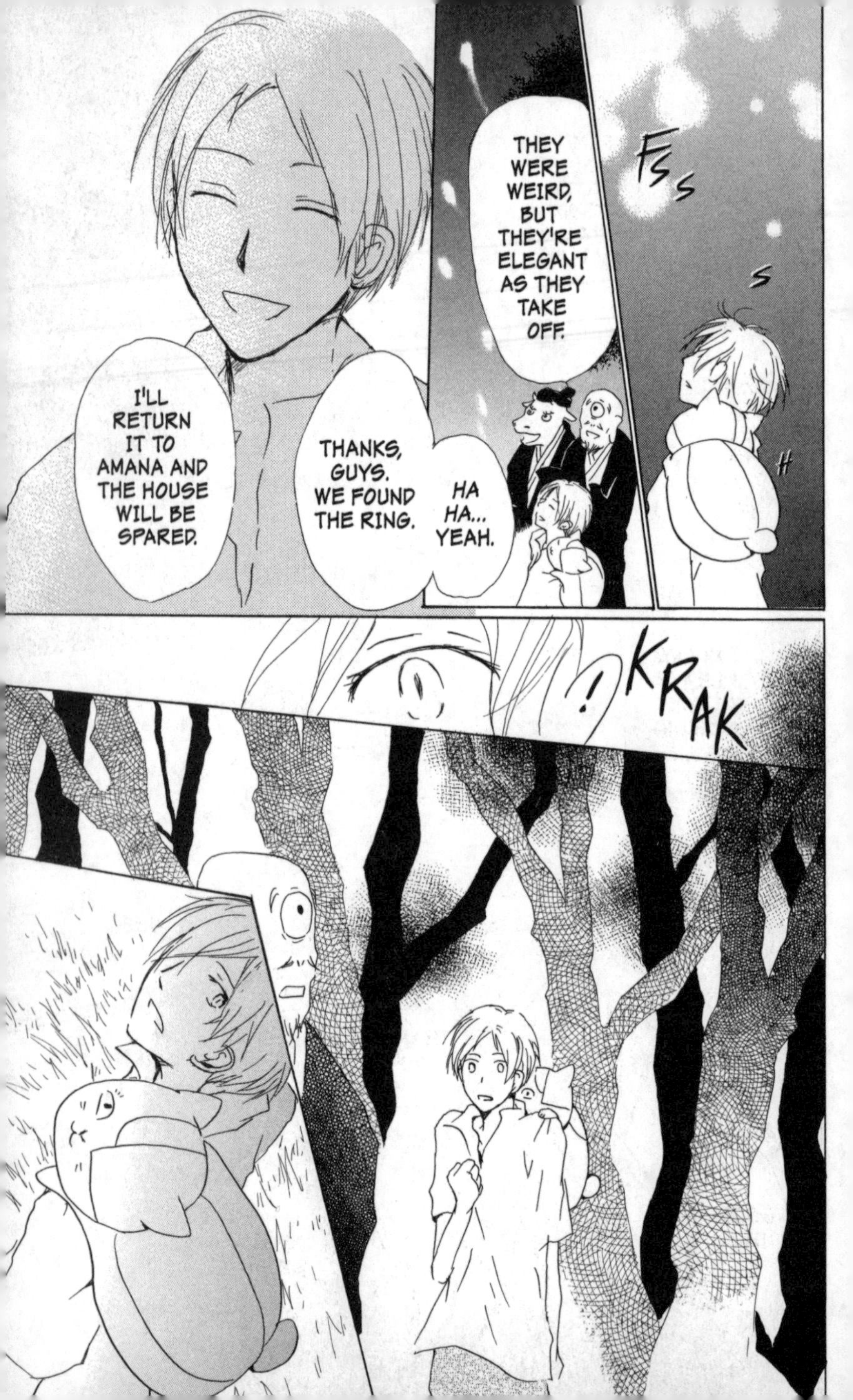
FSSS
S
H
THEY WERE WEIRD, BUT THEY'RE ELEGANT AS THEY TAKE OFF.
HA HA... YEAH.
THANKS, GUYS. WE FOUND THE RING.
I'LL RETURN IT TO AMANA AND THE HOUSE WILL BE SPARED.
KRAK
!

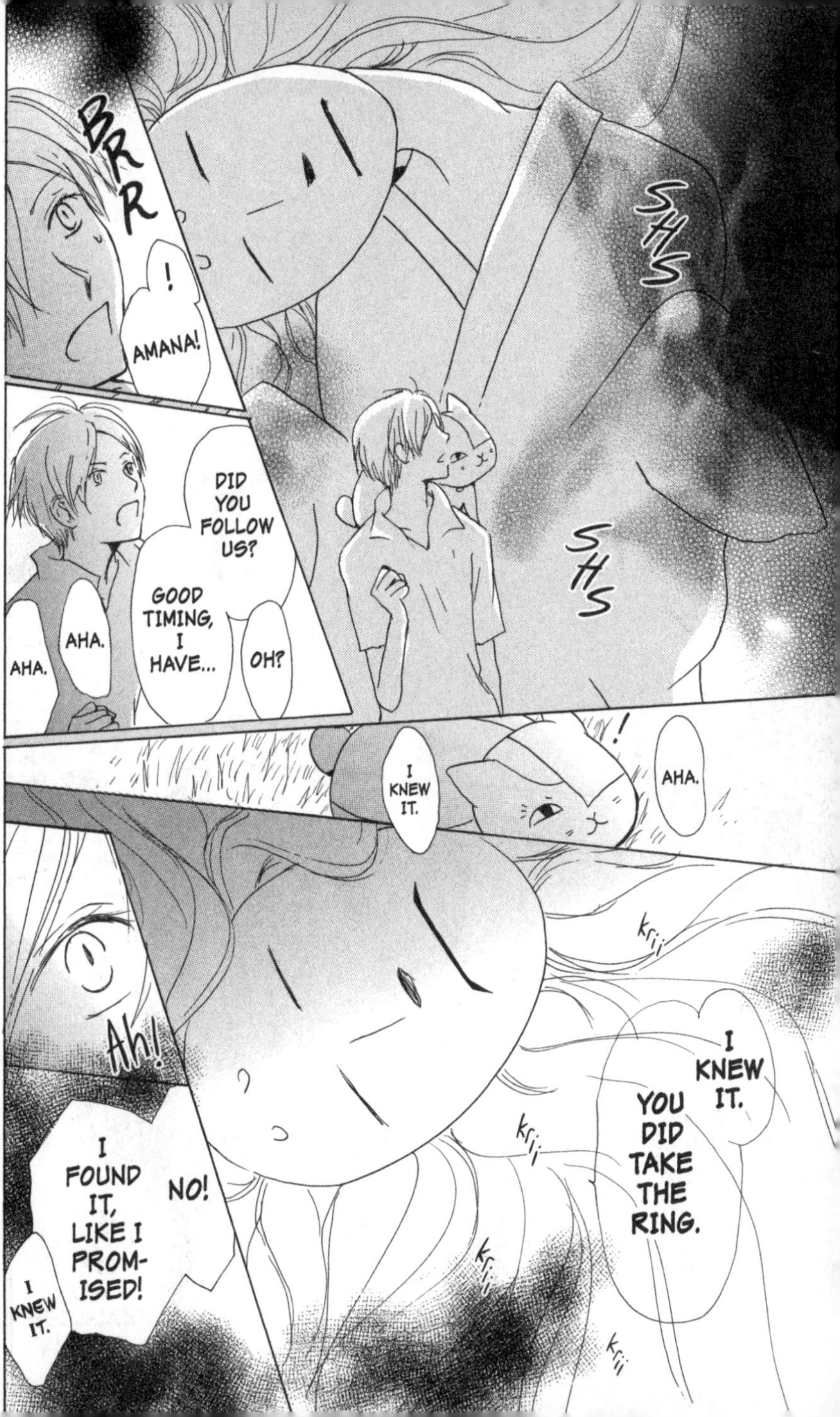
SHS
SHS
BRR
!
AMANA!
DID YOU FOLLOW US?
OH?
GOOD TIMING, I HAVE...
AHA.
AHA.
!
AHA.
I KNEW IT.
krii
krii
krii
krii
I KNEW IT.
YOU DID TAKE THE RING.
Ah!
NO!
I FOUND IT, LIKE I PROMISED!
I KNEW IT.

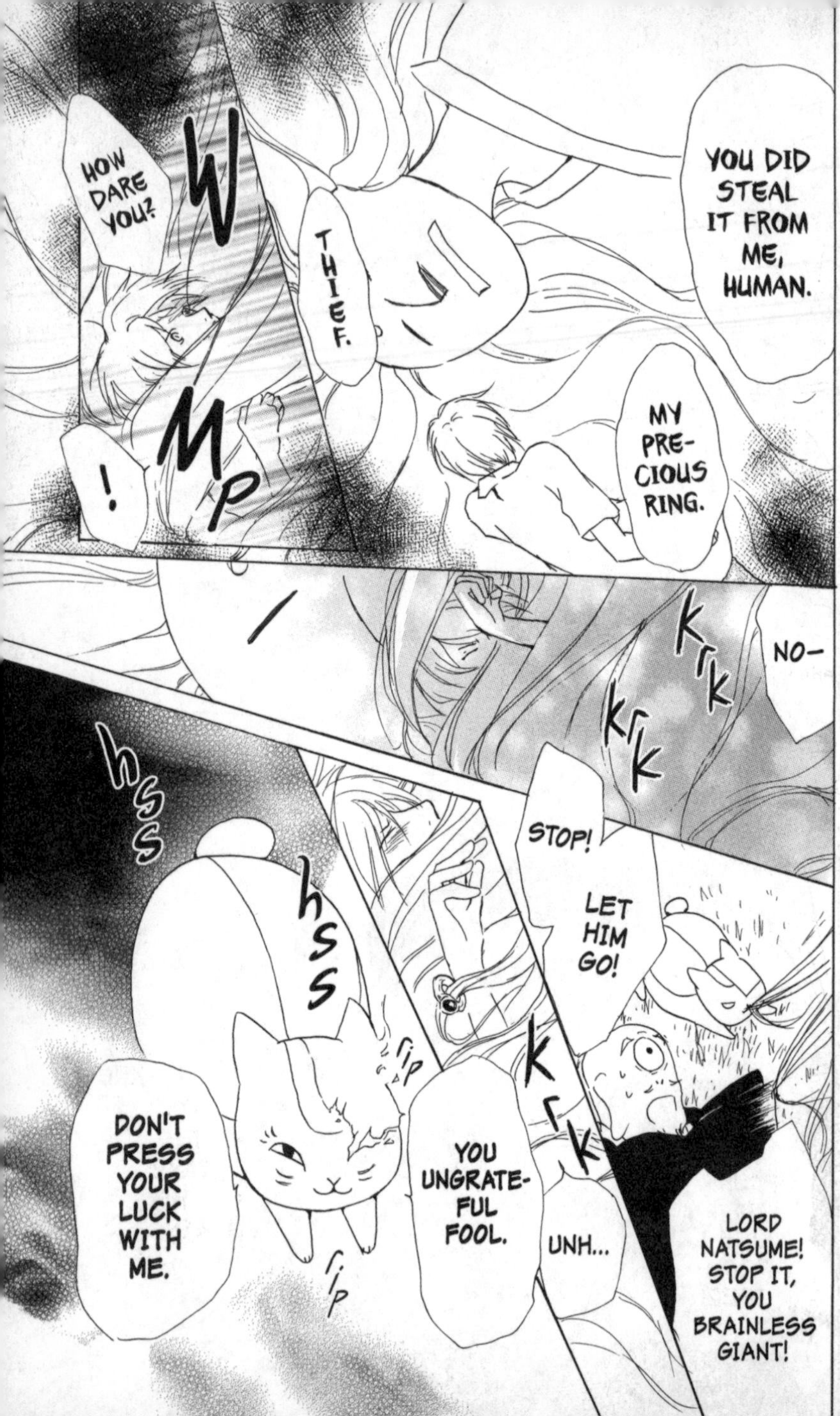
YOU DID STEAL IT FROM ME, HUMAN.
MY PRECIOUS RING.
THIEF.
HOW DARE YOU!?
WMP
!
NO-
KRK
KRK
STOP!
LET HIM GO!
KRK
LORD NATSUME! STOP IT, YOU BRAINLESS GIANT!
UNH...
YOU UNGRATEFUL FOOL.
rip
hss
hss
DON'T PRESS YOUR LUCK WITH ME.
rip

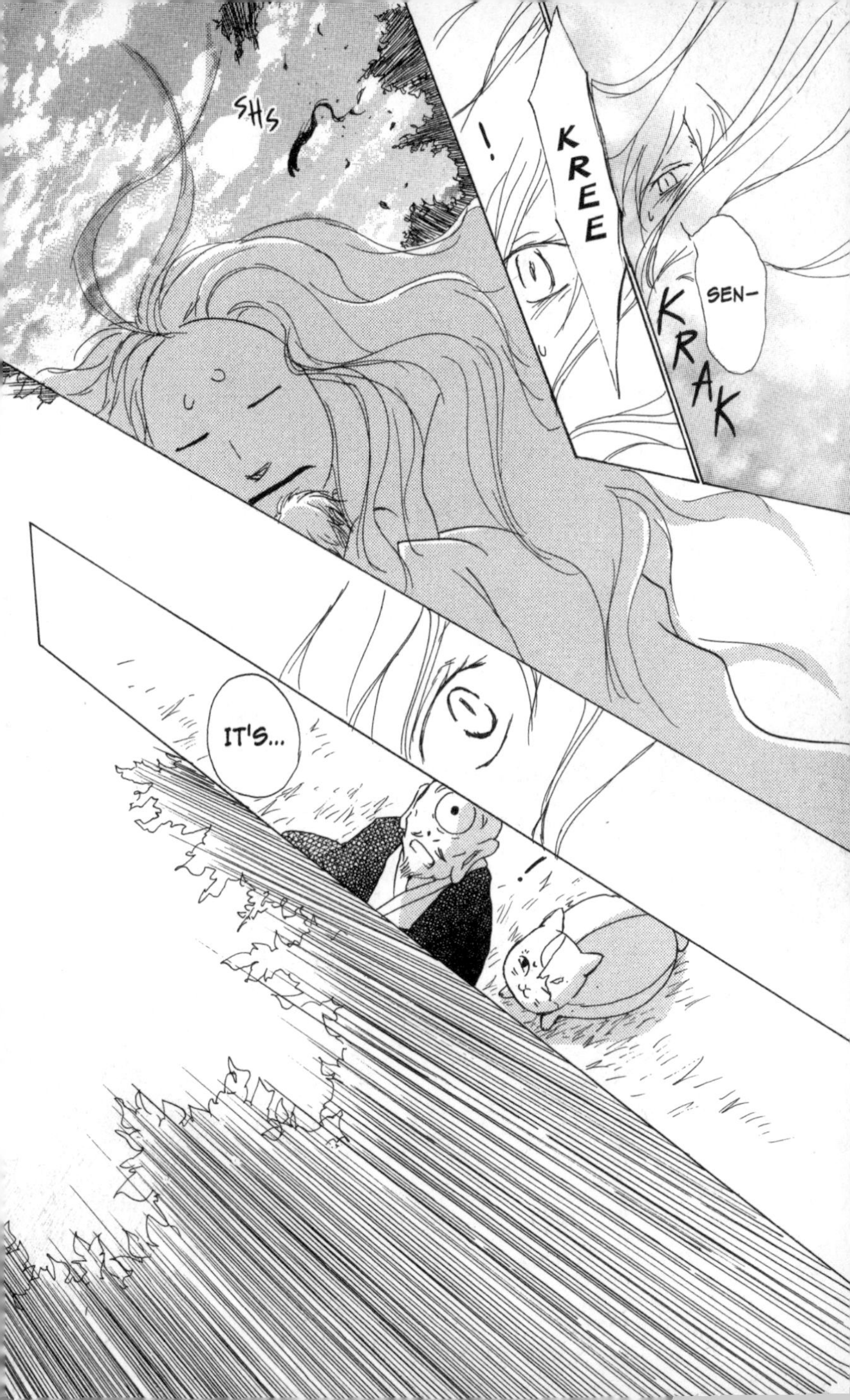

SEN-
KRAK
!
KREE
SHS
IT'S...
!

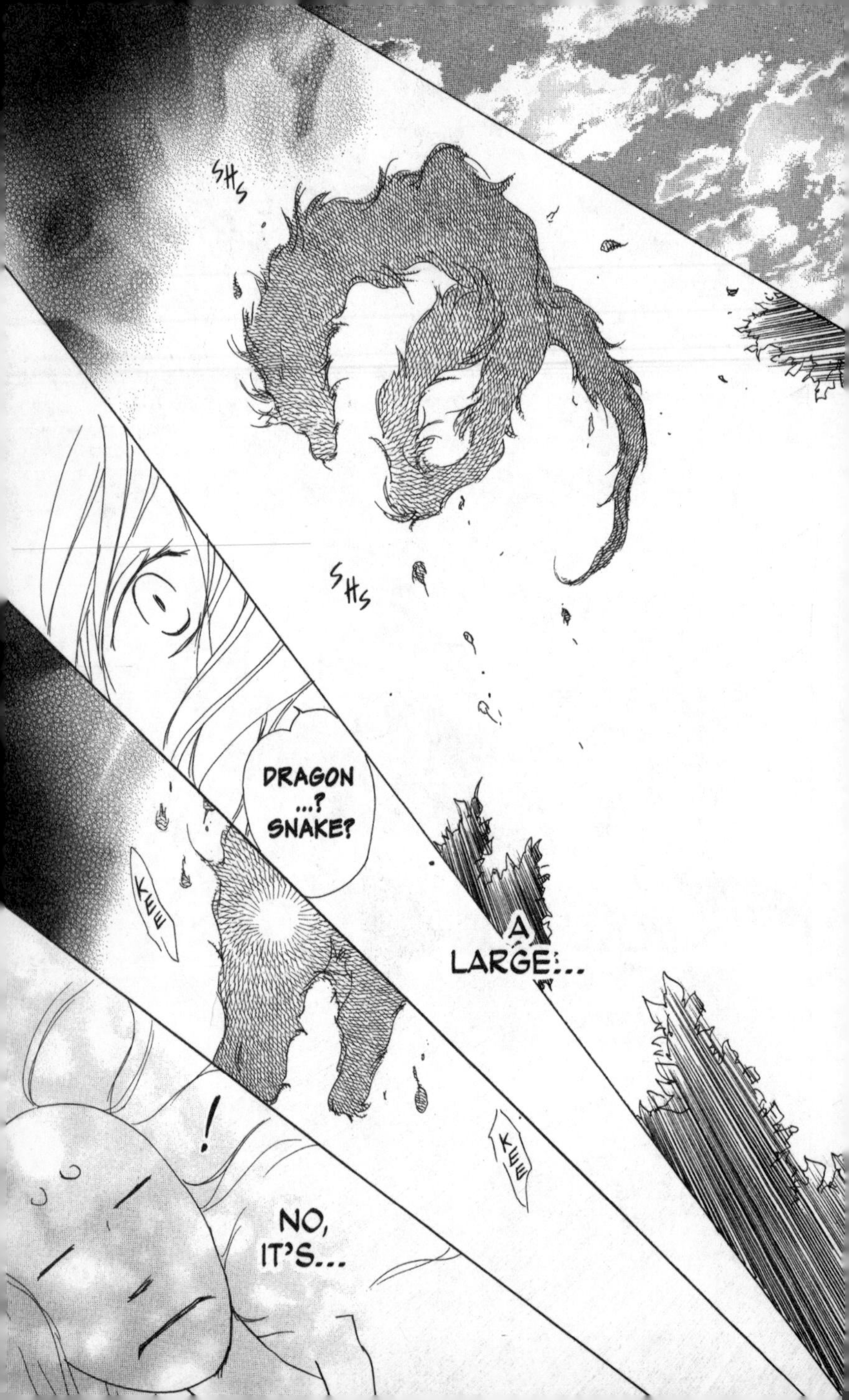
SHS
SHS
DRAGON ...? SNAKE?
A LARGE...
KEE
KEE
!
NO, IT'S...

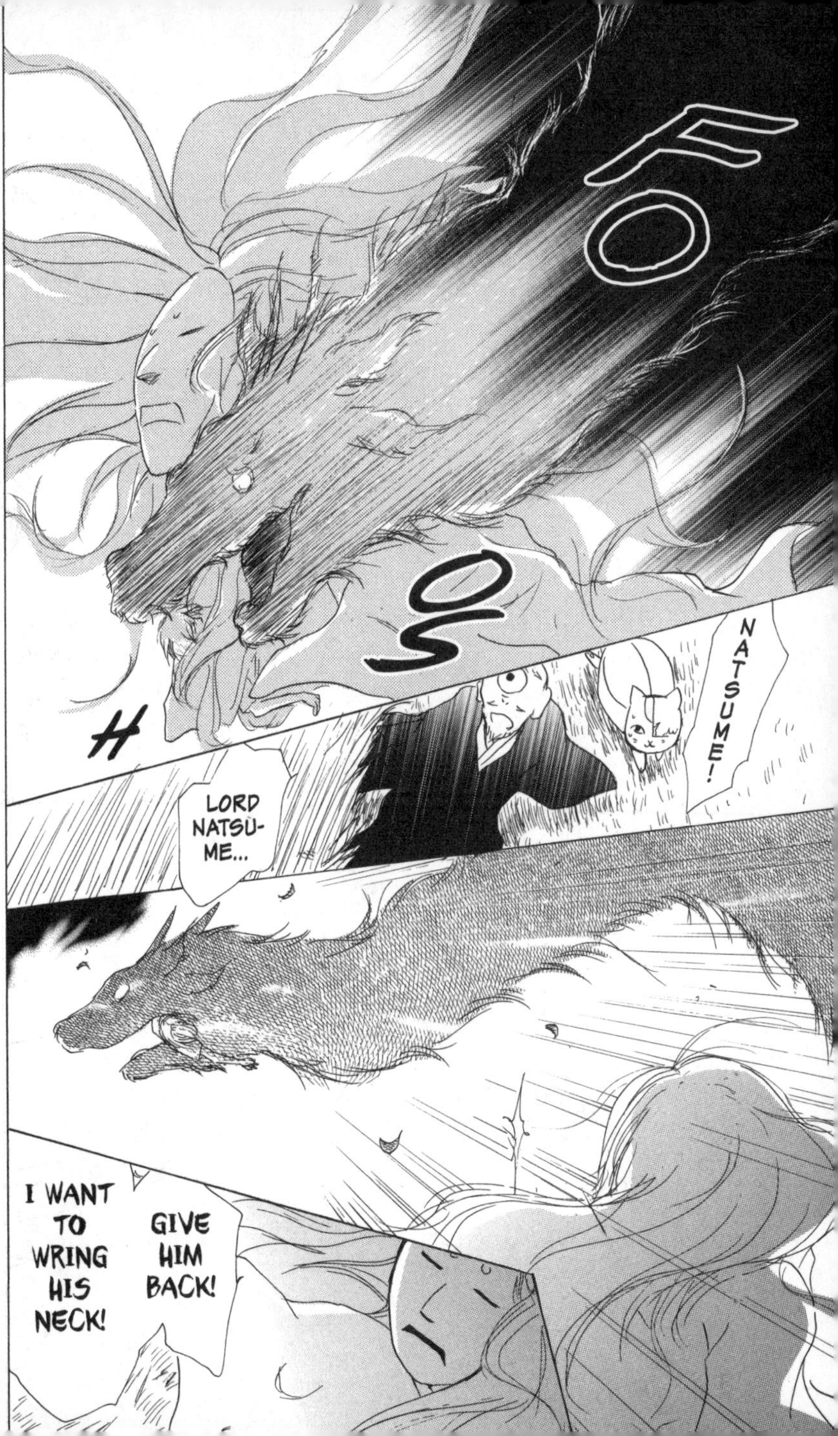
FOOSH
NATSUME!
LORD NATSUME...
GIVE HIM BACK!
I WANT TO WRING HIS NECK!

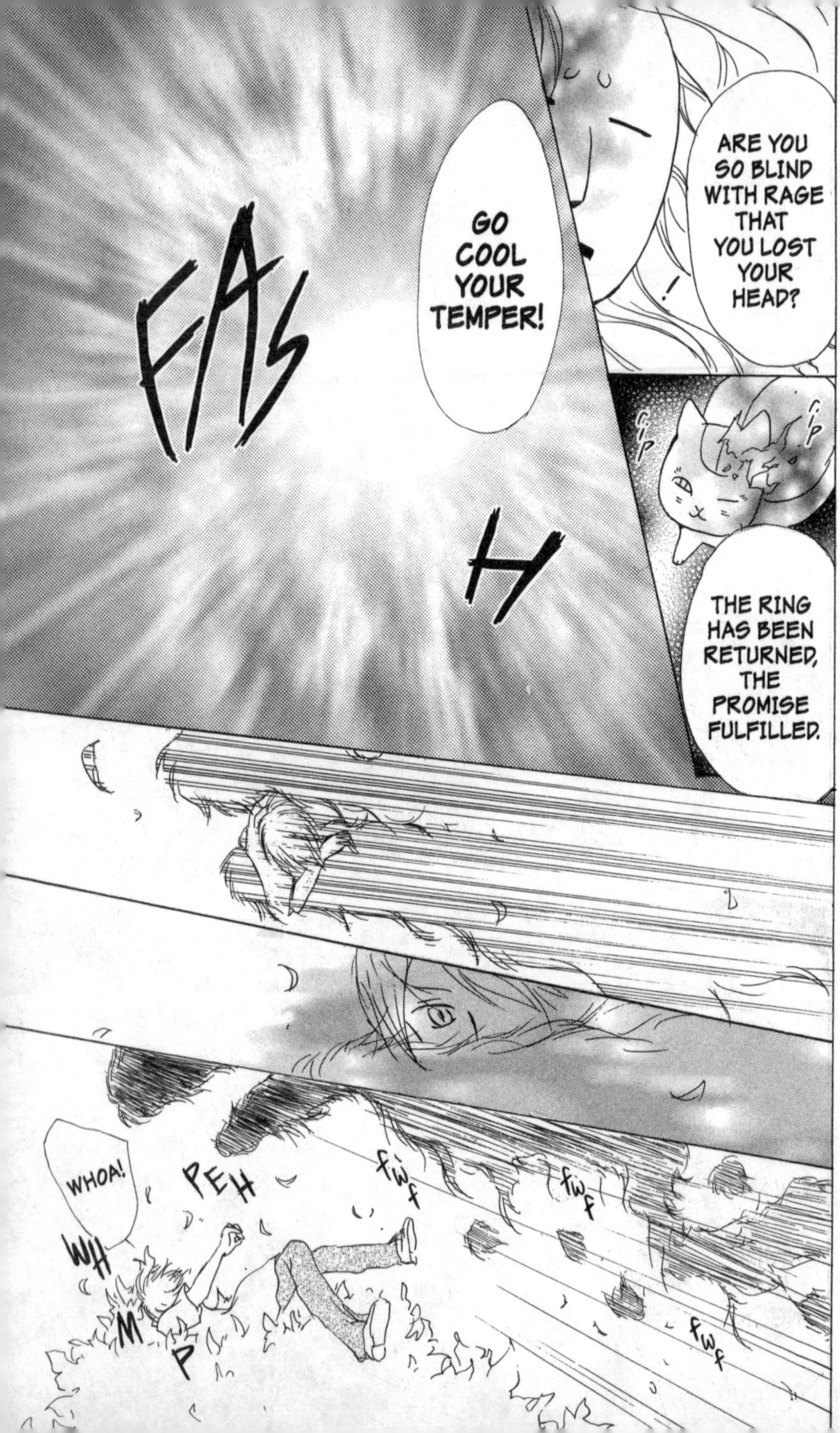
ARE YOU SO BLIND WITH RAGE THAT YOU LOST YOUR HEAD?
!
THE RING HAS BEEN RETURNED, THE PROMISE FULFILLED.
GO COOL YOUR TEMPER!
FASH
fwf
fwf
fwf
PEH
WHOA!
WHMP

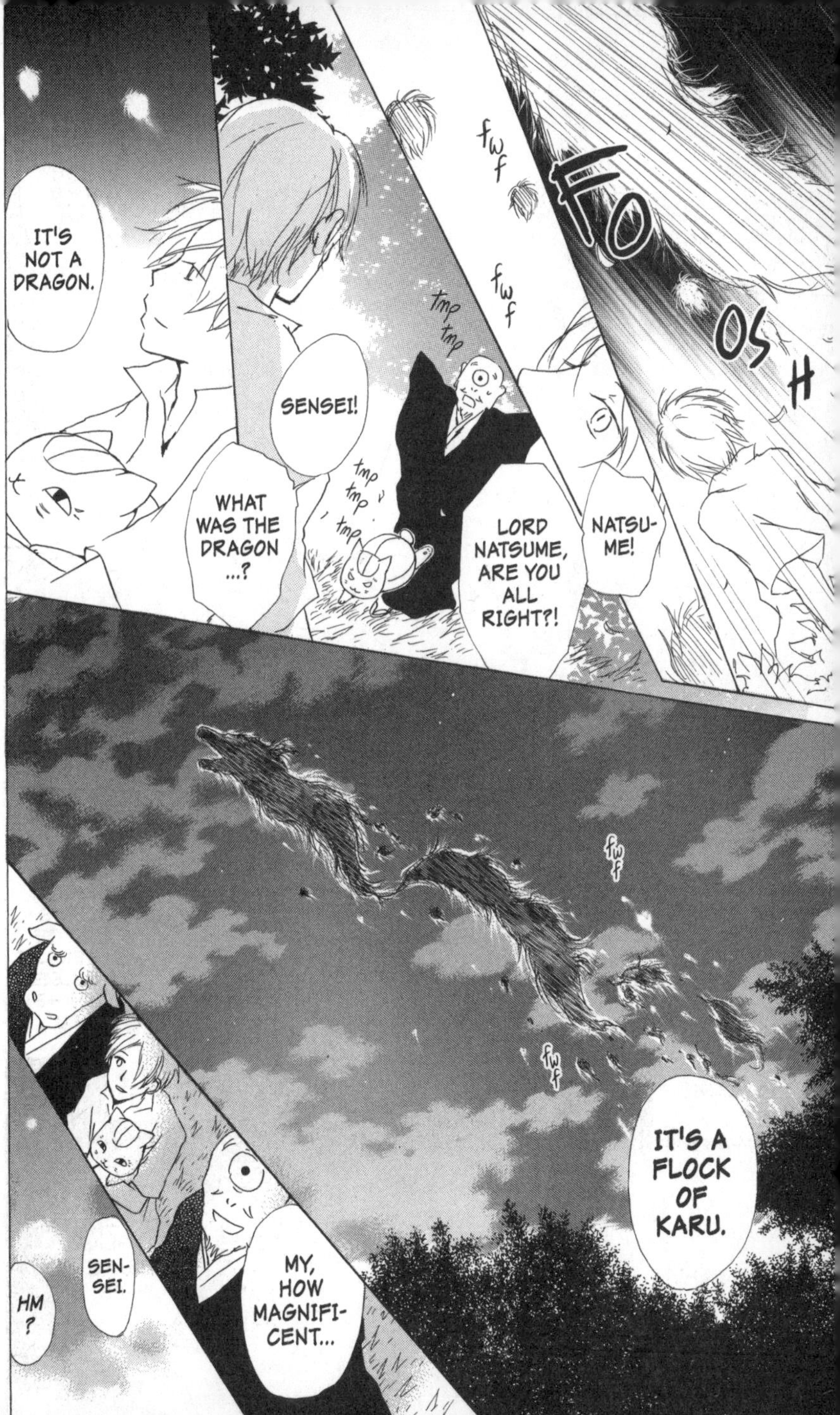
FOOSH
fwf
fwf
NATSU-ME!
LORD NATSUME, ARE YOU ALL RIGHT?!
tmp tmp
SENSEI!
tmp tmp tmp
WHAT WAS THE DRAGON ...?
IT'S NOT A DRAGON.
fwf
fwf
IT'S A FLOCK OF KARU.
MY, HOW MAGNIFI-CENT...
SEN-SEI.
HM ?

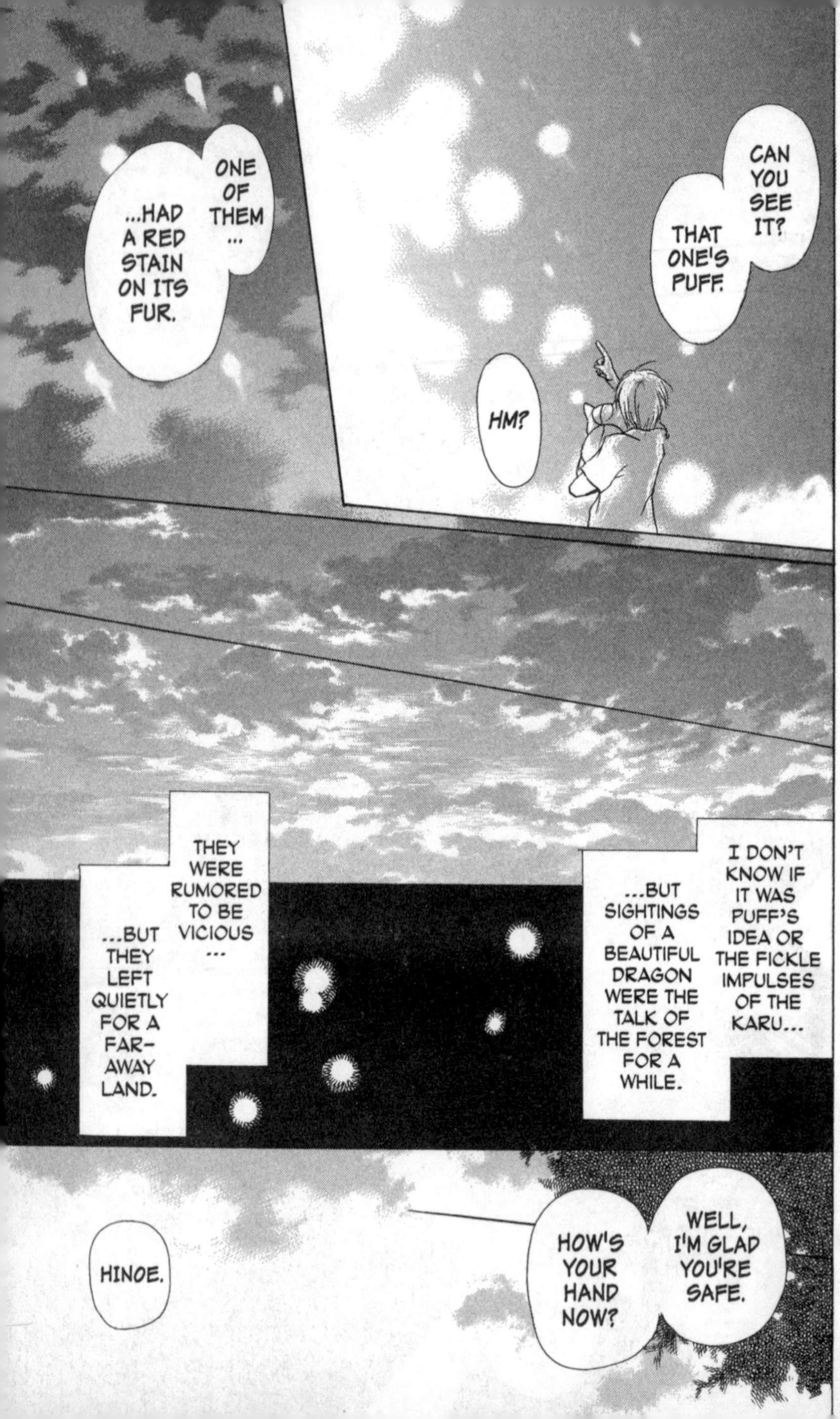
CAN YOU SEE IT?
THAT ONE'S PUFF.
HM?
ONE OF THEM...
...HAD A RED STAIN ON ITS FUR.
I DON'T KNOW IF IT WAS PUFF'S IDEA OR THE FICKLE IMPULSES OF THE KARU...
...BUT SIGHTINGS OF A BEAUTIFUL DRAGON WERE THE TALK OF THE FOREST FOR A WHILE.
THEY WERE RUMORED TO BE VICIOUS...
...BUT THEY LEFT QUIETLY FOR A FAR-AWAY LAND.
WELL, I'M GLAD YOU'RE SAFE.
HOW'S YOUR HAND NOW?
HINOE.

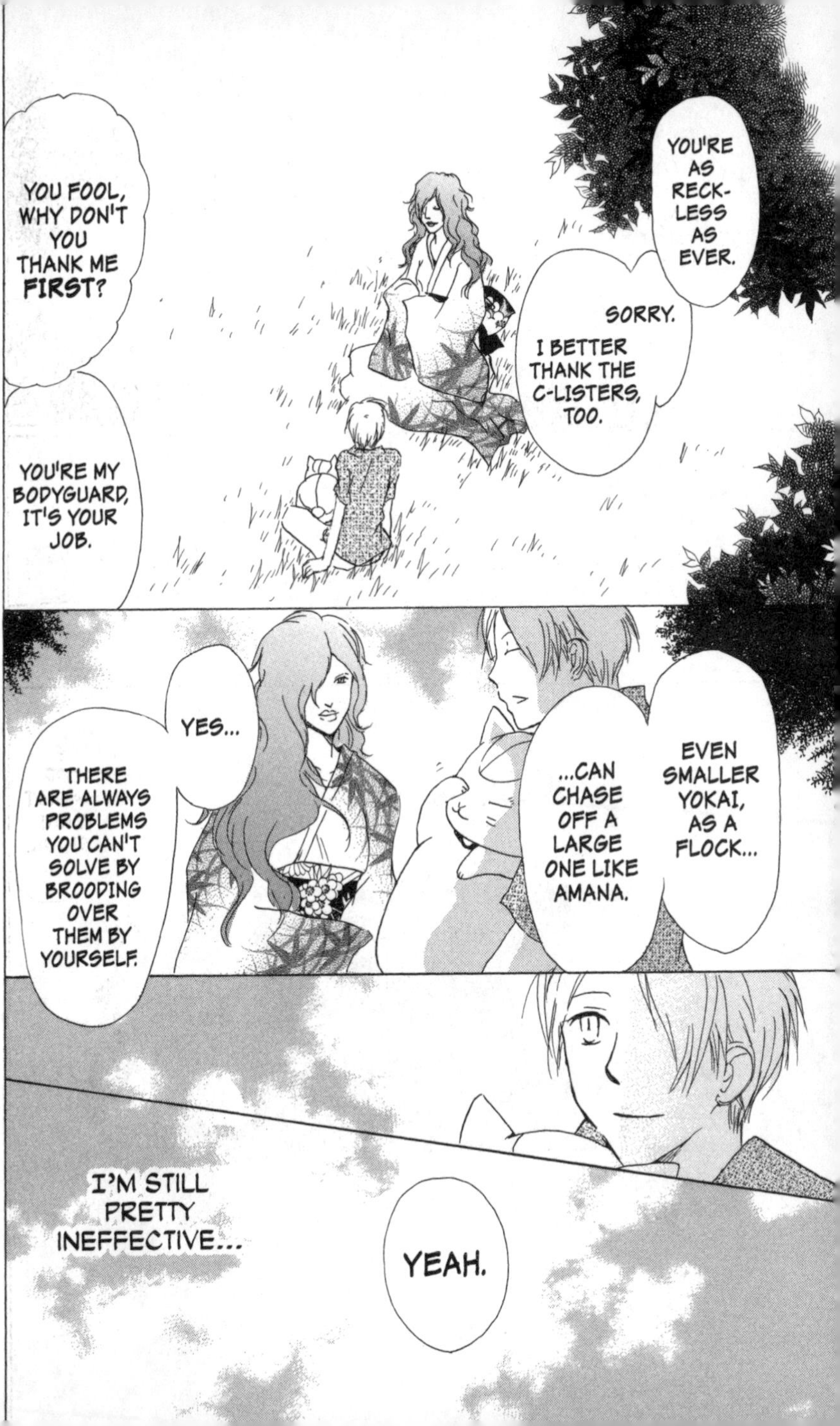
YOU'RE AS RECK-LESS AS EVER.
SORRY.
I BETTER THANK THE C-LISTERS, TOO.
YOU FOOL, WHY DON'T YOU THANK ME FIRST?
YOU'RE MY BODYGUARD, IT'S YOUR JOB.
EVEN SMALLER YOKAI, AS A FLOCK...
...CAN CHASE OFF A LARGE ONE LIKE AMANA.
YES...
THERE ARE ALWAYS PROBLEMS YOU CAN'T SOLVE BY BROODING OVER THEM BY YOURSELF.
YEAH.
I'M STILL PRETTY INEFFECTIVE...

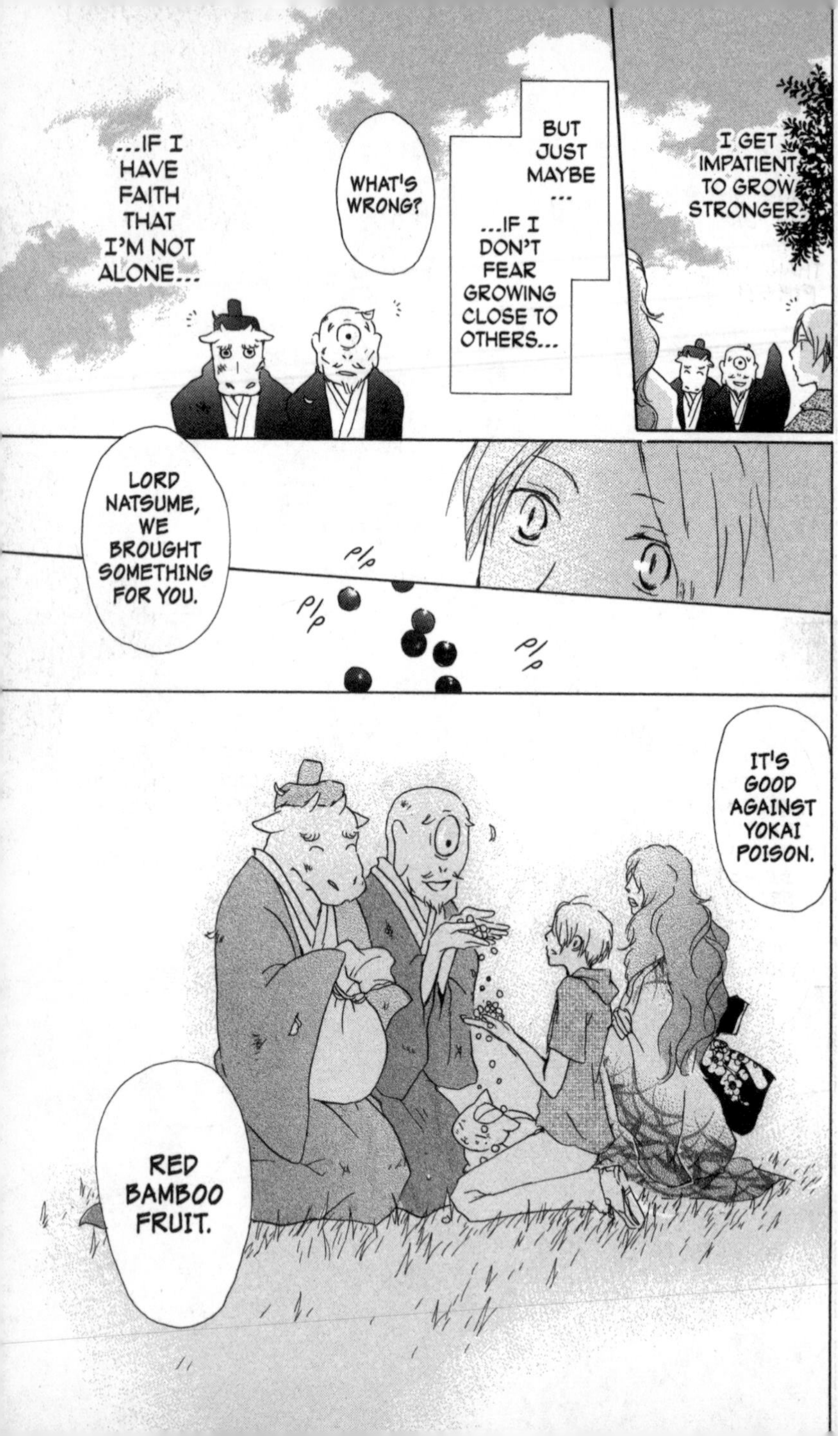
I GET IMPATIENT TO GROW STRONGER.
BUT JUST MAYBE ...
...IF I DON'T FEAR GROWING CLOSE TO OTHERS...
WHAT'S WRONG?
...IF I HAVE FAITH THAT I'M NOT ALONE...
LORD NATSUME, WE BROUGHT SOMETHING FOR YOU.
IT'S GOOD AGAINST YOKAI POISON.
RED BAMBOO FRUIT.

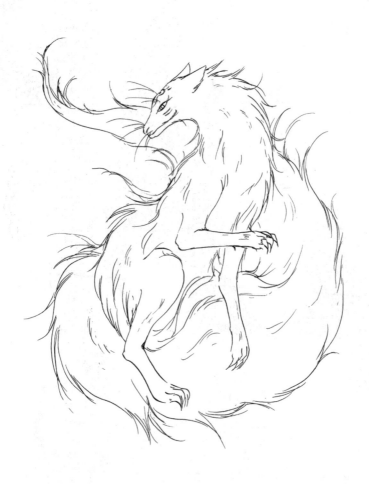

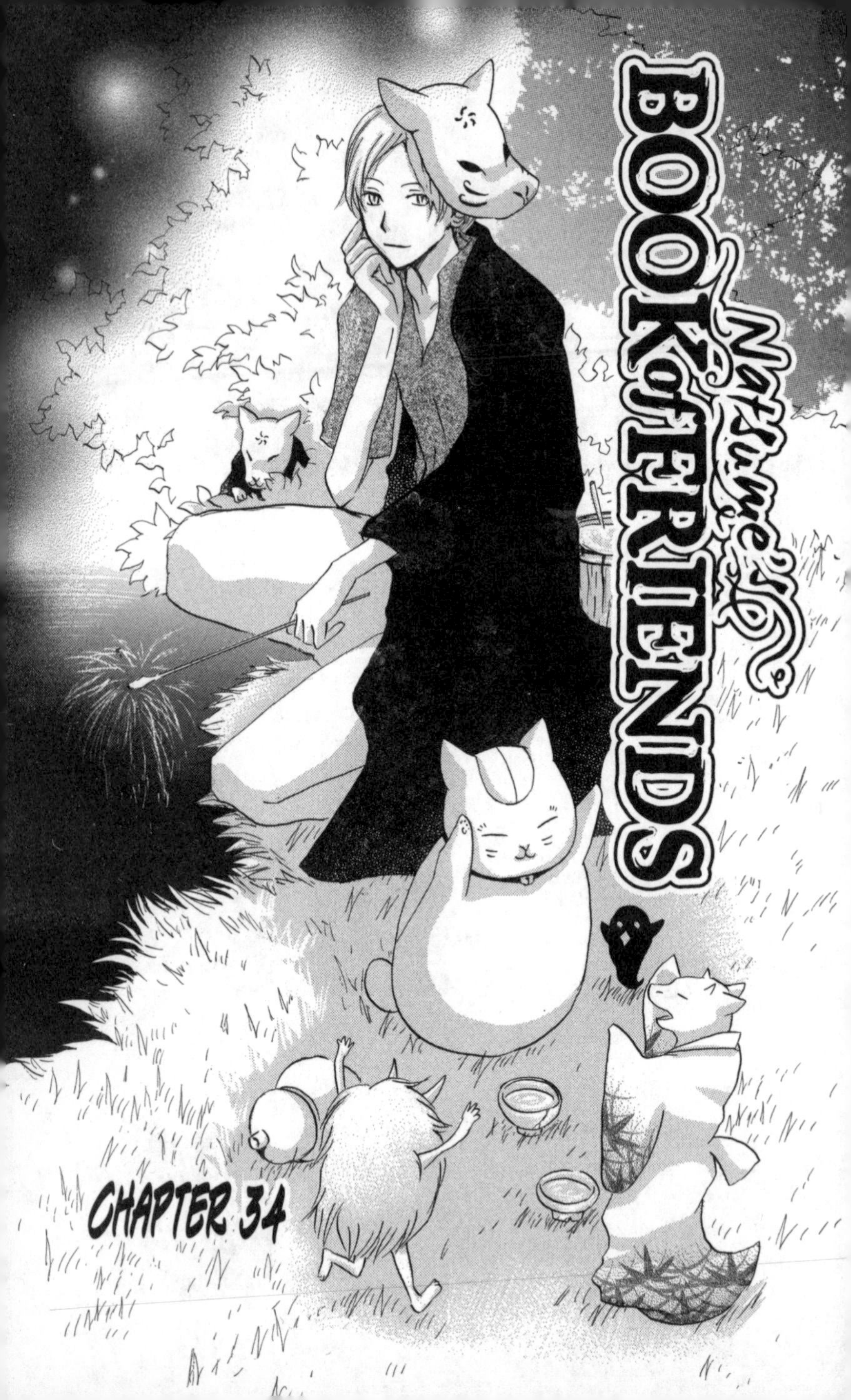
Natsume's Book of Friends
Chapter 34

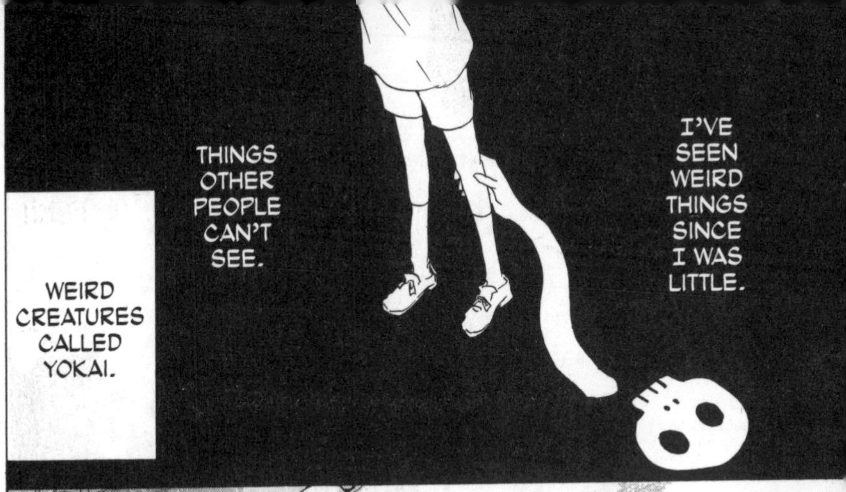
I'VE SEEN WEIRD THINGS SINCE I WAS LITTLE.
THINGS OTHER PEOPLE CAN'T SEE.
WEIRD CREATURES CALLED YOKAI.

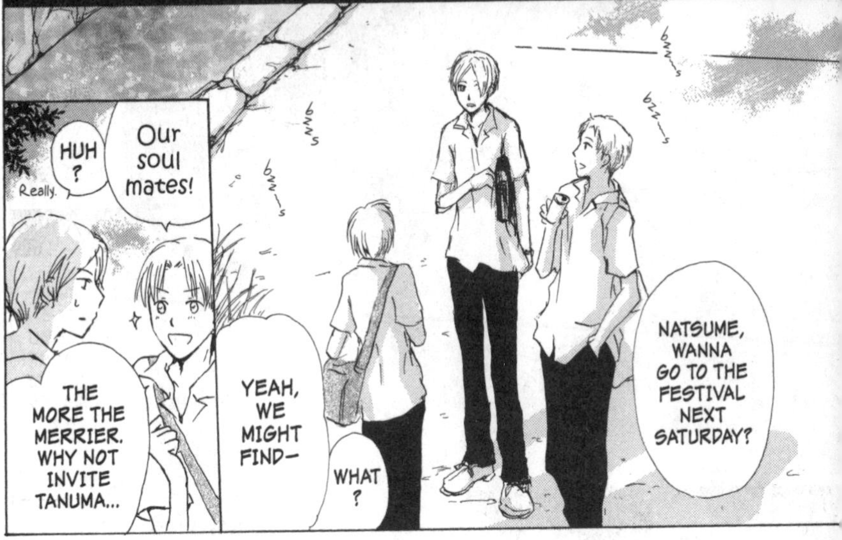
NATSUME, WANNA GO TO THE FESTIVAL NEXT SATURDAY?
WHAT?
YEAH, WE MIGHT FIND—
Our soul mates!
HUH?
Really.
THE MORE THE MERRIER. WHY NOT INVITE TANUMA...

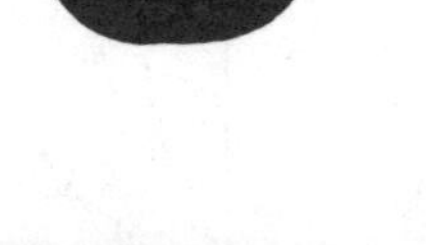

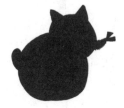

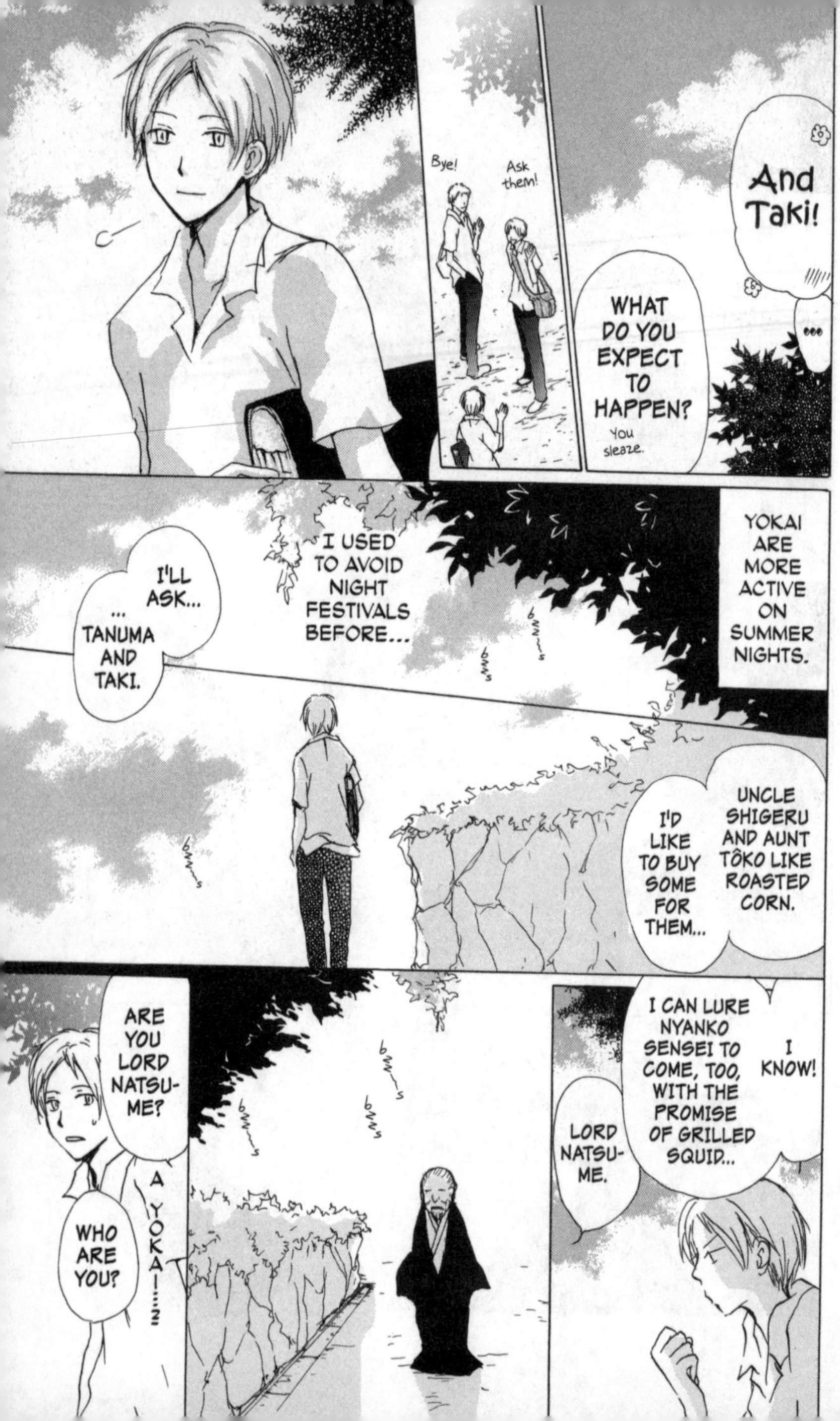
And Taki!
...
WHAT DO YOU EXPECT TO HAPPEN? You sleaze.
Ask them!
Bye!
YOKAI ARE MORE ACTIVE ON SUMMER NIGHTS.
I USED TO AVOID NIGHT FESTIVALS BEFORE...
bzzz
I'LL ASK... ...TANUMA AND TAKI.
UNCLE SHIGERU AND AUNT TÔKO LIKE ROASTED CORN.
I'D LIKE TO BUY SOME FOR THEM...
bzzz
I KNOW!
I CAN LURE NYANKO SENSEI TO COME, TOO, WITH THE PROMISE OF GRILLED SQUID...
LORD NATSUME.
bzzz
ARE YOU LORD NATSUME?
A YOKAI...?!
WHO ARE YOU?

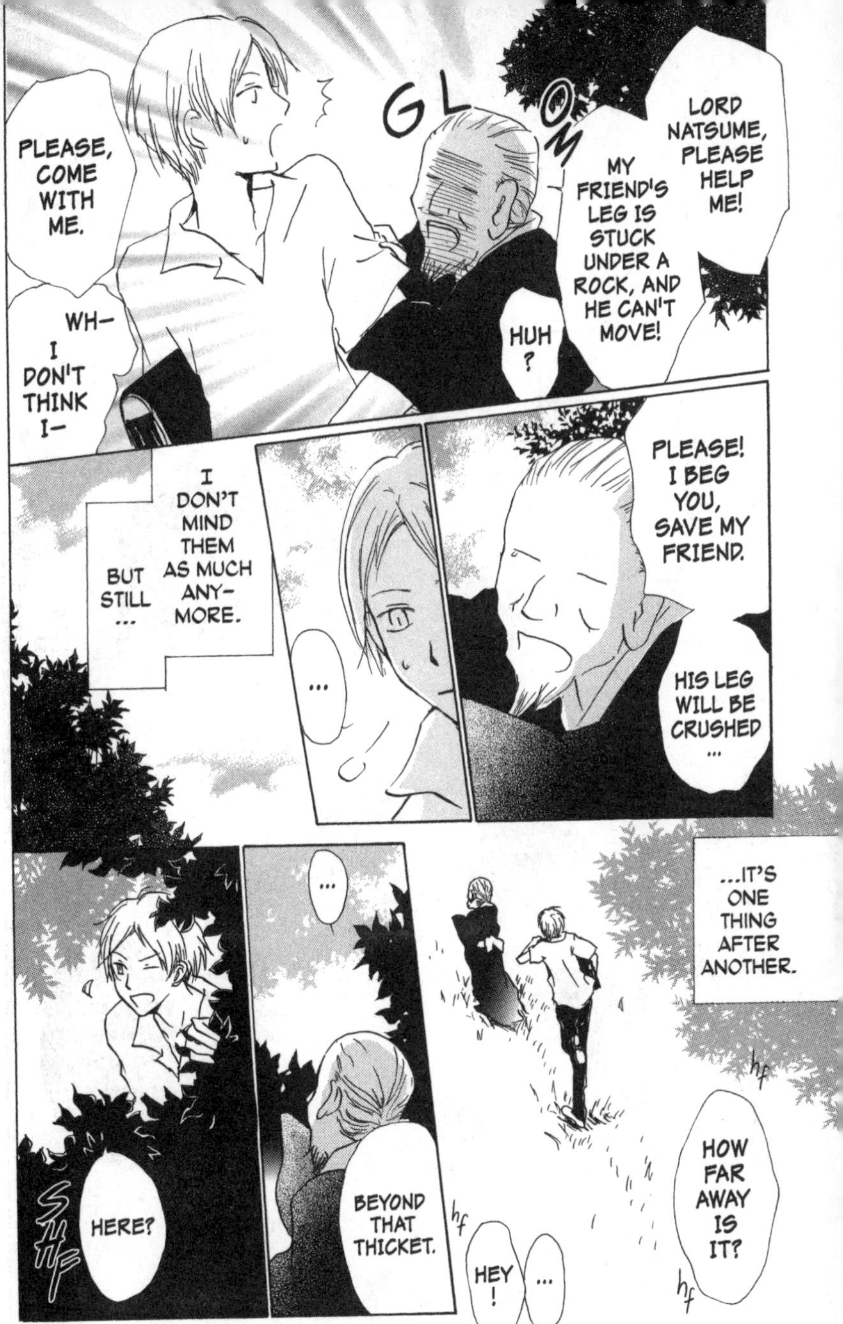
LORD NATSUME, PLEASE HELP ME!
GLOM
MY FRIEND'S LEG IS STUCK UNDER A ROCK, AND HE CAN'T MOVE!
PLEASE, COME WITH ME.
HUH?
WH— I DON'T THINK I—
PLEASE! I BEG YOU, SAVE MY FRIEND.
HIS LEG WILL BE CRUSHED...
...
I DON'T MIND THEM AS MUCH ANY-MORE.
BUT STILL...
...IT'S ONE THING AFTER ANOTHER.
hf
HOW FAR AWAY IS IT?
hf
hf
HEY!
...
...
BEYOND THAT THICKET.
SHF
HERE?

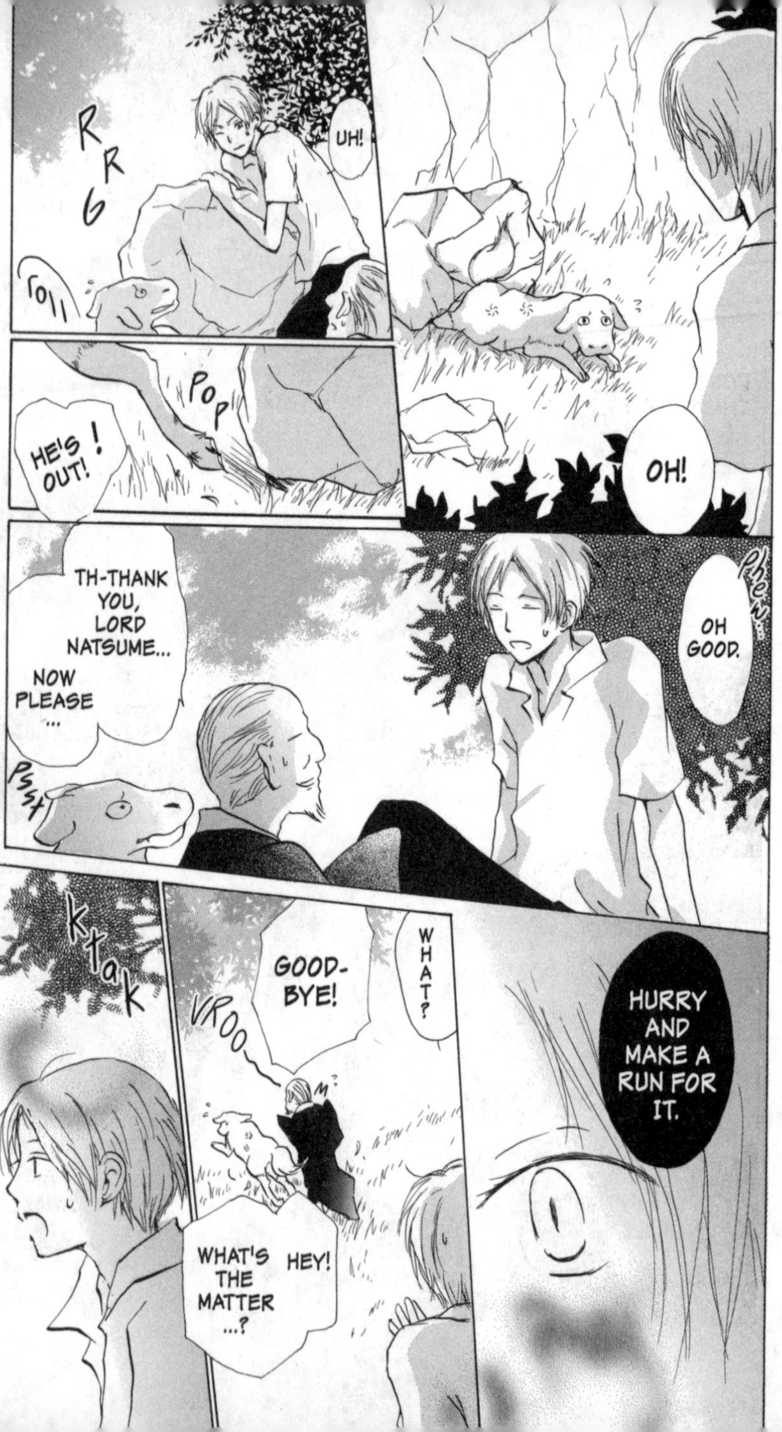
UH!
RRG
roll
POP
HE'S OUT! !
OH!
Phew...
OH GOOD.
TH-THANK YOU, LORD NATSUME...
NOW PLEASE ...
Psst
HURRY AND MAKE A RUN FOR IT.
HEY!
WHAT'S THE MATTER ...?
WHAT?
GOOD-BYE!
VROOM
ktak

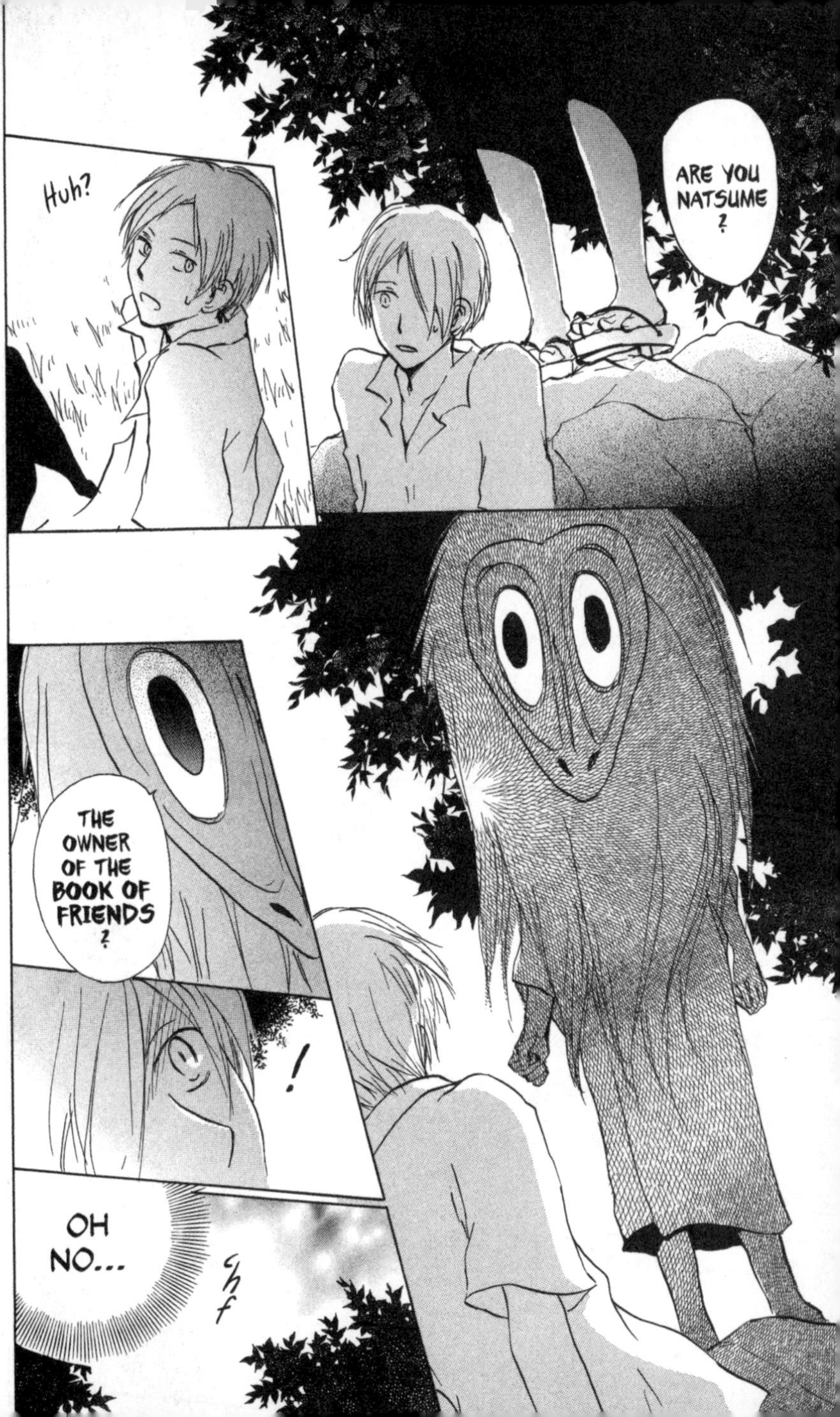
ARE YOU NATSUME ?
Huh?
THE OWNER OF THE BOOK OF FRIENDS ?
!
OH NO...
chf

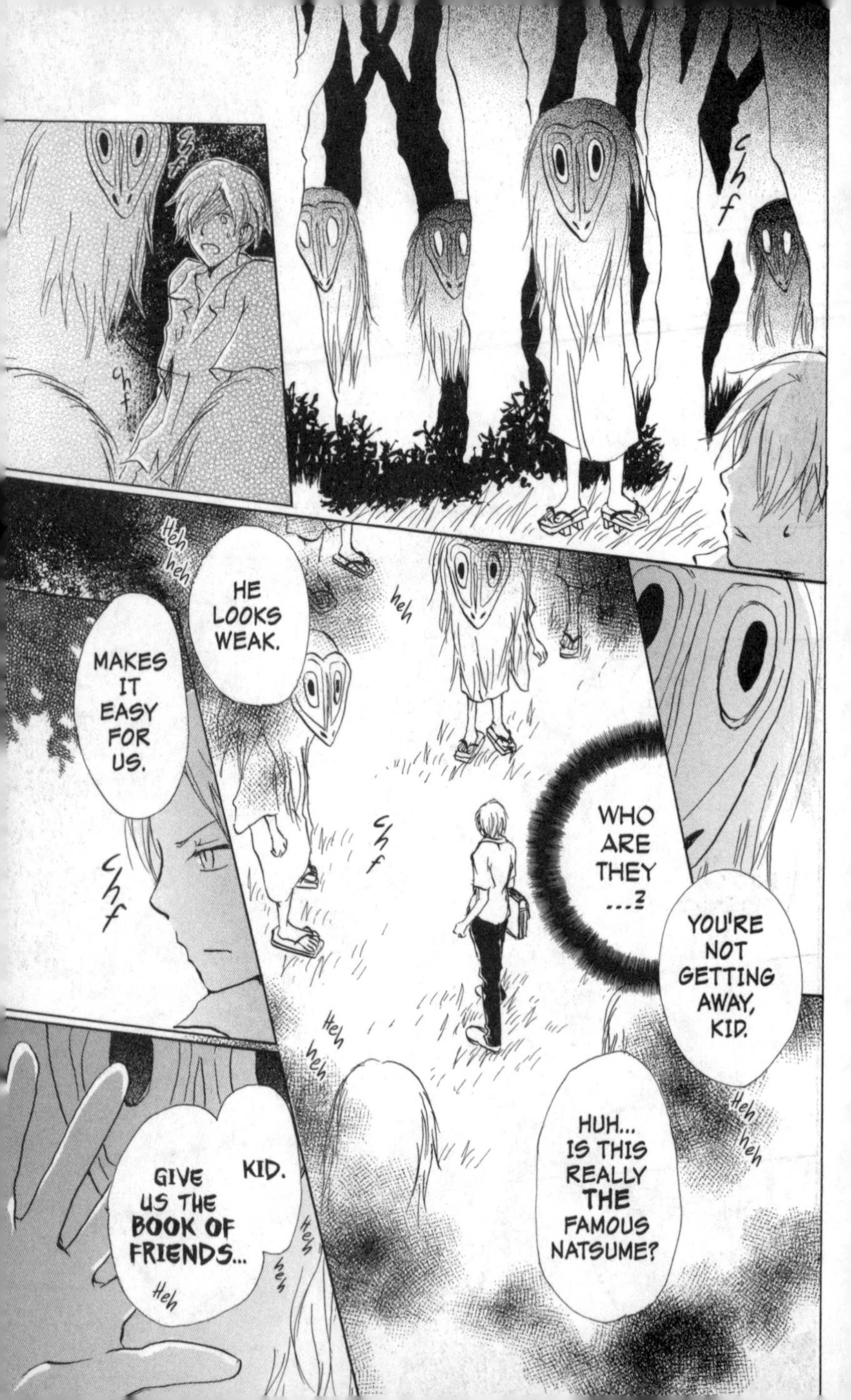
chf
chf
WHO ARE THEY ...?
YOU'RE NOT GETTING AWAY, KID.
Heh heh
HUH... IS THIS REALLY THE FAMOUS NATSUME?
heh
Heh heh
HE LOOKS WEAK.
MAKES IT EASY FOR US.
chf
chf
Heh heh
KID.
GIVE US THE BOOK OF FRIENDS...
Heh heh

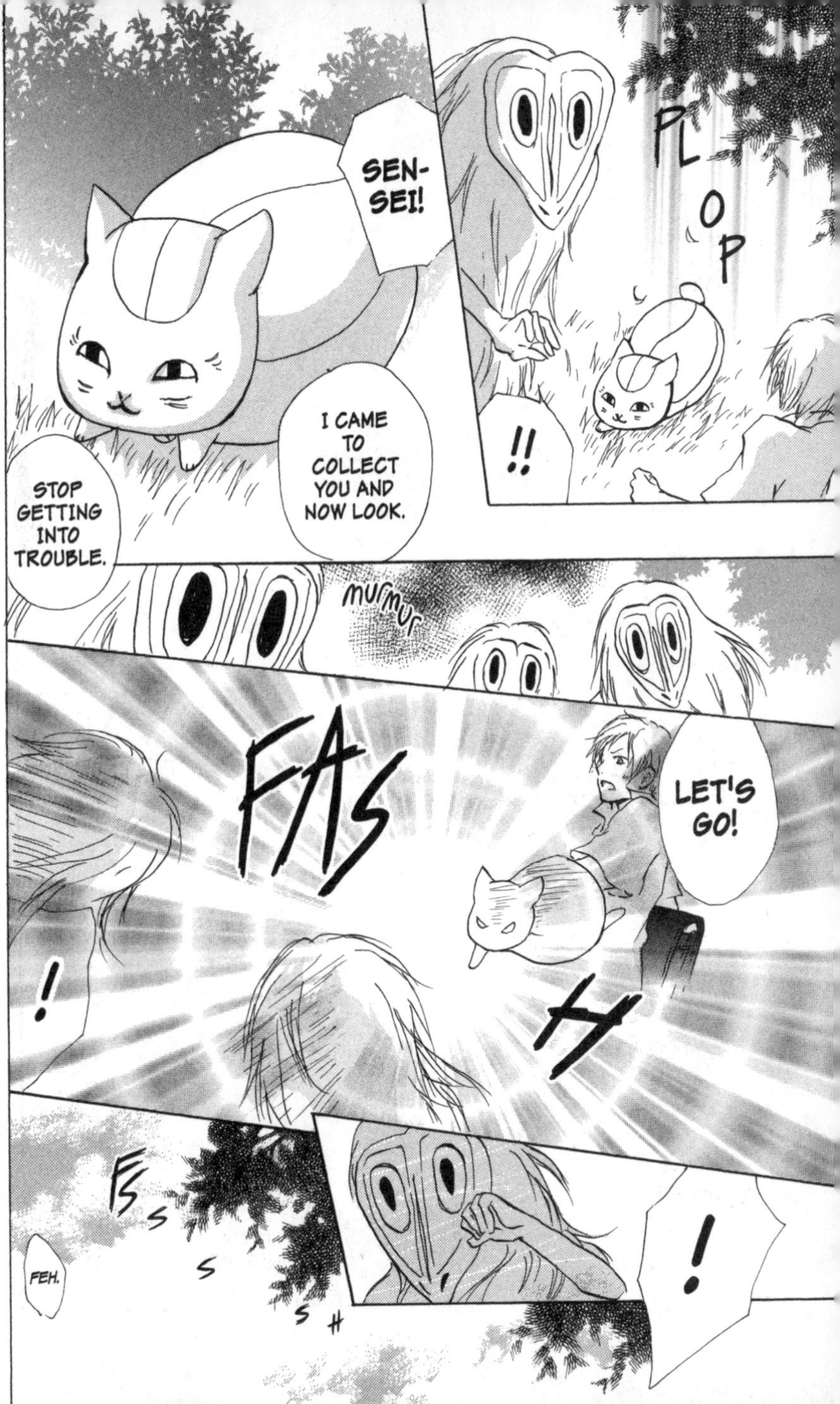
PLOP
!!
SEN-SEI!
I CAME TO COLLECT YOU AND NOW LOOK.
STOP GETTING INTO TROUBLE.
murmur
LET'S GO!
FAS
H
!
!
FSSSSH
FEH.

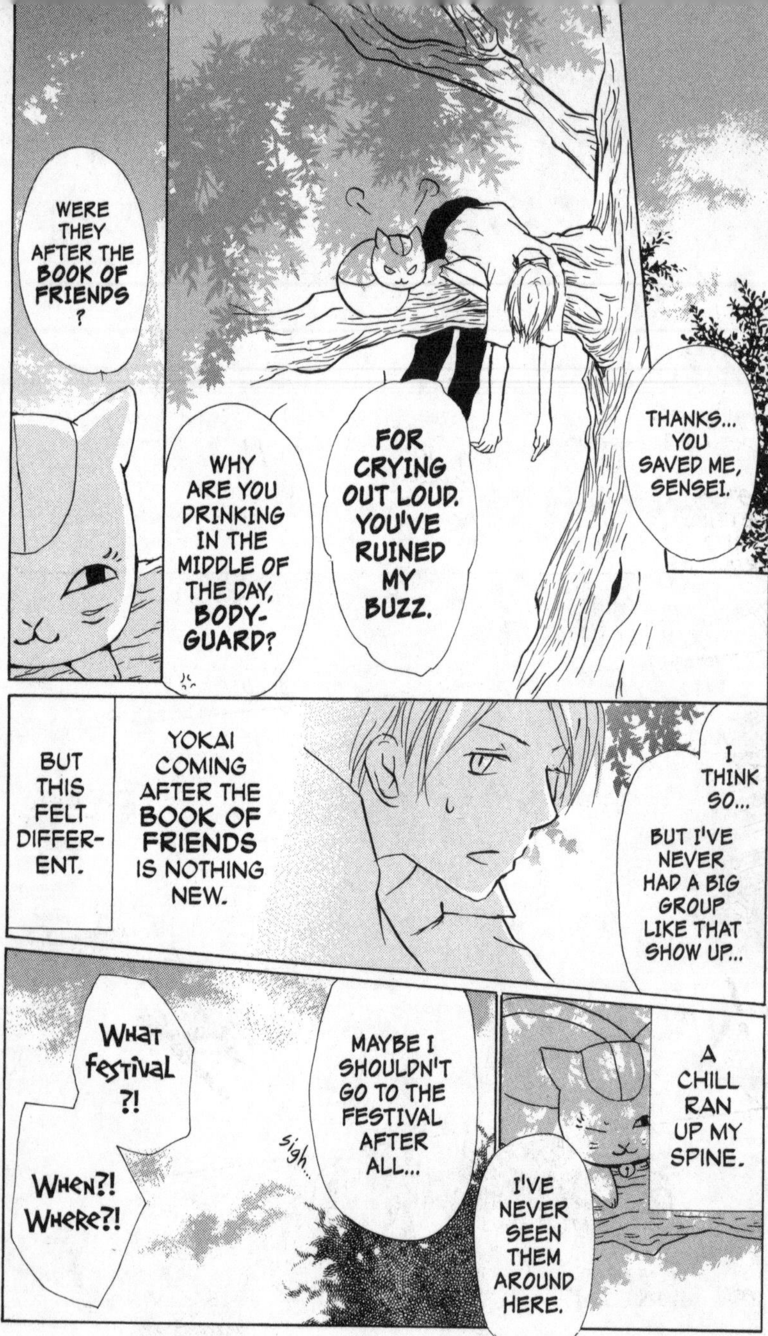
THANKS... YOU SAVED ME, SENSEI.
FOR CRYING OUT LOUD. YOU'VE RUINED MY BUZZ.
WHY ARE YOU DRINKING IN THE MIDDLE OF THE DAY, BODY-GUARD?
WERE THEY AFTER THE BOOK OF FRIENDS?
I THINK SO...
BUT I'VE NEVER HAD A BIG GROUP LIKE THAT SHOW UP...
YOKAI COMING AFTER THE BOOK OF FRIENDS IS NOTHING NEW.
BUT THIS FELT DIFFER-ENT.
A CHILL RAN UP MY SPINE.
I'VE NEVER SEEN THEM AROUND HERE.
MAYBE I SHOULDN'T GO TO THE FESTIVAL AFTER ALL...
sigh...
What festival?!
When?! Where?!

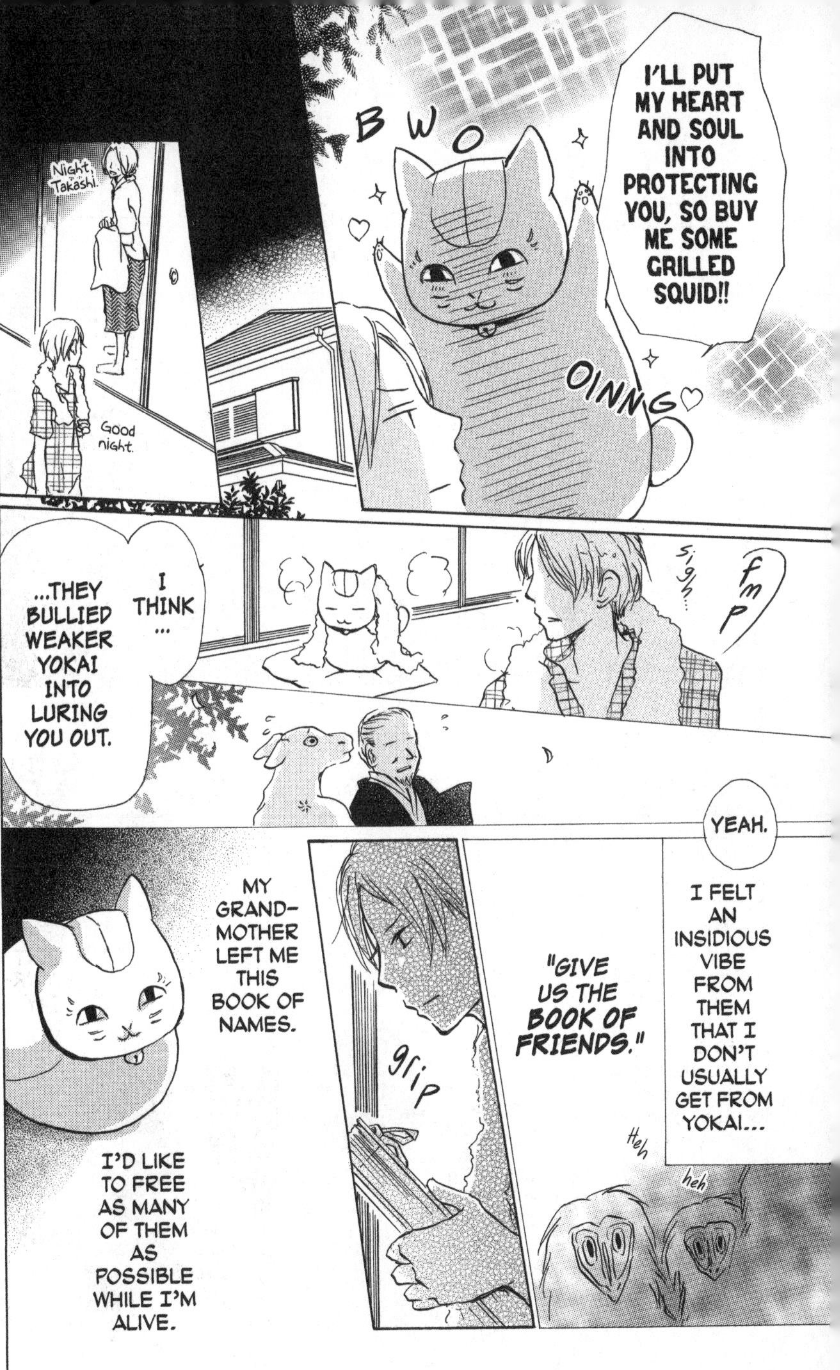
I'LL PUT MY HEART AND SOUL INTO PROTECTING YOU, SO BUY ME SOME GRILLED SQUID!!
BWO
OINNG♡
Night, Takashi.
Good night.
sigh...
fmp
I THINK...
...THEY BULLIED WEAKER YOKAI INTO LURING YOU OUT.
YEAH.
I FELT AN INSIDIOUS VIBE FROM THEM THAT I DON'T USUALLY GET FROM YOKAI...
Heh
heh
"GIVE US THE BOOK OF FRIENDS."
grip
MY GRANDMOTHER LEFT ME THIS BOOK OF NAMES.
I'D LIKE TO FREE AS MANY OF THEM AS POSSIBLE WHILE I'M ALIVE.

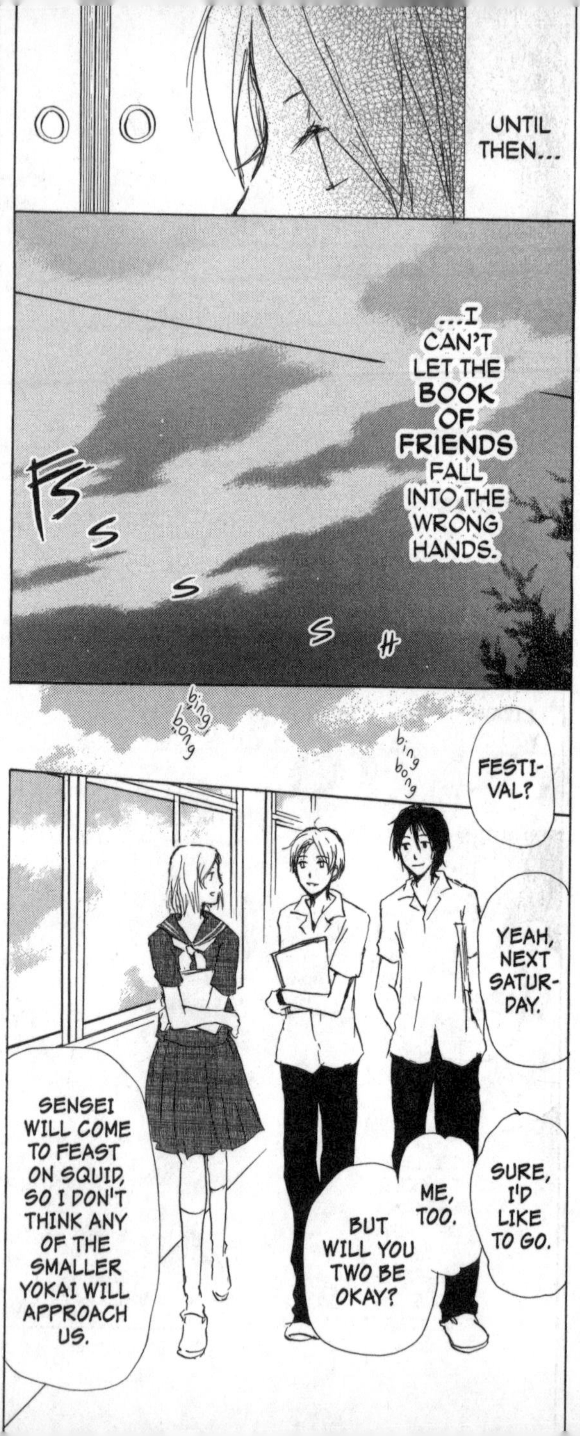
UNTIL THEN...
...I CAN'T LET THE BOOK OF FRIENDS FALL INTO THE WRONG HANDS.
FSSSSH
bing bong
bing bong
FESTIVAL?
YEAH, NEXT SATURDAY.
SURE, I'D LIKE TO GO.
ME, TOO.
BUT WILL YOU TWO BE OKAY?
SENSEI WILL COME TO FEAST ON SQUID, SO I DON'T THINK ANY OF THE SMALLER YOKAI WILL APPROACH US.

## 03

### ❀ Kitty Merchandise

There have been more opportunities to produce Nyanko Sensei merchandise. It's really been a blessing. They've been so meticulous in the design of these items. Amazingly enough, they turned that ugly-creepy cat into little mascots emanating an adorable aura. I can't believe that my heart could go pitter-pat for Nyanko Sensei! I won't let him get the better of me!

Speaking of adorable, my readers sometimes send me their handmade versions of Nyanko Sensei. I've made a box styled like a traditional Japanese room, and named it "the Kitty Box," which is now full of all the cute little kitties that traveled from their various homes. It's truly my treasure box.

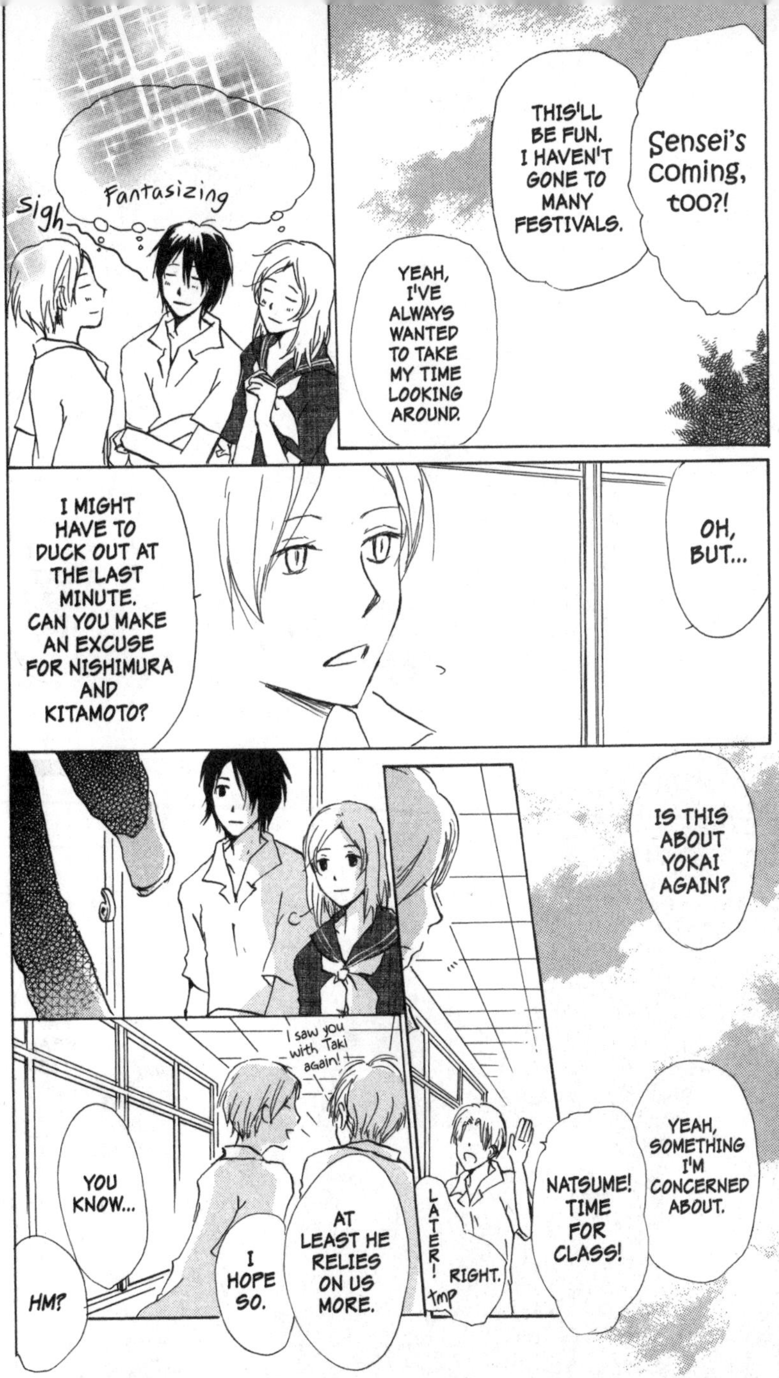

Sensei's coming, too?!
THIS'LL BE FUN. I HAVEN'T GONE TO MANY FESTIVALS.
YEAH, I'VE ALWAYS WANTED TO TAKE MY TIME LOOKING AROUND.
Fantasizing
Sigh
OH, BUT...
I MIGHT HAVE TO DUCK OUT AT THE LAST MINUTE. CAN YOU MAKE AN EXCUSE FOR NISHIMURA AND KITAMOTO?
IS THIS ABOUT YOKAI AGAIN?
YEAH, SOMETHING I'M CONCERNED ABOUT.
NATSUME! TIME FOR CLASS!
RIGHT.
LATER!
tmp
I saw you with Taki again!
AT LEAST HE RELIES ON US MORE.
I HOPE SO.
YOU KNOW...
HM?

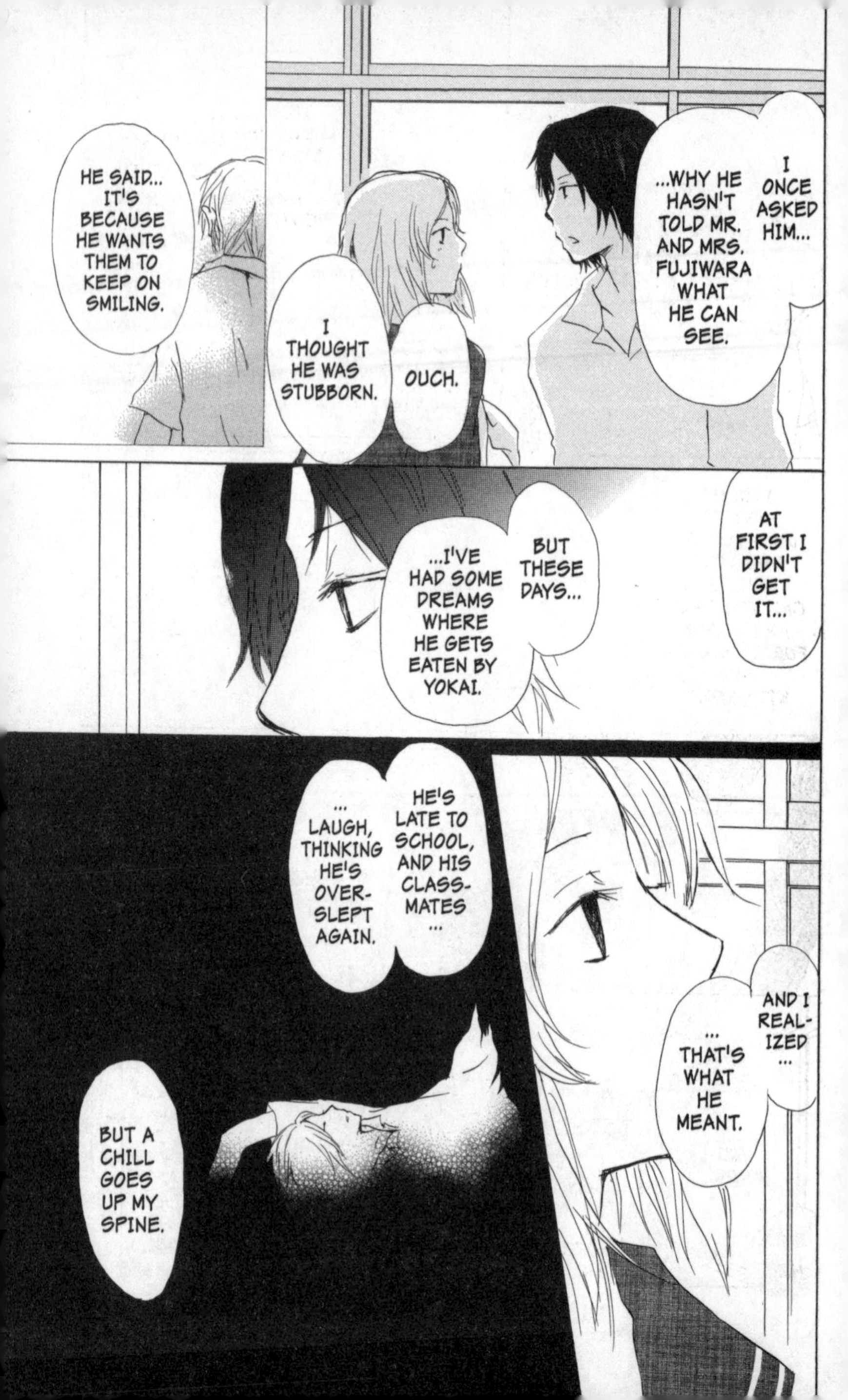
I ONCE ASKED HIM...
...WHY HE HASN'T TOLD MR. AND MRS. FUJIWARA WHAT HE CAN SEE.
OUCH.
I THOUGHT HE WAS STUBBORN.
HE SAID... IT'S BECAUSE HE WANTS THEM TO KEEP ON SMILING.
AT FIRST I DIDN'T GET IT...
BUT THESE DAYS...
...I'VE HAD SOME DREAMS WHERE HE GETS EATEN BY YOKAI.
AND I REALIZED...
...THAT'S WHAT HE MEANT.
HE'S LATE TO SCHOOL, AND HIS CLASS-MATES...
...LAUGH, THINKING HE'S OVER-SLEPT AGAIN.
BUT A CHILL GOES UP MY SPINE.

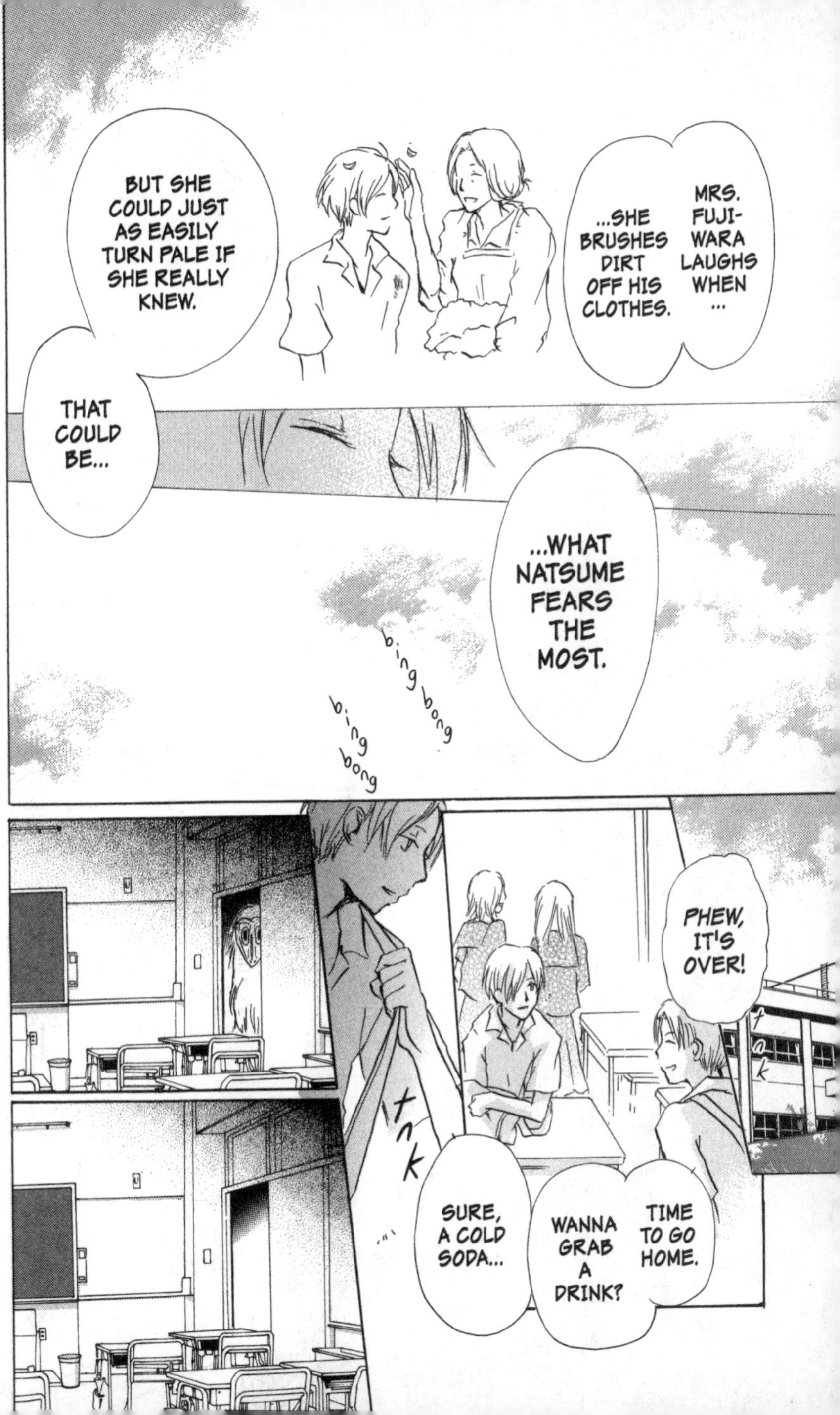
MRS. FUJI-WARA LAUGHS WHEN ...
...SHE BRUSHES DIRT OFF HIS CLOTHES.
BUT SHE COULD JUST AS EASILY TURN PALE IF SHE REALLY KNEW.
THAT COULD BE...
...WHAT NATSUME FEARS THE MOST.
bing bong
bing bong
PHEW, IT'S OVER!
TIME TO GO HOME.
WANNA GRAB A DRINK?
SURE, A COLD SODA...

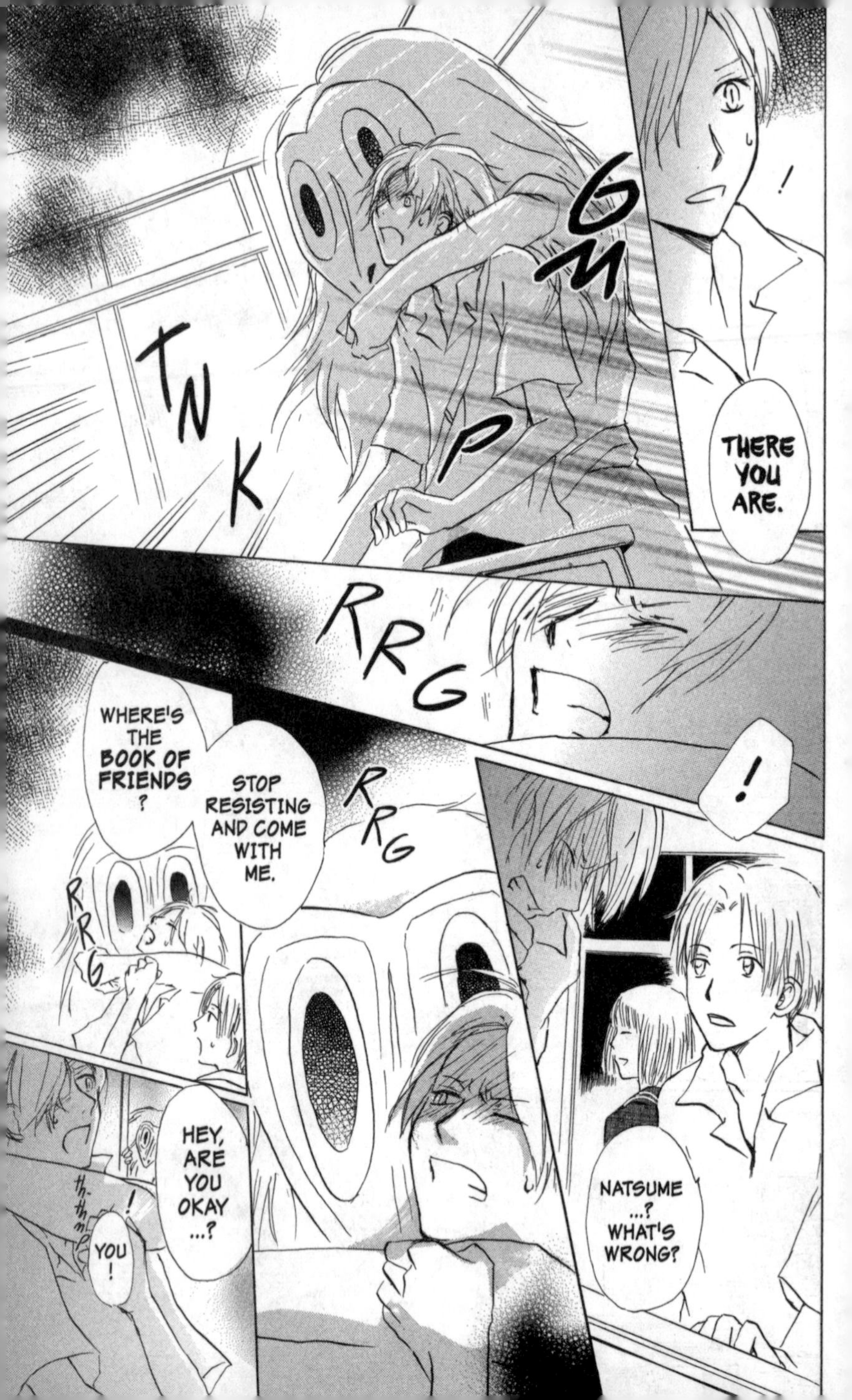
!
THERE YOU ARE.
GOMP
TNK
RRRG
!
NATSUME ...? WHAT'S WRONG?
RRRG
WHERE'S THE BOOK OF FRIENDS?
STOP RESISTING AND COME WITH ME.
RRRG
HEY, ARE YOU OKAY ...?
!
YOU!

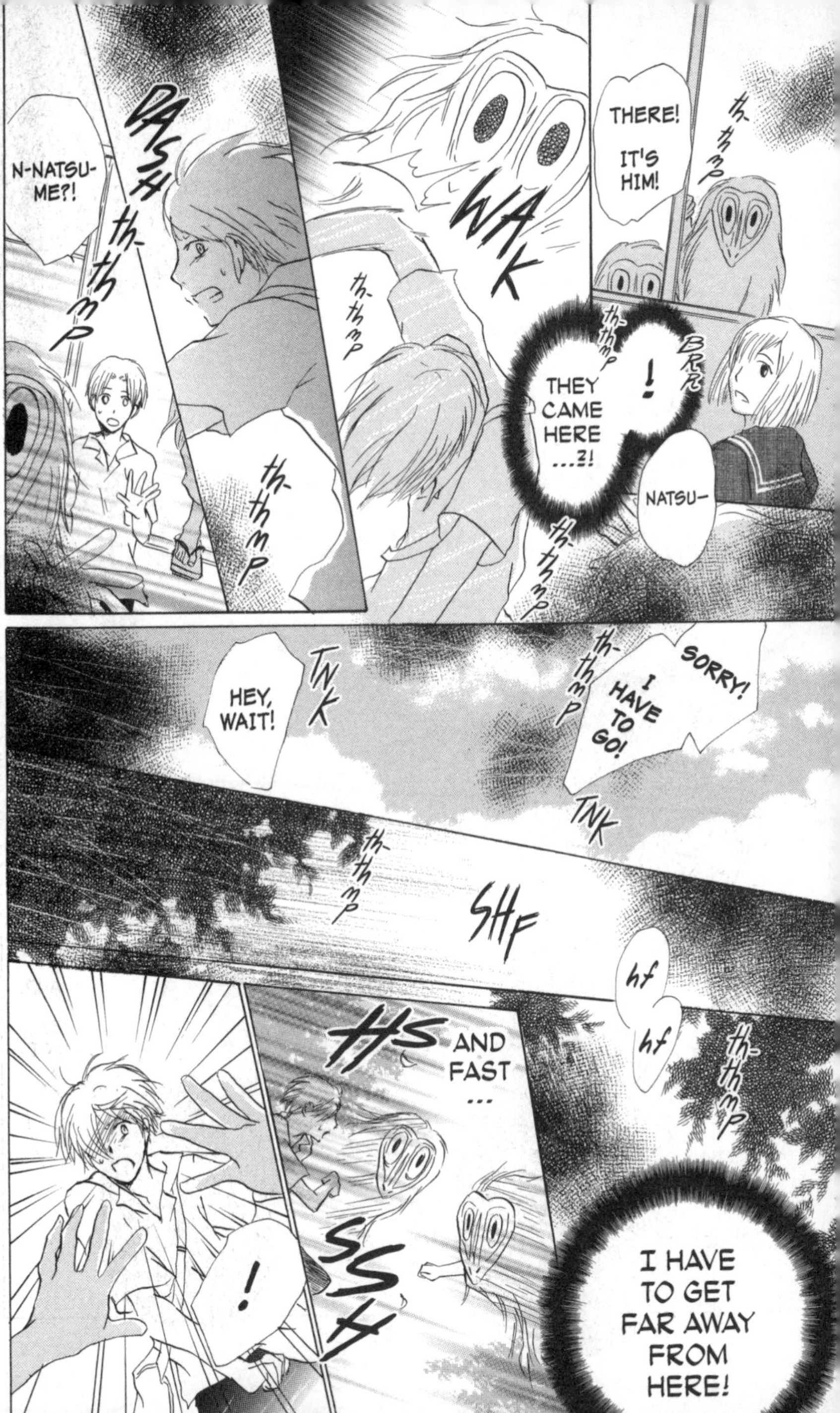
THERE! IT'S HIM!
th-thmp
BRR
th-thmp
!
THEY CAME HERE ...?!
NATSU-
th-thmp
WAK
th-thmp
th-thmp
DASH
th-thmp
N-NATSU-ME?!
SORRY! I HAVE TO GO!
th-thmp
TNK
TNK
HEY, WAIT!
th-thmp
SHF
hf
hf
th-thmp
I HAVE TO GET FAR AWAY FROM HERE!
HS
AND FAST ...
SSH
!

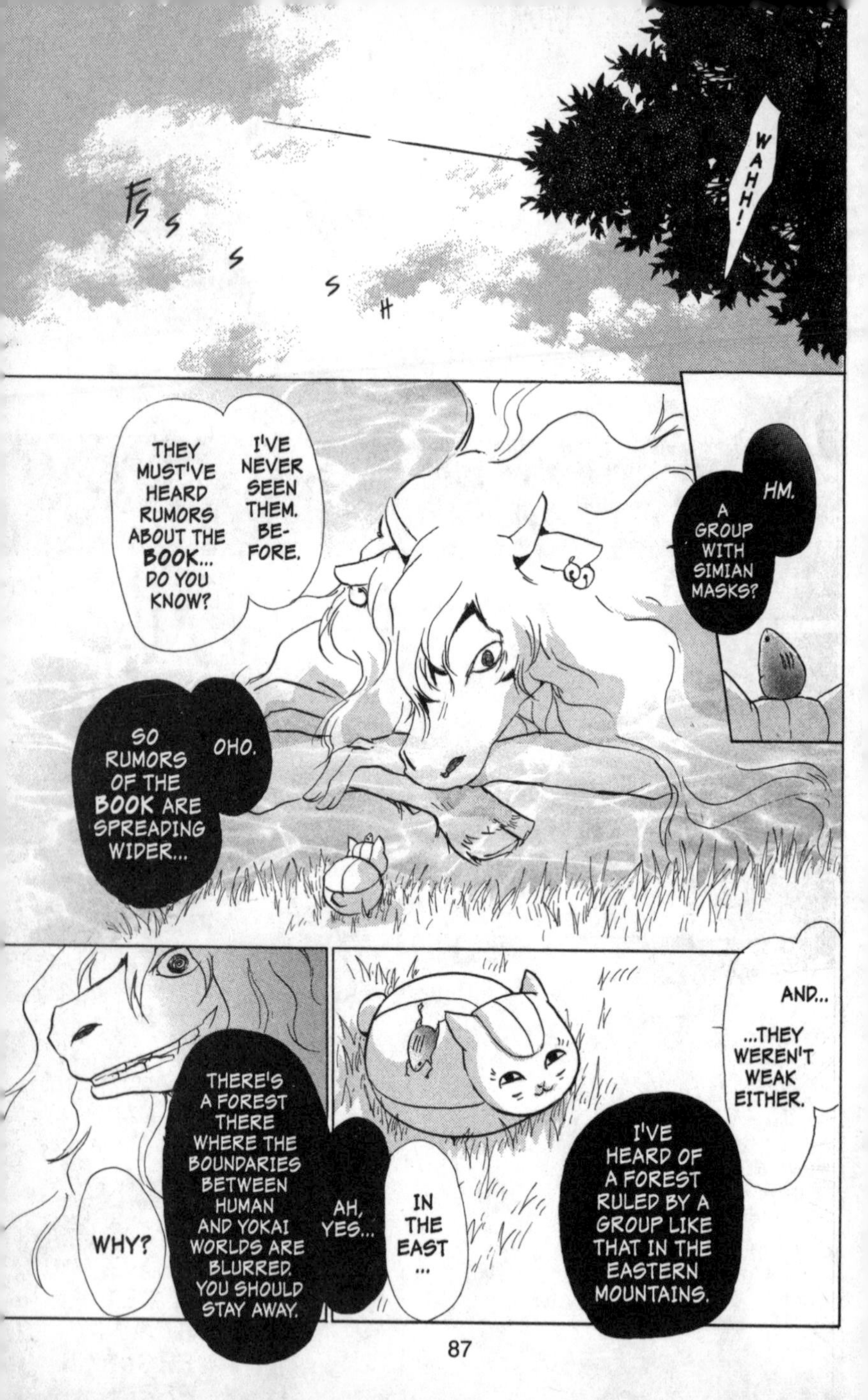
WAHH!
FSSSSH
HM.
A GROUP WITH SIMIAN MASKS?
I'VE NEVER SEEN THEM. BE-FORE.
THEY MUST'VE HEARD RUMORS ABOUT THE BOOK... DO YOU KNOW?
OHO.
SO RUMORS OF THE BOOK ARE SPREADING WIDER...
AND...
...THEY WEREN'T WEAK EITHER.
I'VE HEARD OF A FOREST RULED BY A GROUP LIKE THAT IN THE EASTERN MOUNTAINS.
IN THE EAST...
AH, YES...
THERE'S A FOREST THERE WHERE THE BOUNDARIES BETWEEN HUMAN AND YOKAI WORLDS ARE BLURRED. YOU SHOULD STAY AWAY.
WHY?

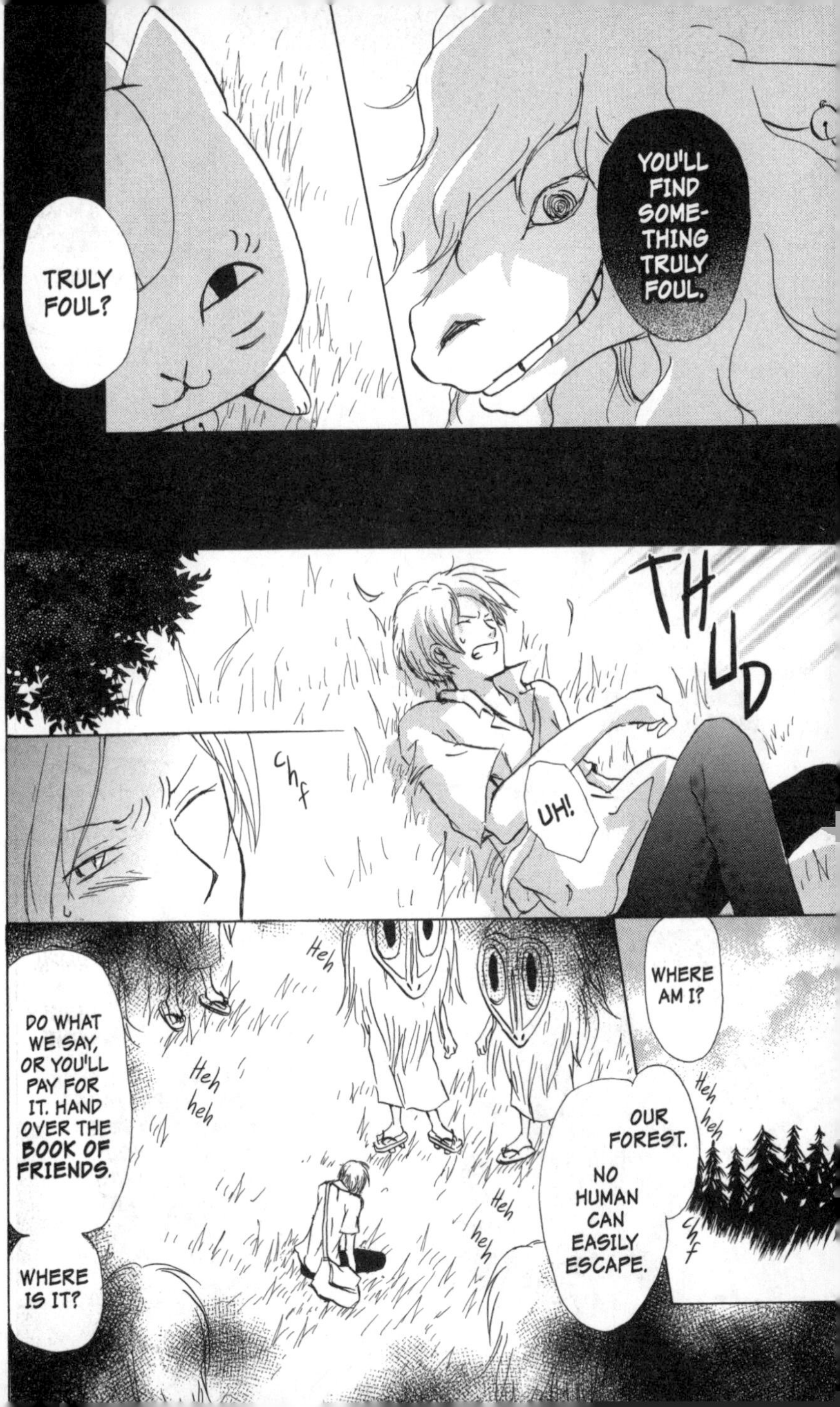
YOU'LL FIND SOME-THING TRULY FOUL.
TRULY FOUL?
THUD
UH!
chf
WHERE AM I?
Heh heh
chf
OUR FOREST.
NO HUMAN CAN EASILY ESCAPE.
Heh heh
Heh
Heh heh
DO WHAT WE SAY, OR YOU'LL PAY FOR IT. HAND OVER THE BOOK OF FRIENDS.
WHERE IS IT?

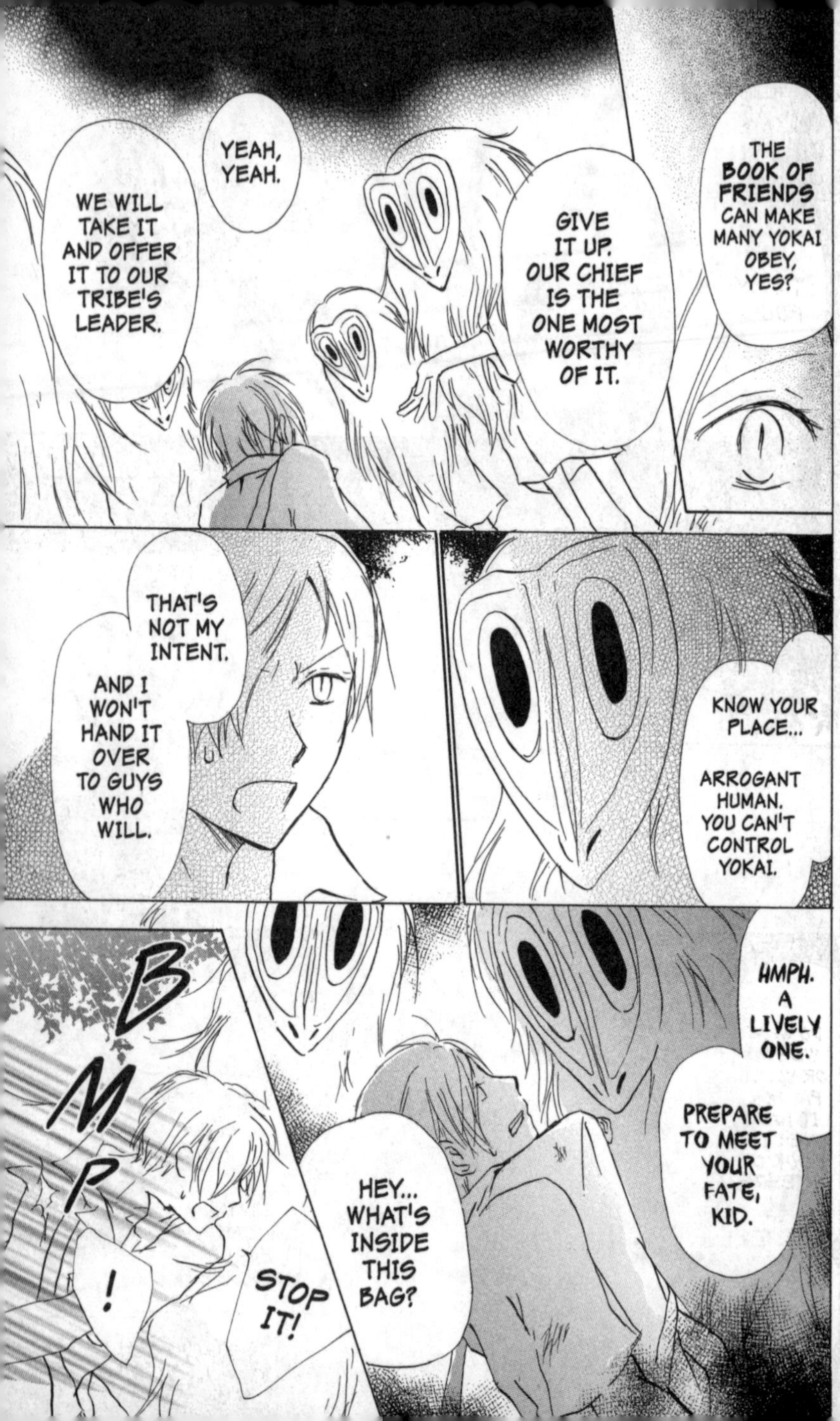
THE BOOK OF FRIENDS CAN MAKE MANY YOKAI OBEY, YES?
GIVE IT UP. OUR CHIEF IS THE ONE MOST WORTHY OF IT.
YEAH, YEAH.
WE WILL TAKE IT AND OFFER IT TO OUR TRIBE'S LEADER.
KNOW YOUR PLACE...
ARROGANT HUMAN. YOU CAN'T CONTROL YOKAI.
THAT'S NOT MY INTENT.
AND I WON'T HAND IT OVER TO GUYS WHO WILL.
HMPH. A LIVELY ONE.
PREPARE TO MEET YOUR FATE, KID.
HEY... WHAT'S INSIDE THIS BAG?
STOP IT!
BMP
!

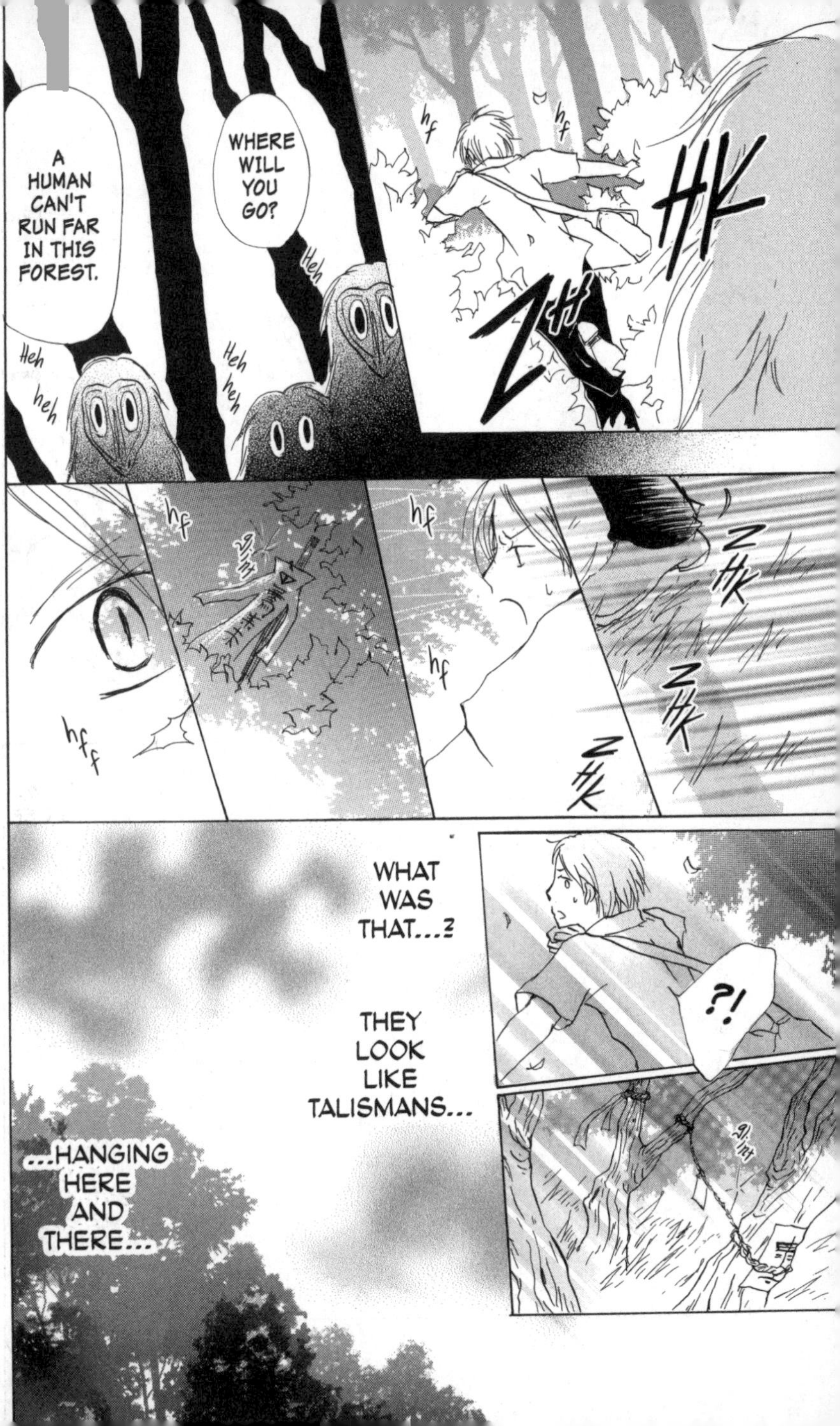
hf
hf
ZHK
WHERE WILL YOU GO?
Heh
A HUMAN CAN'T RUN FAR IN THIS FOREST.
Heh heh
Heh heh
ZHK
ZHK
ZHK
hf
hf
hf
hff
?!
WHAT WAS THAT...?
THEY LOOK LIKE TALISMANS...
...HANGING HERE AND THERE...

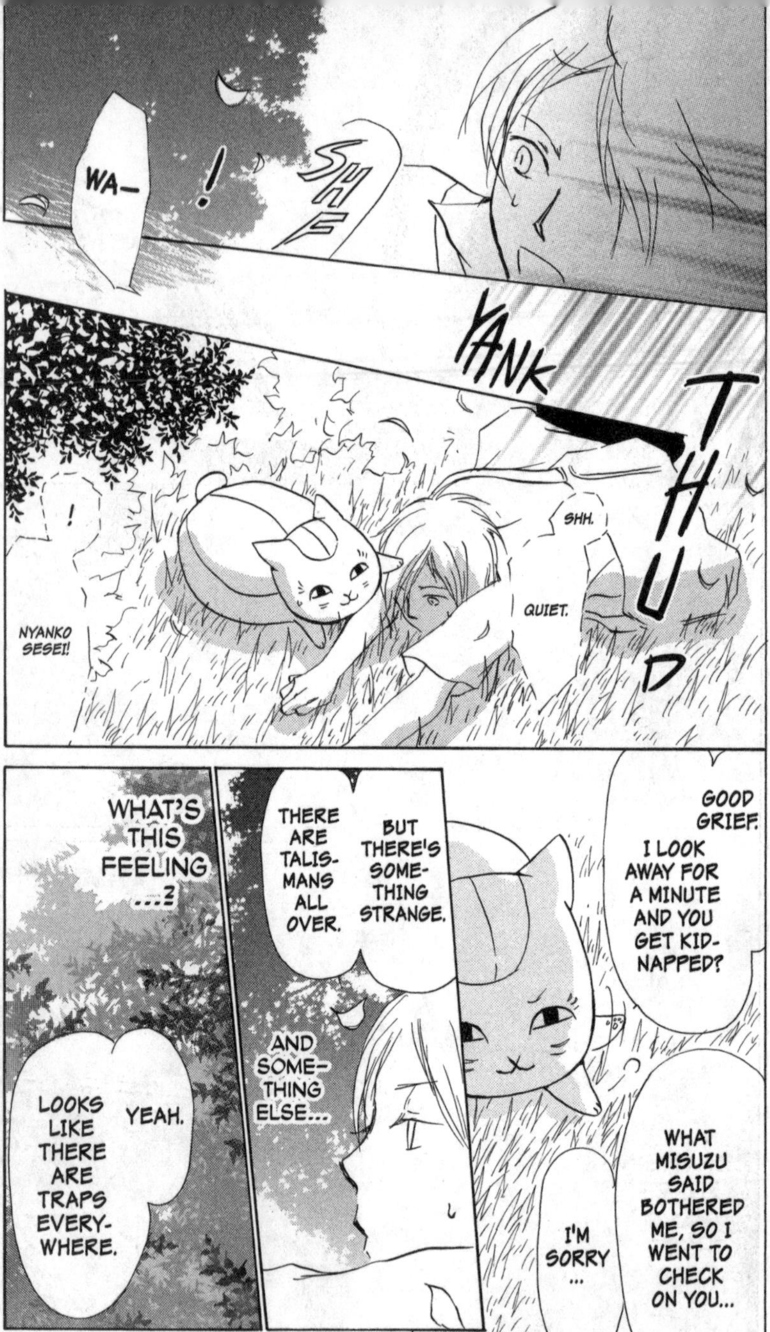
SHF
!
WA—
YANK
THUD
SHH.
QUIET.
!
NYANKO SESEI!
GOOD GRIEF. I LOOK AWAY FOR A MINUTE AND YOU GET KIDNAPPED?
WHAT MISUZU SAID BOTHERED ME, SO I WENT TO CHECK ON YOU...
I'M SORRY...
BUT THERE'S SOMETHING STRANGE.
THERE ARE TALISMANS ALL OVER.
AND SOMETHING ELSE...
WHAT'S THIS FEELING...?
YEAH.
LOOKS LIKE THERE ARE TRAPS EVERYWHERE.

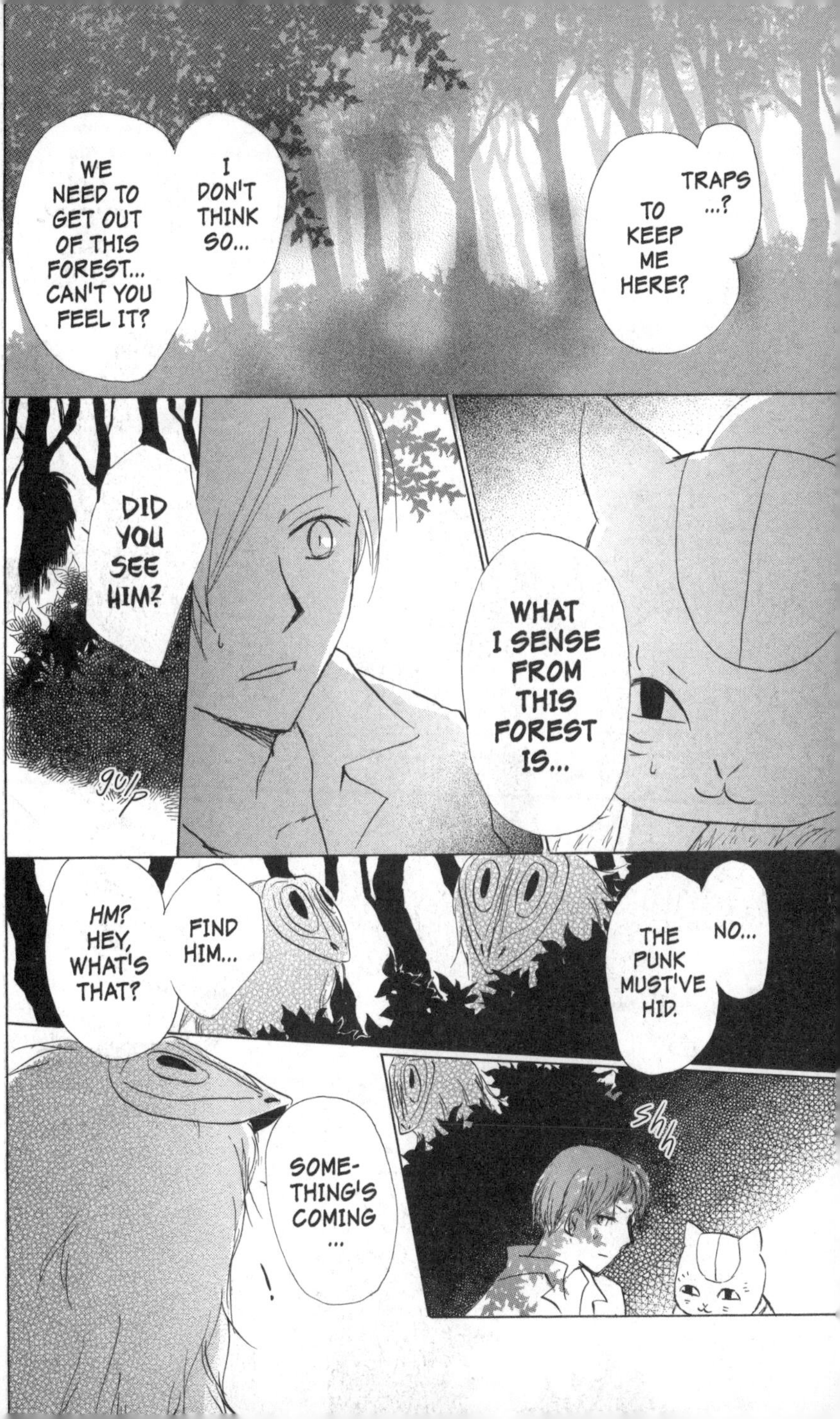
TRAPS ...? TO KEEP ME HERE?
I DON'T THINK SO...
WE NEED TO GET OUT OF THIS FOREST... CAN'T YOU FEEL IT?
WHAT I SENSE FROM THIS FOREST IS...
DID YOU SEE HIM?
gulp
NO... THE PUNK MUST'VE HID.
FIND HIM...
HM? HEY, WHAT'S THAT?
shh
SOME-THING'S COMING ...
!

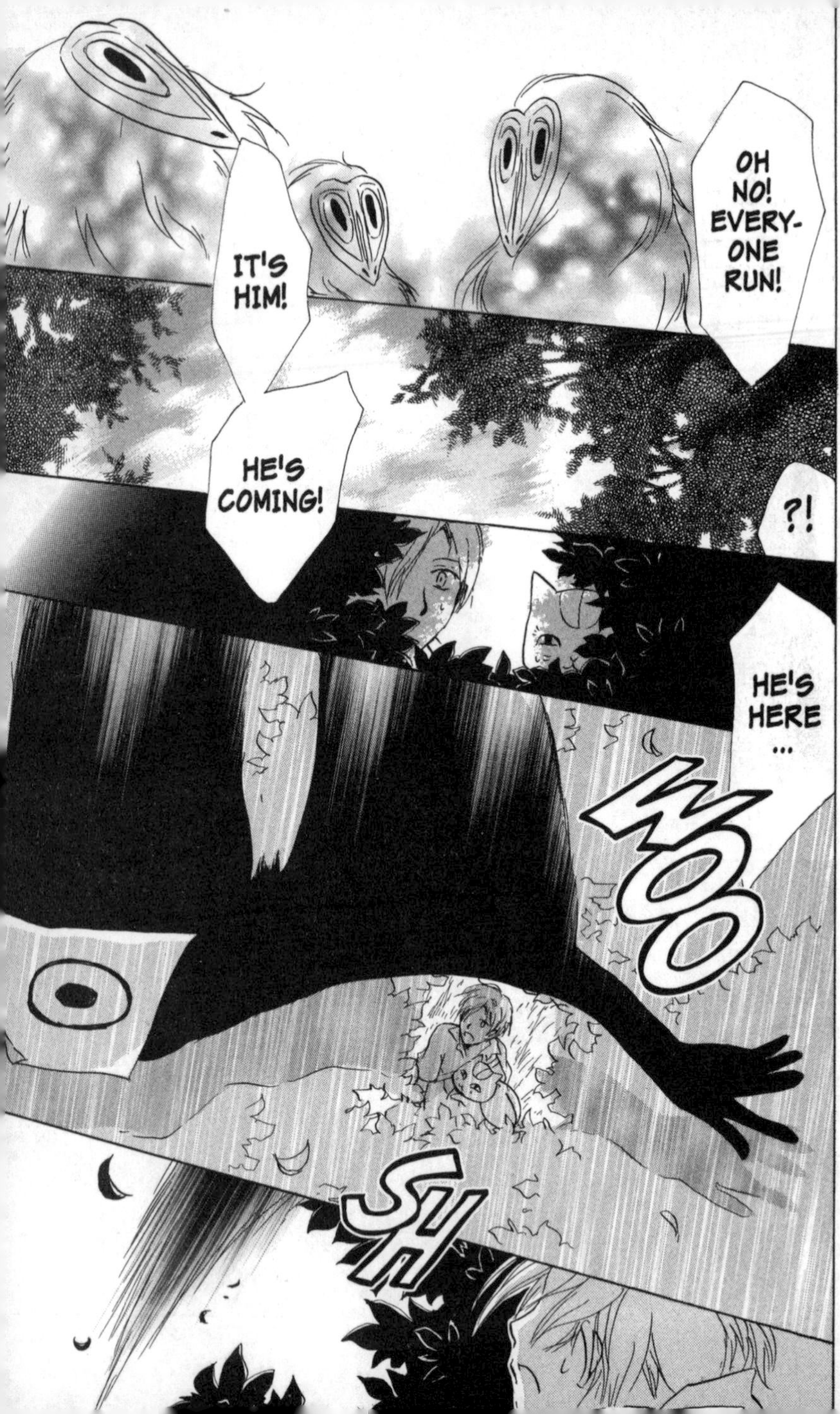
OH NO! EVERY-ONE RUN!
IT'S HIM!
HE'S COMING!
?!
HE'S HERE ...
WOO
SH

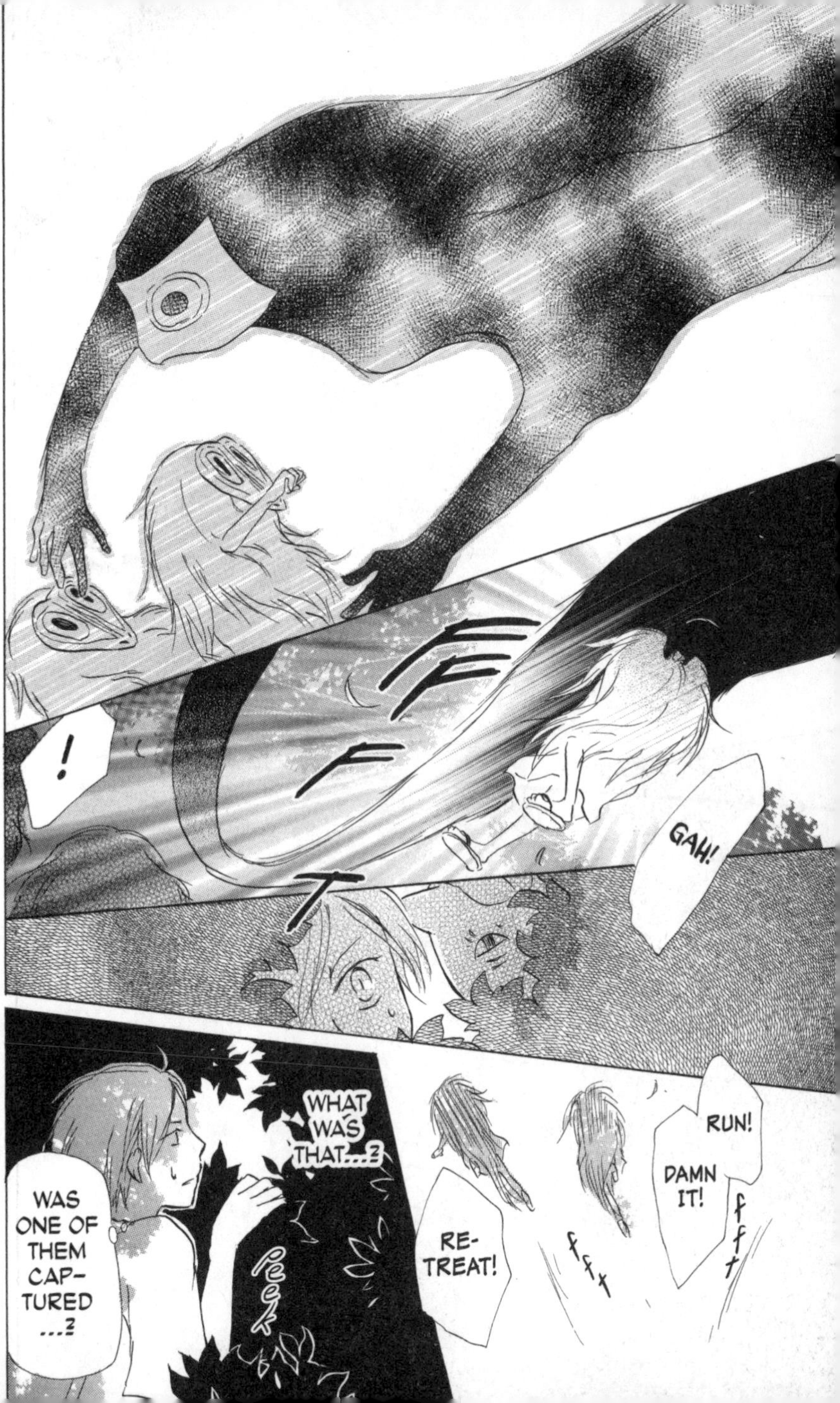
GAH!
FFFT
!
RUN!
DAMN IT!
fft
RE-TREAT!
fft
WHAT WAS THAT...?
peek
WAS ONE OF THEM CAP-TURED ...?

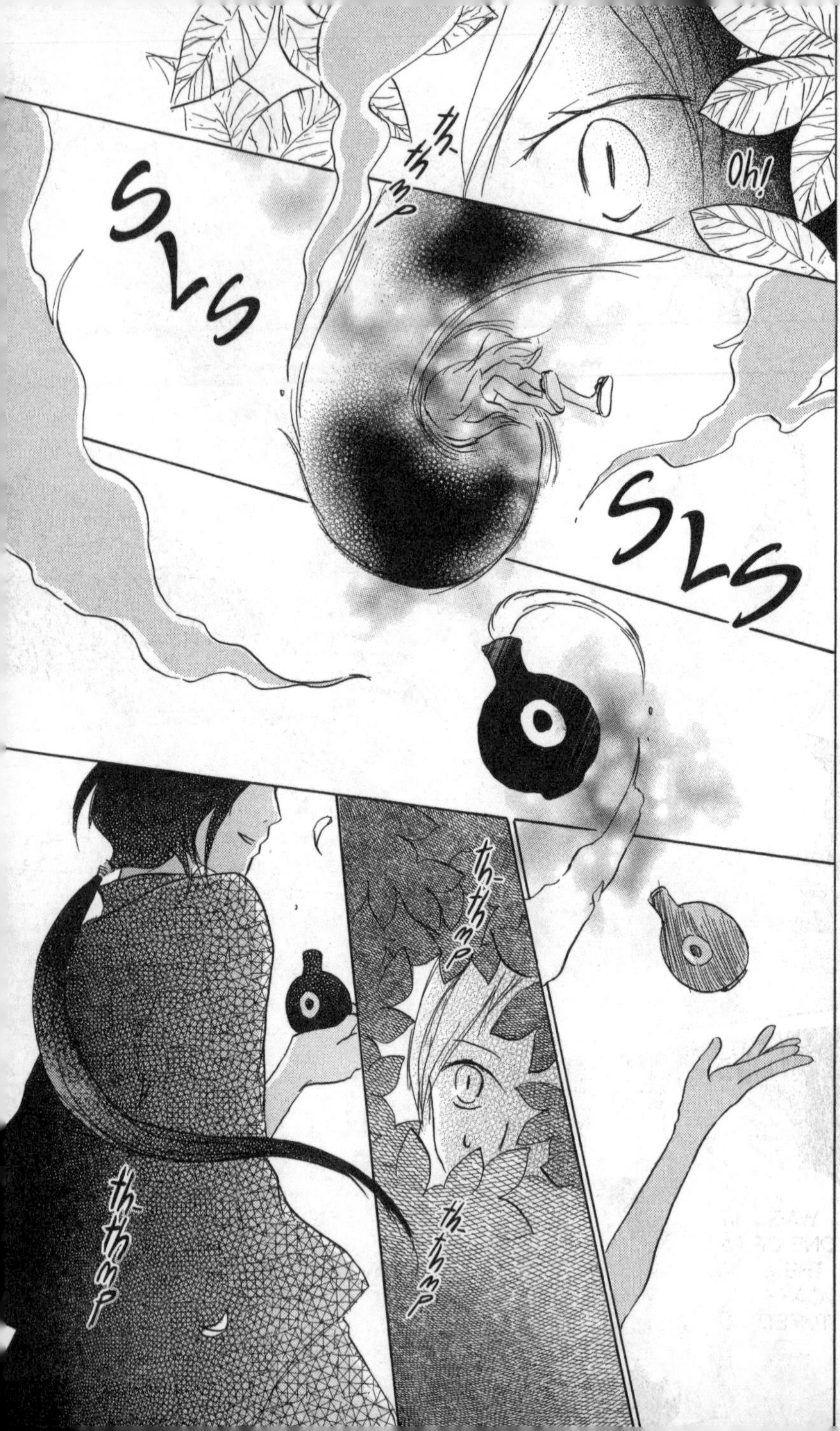
Oh!
th-thump
th-thump
th-thump
th-thump

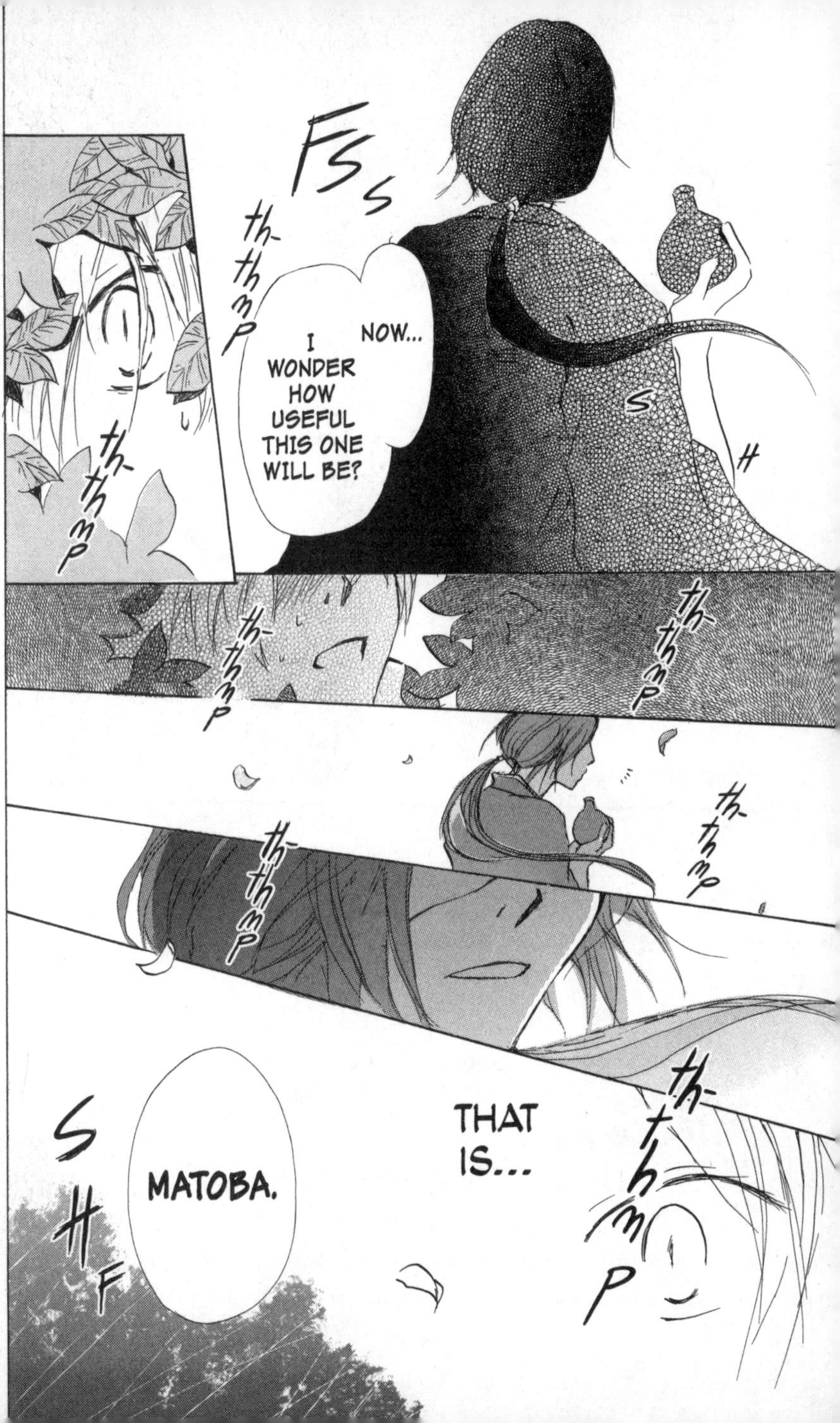

SH
FSS S
NOW... I WONDER HOW USEFUL THIS ONE WILL BE?
th-thump
th-thump
th-thump
th-thump
th-thump
th-thump
th-thump
THAT IS...
MATOBA.
SHF

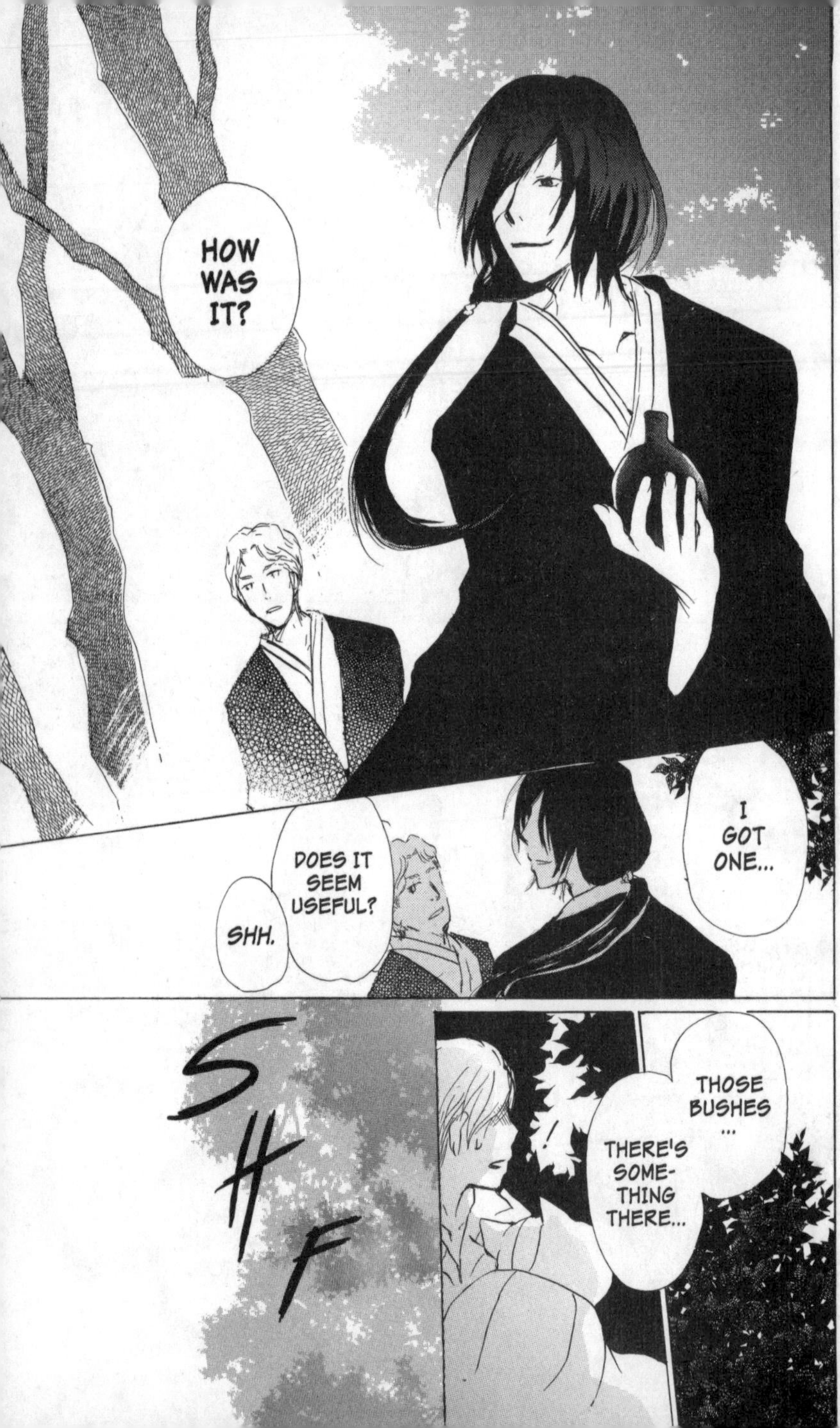
HOW WAS IT?
I GOT ONE...
DOES IT SEEM USEFUL?
SHH.
THOSE BUSHES ...
THERE'S SOME-THING THERE...
SHF

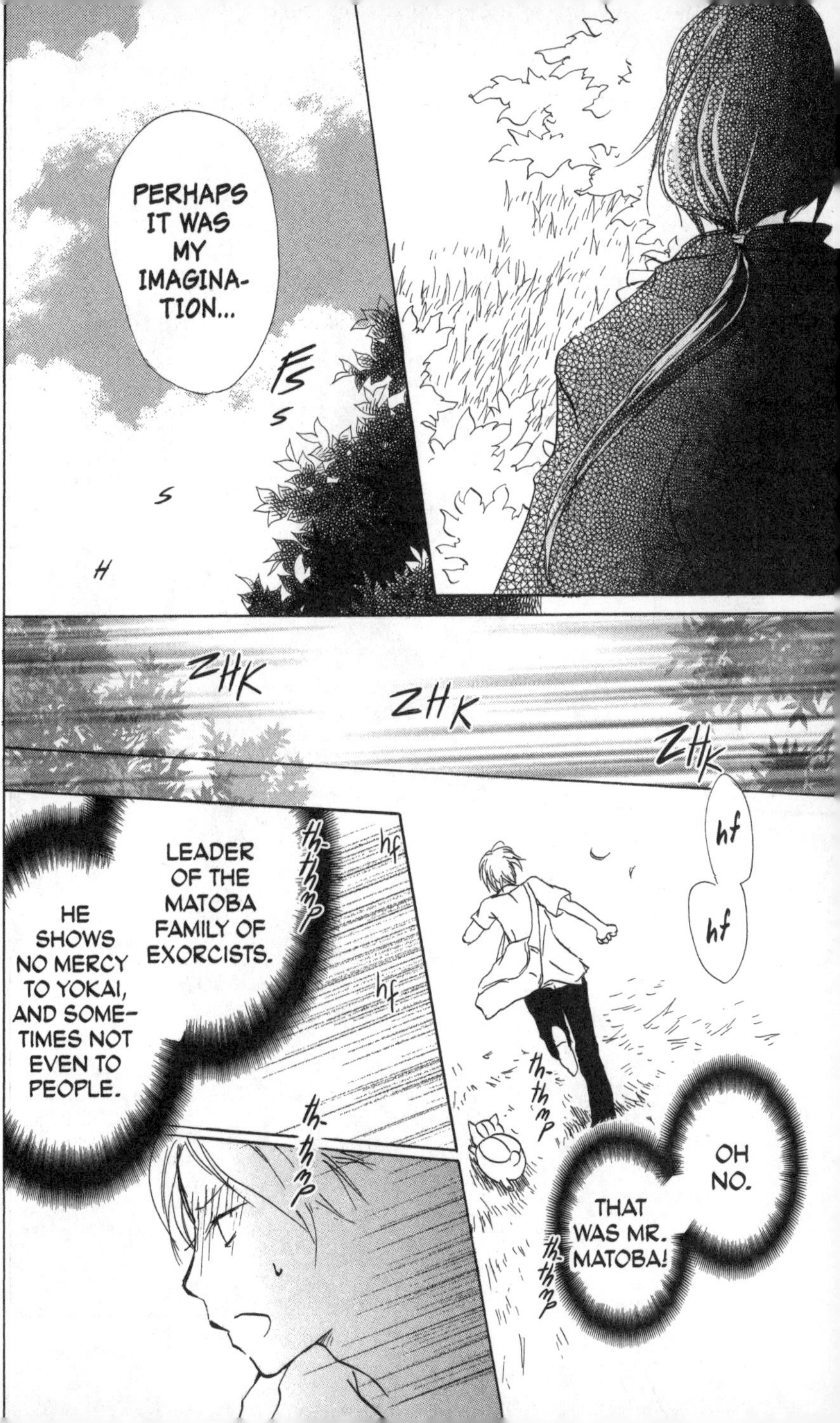
PERHAPS IT WAS MY IMAGINATION...
FSSH
ZHK
ZHK
ZHK
hf
hf
th-thmp
th-thmp
OH NO.
THAT WAS MR. MATOBA!
LEADER OF THE MATOBA FAMILY OF EXORCISTS.
HE SHOWS NO MERCY TO YOKAI, AND SOME-TIMES NOT EVEN TO PEOPLE.
hf
hf
th-thmp
th-thmp

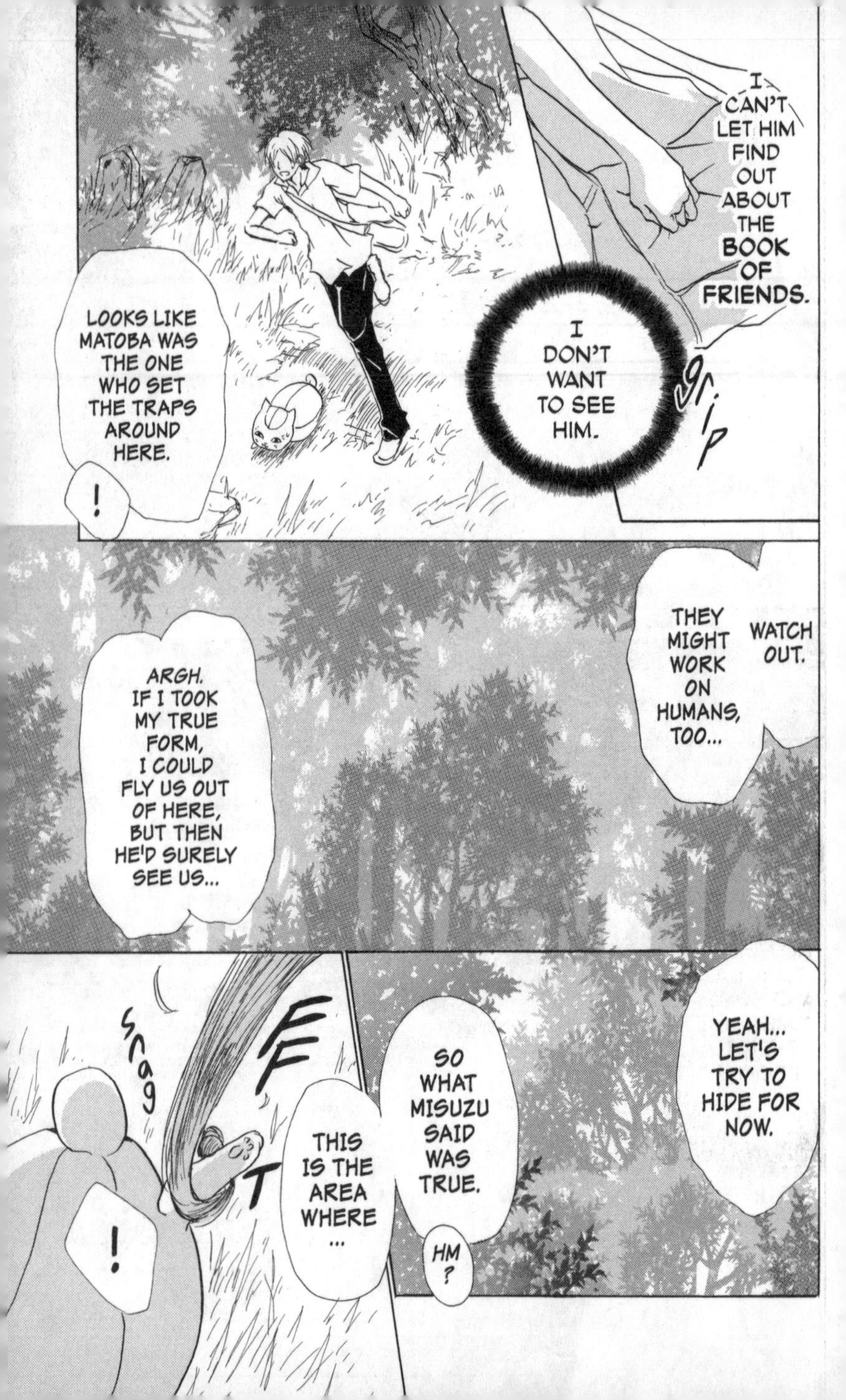
I CAN'T LET HIM FIND OUT ABOUT THE BOOK OF FRIENDS.
I DON'T WANT TO SEE HIM.
grip
LOOKS LIKE MATOBA WAS THE ONE WHO SET THE TRAPS AROUND HERE.
!
WATCH OUT.
THEY MIGHT WORK ON HUMANS, TOO...
ARGH. IF I TOOK MY TRUE FORM, I COULD FLY US OUT OF HERE, BUT THEN HE'D SURELY SEE US...
YEAH... LET'S TRY TO HIDE FOR NOW.
SO WHAT MISUZU SAID WAS TRUE.
HM?
THIS IS THE AREA WHERE ...
FFT
snag
!

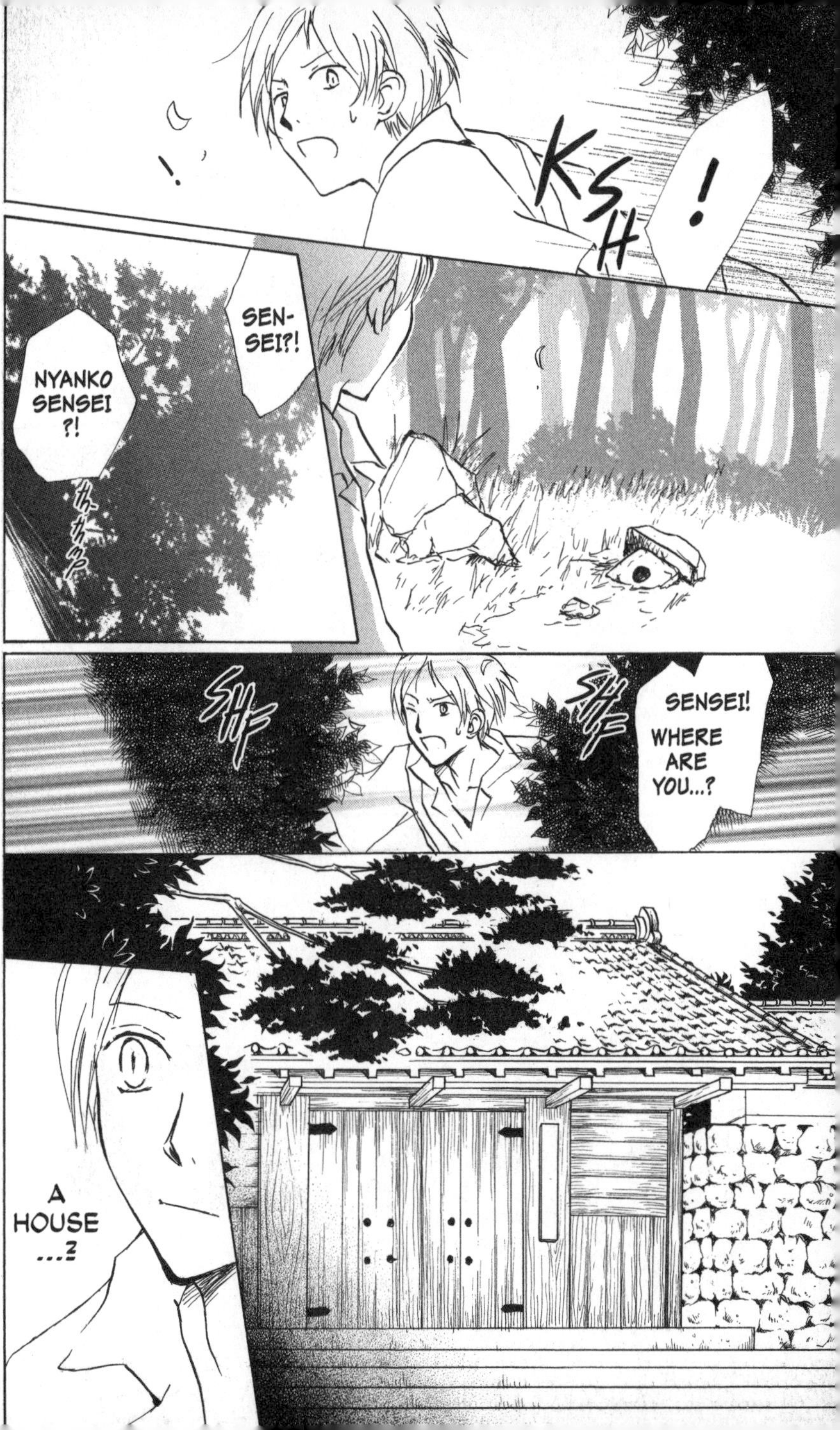
!
KSH
!
SEN-SEI?!
NYANKO SENSEI ?!
th-thmp
SENSEI! WHERE ARE YOU...?
SHF
SHF
A HOUSE ...?

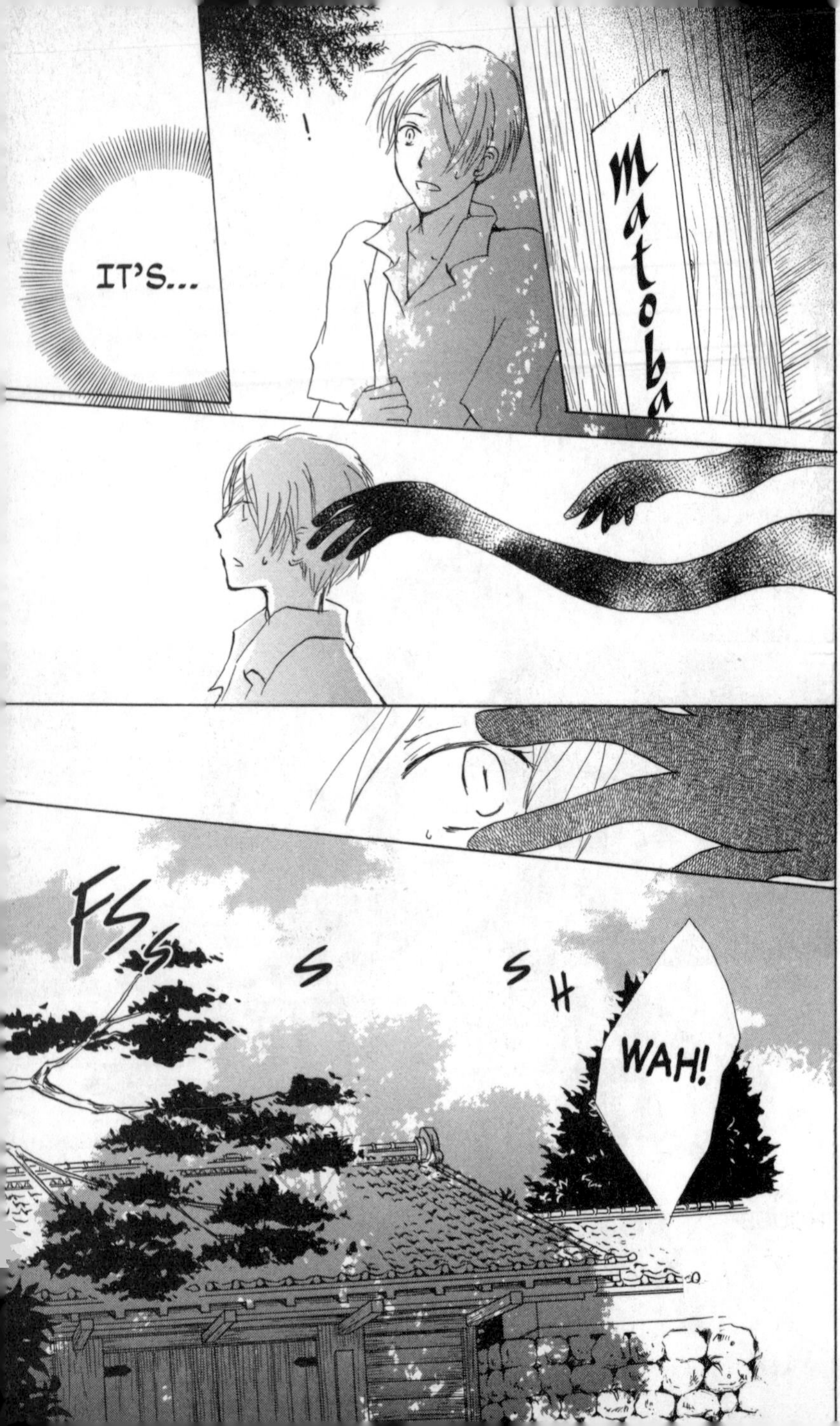
Matoba
!
IT'S...
FSSSH
WAH!

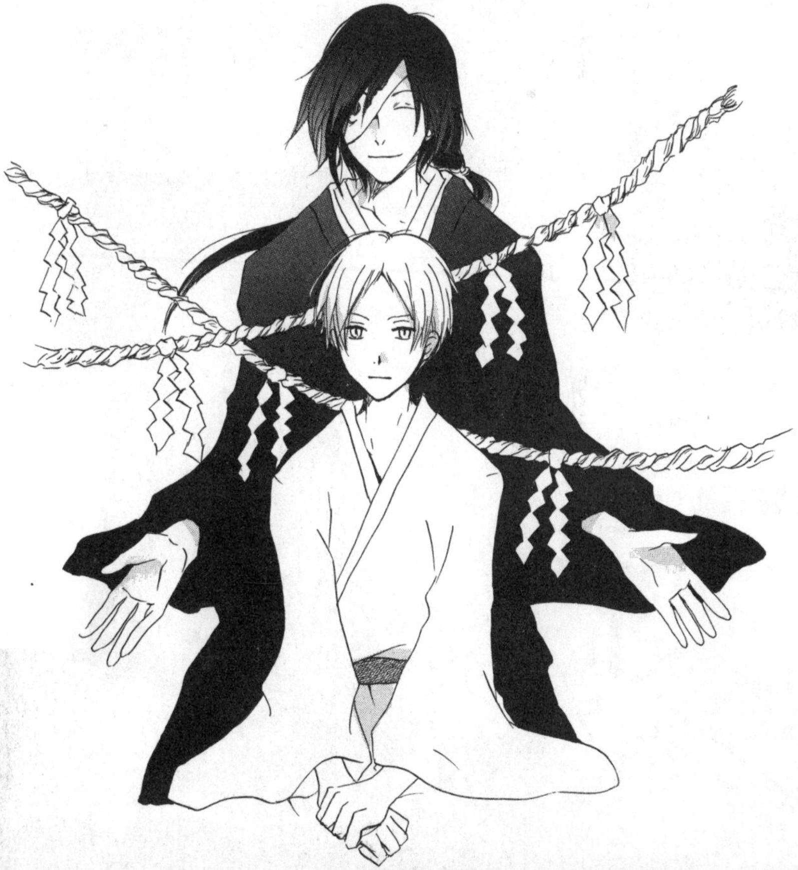

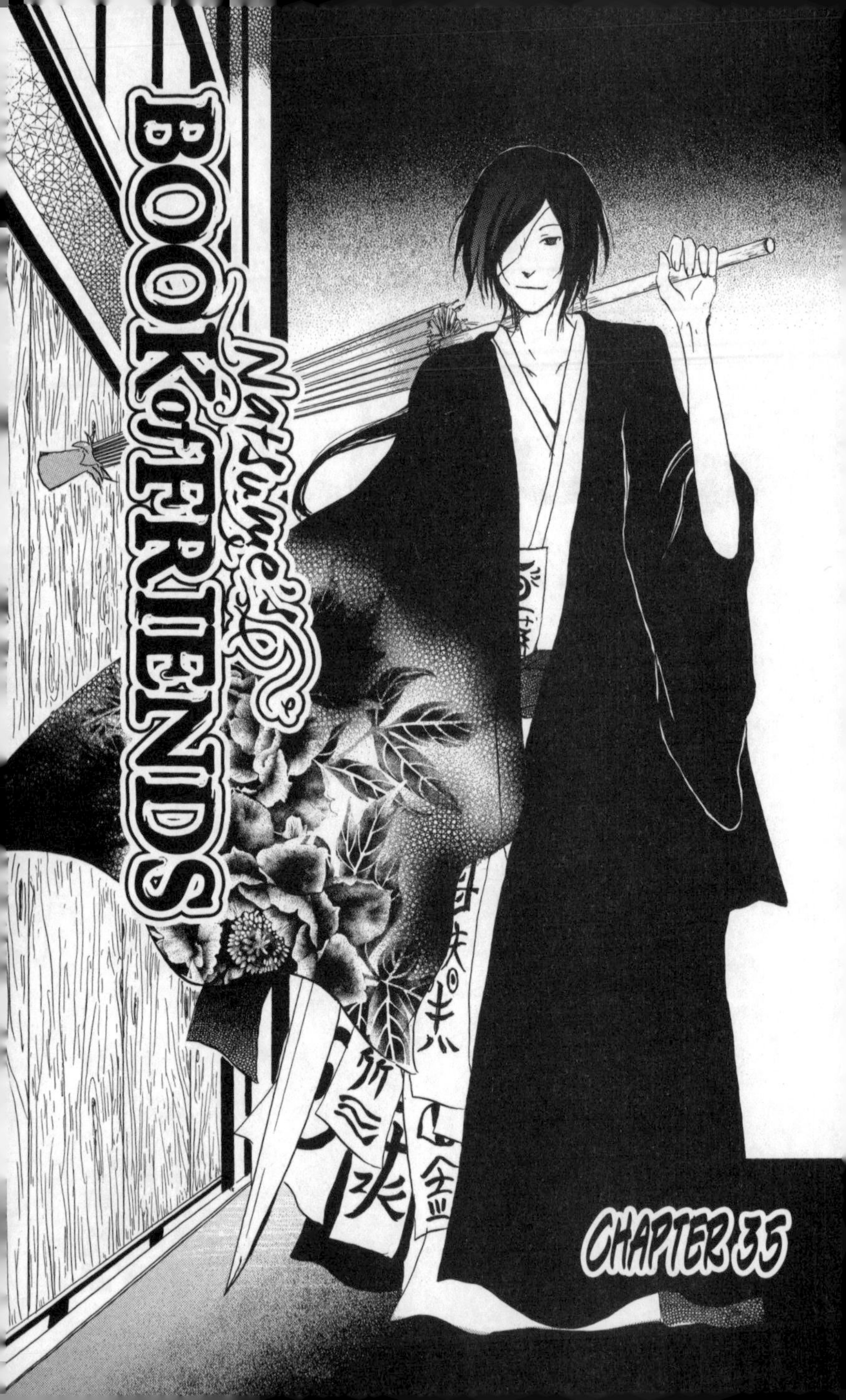
Natsume's
BOOK of FRIENDS
CHAPTER 35

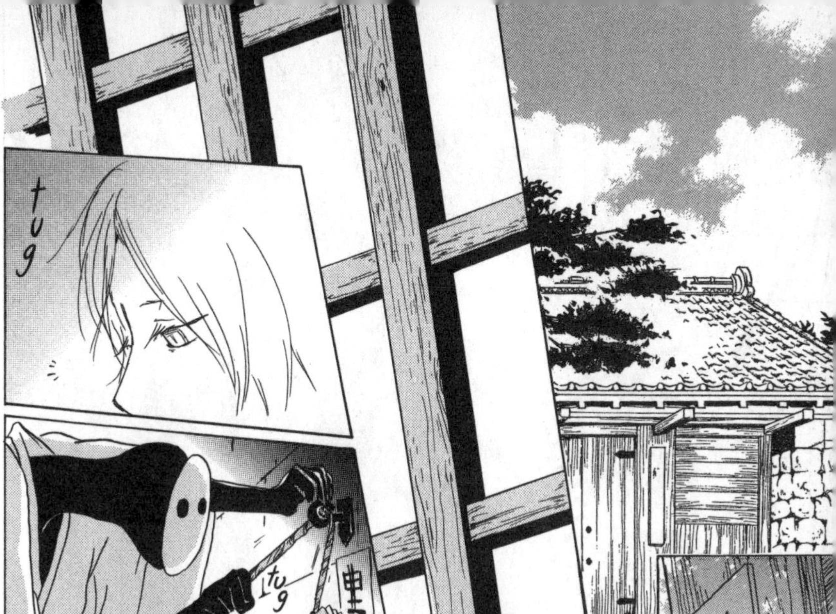
Matoba
tug
tug
!
HEY!

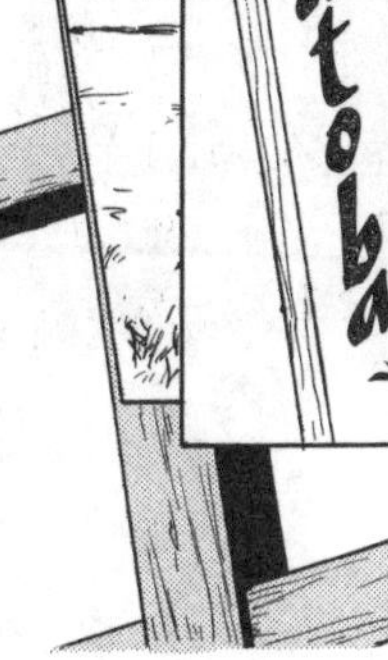

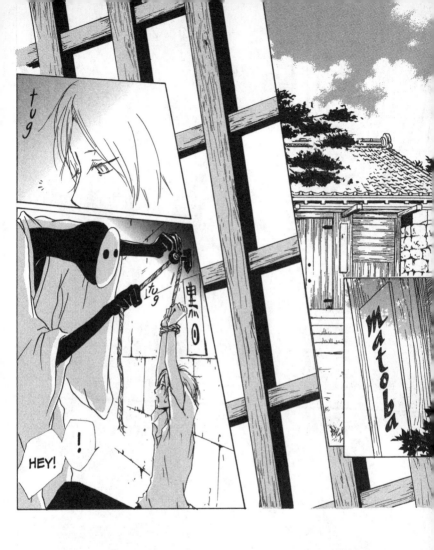

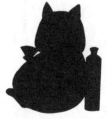

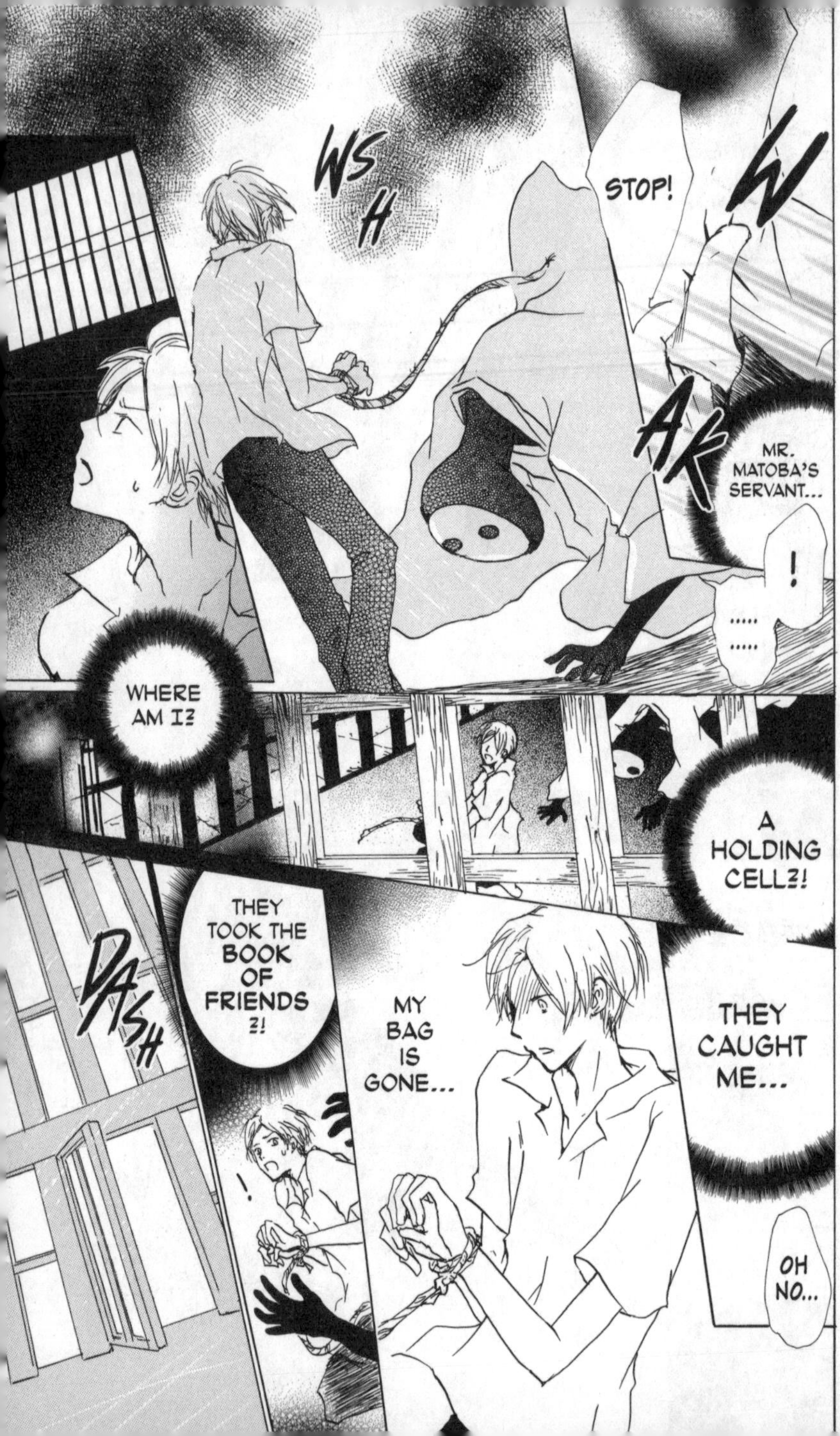
W
STOP!
WSH
AK
MR. MATOBA'S SERVANT...
!
.....
.....
A HOLDING CELL?!
WHERE AM I?
THEY CAUGHT ME...
OH NO...
MY BAG IS GONE...
THEY TOOK THE BOOK OF FRIENDS ?!
!
DASH

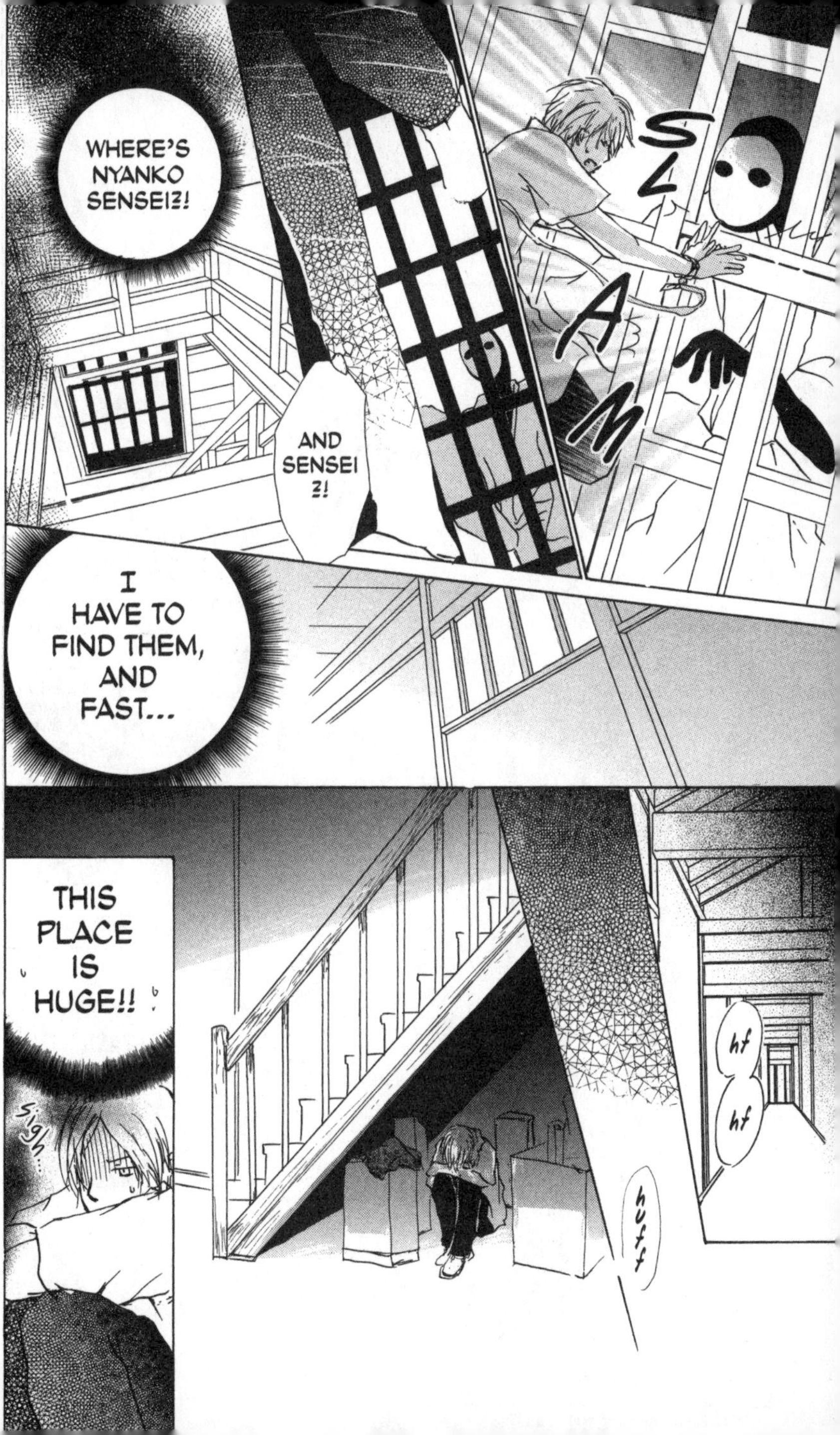
SLAM
WHERE'S NYANKO SENSEI?!
AND SENSEI?!
I HAVE TO FIND THEM, AND FAST...
hf
hf
huff
THIS PLACE IS HUGE!!
sigh...

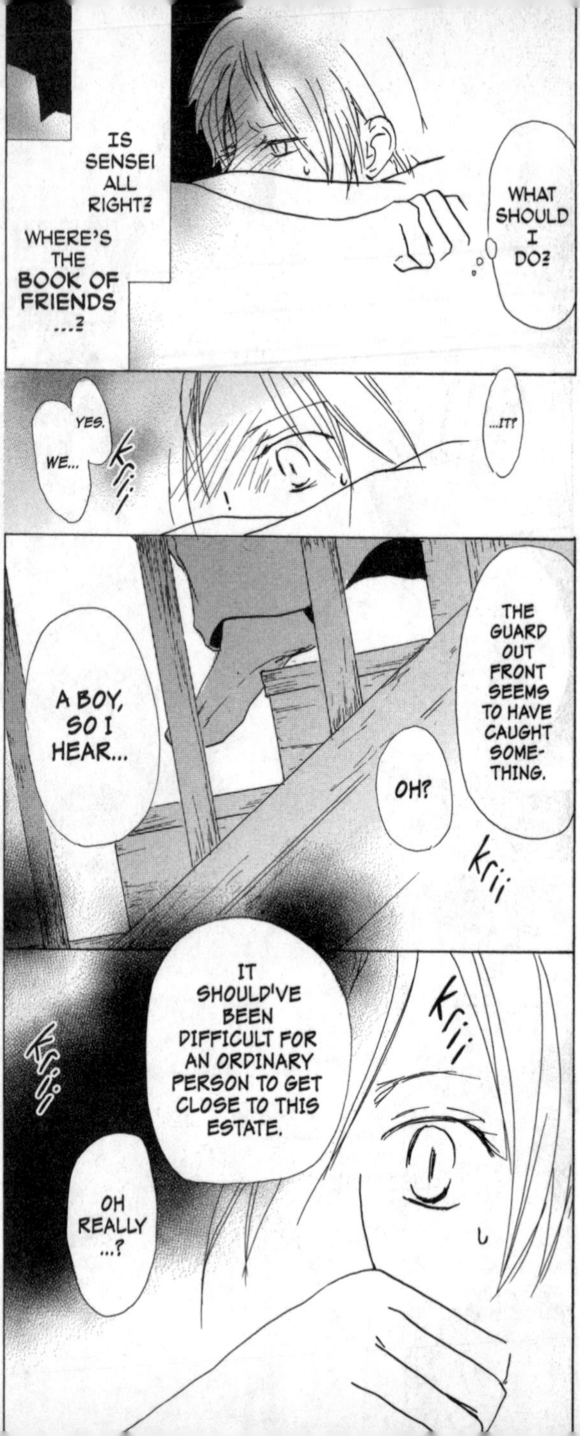
WHAT SHOULD I DO?
IS SENSEI ALL RIGHT?
WHERE'S THE BOOK OF FRIENDS ...?
...IT?
YES.
WE...
Krii
THE GUARD OUT FRONT SEEMS TO HAVE CAUGHT SOME-THING.
OH?
A BOY, SO I HEAR...
Krii
Krii
IT SHOULD'VE BEEN DIFFICULT FOR AN ORDINARY PERSON TO GET CLOSE TO THIS ESTATE.
OH REALLY ...?
Krii

## 04

**❋Kitty paw pads**

When they were creating the character sheets for the anime, some minor design changes from the manga were necessary. They took the pains to go over every single one with me. When I met the director and the other staff, I knew that I could trust them completely and felt comfortable letting them do whatever they felt was necessary. But they were very concerned about my opinions, which was touching. One memorable example was the question of whether they could have one less "toe bean" on Nyanko Sensei's paw. I was astonished—they were actually going to bother drawing in the paw pads on such short, tiny, moving legs?! It made me happy that they were so concerned over something as small as one fewer toe bean. I doodled a three-toed paw pad on the edge of the page I was working on at the time, to try it out. Now I think of this every time I draw Sensei's paw pad. These tiny little differences between the anime and the manga are so endearing.

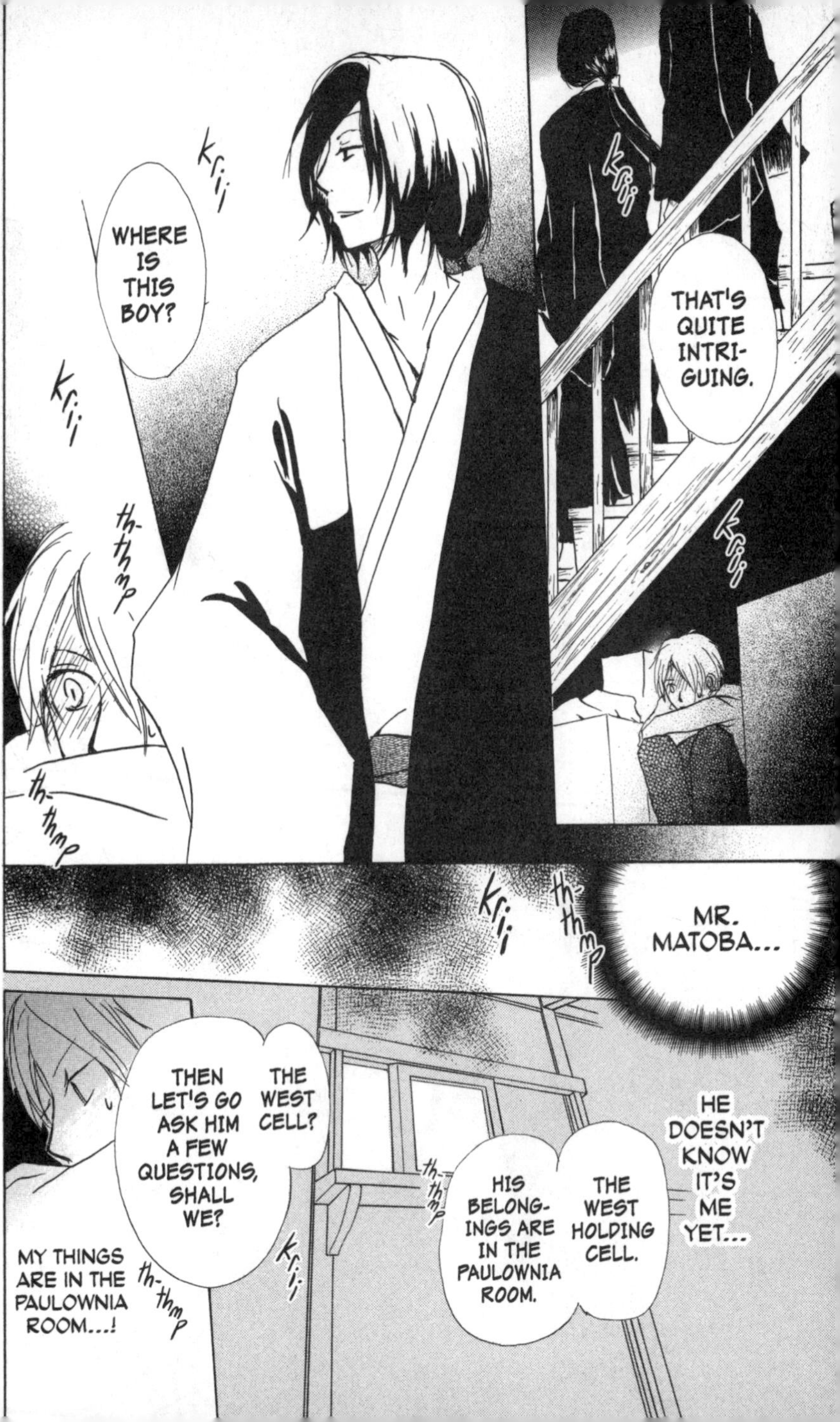
kriii
THAT'S QUITE INTRI-GUING.
kriii
kriii
WHERE IS THIS BOY?
kriii
th-thmp
th-thmp
MR. MATOBA...
th-thmp
kriii
HE DOESN'T KNOW IT'S ME YET...
THE WEST HOLDING CELL.
HIS BELONG-INGS ARE IN THE PAULOWNIA ROOM.
th-thmp
THE WEST CELL?
THEN LET'S GO ASK HIM A FEW QUESTIONS, SHALL WE?
kriii
th-thmp
MY THINGS ARE IN THE PAULOWNIA ROOM...!

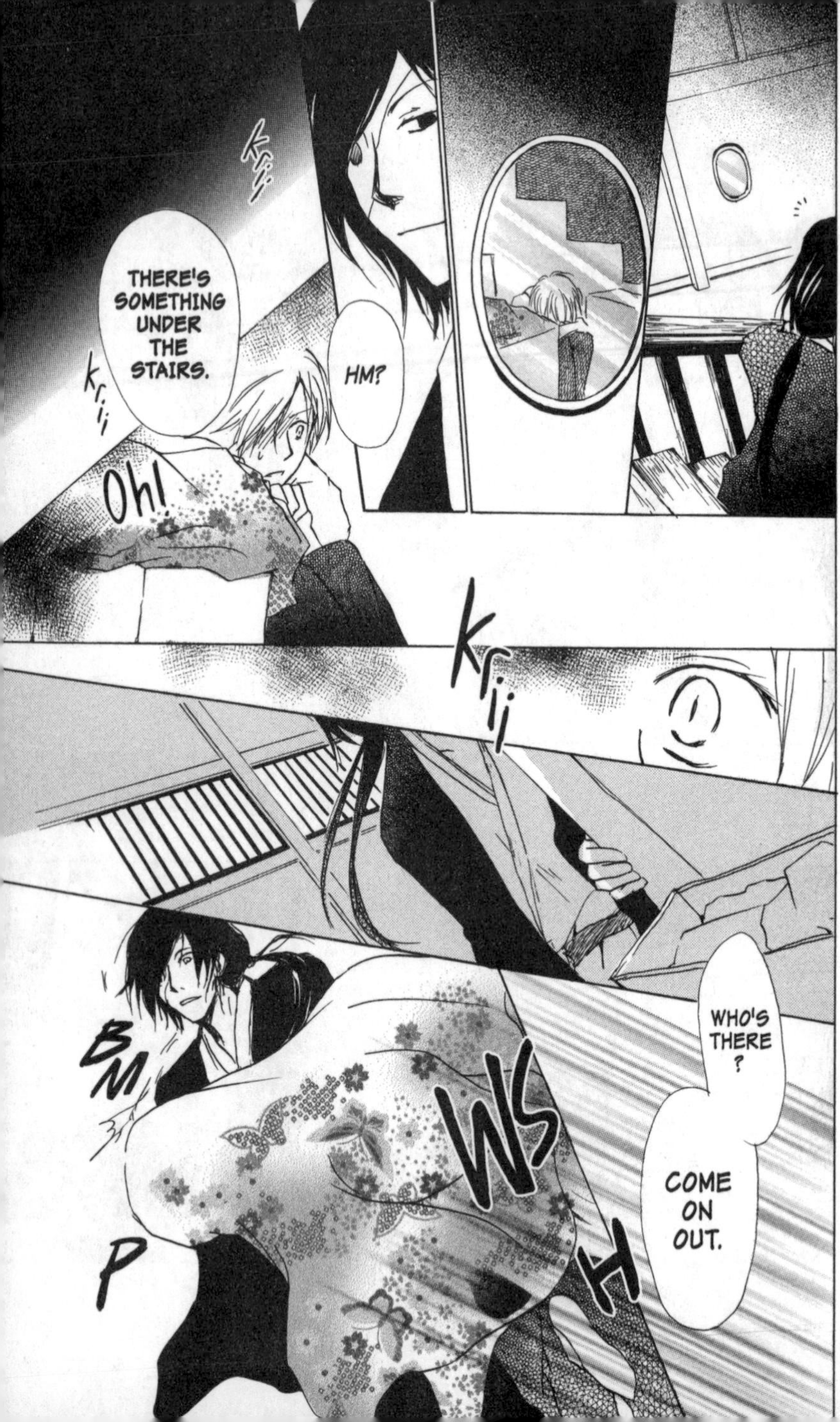
HM?
Kriii
THERE'S SOMETHING UNDER THE STAIRS.
Kriii
Oh!
Kriii
WHO'S THERE?
COME ON OUT.
WSH
BMP

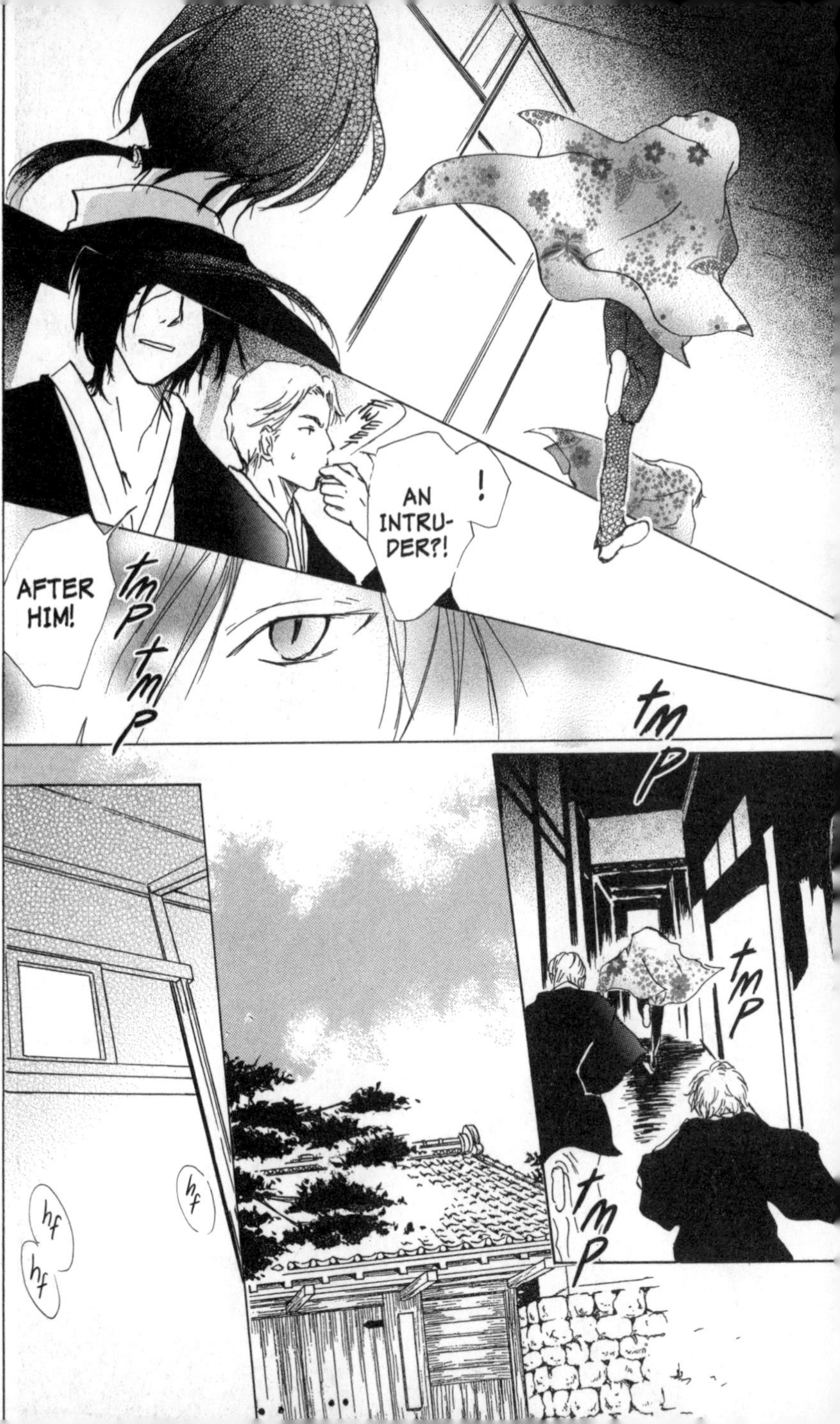
!
AN INTRUDER?!
AFTER HIM!
tmp tmp
tmp
tmp
tmp
hf
hf hf

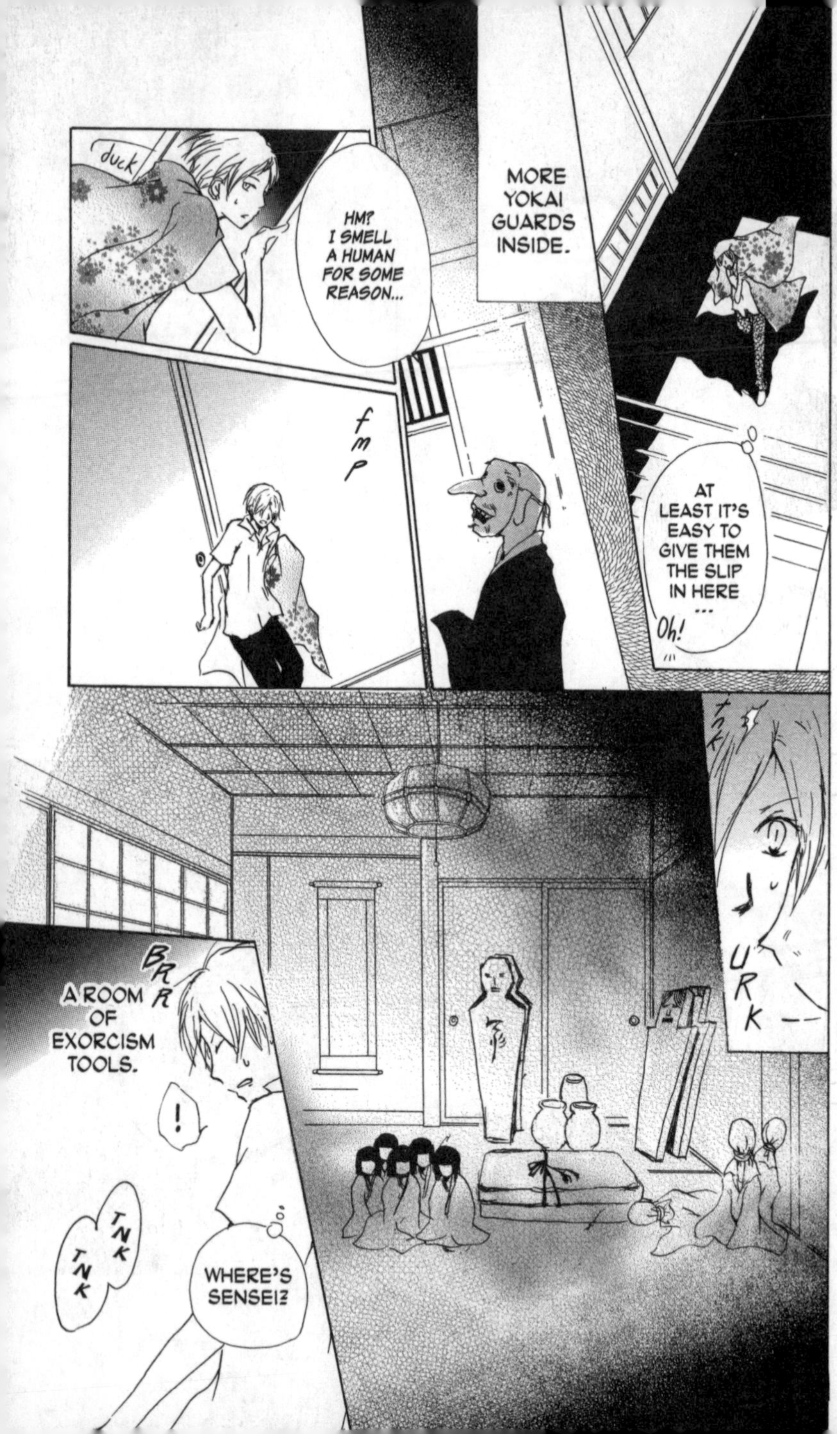
MORE YOKAI GUARDS INSIDE.
AT LEAST IT'S EASY TO GIVE THEM THE SLIP IN HERE...
Oh!
duck
HM? I SMELL A HUMAN FOR SOME REASON...
fmp
tnk
URK
BRR
A ROOM OF EXORCISM TOOLS.
!
TNK TNK
WHERE'S SENSEI!?

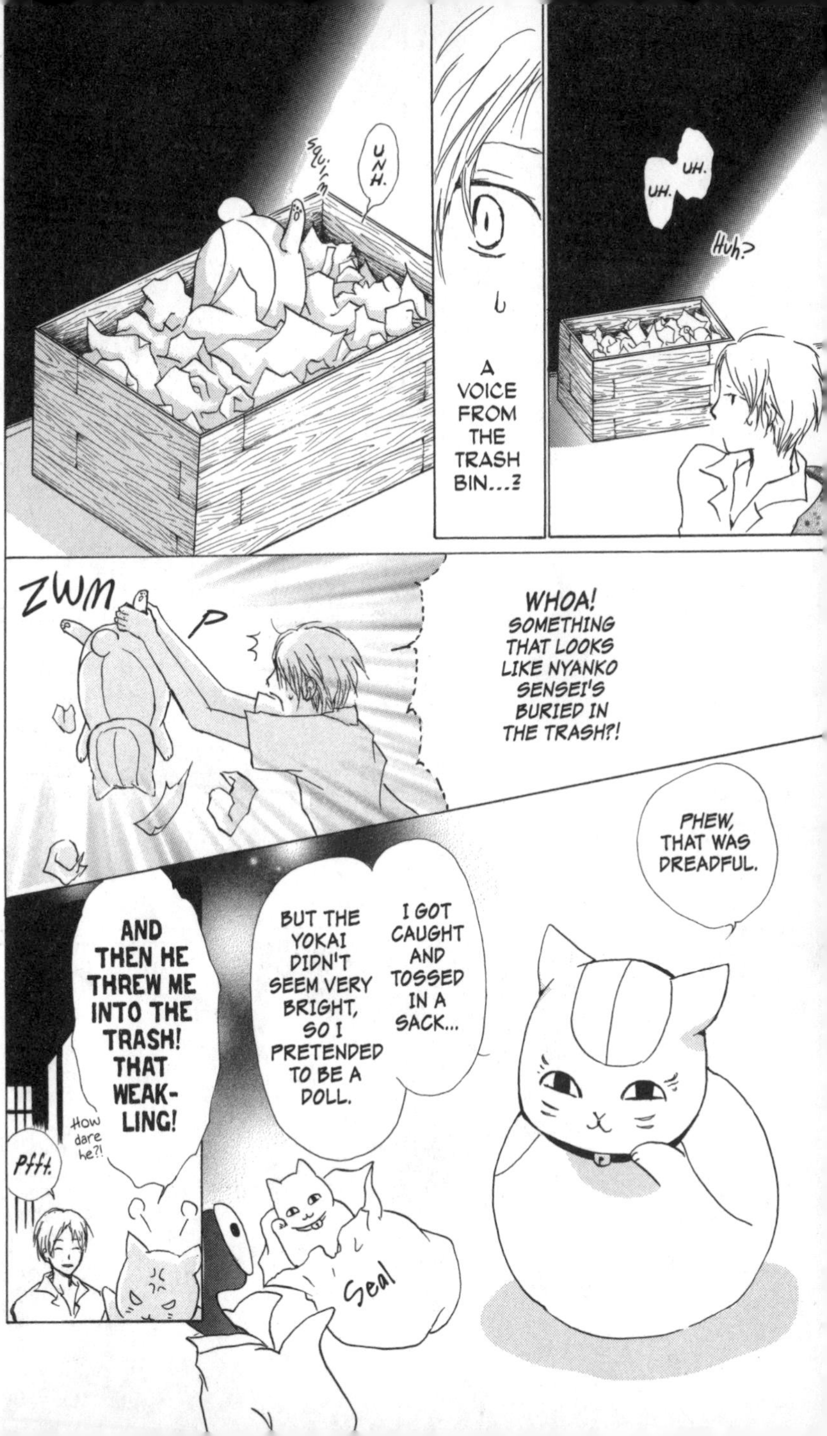
UH.
UH.
Huh?
A VOICE FROM THE TRASH BIN...?
UNH.
squirm
WHOA! SOMETHING THAT LOOKS LIKE NYANKO SENSEI'S BURIED IN THE TRASH?!
P
ZWM
PHEW, THAT WAS DREADFUL.
I GOT CAUGHT AND TOSSED IN A SACK...
BUT THE YOKAI DIDN'T SEEM VERY BRIGHT, SO I PRETENDED TO BE A DOLL.
Seal
AND THEN HE THREW ME INTO THE TRASH! THAT WEAK-LING!
How dare he?!
Pfft.

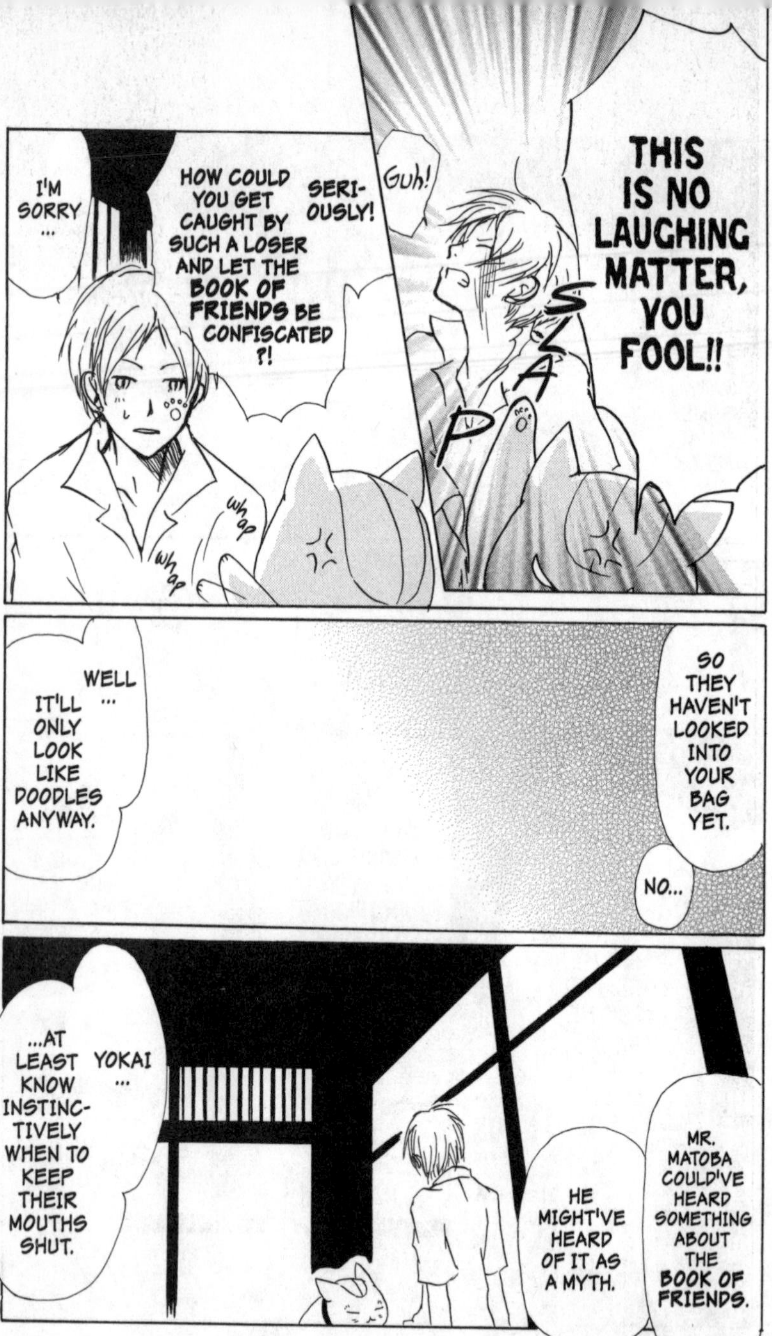

THIS IS NO LAUGHING MATTER, YOU FOOL!!
Guh!
SLAP
SERIOUSLY!
HOW COULD YOU GET CAUGHT BY SUCH A LOSER AND LET THE BOOK OF FRIENDS BE CONFISCATED?!
I'M SORRY...
whap
whap
SO THEY HAVEN'T LOOKED INTO YOUR BAG YET.
NO...
WELL... IT'LL ONLY LOOK LIKE DOODLES ANYWAY.
MR. MATOBA COULD'VE HEARD SOMETHING ABOUT THE BOOK OF FRIENDS.
HE MIGHT'VE HEARD OF IT AS A MYTH.
YOKAI...
...AT LEAST KNOW INSTINCTIVELY WHEN TO KEEP THEIR MOUTHS SHUT.

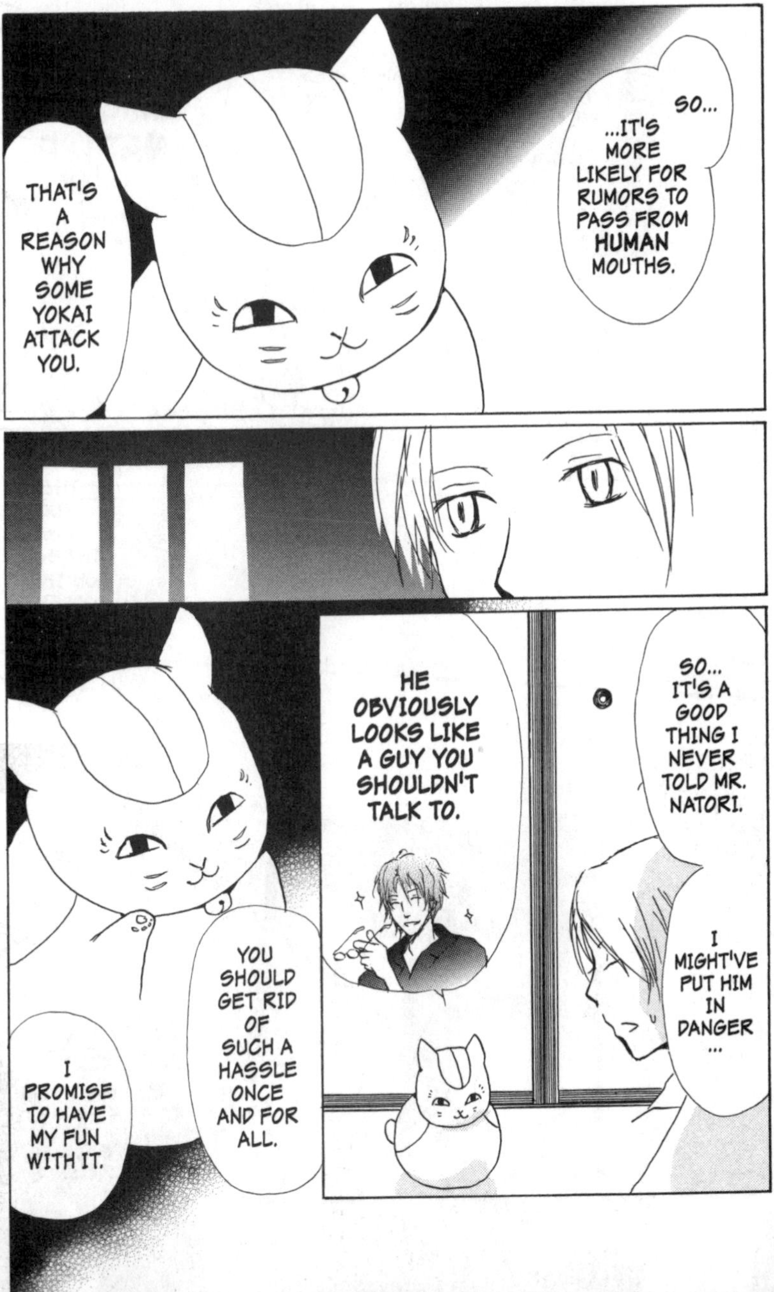
SO... ...IT'S MORE LIKELY FOR RUMORS TO PASS FROM **HUMAN** MOUTHS.
THAT'S A REASON WHY SOME YOKAI ATTACK YOU.
SO... IT'S A GOOD THING I NEVER TOLD MR. NATORI.
I MIGHT'VE PUT HIM IN DANGER ...
HE OBVIOUSLY LOOKS LIKE A GUY YOU SHOULDN'T TALK TO.
YOU SHOULD GET RID OF SUCH A HASSLE ONCE AND FOR ALL.
I PROMISE TO HAVE MY FUN WITH IT.

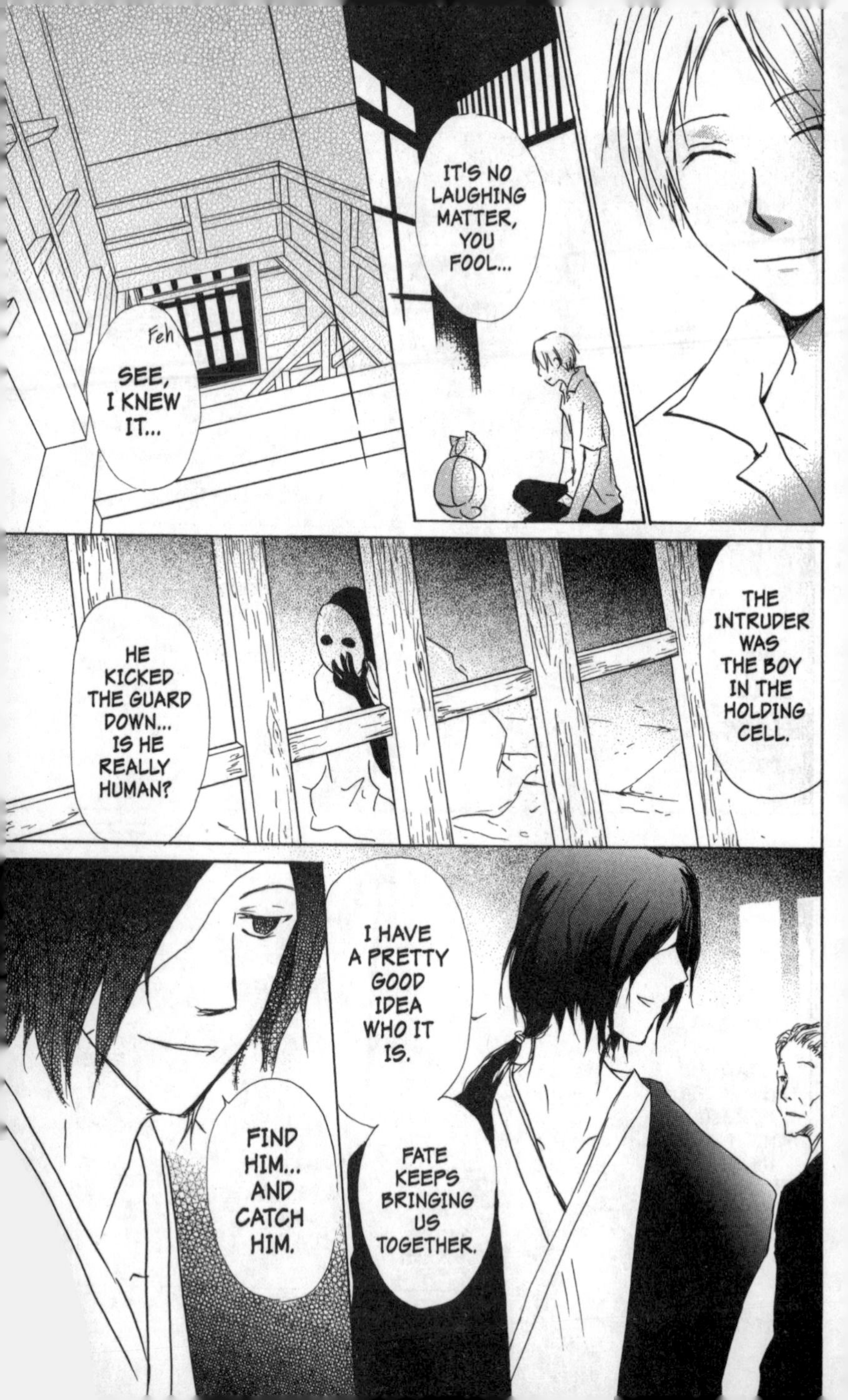
IT'S NO LAUGHING MATTER, YOU FOOL...
Feh
SEE, I KNEW IT...
THE INTRUDER WAS THE BOY IN THE HOLDING CELL.
HE KICKED THE GUARD DOWN... IS HE REALLY HUMAN?
I HAVE A PRETTY GOOD IDEA WHO IT IS.
FATE KEEPS BRINGING US TOGETHER.
FIND HIM... AND CATCH HIM.

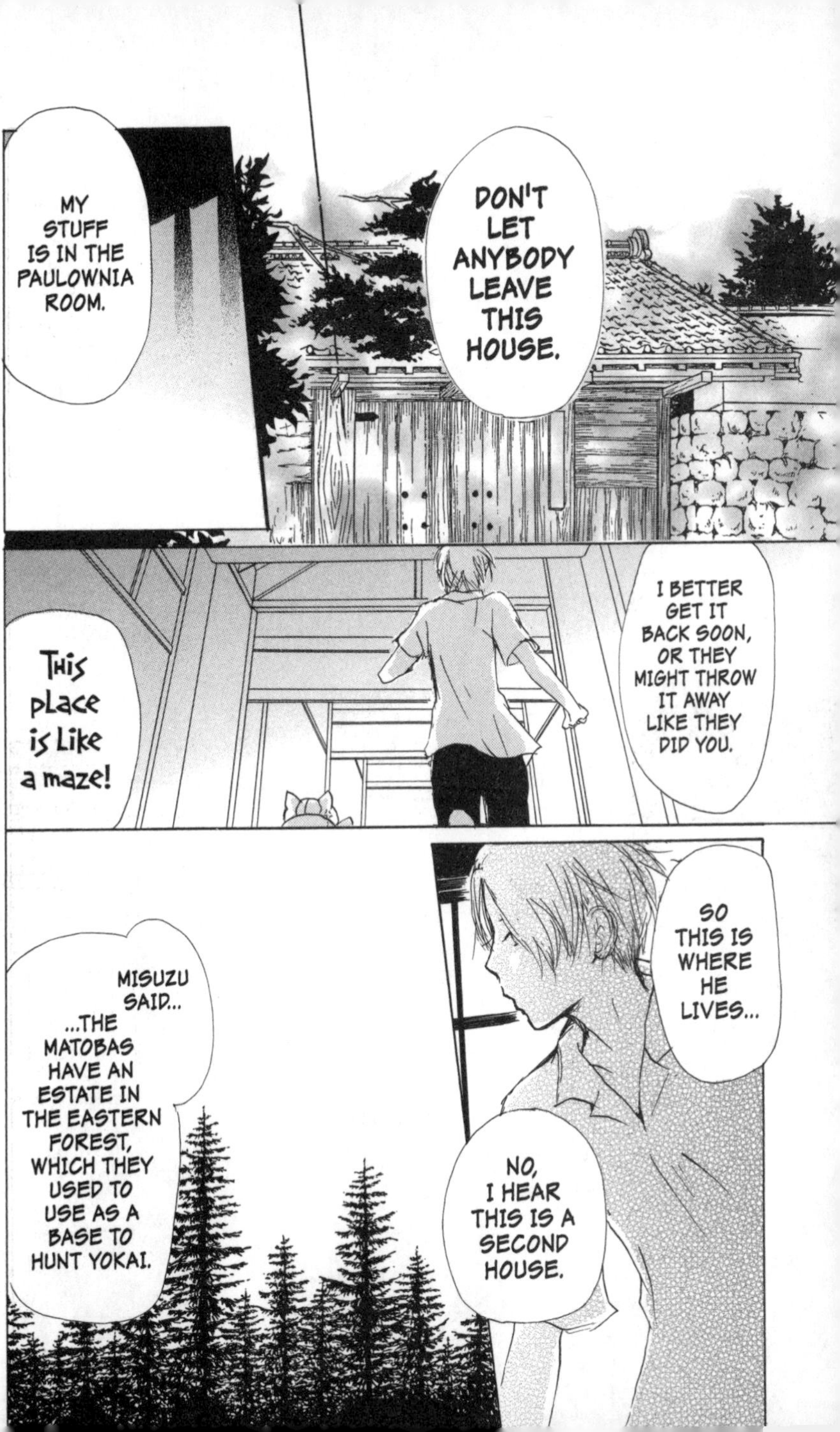
DON'T LET ANYBODY LEAVE THIS HOUSE.
MY STUFF IS IN THE PAULOWNIA ROOM.
I BETTER GET IT BACK SOON, OR THEY MIGHT THROW IT AWAY LIKE THEY DID YOU.
This place is like a maze!
SO THIS IS WHERE HE LIVES...
NO, I HEAR THIS IS A SECOND HOUSE.
MISUZU SAID...
...THE MATOBAS HAVE AN ESTATE IN THE EASTERN FOREST, WHICH THEY USED TO USE AS A BASE TO HUNT YOKAI.

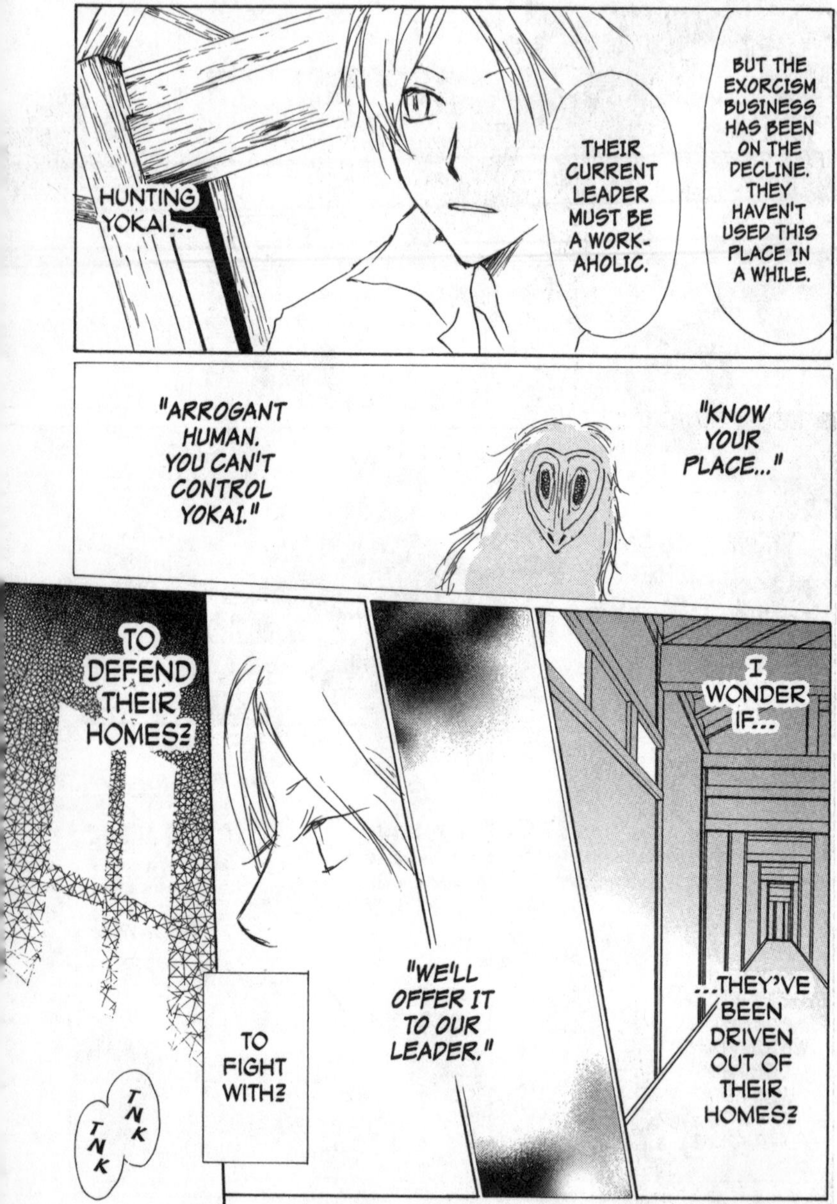
BUT THE EXORCISM BUSINESS HAS BEEN ON THE DECLINE. THEY HAVEN'T USED THIS PLACE IN A WHILE.
THEIR CURRENT LEADER MUST BE A WORK-AHOLIC.
HUNTING YOKAI...
"KNOW YOUR PLACE..."
"ARROGANT HUMAN. YOU CAN'T CONTROL YOKAI."
I WONDER IF...
...THEY'VE BEEN DRIVEN OUT OF THEIR HOMES?
"WE'LL OFFER IT TO OUR LEADER."
TO DEFEND THEIR HOMES?
TO FIGHT WITH?
TNK TNK

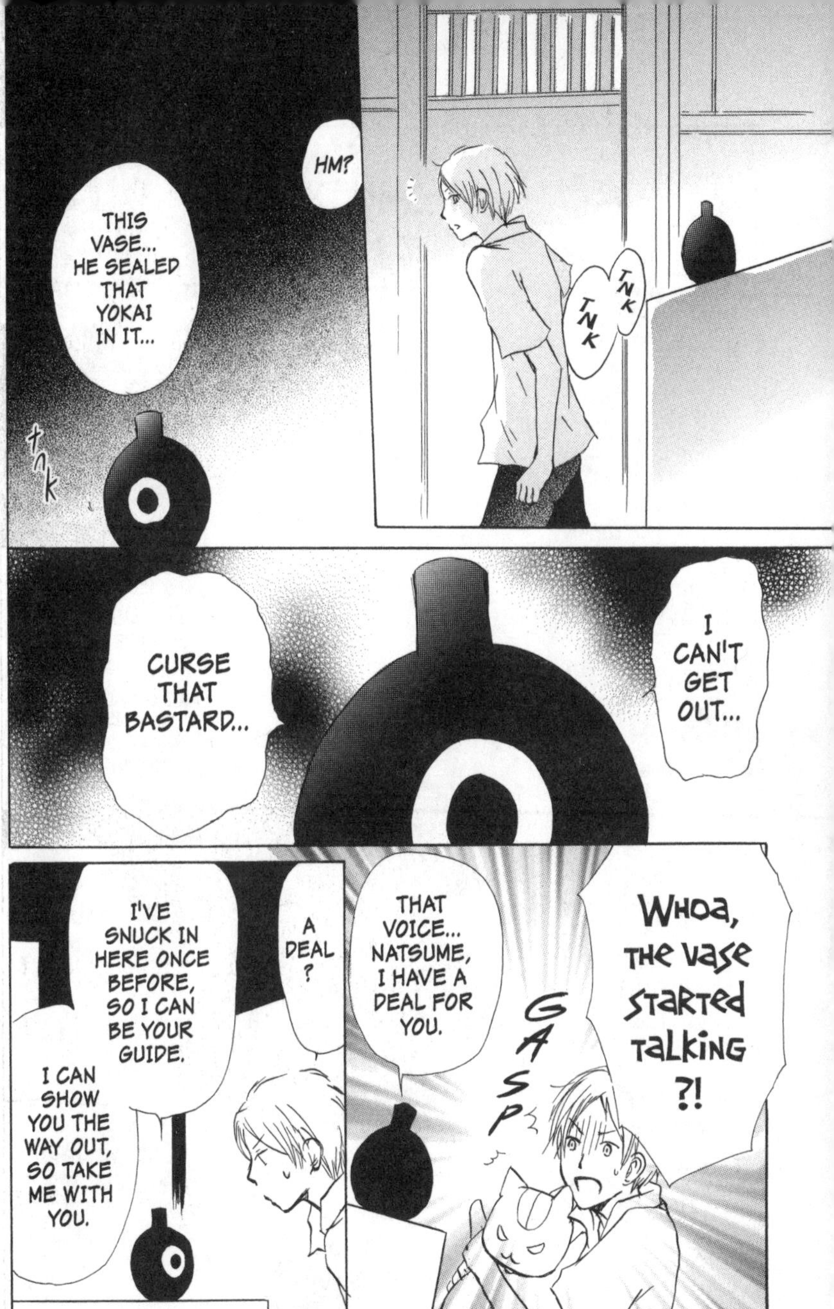
TNK TNK
HM?
THIS VASE... HE SEALED THAT YOKAI IN IT...
TNK
I CAN'T GET OUT...
CURSE THAT BASTARD...
WHOA, THE VASE STARTED TALKING?!
GASP
THAT VOICE... NATSUME, I HAVE A DEAL FOR YOU.
A DEAL?
I'VE SNUCK IN HERE ONCE BEFORE, SO I CAN BE YOUR GUIDE.
I CAN SHOW YOU THE WAY OUT, SO TAKE ME WITH YOU.

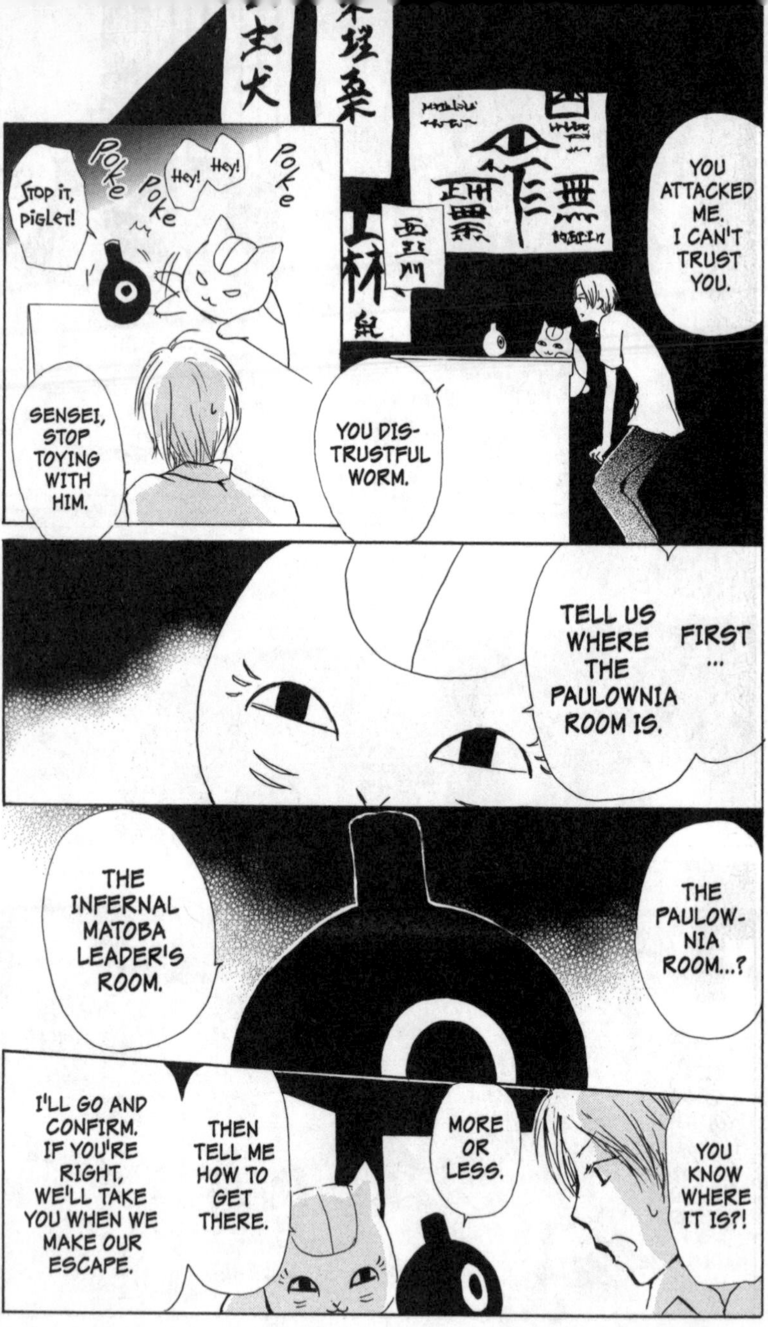
YOU ATTACKED ME. I CAN'T TRUST YOU.
YOU DIS-TRUSTFUL WORM.
Poke
Hey!
Hey!
Poke
Poke
Stop it, piglet!
SENSEI, STOP TOYING WITH HIM.
FIRST...
TELL US WHERE THE PAULOWNIA ROOM IS.
THE PAULOW-NIA ROOM...?
THE INFERNAL MATOBA LEADER'S ROOM.
YOU KNOW WHERE IT IS?!
MORE OR LESS.
THEN TELL ME HOW TO GET THERE.
I'LL GO AND CONFIRM. IF YOU'RE RIGHT, WE'LL TAKE YOU WHEN WE MAKE OUR ESCAPE.

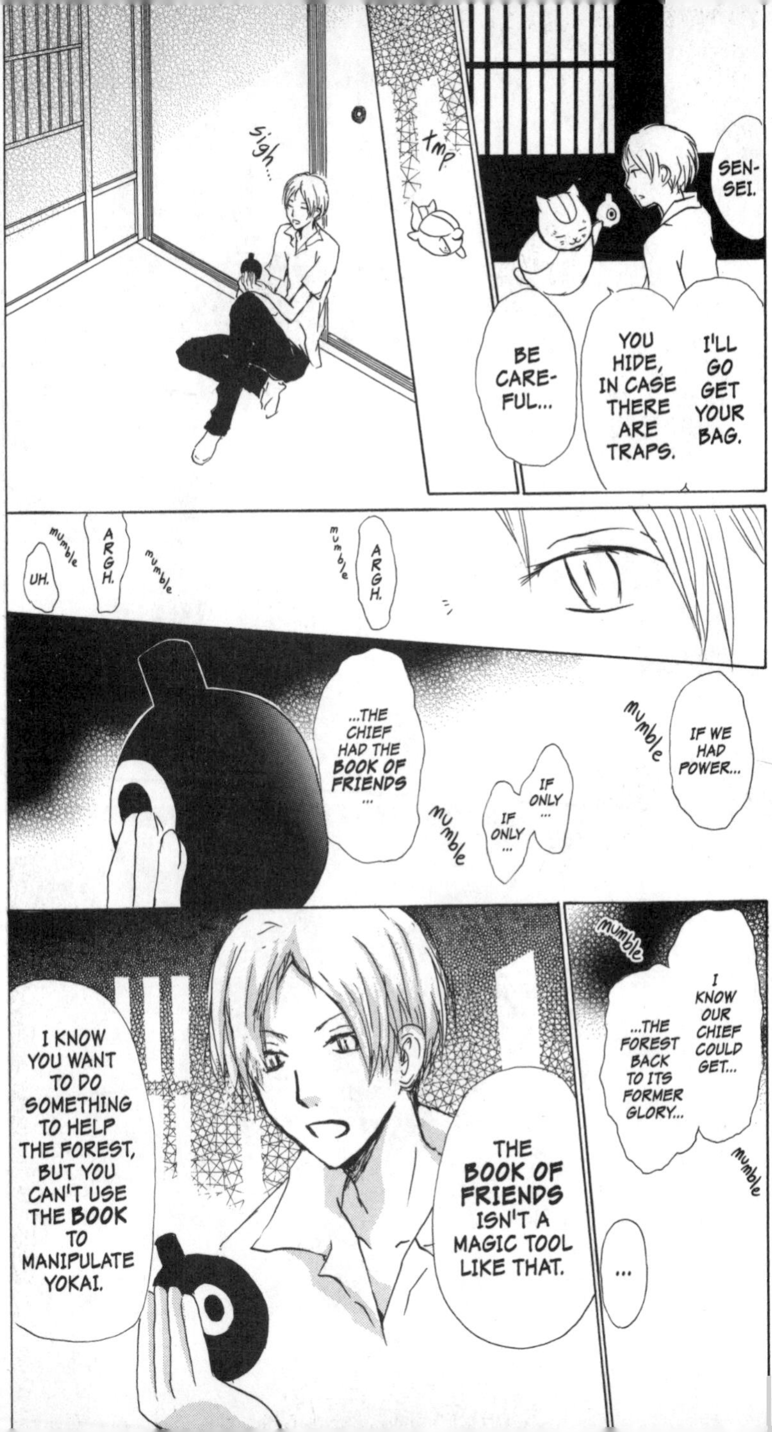
SEN-SEI.
I'LL GO GET YOUR BAG.
YOU HIDE, IN CASE THERE ARE TRAPS.
BE CARE-FUL...
xmp
sigh...
mumble
ARGH.
mumble
ARGH.
mumble
UH.
mumble
IF WE HAD POWER...
IF ONLY...
IF ONLY...
mumble
...THE CHIEF HAD THE BOOK OF FRIENDS...
mumble
I KNOW OUR CHIEF COULD GET...
...THE FOREST BACK TO ITS FORMER GLORY...
mumble
...
THE BOOK OF FRIENDS ISN'T A MAGIC TOOL LIKE THAT.
I KNOW YOU WANT TO DO SOMETHING TO HELP THE FOREST, BUT YOU CAN'T USE THE BOOK TO MANIPULATE YOKAI.

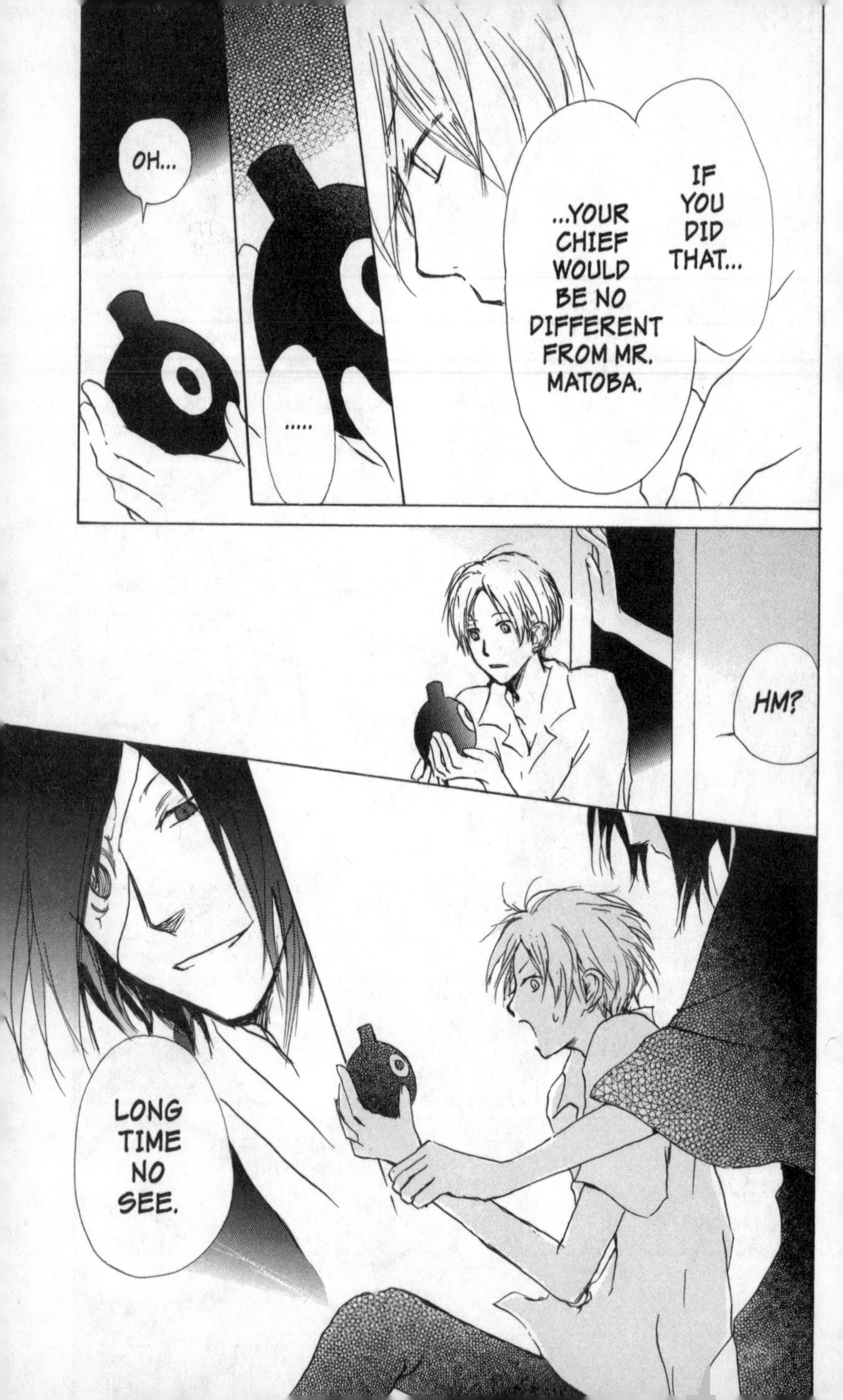
IF YOU DID THAT...
...YOUR CHIEF WOULD BE NO DIFFERENT FROM MR. MATOBA.
.....
OH...
HM?
LONG TIME NO SEE.

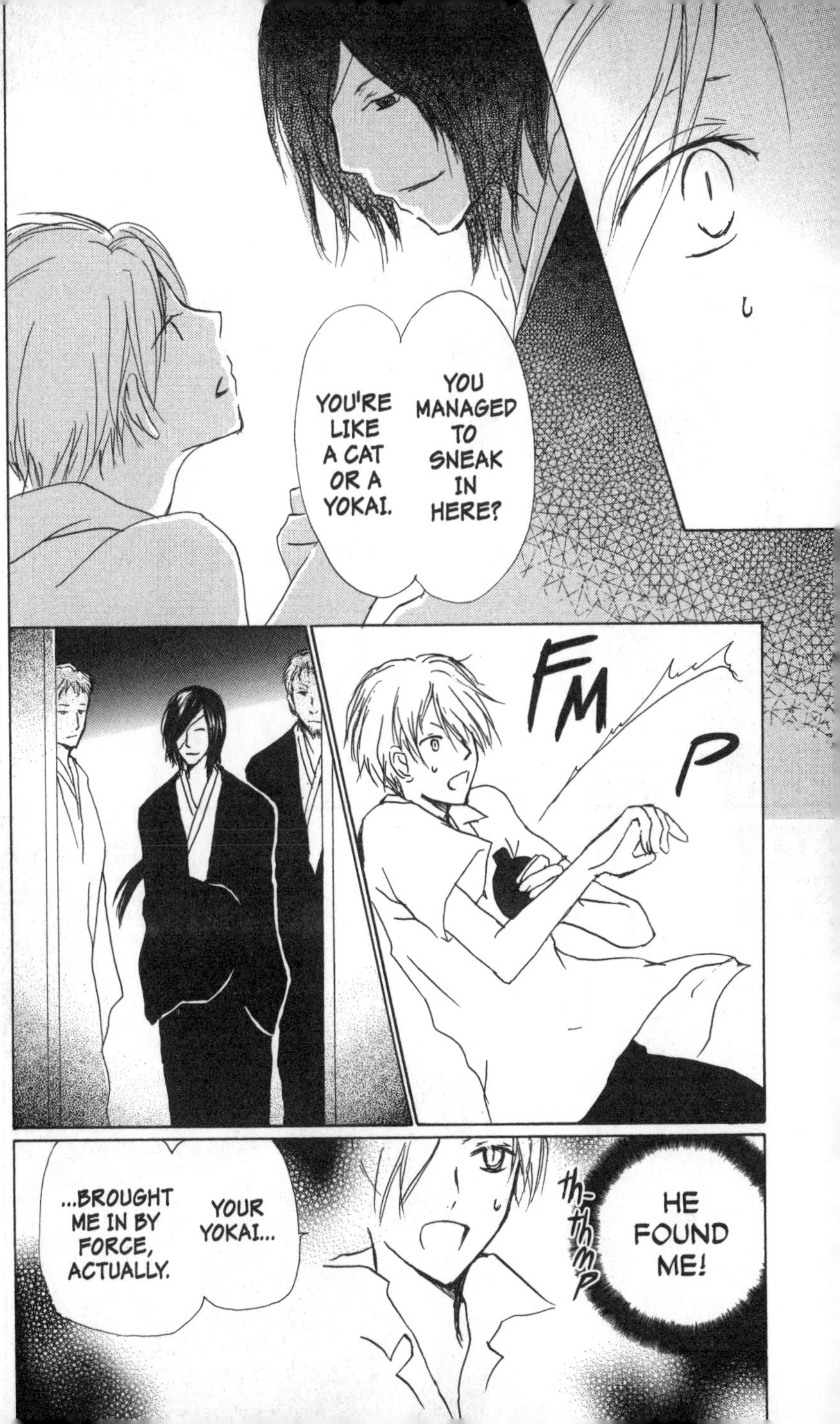
YOU MANAGED TO SNEAK IN HERE?
YOU'RE LIKE A CAT OR A YOKAI.
FMP
HE FOUND ME!
th-thmp
YOUR YOKAI...
...BROUGHT ME IN BY FORCE, ACTUALLY.

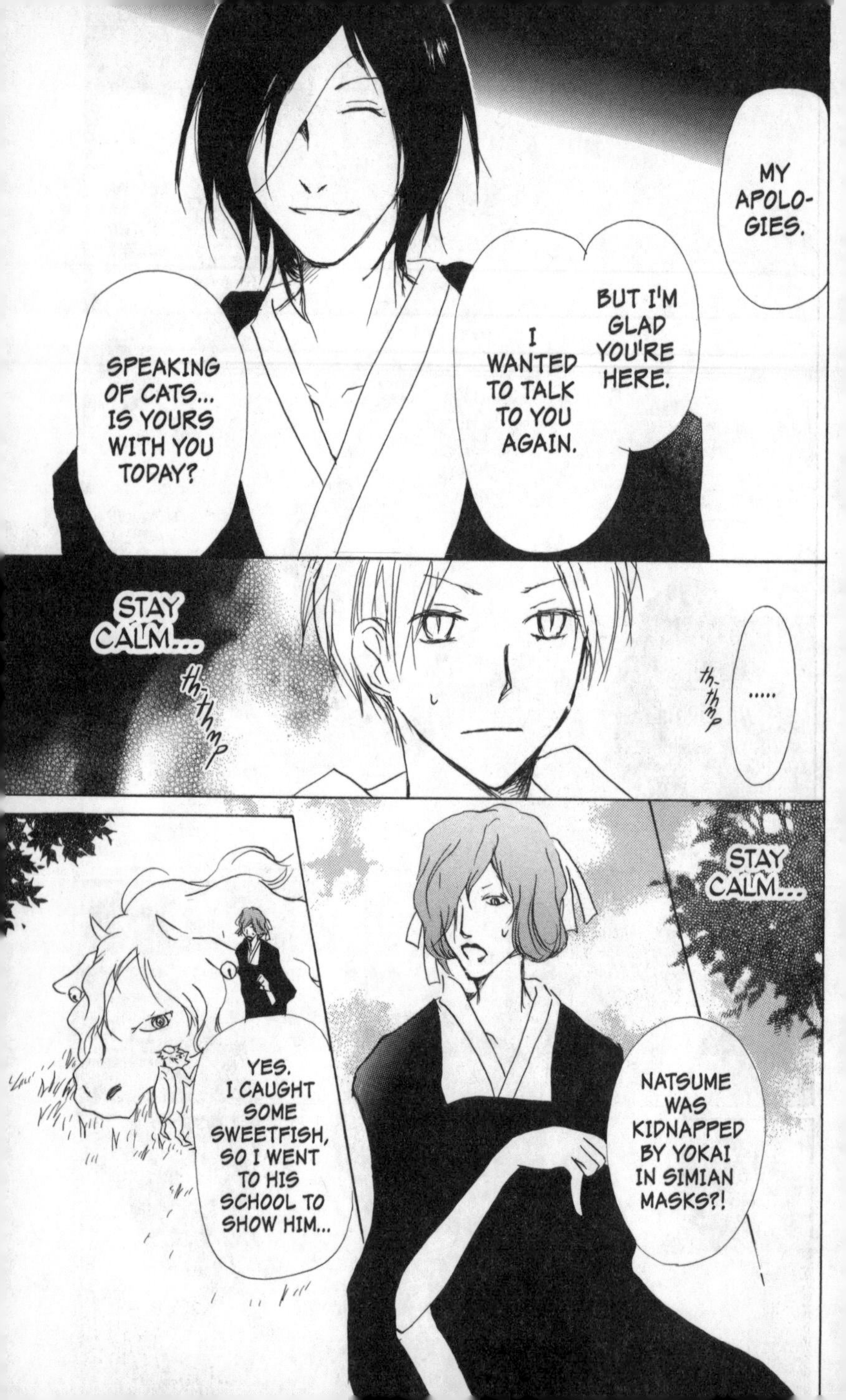

MY APOLOGIES.
BUT I'M GLAD YOU'RE HERE.
I WANTED TO TALK TO YOU AGAIN.
SPEAKING OF CATS... IS YOURS WITH YOU TODAY?
.....
th-thmp
STAY CALM...
th-thmp
STAY CALM...
NATSUME WAS KIDNAPPED BY YOKAI IN SIMIAN MASKS?!
YES. I CAUGHT SOME SWEETFISH, SO I WENT TO HIS SCHOOL TO SHOW HIM...

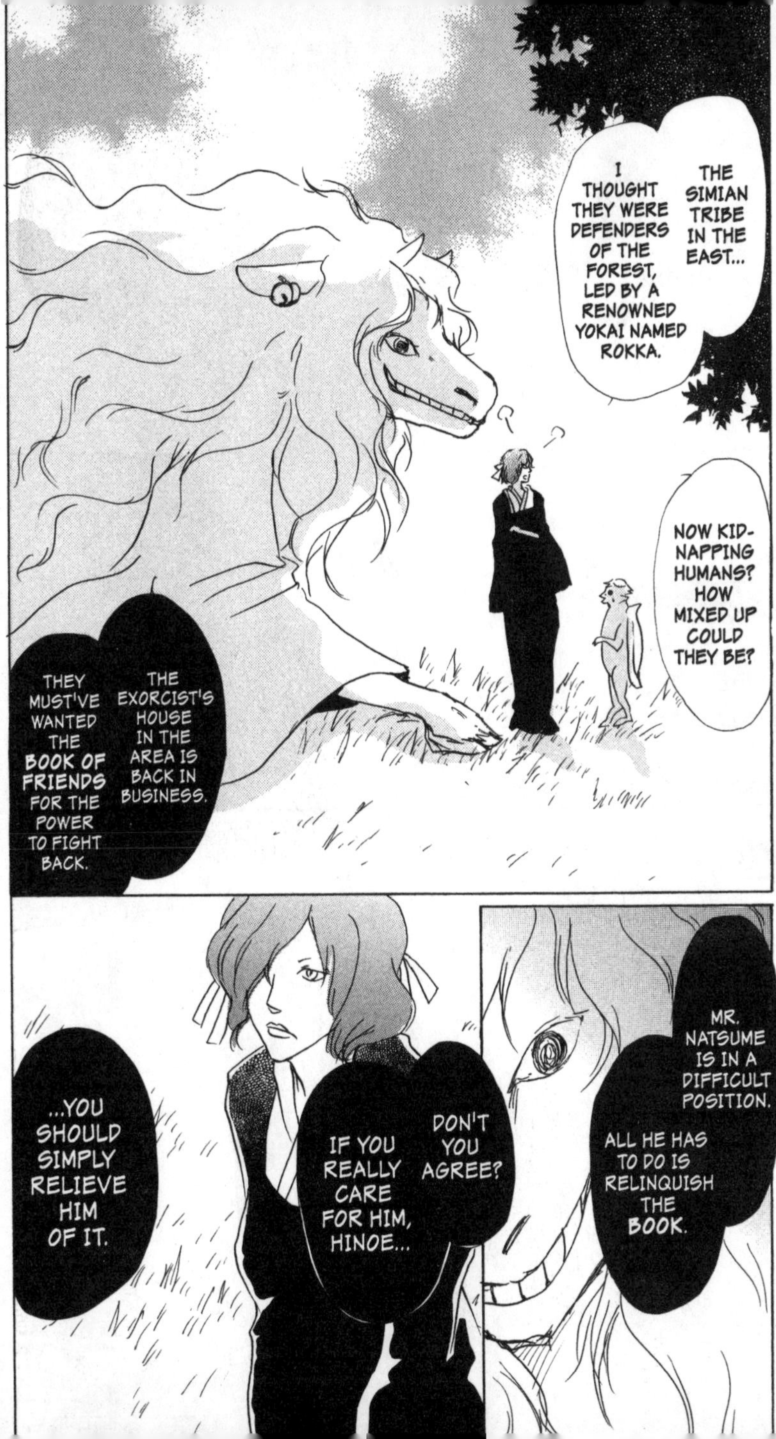
THE SIMIAN TRIBE IN THE EAST...
I THOUGHT THEY WERE DEFENDERS OF THE FOREST, LED BY A RENOWNED YOKAI NAMED ROKKA.
NOW KID-NAPPING HUMANS? HOW MIXED UP COULD THEY BE?
THE EXORCIST'S HOUSE IN THE AREA IS BACK IN BUSINESS.
THEY MUST'VE WANTED THE BOOK OF FRIENDS FOR THE POWER TO FIGHT BACK.
MR. NATSUME IS IN A DIFFICULT POSITION.
ALL HE HAS TO DO IS RELINQUISH THE BOOK.
DON'T YOU AGREE?
IF YOU REALLY CARE FOR HIM, HINOE...
...YOU SHOULD SIMPLY RELIEVE HIM OF IT.

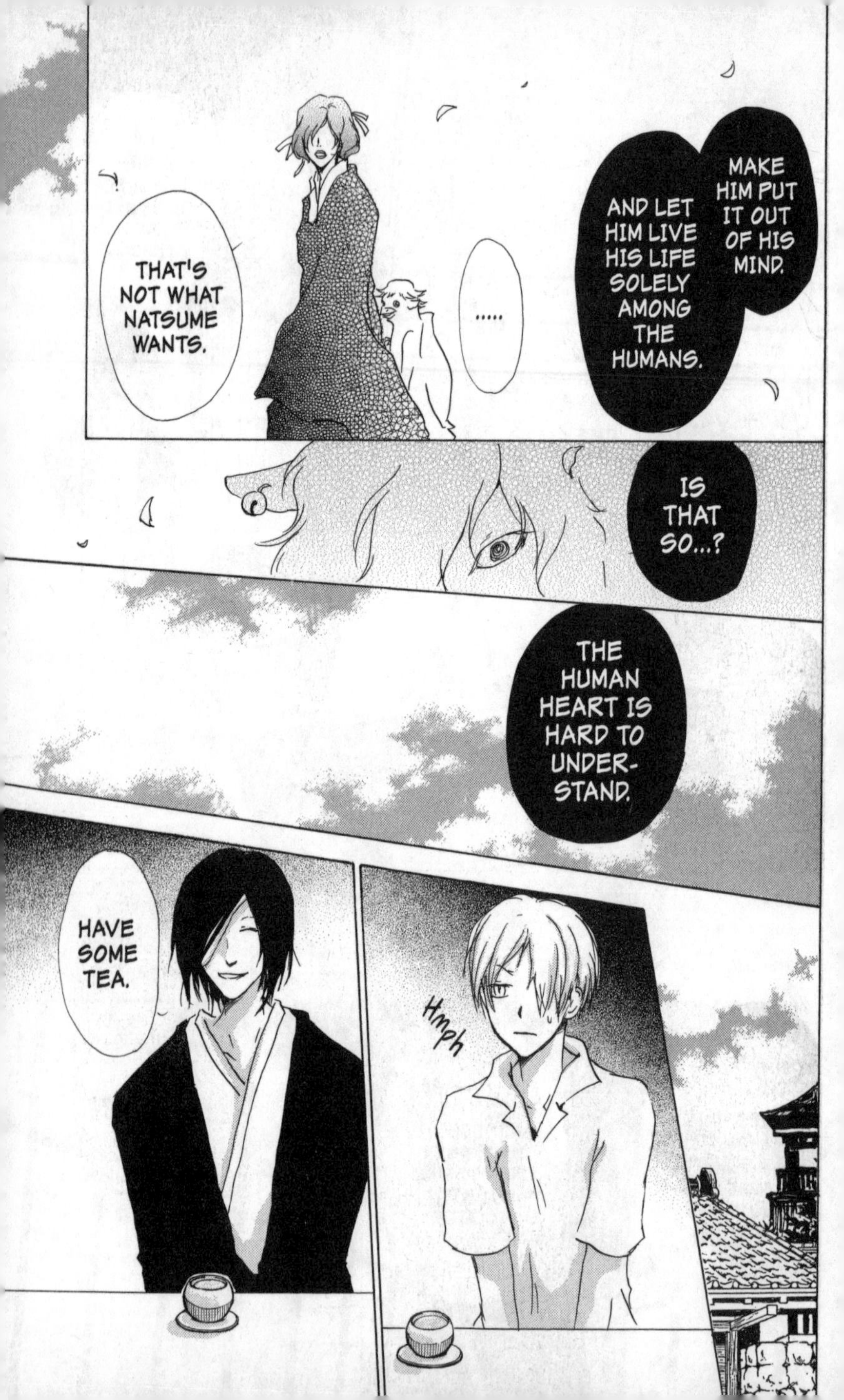
MAKE HIM PUT IT OUT OF HIS MIND.
AND LET HIM LIVE HIS LIFE SOLELY AMONG THE HUMANS.
.....
THAT'S NOT WHAT NATSUME WANTS.
IS THAT SO...?
THE HUMAN HEART IS HARD TO UNDER-STAND.
Hmph
HAVE SOME TEA.

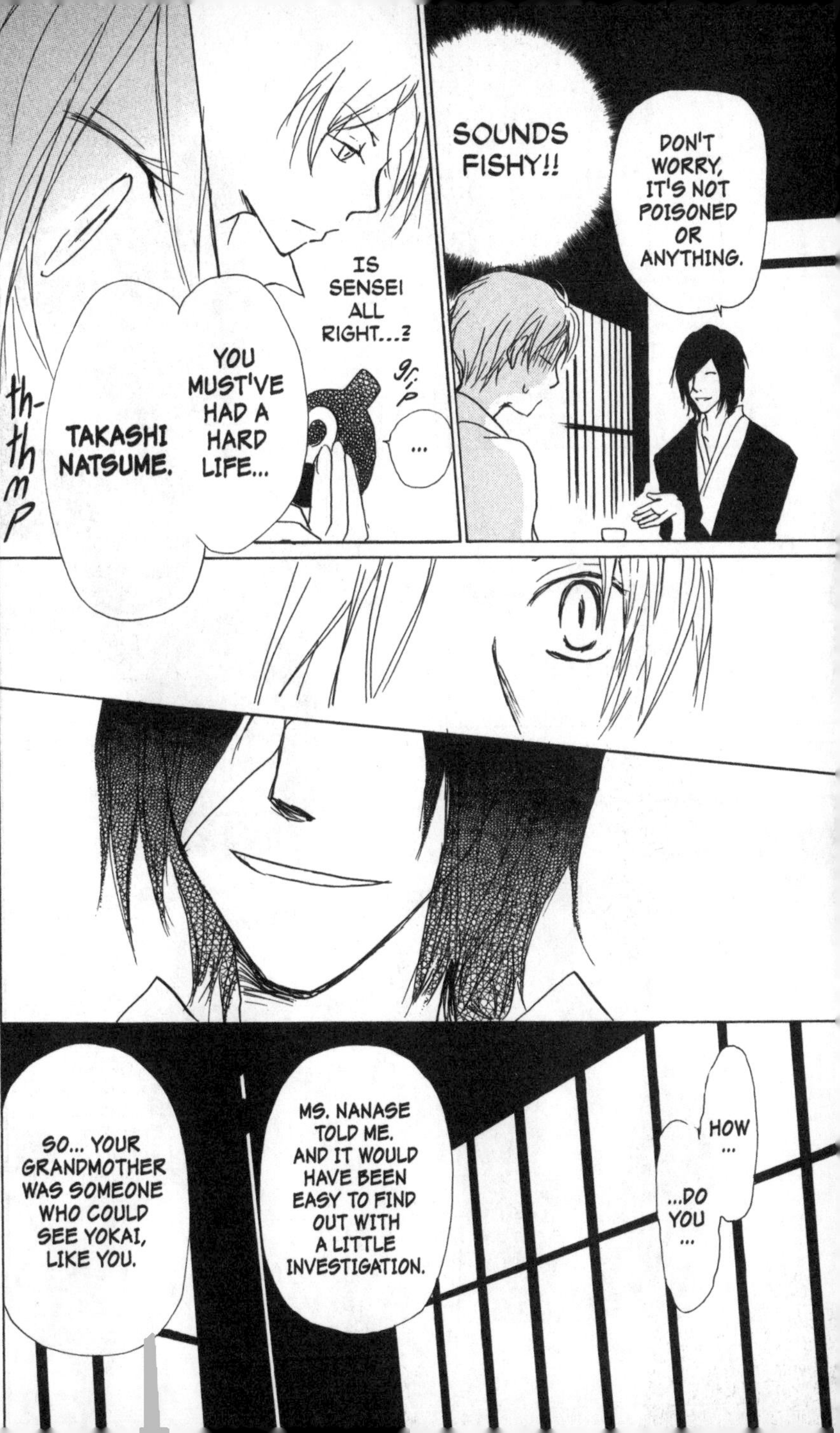
DON'T WORRY, IT'S NOT POISONED OR ANYTHING.
SOUNDS FISHY!!
IS SENSEI ALL RIGHT...?
grip
...
YOU MUST'VE HAD A HARD LIFE...
TAKASHI NATSUME.
th-thmp
HOW... ...DO YOU...
MS. NANASE TOLD ME. AND IT WOULD HAVE BEEN EASY TO FIND OUT WITH A LITTLE INVESTIGATION.
SO... YOUR GRANDMOTHER WAS SOMEONE WHO COULD SEE YOKAI, LIKE YOU.

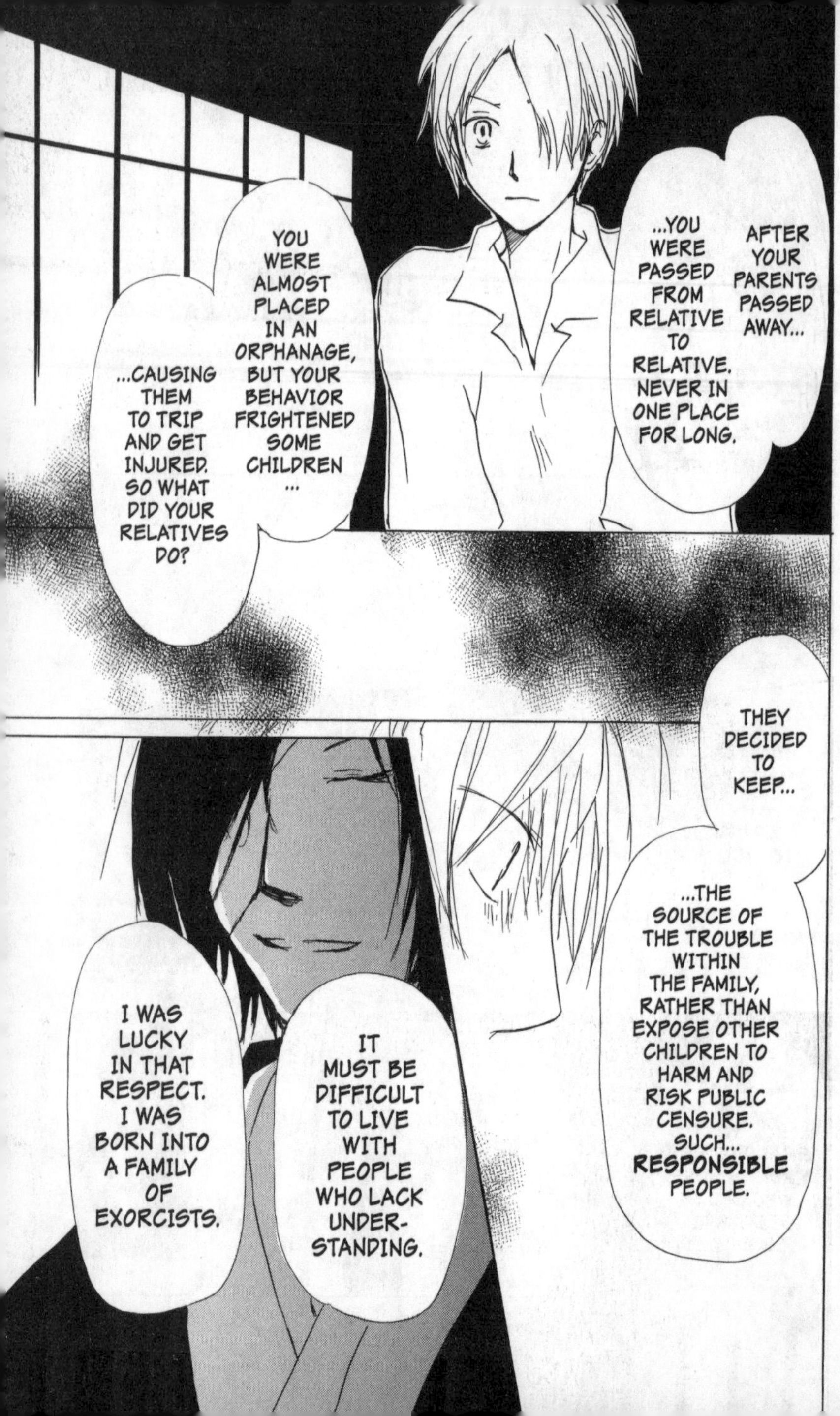
AFTER YOUR PARENTS PASSED AWAY...
...YOU WERE PASSED FROM RELATIVE TO RELATIVE. NEVER IN ONE PLACE FOR LONG.
YOU WERE ALMOST PLACED IN AN ORPHANAGE, BUT YOUR BEHAVIOR FRIGHTENED SOME CHILDREN ...
...CAUSING THEM TO TRIP AND GET INJURED. SO WHAT DID YOUR RELATIVES DO?
THEY DECIDED TO KEEP...
...THE SOURCE OF THE TROUBLE WITHIN THE FAMILY, RATHER THAN EXPOSE OTHER CHILDREN TO HARM AND RISK PUBLIC CENSURE. SUCH... RESPONSIBLE PEOPLE.
IT MUST BE DIFFICULT TO LIVE WITH PEOPLE WHO LACK UNDER-STANDING.
I WAS LUCKY IN THAT RESPECT. I WAS BORN INTO A FAMILY OF EXORCISTS.

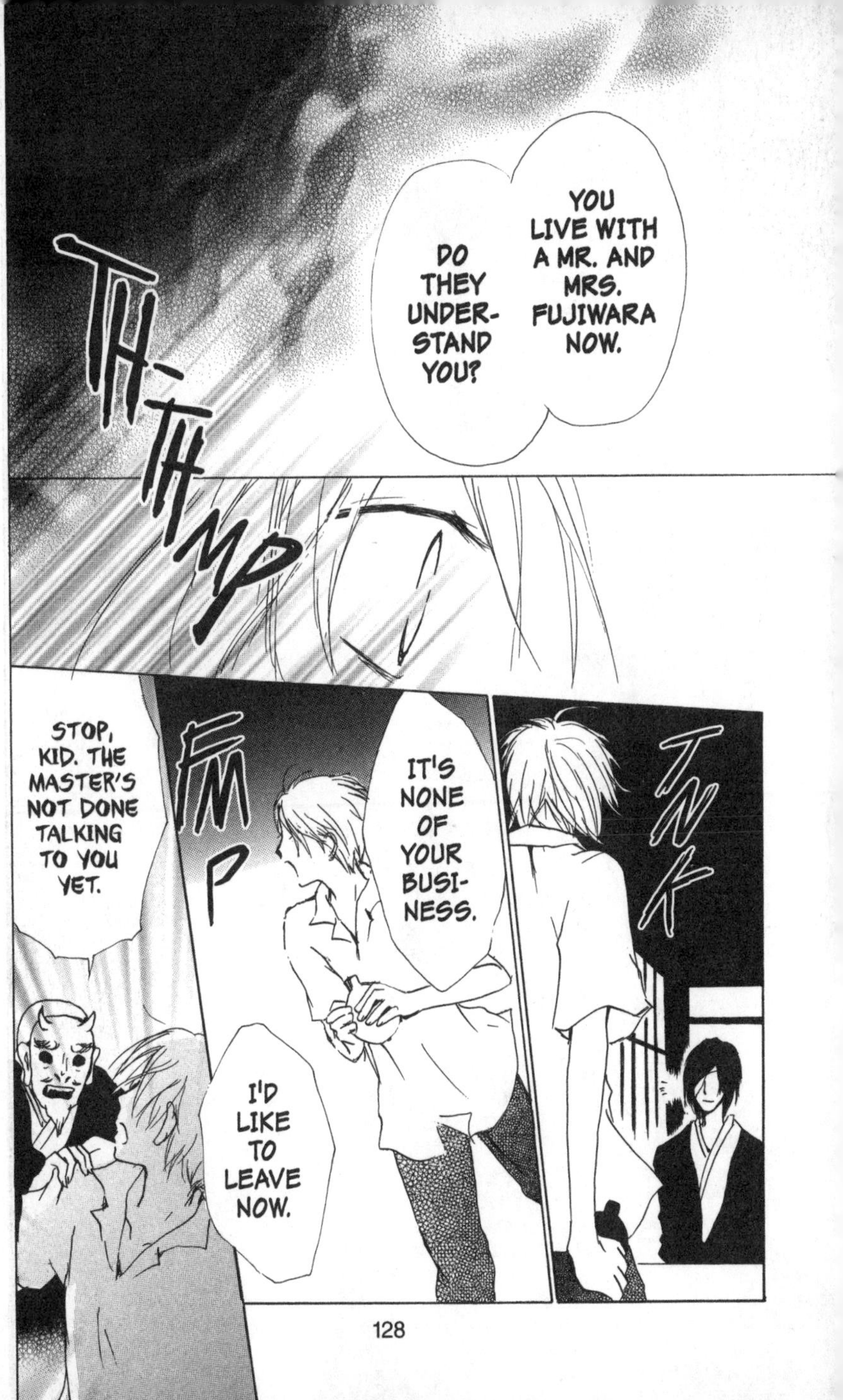
YOU LIVE WITH A MR. AND MRS. FUJIWARA NOW.
DO THEY UNDERSTAND YOU?
TH-THMP
TNK
IT'S NONE OF YOUR BUSINESS.
FMP
I'D LIKE TO LEAVE NOW.
STOP, KID. THE MASTER'S NOT DONE TALKING TO YOU YET.

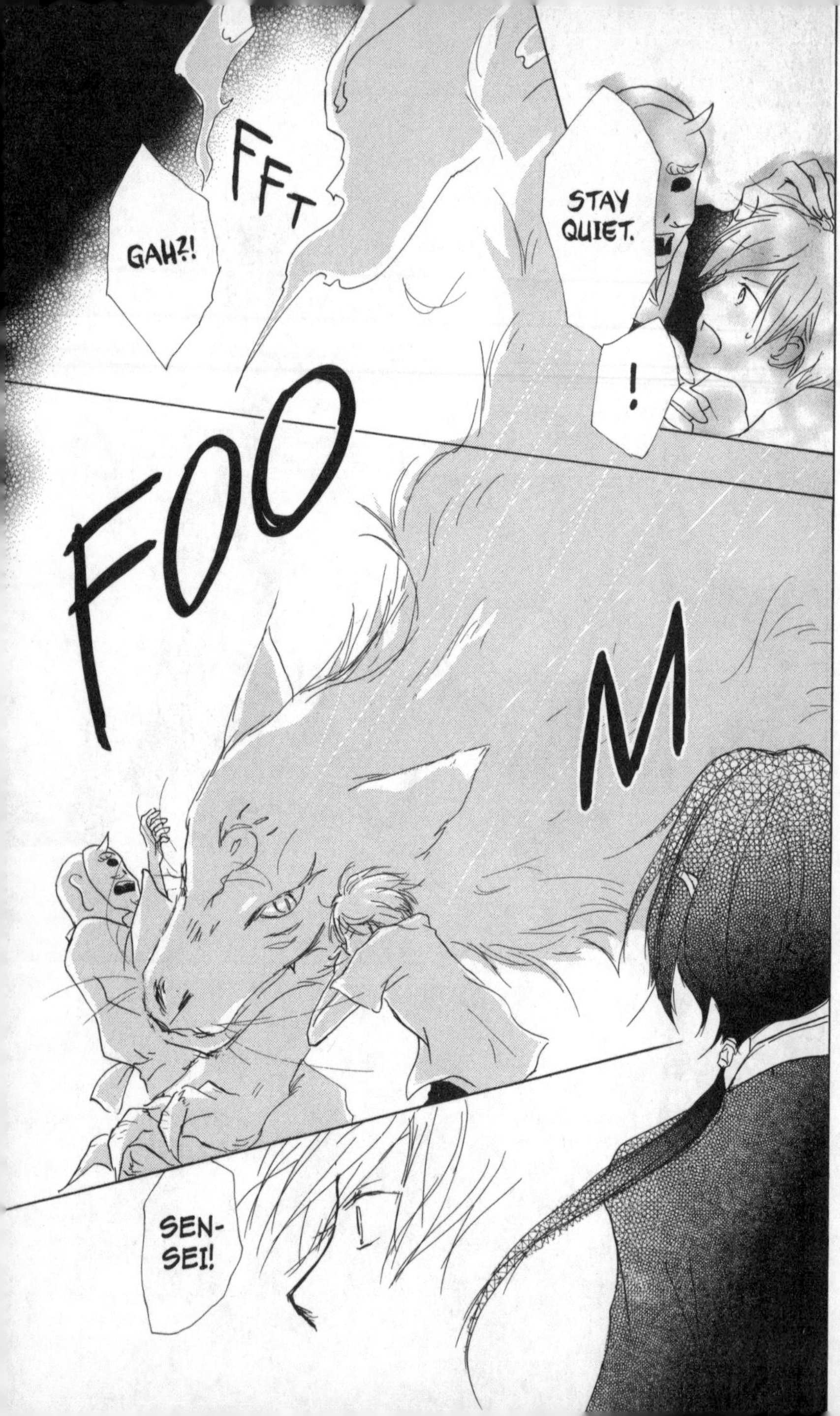
STAY QUIET.
!
FFT
GAH?!
FOOM
SEN-SEI!

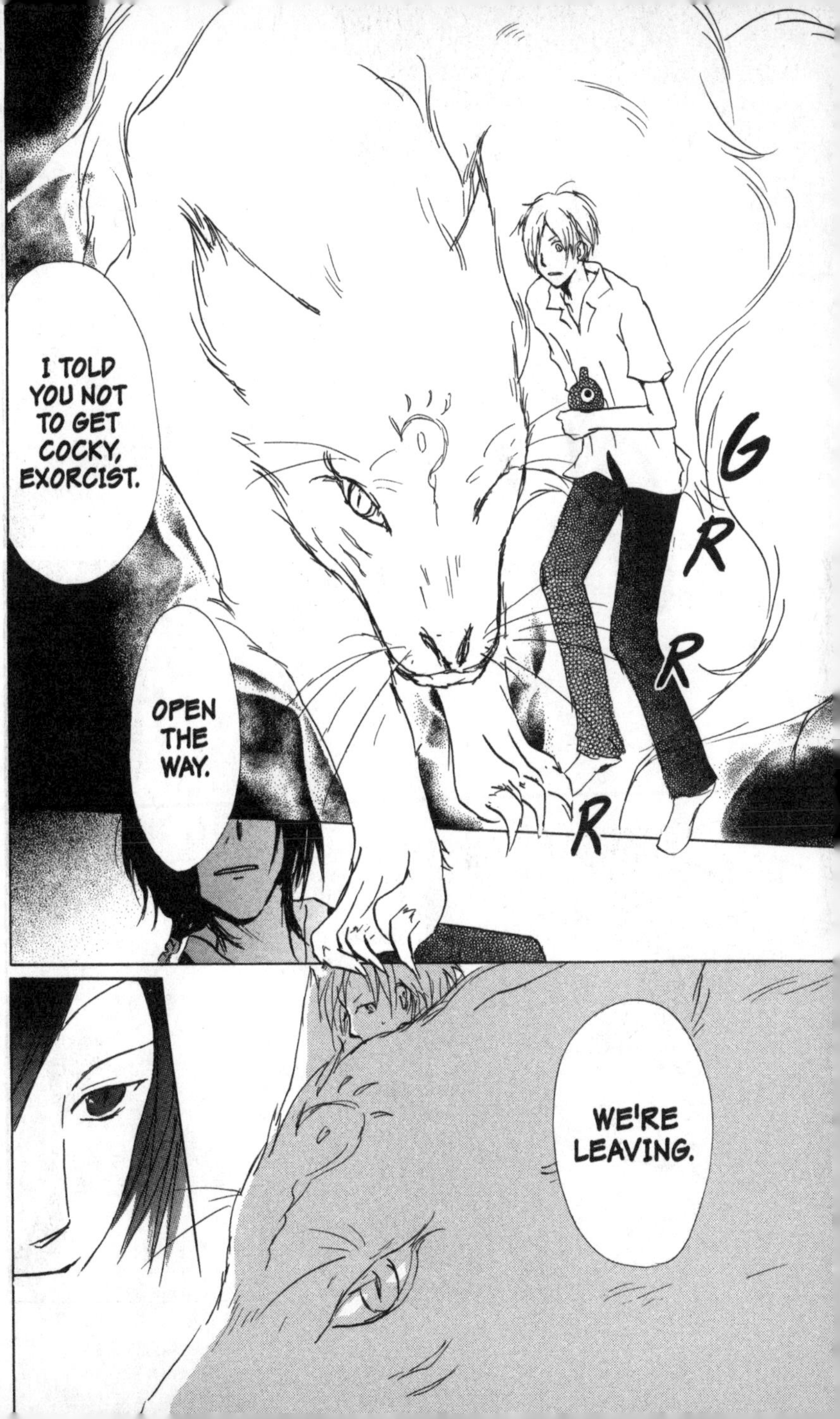
GRRRR
I TOLD YOU NOT TO GET COCKY, EXORCIST.
OPEN THE WAY.
WE'RE LEAVING.

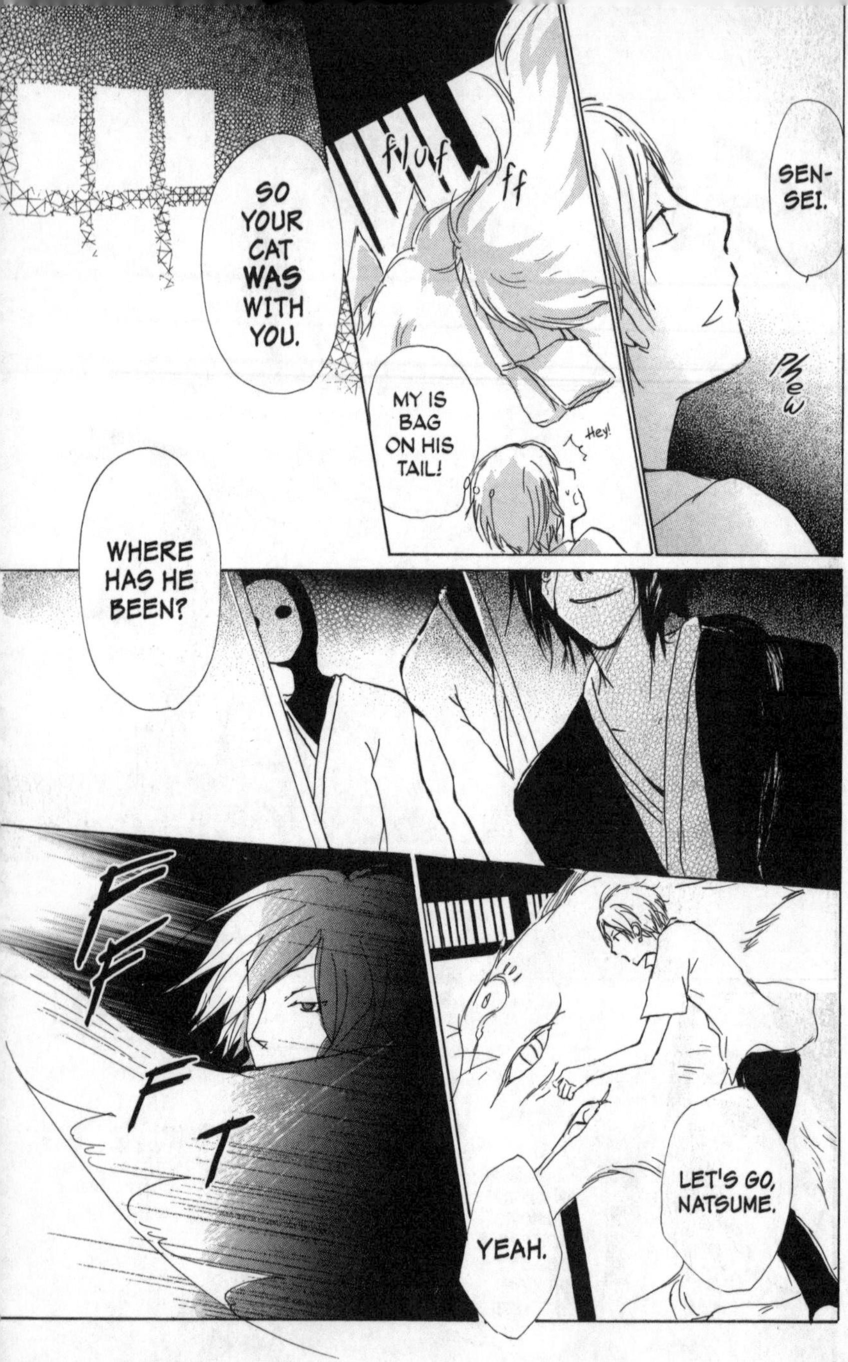
SEN-SEI.
Phew
fluff
Hey!
MY IS BAG ON HIS TAIL!
SO YOUR CAT WAS WITH YOU.
WHERE HAS HE BEEN?
LET'S GO, NATSUME.
YEAH.
FFFT

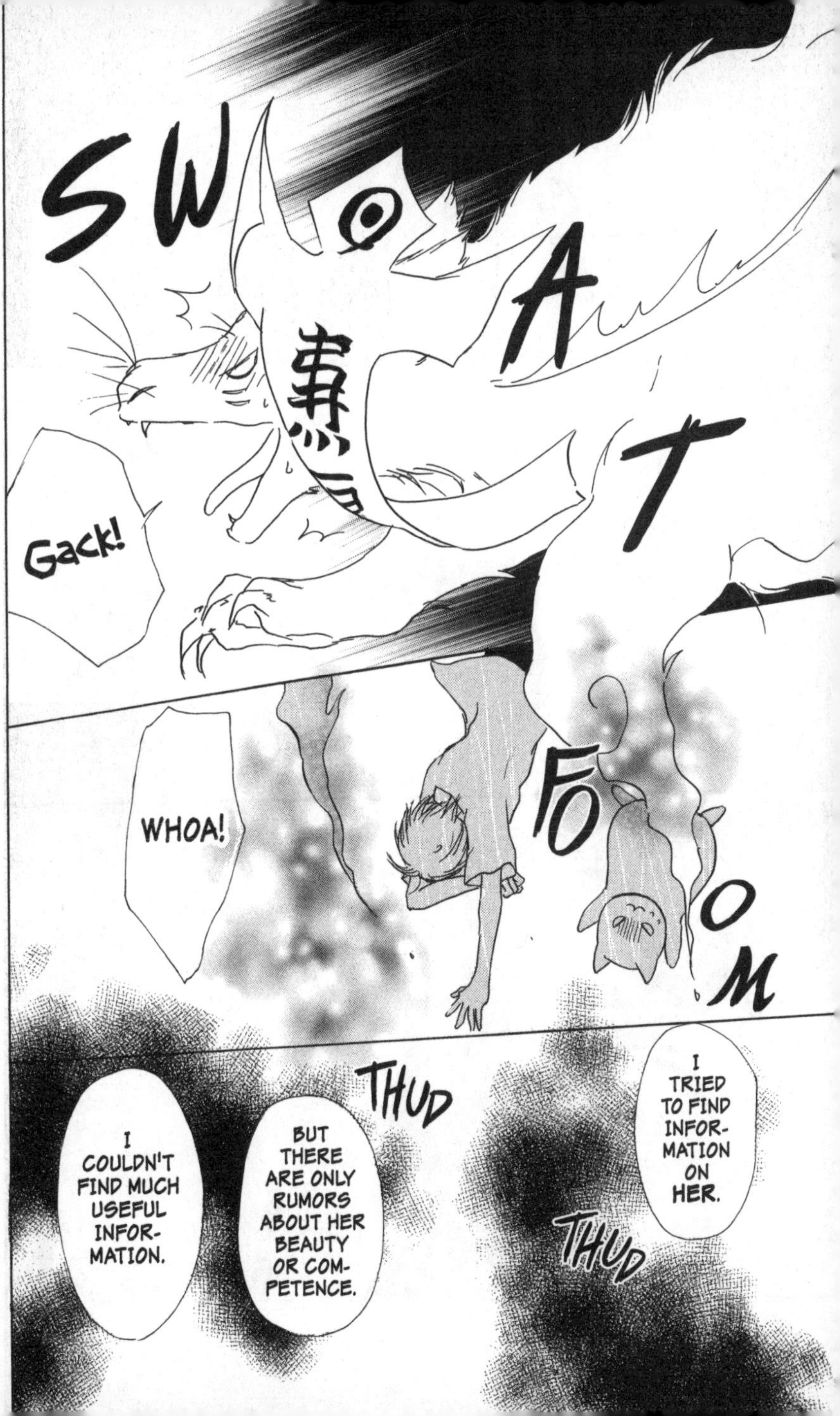
SWOAT
Gack!
FOOM
WHOA!
I TRIED TO FIND INFOR-MATION ON HER.
THUD
THUD
BUT THERE ARE ONLY RUMORS ABOUT HER BEAUTY OR COM-PETENCE.
I COULDN'T FIND MUCH USEFUL INFOR-MATION.

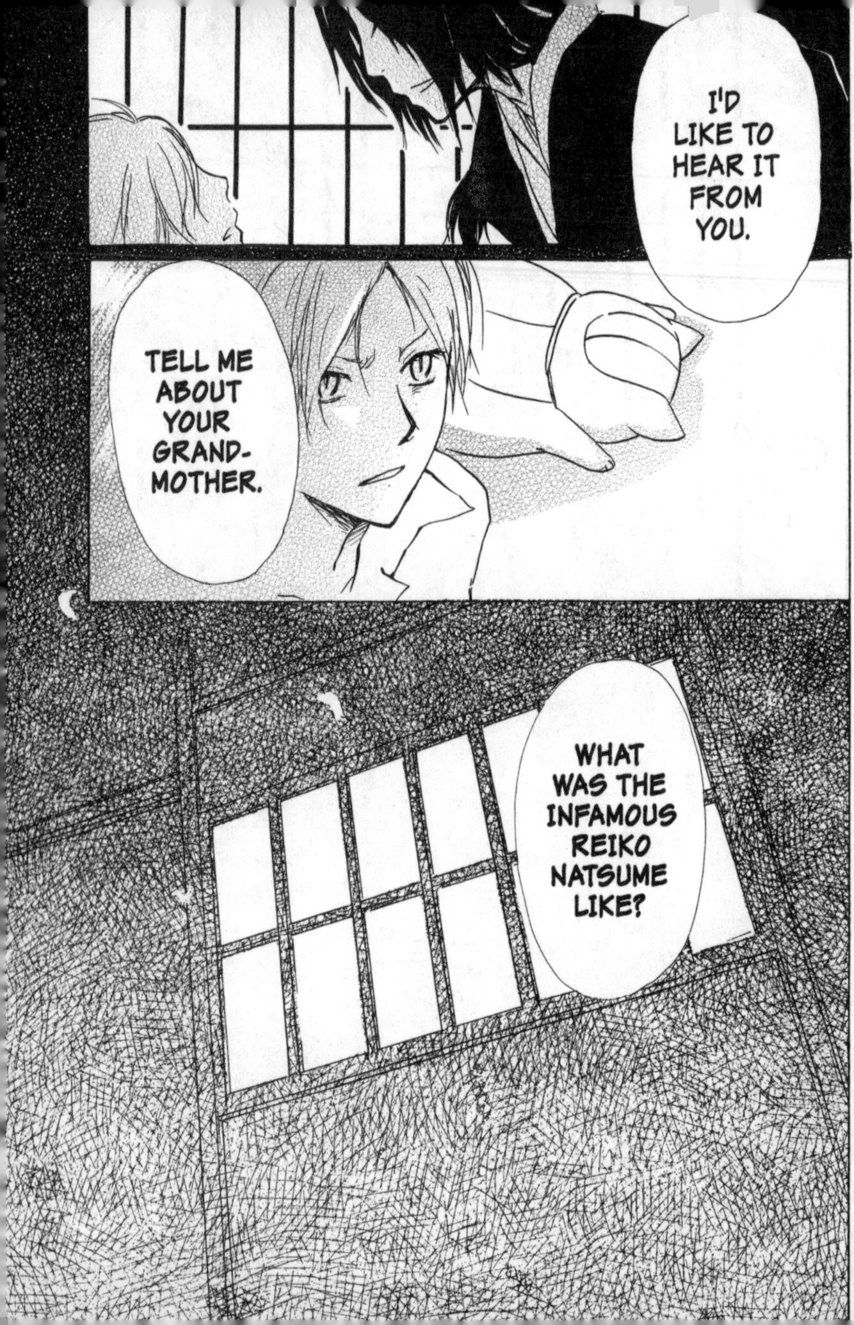
I'D LIKE TO HEAR IT FROM YOU.
TELL ME ABOUT YOUR GRAND-MOTHER.
WHAT WAS THE INFAMOUS REIKO NATSUME LIKE?

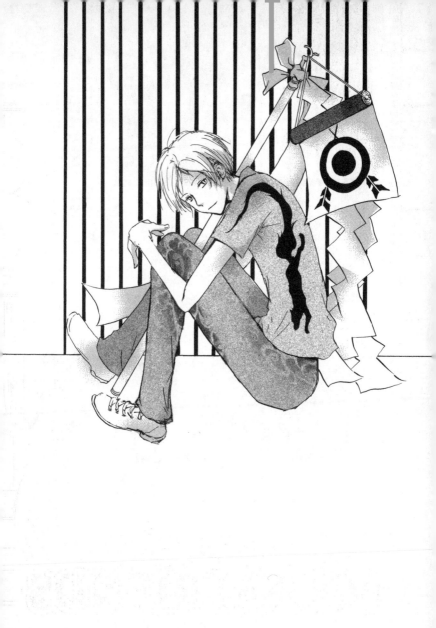

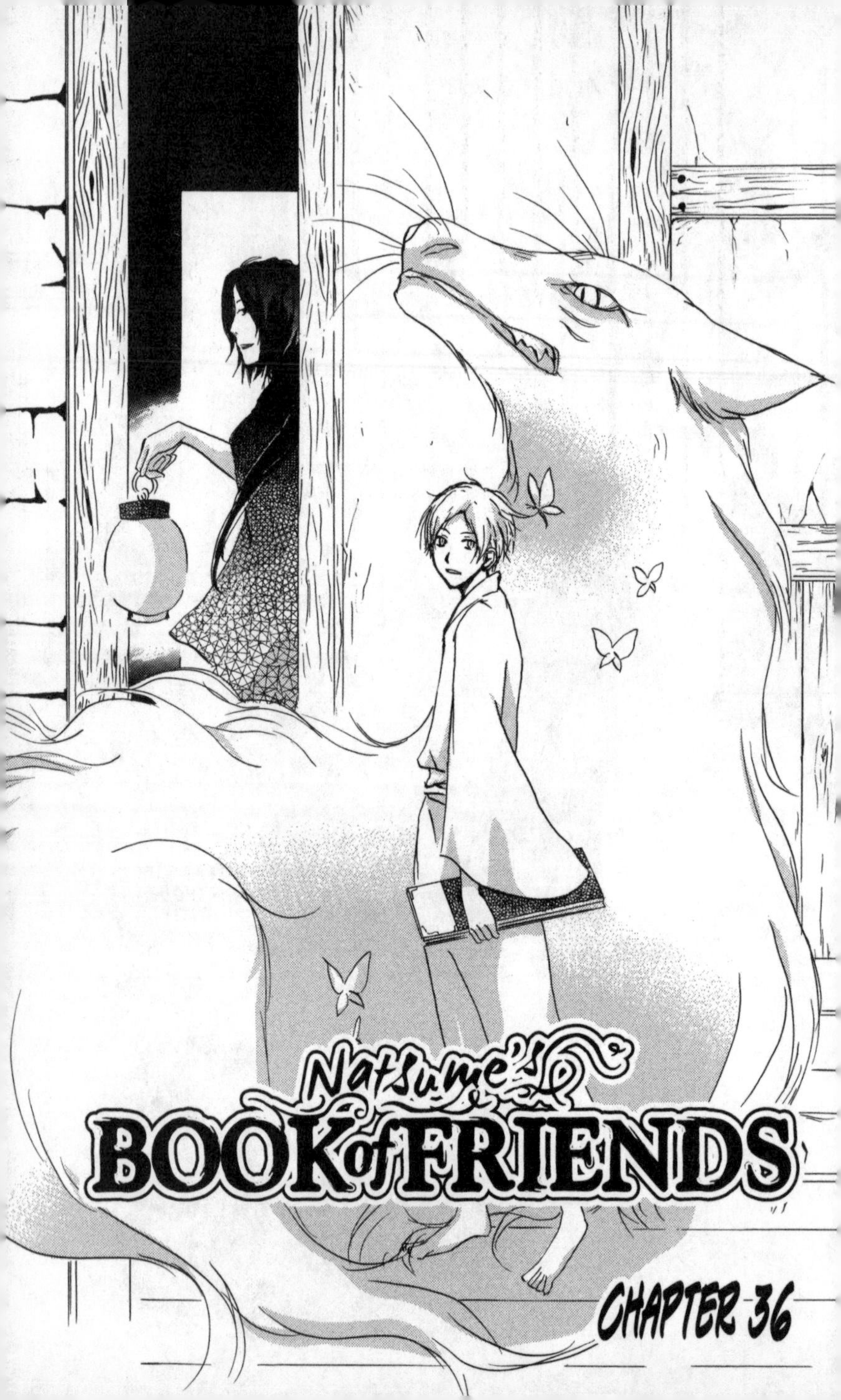
Natsume's
BOOK of FRIENDS
CHAPTER 36

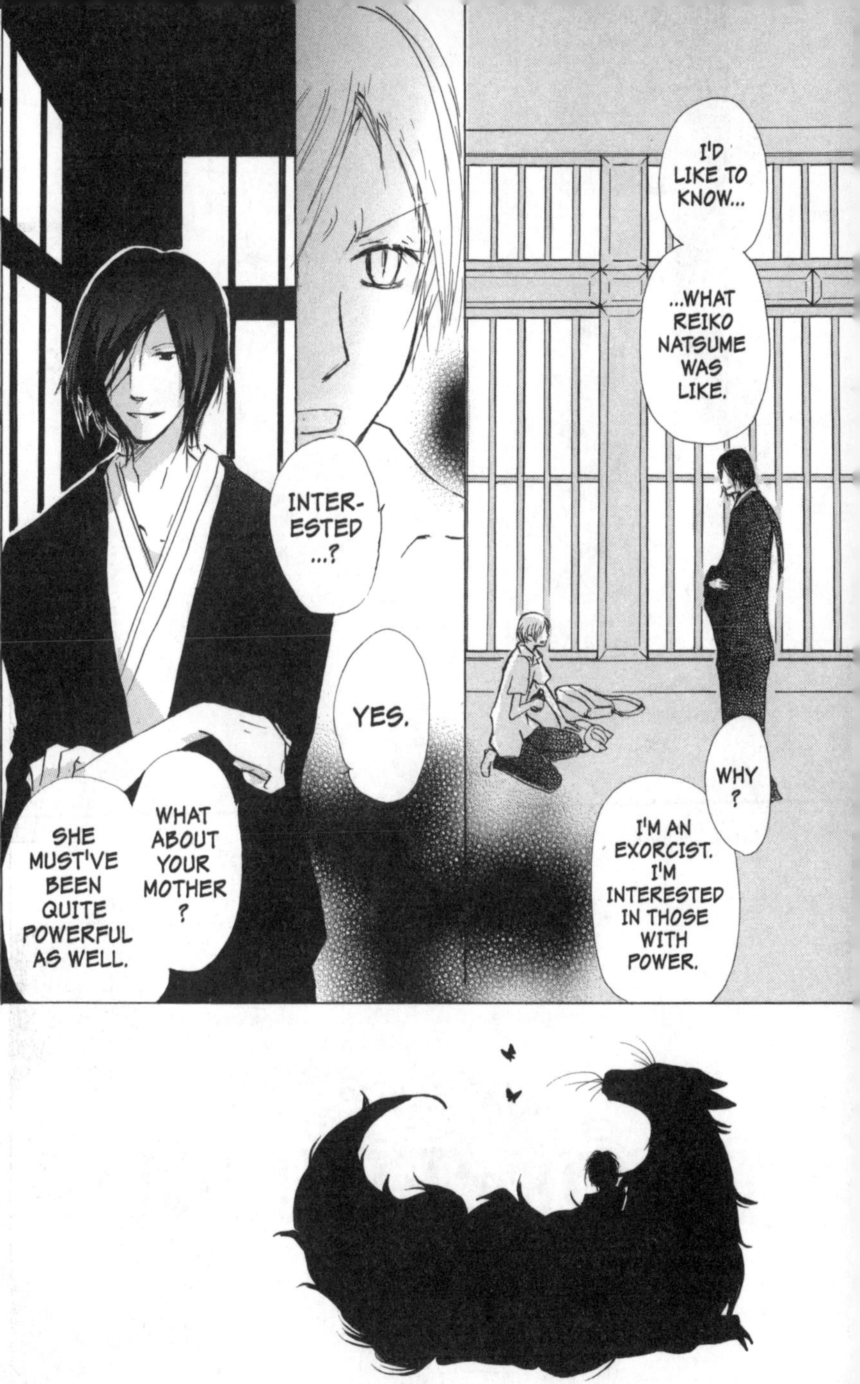
I'D LIKE TO KNOW...
...WHAT REIKO NATSUME WAS LIKE.
WHY?
I'M AN EXORCIST. I'M INTERESTED IN THOSE WITH POWER.
INTER-ESTED ...?
YES.
WHAT ABOUT YOUR MOTHER?
SHE MUST'VE BEEN QUITE POWERFUL AS WELL.

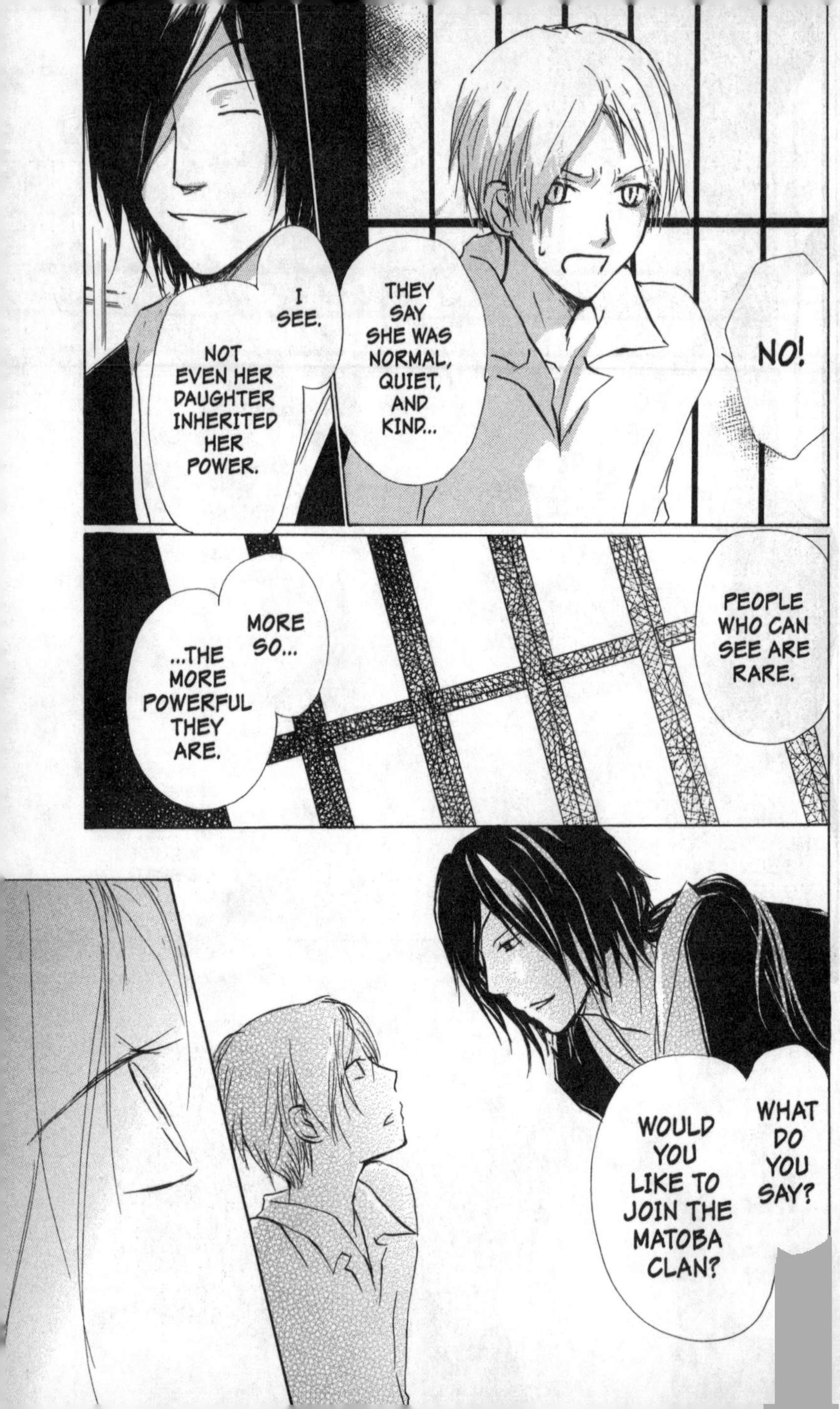
NO!
THEY SAY SHE WAS NORMAL, QUIET, AND KIND...
I SEE.
NOT EVEN HER DAUGHTER INHERITED HER POWER.
PEOPLE WHO CAN SEE ARE RARE.
MORE SO...
...THE MORE POWERFUL THEY ARE.
WHAT DO YOU SAY?
WOULD YOU LIKE TO JOIN THE MATOBA CLAN?

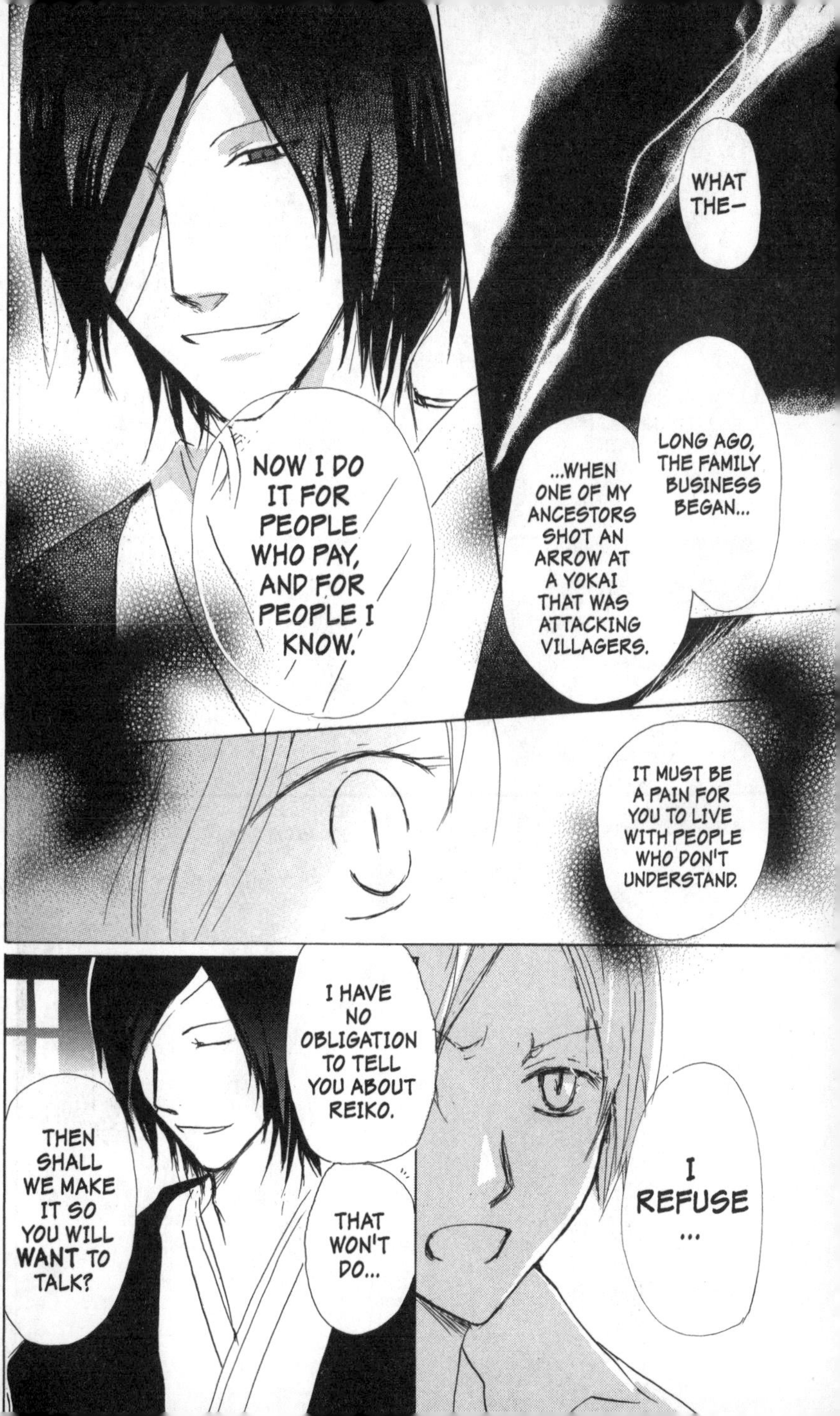
WHAT THE—
LONG AGO, THE FAMILY BUSINESS BEGAN...
...WHEN ONE OF MY ANCESTORS SHOT AN ARROW AT A YOKAI THAT WAS ATTACKING VILLAGERS.
NOW I DO IT FOR PEOPLE WHO PAY, AND FOR PEOPLE I KNOW.
IT MUST BE A PAIN FOR YOU TO LIVE WITH PEOPLE WHO DON'T UNDERSTAND.
I REFUSE...
I HAVE NO OBLIGATION TO TELL YOU ABOUT REIKO.
THAT WON'T DO...
THEN SHALL WE MAKE IT SO YOU WILL WANT TO TALK?

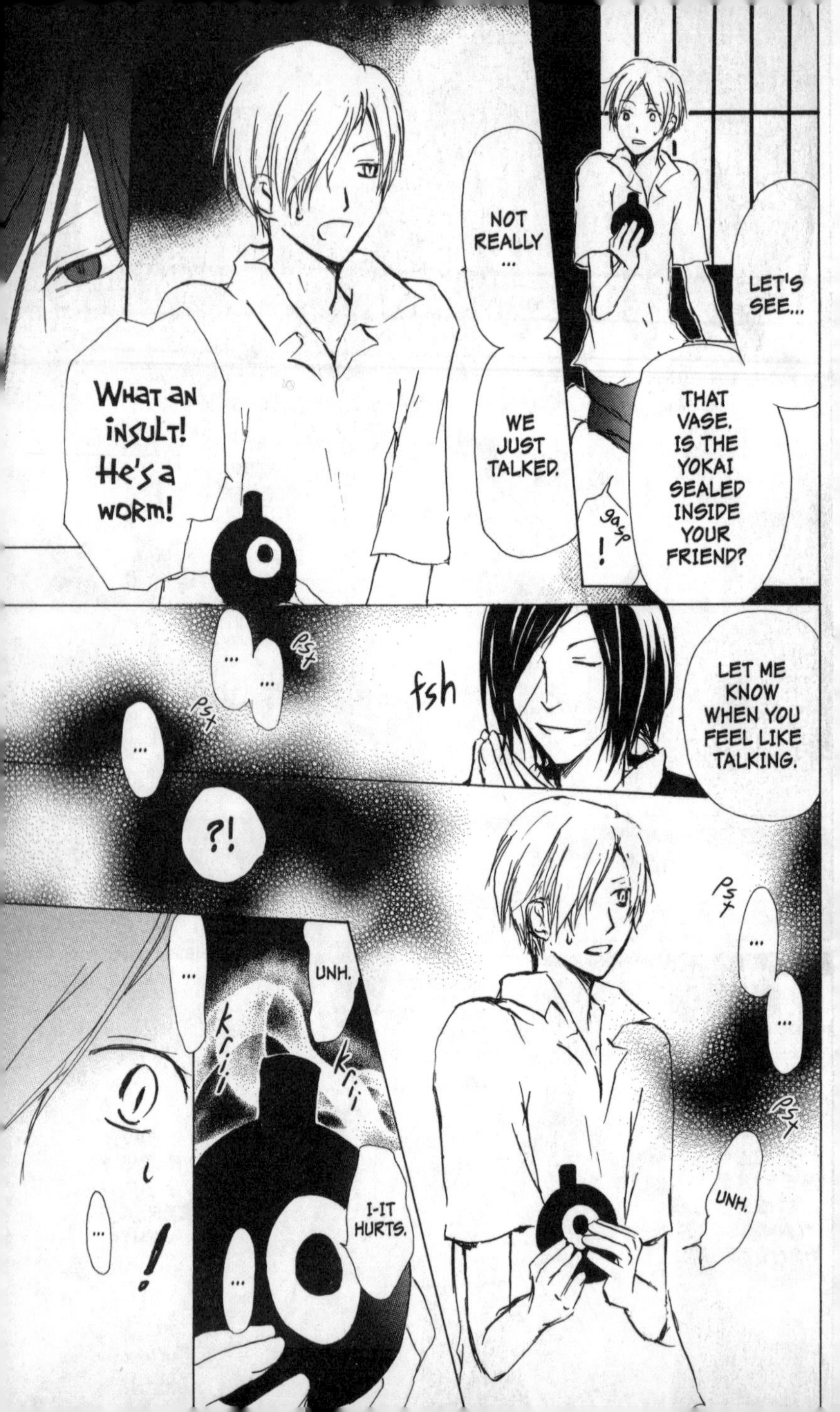

LET'S SEE...
THAT VASE. IS THE YOKAI SEALED INSIDE YOUR FRIEND?
gasp
!
NOT REALLY...
WE JUST TALKED.
What an insult! He's a worm!
LET ME KNOW WHEN YOU FEEL LIKE TALKING.
fsh
pst
...
...
pst
...
?!
pst
...
...
pst
UNH.
...
UNH.
kri
kri
I-IT HURTS.
!
...
...

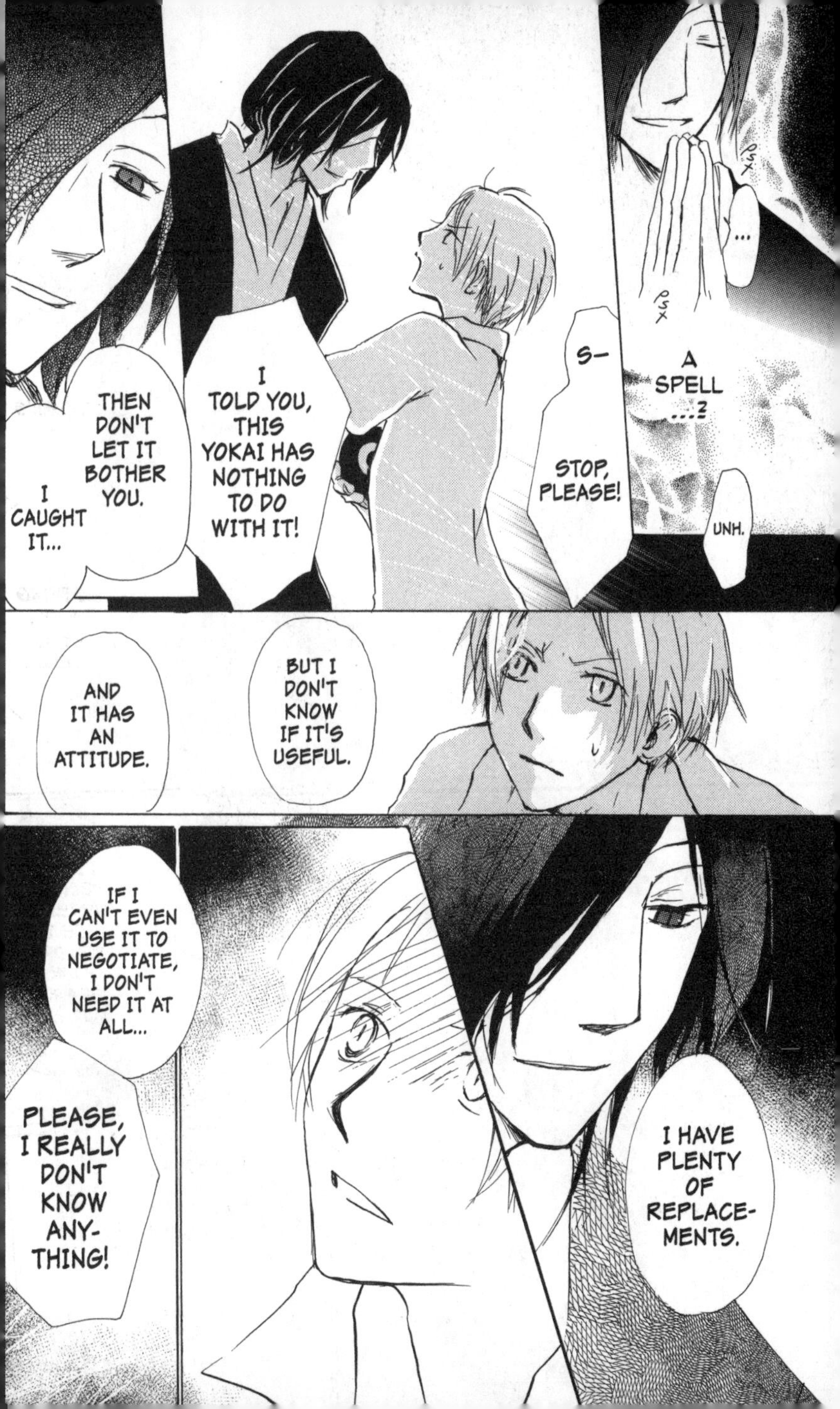
PSX
...
PSX
A SPELL ...?
UNH.
S—
STOP, PLEASE!
I TOLD YOU, THIS YOKAI HAS NOTHING TO DO WITH IT!
THEN DON'T LET IT BOTHER YOU.
I CAUGHT IT...
BUT I DON'T KNOW IF IT'S USEFUL.
AND IT HAS AN ATTITUDE.
IF I CAN'T EVEN USE IT TO NEGOTIATE, I DON'T NEED IT AT ALL...
I HAVE PLENTY OF REPLACE-MENTS.
PLEASE, I REALLY DON'T KNOW ANY-THING!

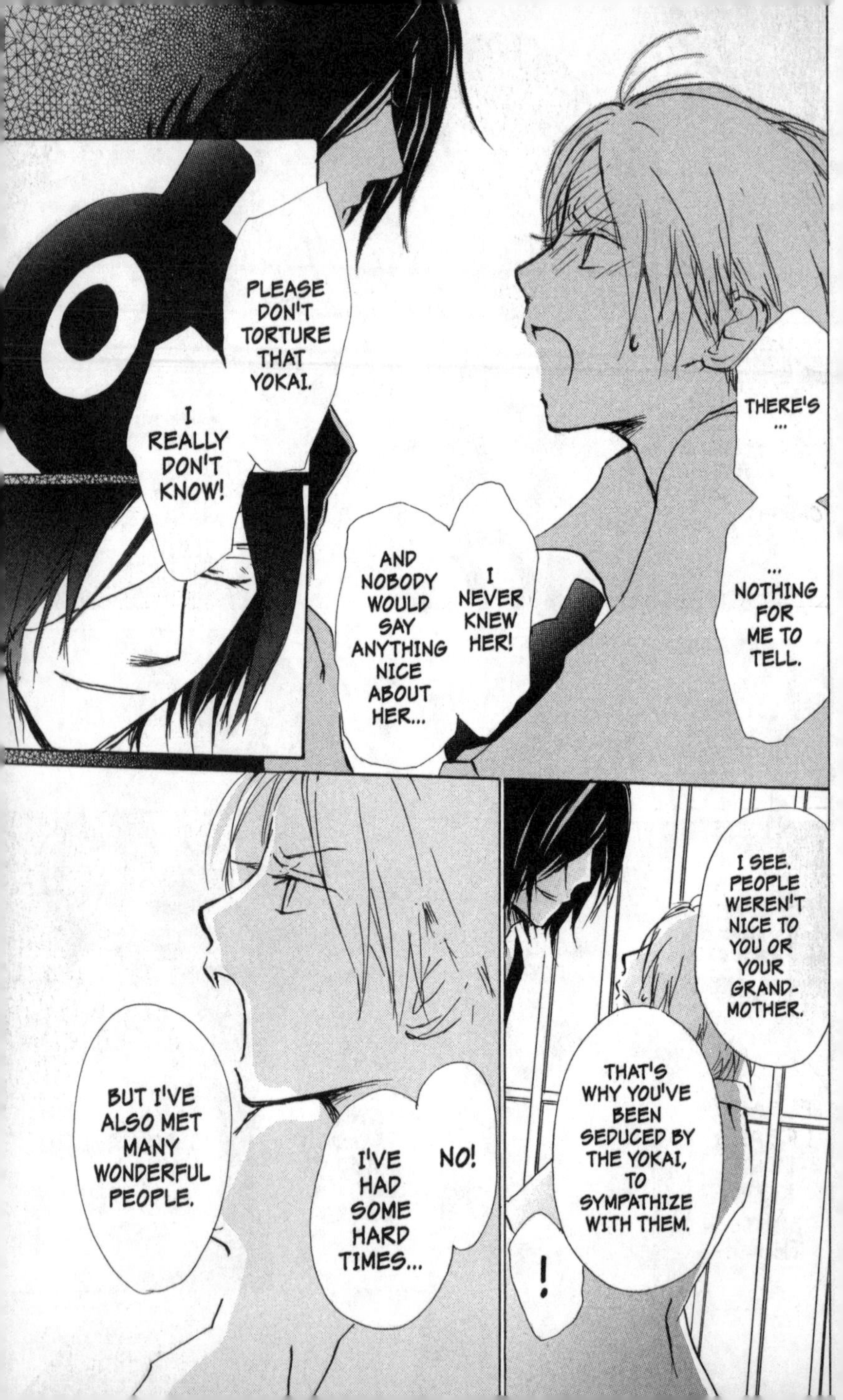
THERE'S ...
... NOTHING FOR ME TO TELL.
I NEVER KNEW HER!
AND NOBODY WOULD SAY ANYTHING NICE ABOUT HER...
PLEASE DON'T TORTURE THAT YOKAI.
I REALLY DON'T KNOW!
I SEE. PEOPLE WEREN'T NICE TO YOU OR YOUR GRAND-MOTHER.
THAT'S WHY YOU'VE BEEN SEDUCED BY THE YOKAI, TO SYMPATHIZE WITH THEM.
!
NO!
I'VE HAD SOME HARD TIMES...
BUT I'VE ALSO MET MANY WONDERFUL PEOPLE.

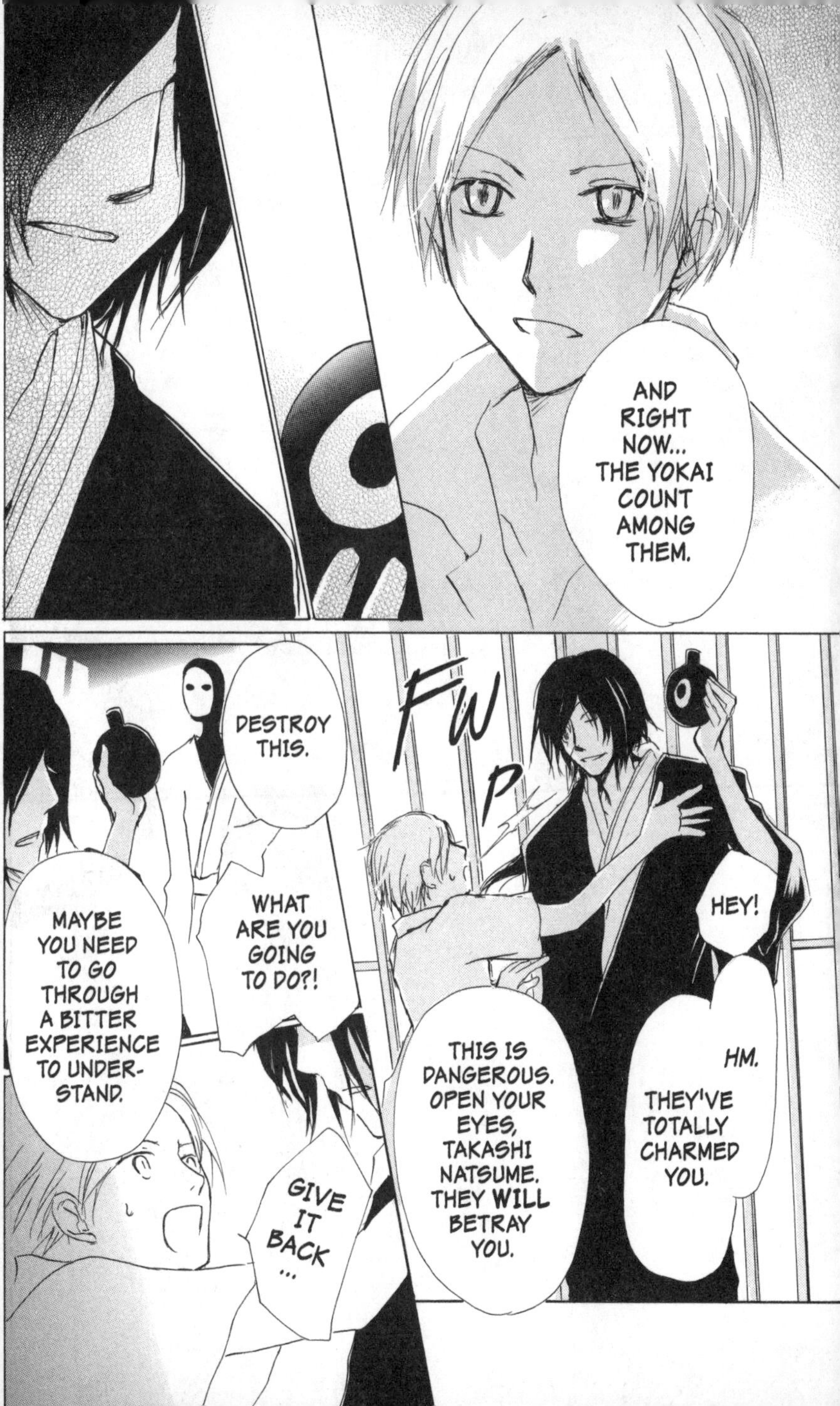
AND RIGHT NOW... THE YOKAI COUNT AMONG THEM.
FWP
HEY!
HM.
THEY'VE TOTALLY CHARMED YOU.
THIS IS DANGEROUS. OPEN YOUR EYES, TAKASHI NATSUME. THEY WILL BETRAY YOU.
DESTROY THIS.
WHAT ARE YOU GOING TO DO?!
MAYBE YOU NEED TO GO THROUGH A BITTER EXPERIENCE TO UNDER-STAND.
GIVE IT BACK...

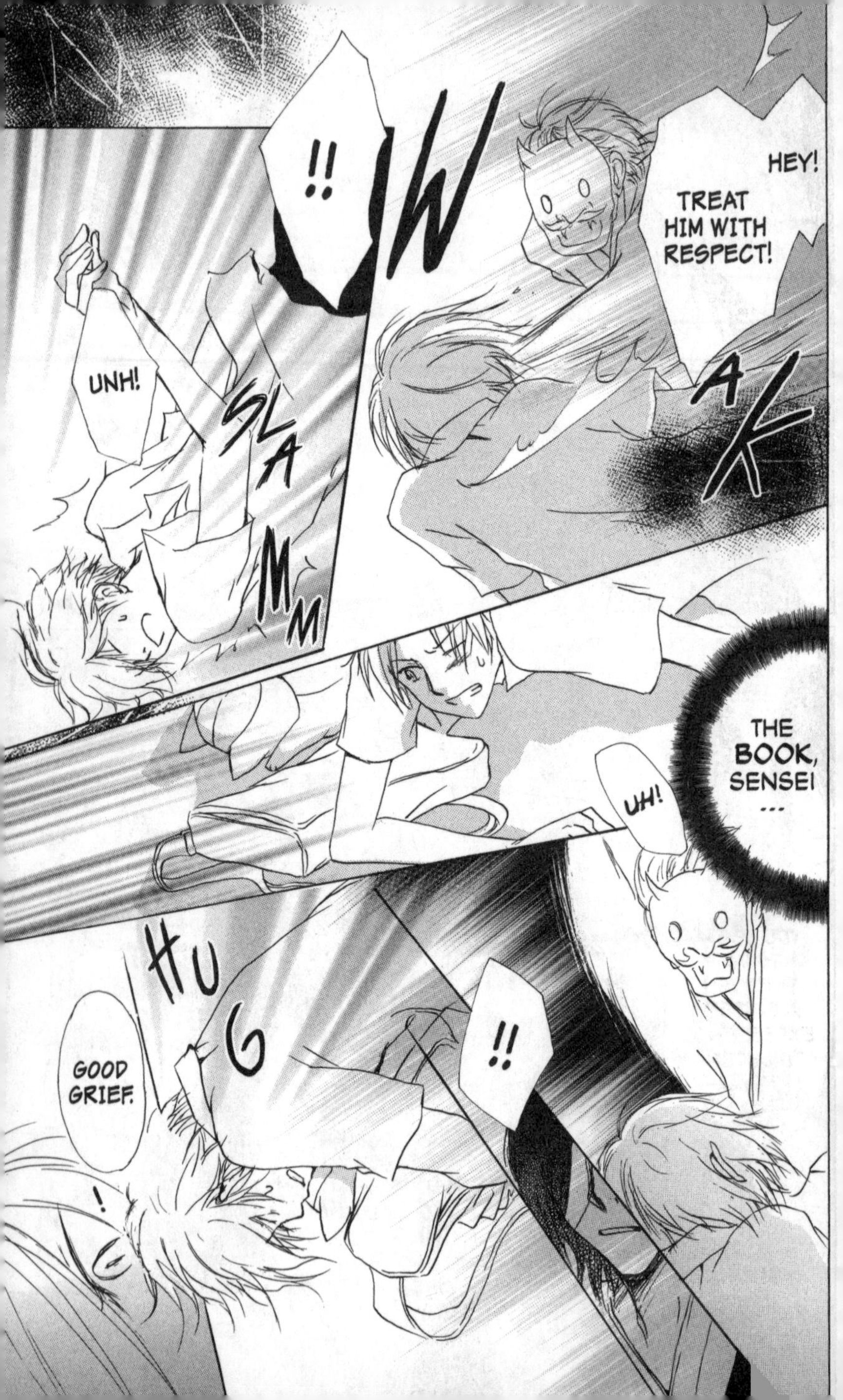
HEY!
TREAT HIM WITH RESPECT!
W
AK
!!
UNH!
SLAMM
THE BOOK, SENSEI ---
UH!
!!
HUG
GOOD GRIEF.
!

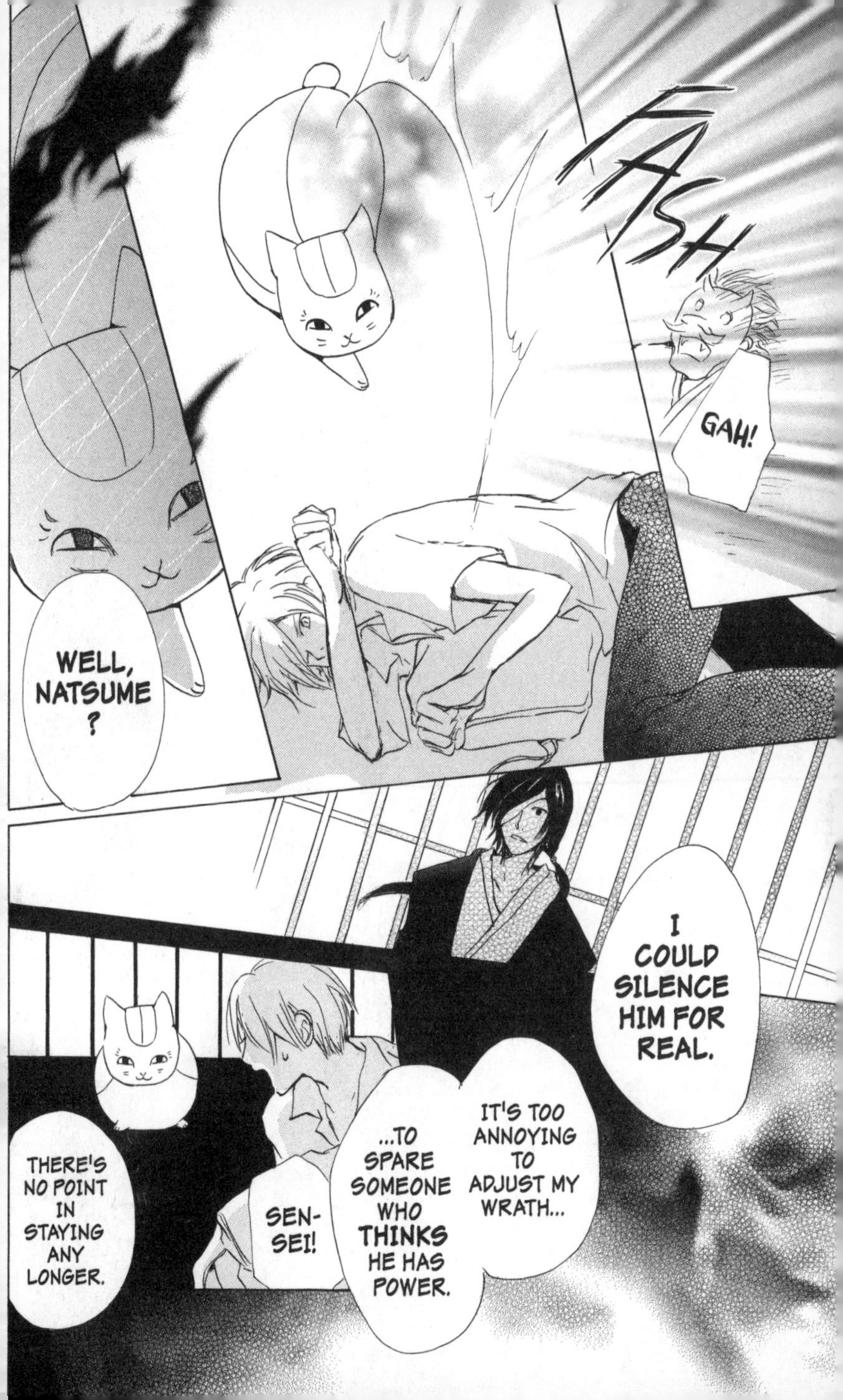
FASH
GAH!
WELL, NATSUME?
I COULD SILENCE HIM FOR REAL.
IT'S TOO ANNOYING TO ADJUST MY WRATH...
...TO SPARE SOMEONE WHO THINKS HE HAS POWER.
SEN-SEI!
THERE'S NO POINT IN STAYING ANY LONGER.

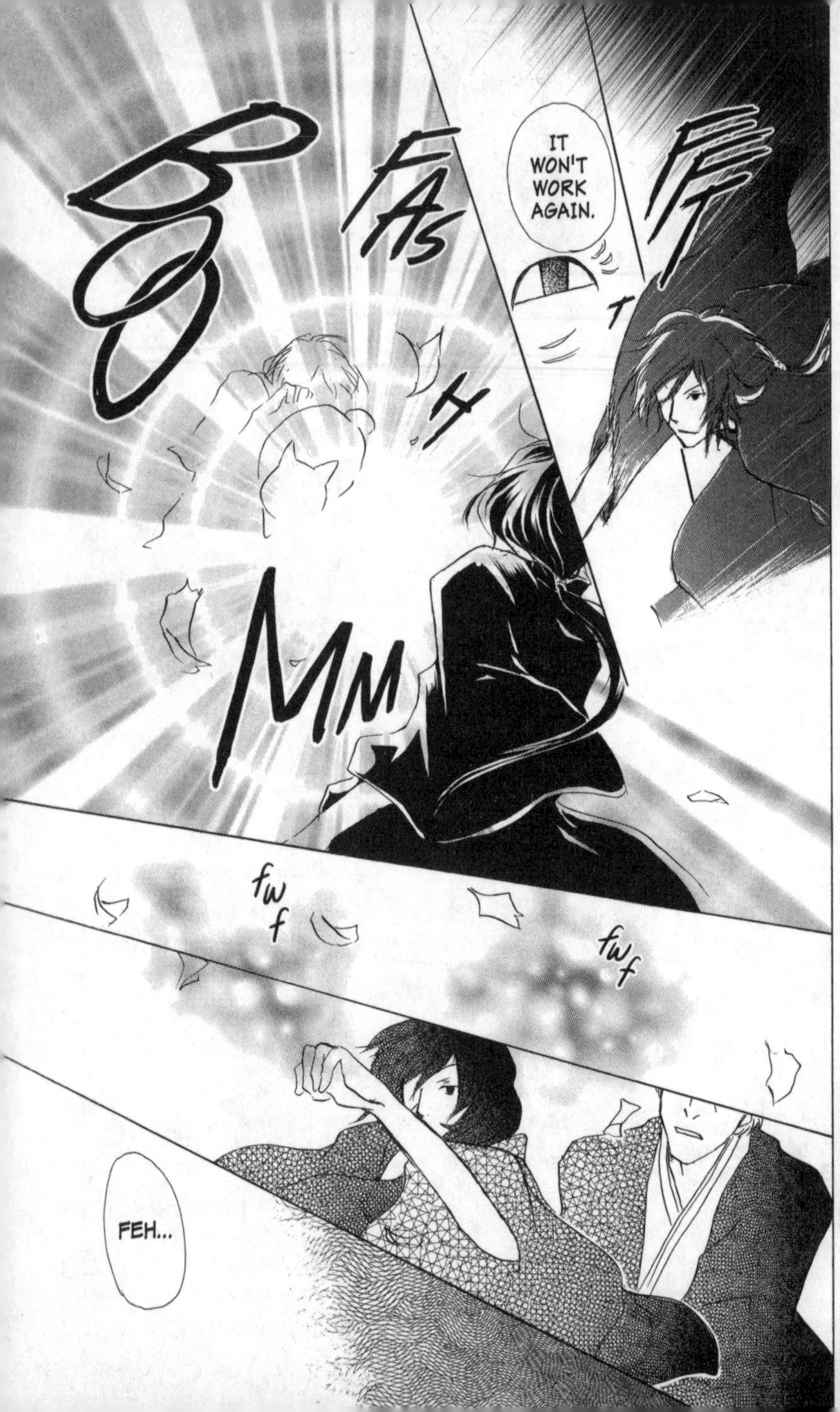
IT WON'T WORK AGAIN.
FFT
FASH
fwf
fwf
FEH...

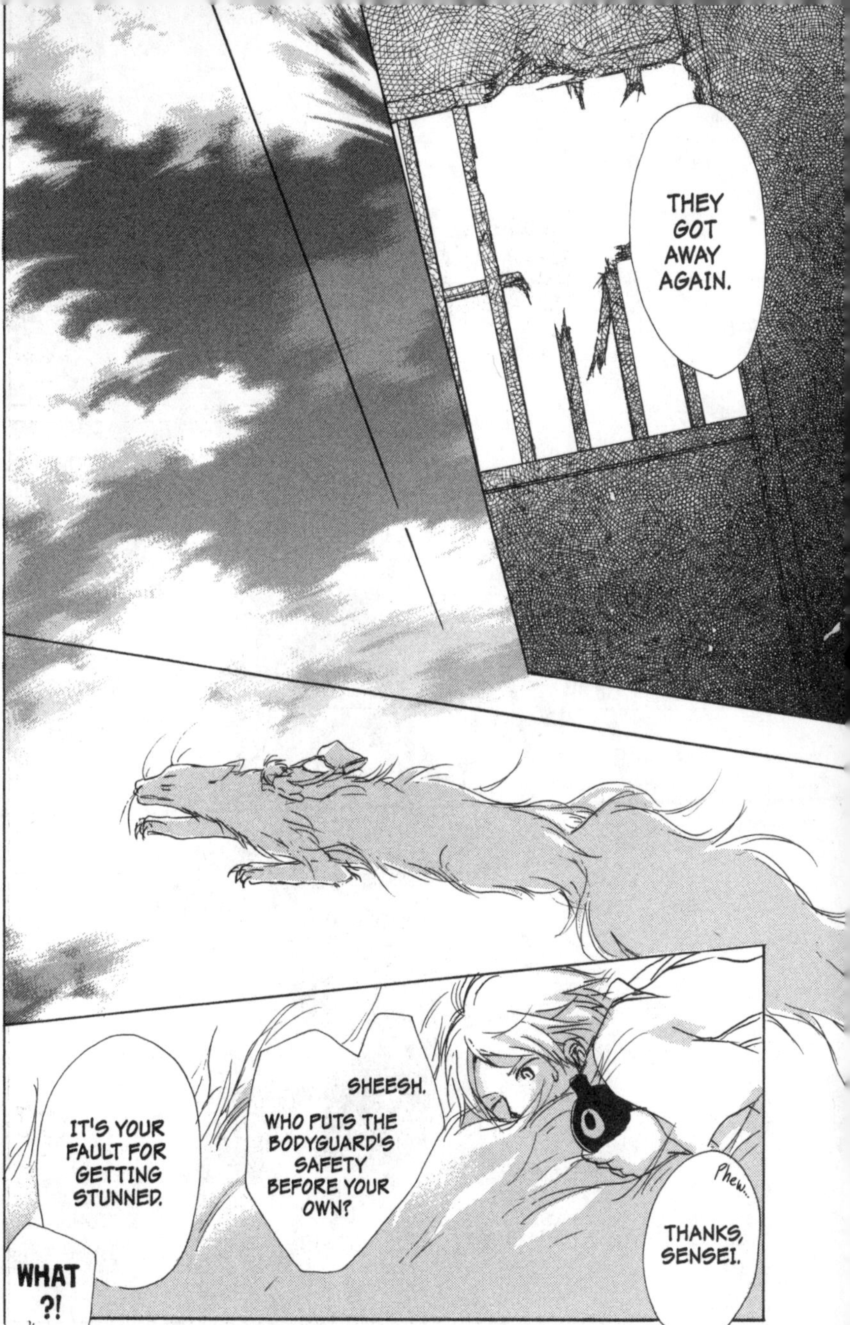
THEY GOT AWAY AGAIN.
Phew...
THANKS, SENSEI.
SHEESH.
WHO PUTS THE BODYGUARD'S SAFETY BEFORE YOUR OWN?
IT'S YOUR FAULT FOR GETTING STUNNED.
WHAT ?!

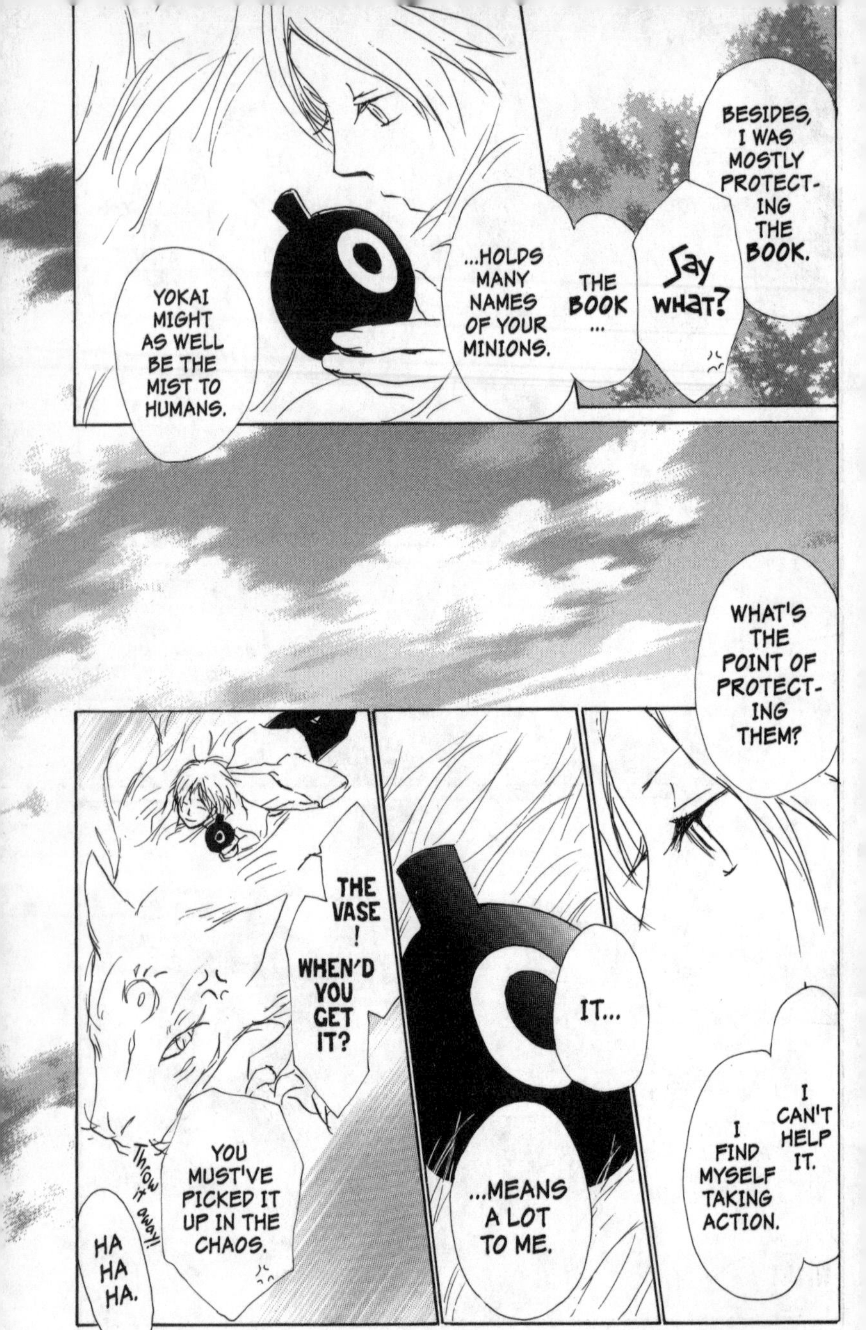
BESIDES, I WAS MOSTLY PROTECTING THE BOOK.
Say WHAT?
THE BOOK...
...HOLDS MANY NAMES OF YOUR MINIONS.
YOKAI MIGHT AS WELL BE THE MIST TO HUMANS.
WHAT'S THE POINT OF PROTECTING THEM?
I CAN'T HELP IT.
I FIND MYSELF TAKING ACTION.
IT...
...MEANS A LOT TO ME.
THE VASE! WHEN'D YOU GET IT?
YOU MUST'VE PICKED IT UP IN THE CHAOS.
Throw it away!
HA HA HA.

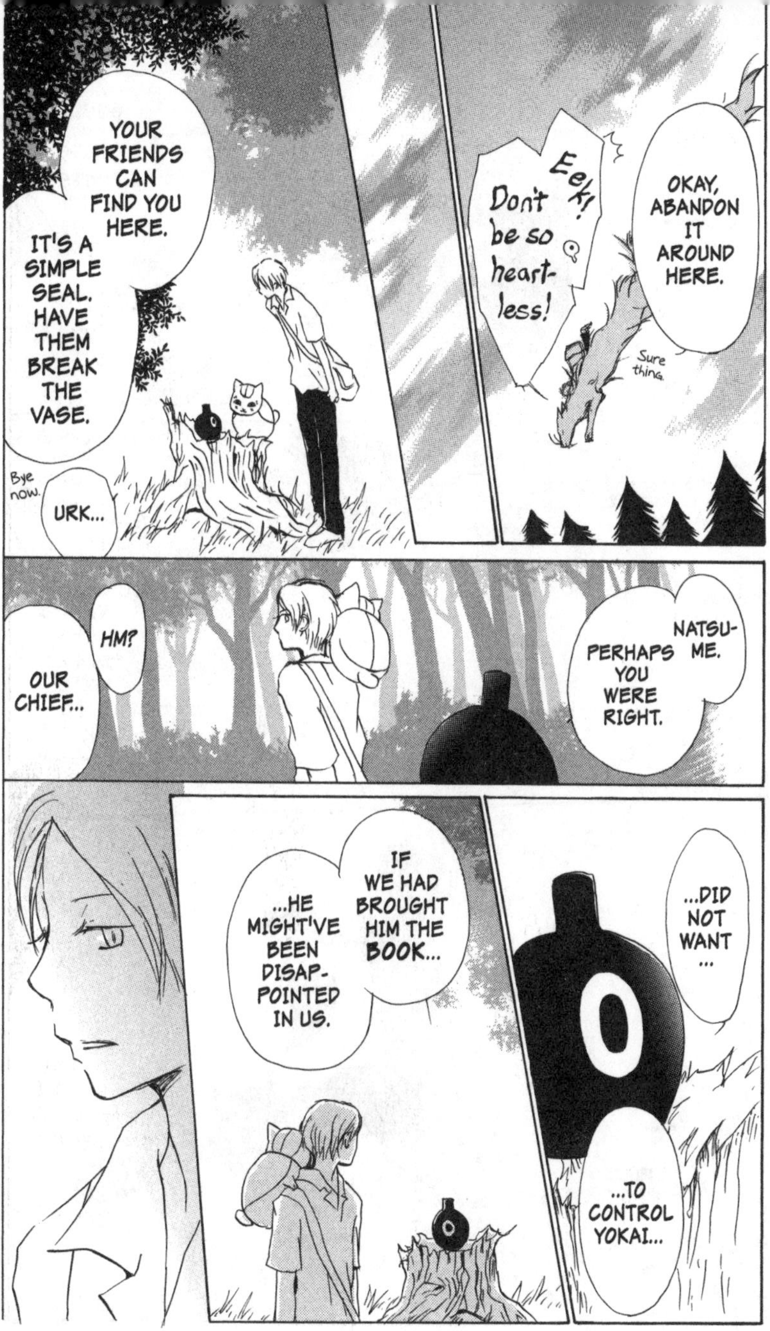
OKAY, ABANDON IT AROUND HERE.
Sure thing.
Eek! Don't be so heart-less!
YOUR FRIENDS CAN FIND YOU HERE.
IT'S A SIMPLE SEAL. HAVE THEM BREAK THE VASE.
Bye now.
URK...
NATSU-ME.
PERHAPS YOU WERE RIGHT.
HM?
OUR CHIEF...
...DID NOT WANT ...
...TO CONTROL YOKAI...
IF WE HAD BROUGHT HIM THE BOOK...
...HE MIGHT'VE BEEN DISAP-POINTED IN US.

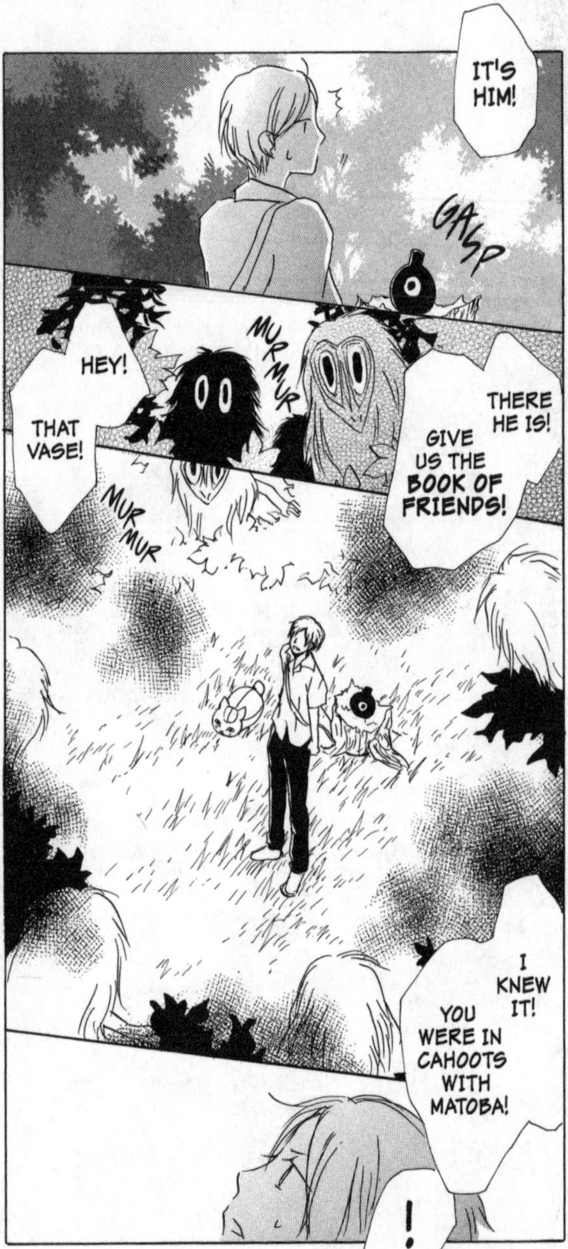
IT'S HIM!
GASP
THERE HE IS!
GIVE US THE BOOK OF FRIENDS!
MURMUR
HEY!
THAT VASE!
MURMUR
I KNEW IT!
YOU WERE IN CAHOOTS WITH MATOBA!
!

## 05

### ❋Letters

Thank you so much for the fan mail. I cherish and read every single one. I almost want to yell out loud, "What should I do with so much delight?!" They provide me with the driving force to keep going.

I apologize that I never have enough time to write replies.

I'll keep working hard to make manga that would convey my gratitude.

Thank you so much.

End of $\frac{1}{4}$ columns.

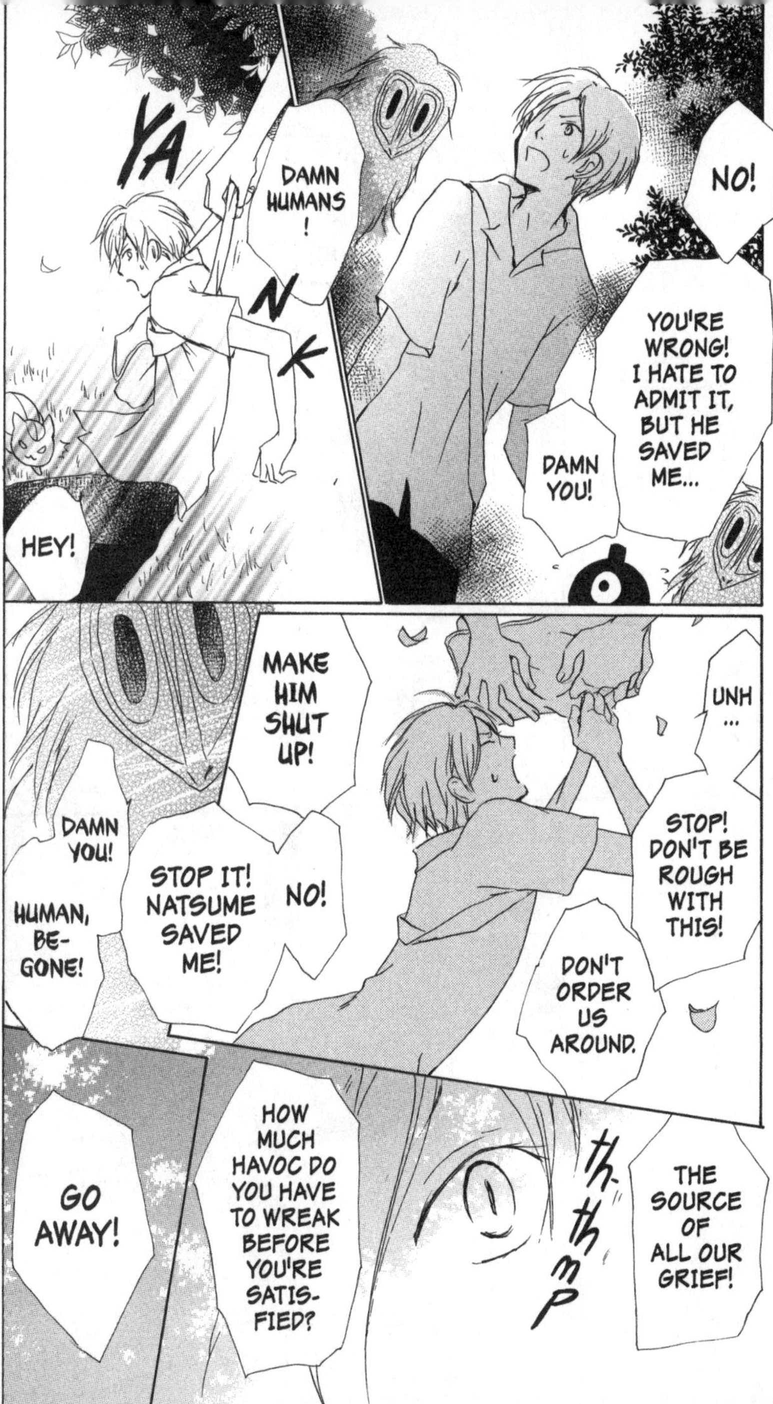
NO!
YOU'RE WRONG! I HATE TO ADMIT IT, BUT HE SAVED ME...
DAMN YOU!
DAMN HUMANS!
YANK
HEY!
UNH...
STOP! DON'T BE ROUGH WITH THIS!
DON'T ORDER US AROUND.
MAKE HIM SHUT UP!
NO!
STOP IT! NATSUME SAVED ME!
DAMN YOU!
HUMAN, BE-GONE!
THE SOURCE OF ALL OUR GRIEF!
th-thump
HOW MUCH HAVOC DO YOU HAVE TO WREAK BEFORE YOU'RE SATIS-FIED?
GO AWAY!

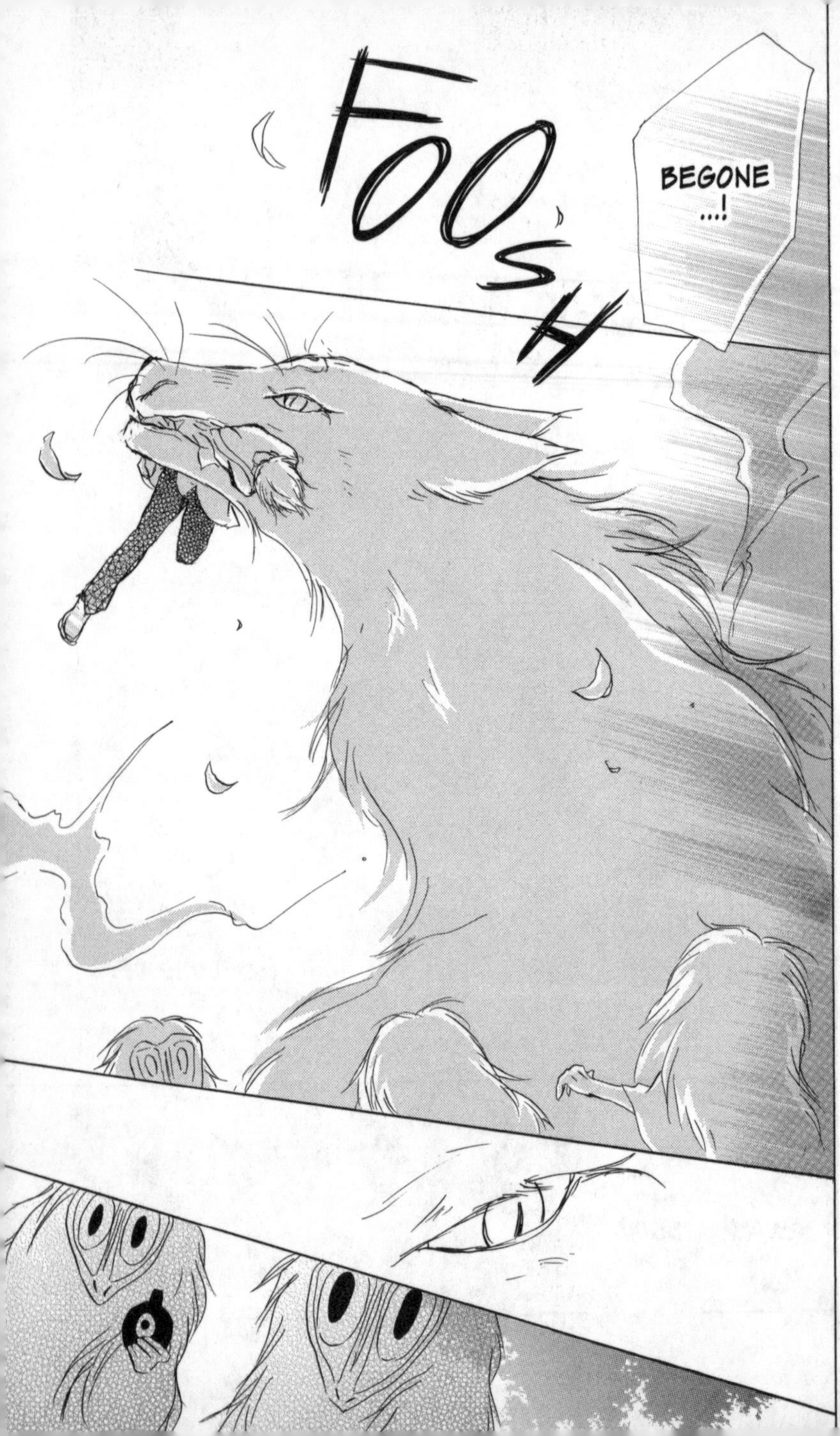
BEGONE
...!
FOOSH

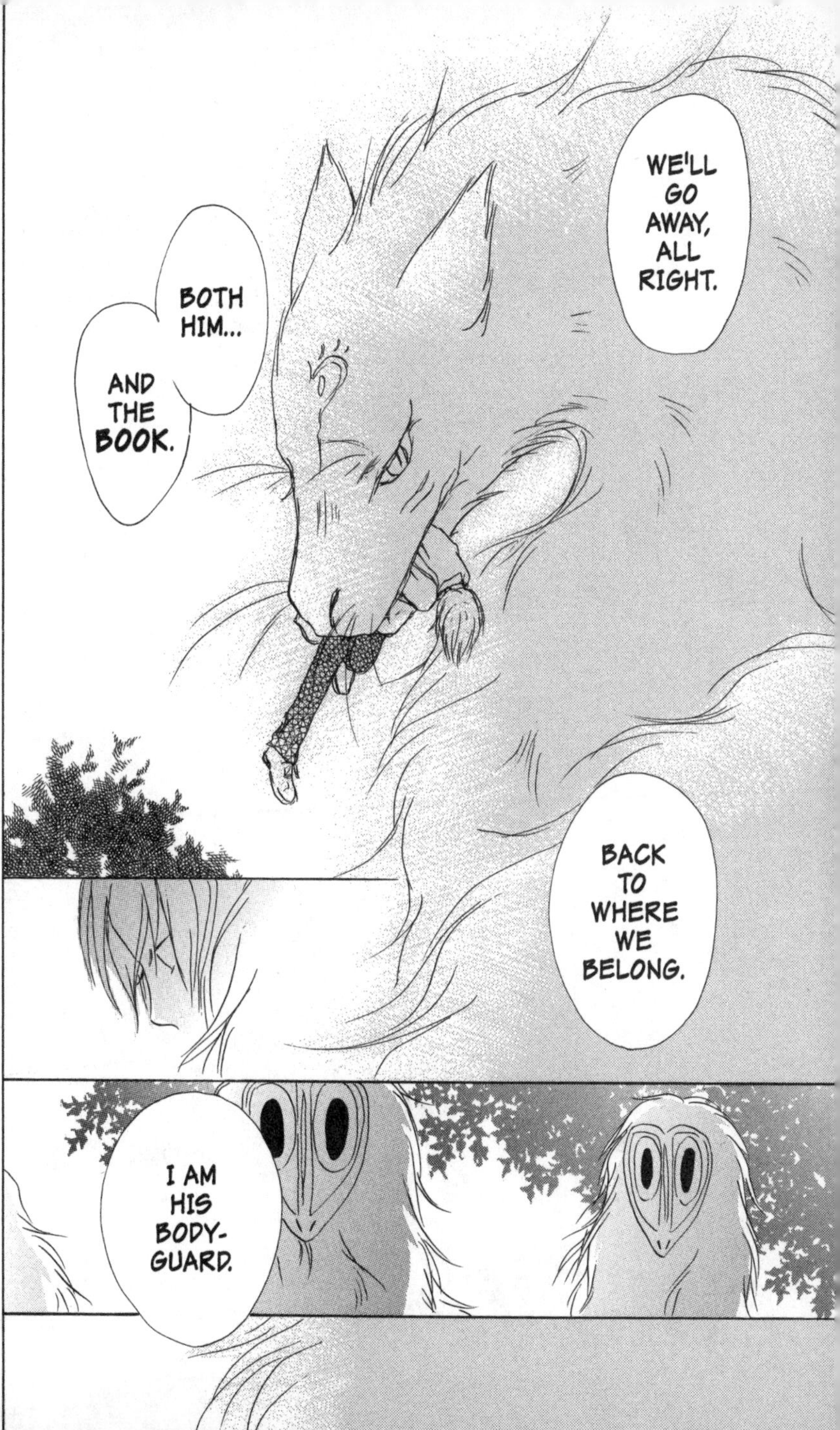
WE'LL GO AWAY, ALL RIGHT.
BOTH HIM...
AND THE BOOK.
BACK TO WHERE WE BELONG.
I AM HIS BODY-GUARD.

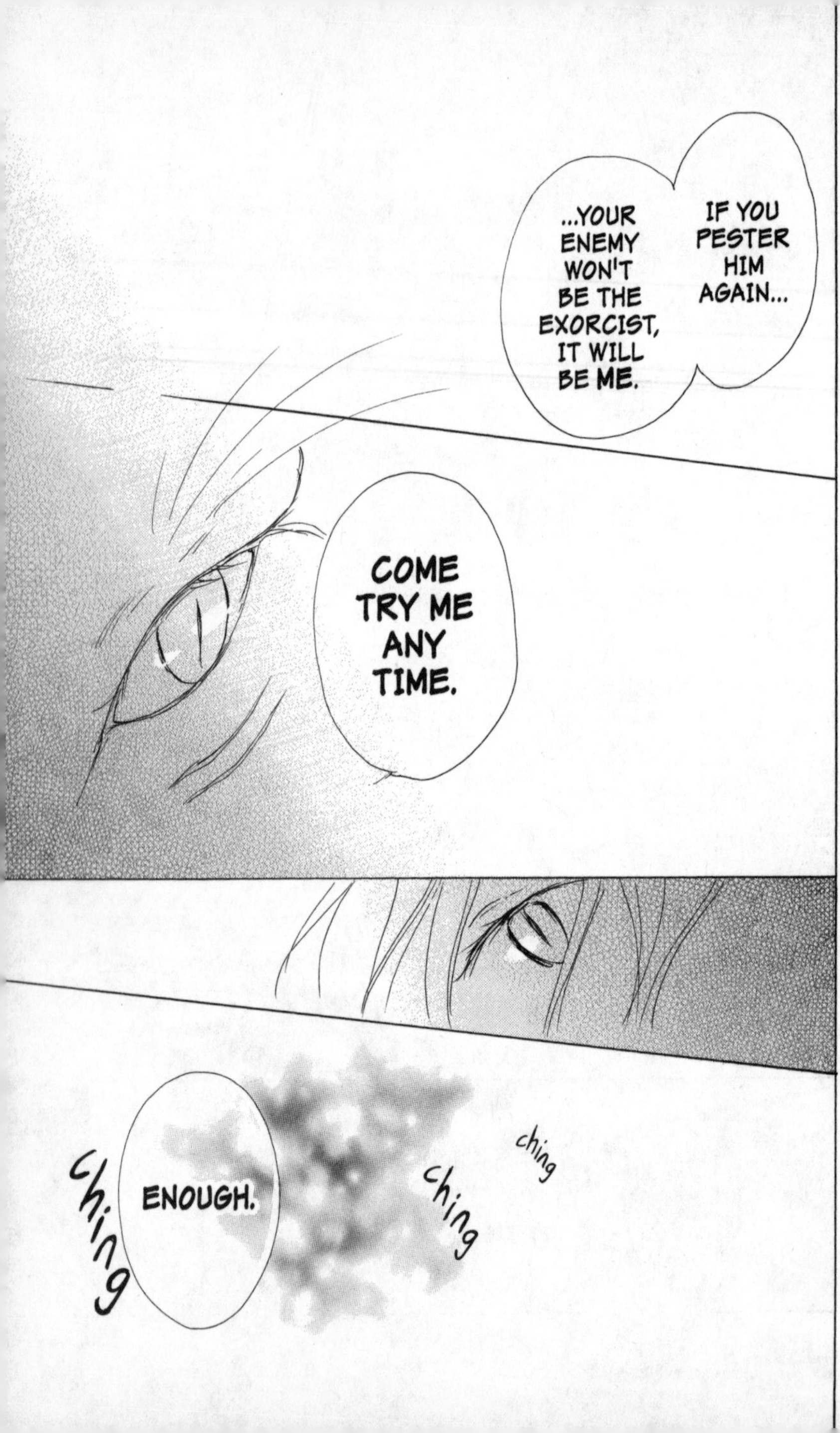
IF YOU PESTER HIM AGAIN...
...YOUR ENEMY WON'T BE THE EXORCIST, IT WILL BE ME.
COME TRY ME ANY TIME.
ching
ching
ENOUGH.
ching

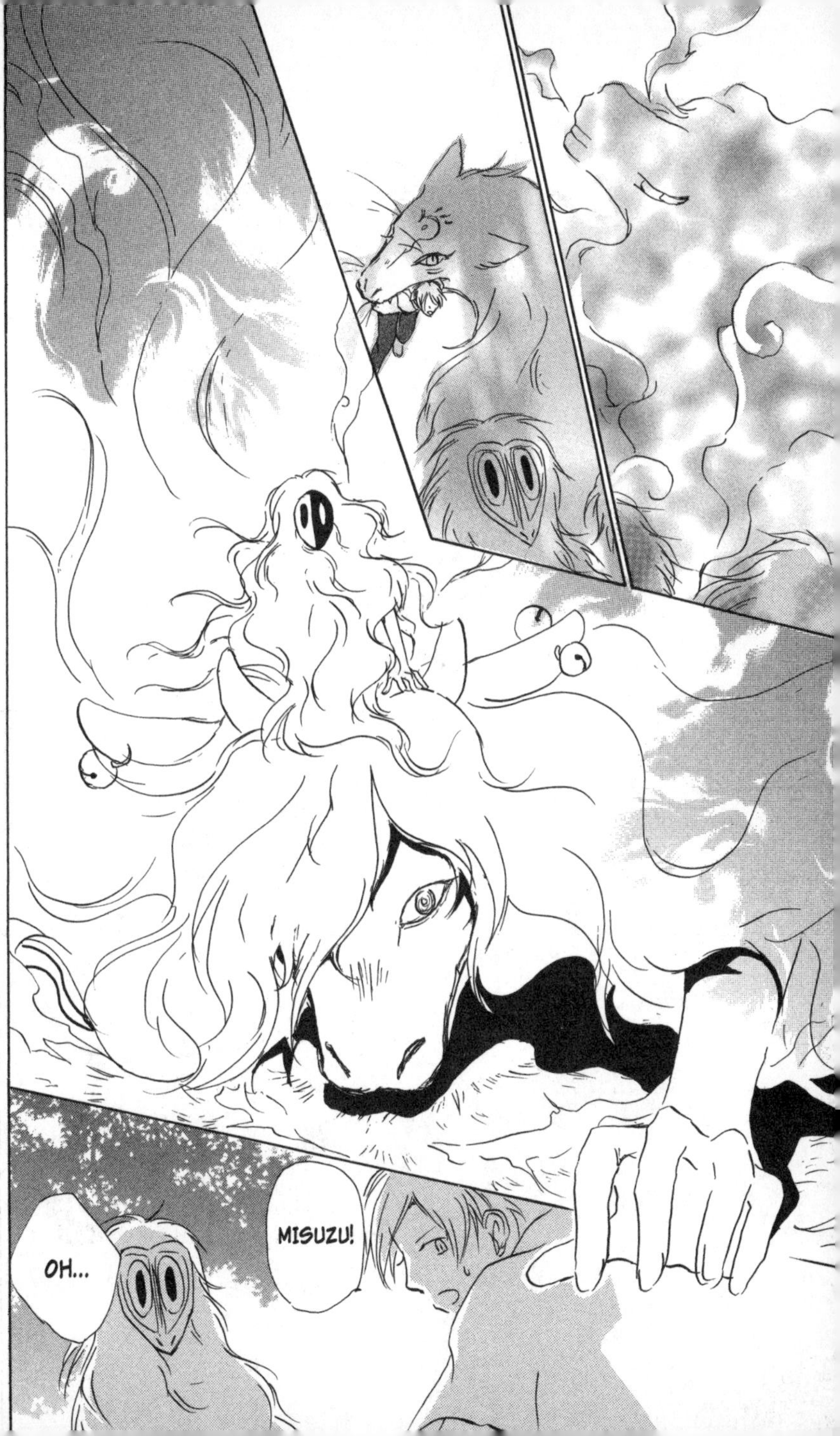
MISUZU!
OH...

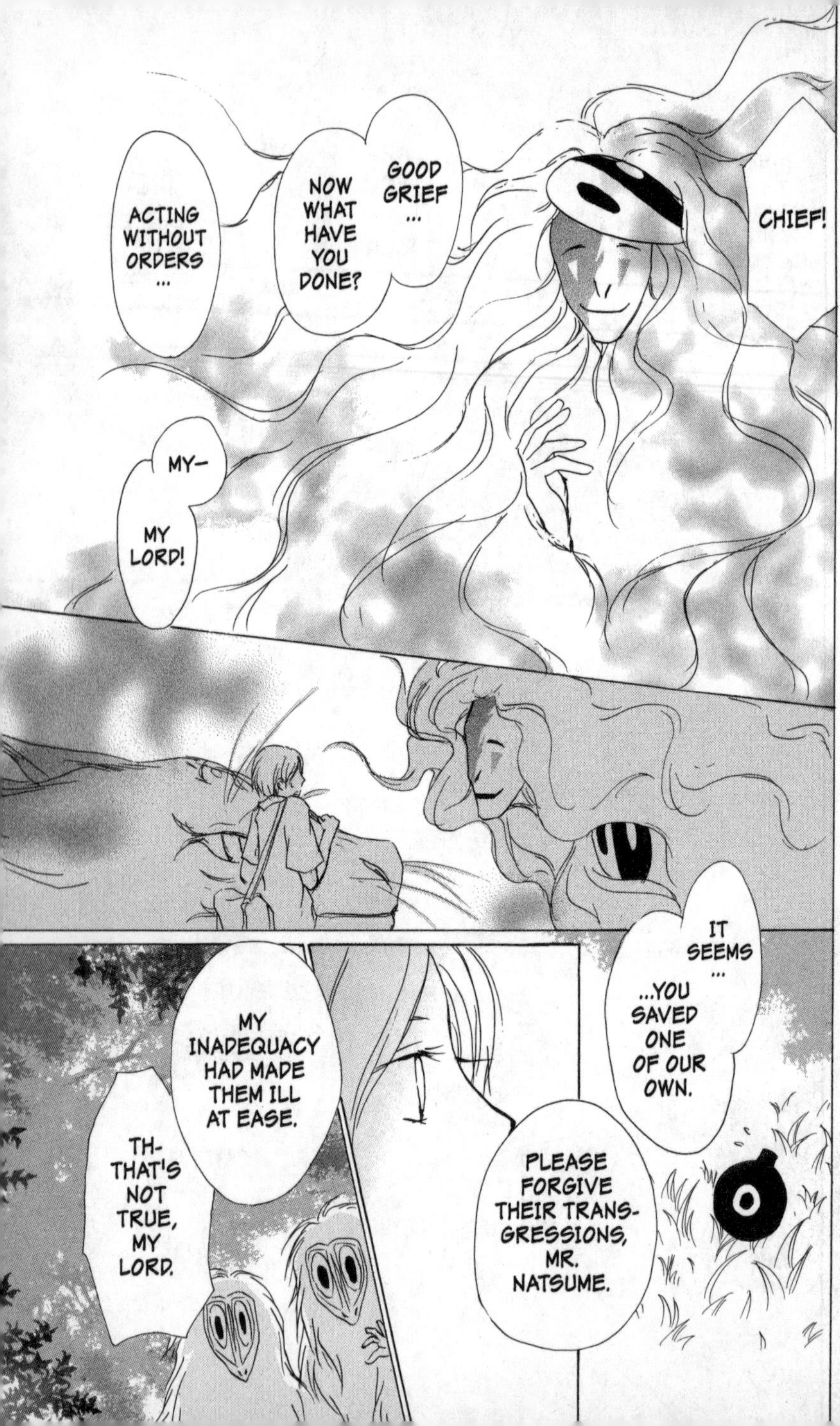
CHIEF!
GOOD GRIEF...
NOW WHAT HAVE YOU DONE?
ACTING WITHOUT ORDERS...
MY—
MY LORD!
IT SEEMS...
...YOU SAVED ONE OF OUR OWN.
PLEASE FORGIVE THEIR TRANSGRESSIONS, MR. NATSUME.
MY INADEQUACY HAD MADE THEM ILL AT EASE.
TH- THAT'S NOT TRUE, MY LORD.

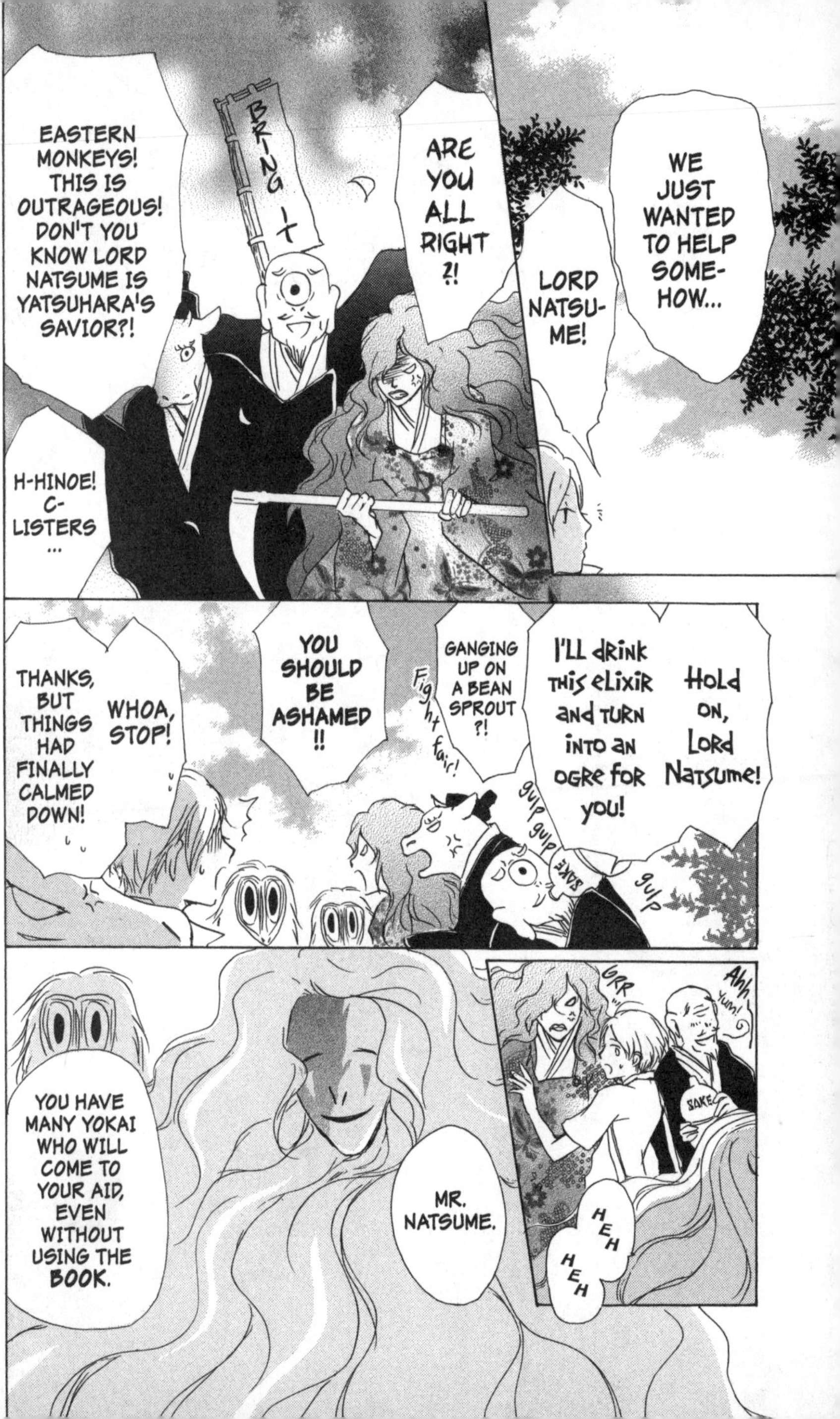
WE JUST WANTED TO HELP SOME-HOW...
LORD NATSU-ME!
ARE YOU ALL RIGHT ?!
BRING IT
EASTERN MONKEYS! THIS IS OUTRAGEOUS! DON'T YOU KNOW LORD NATSUME IS YATSUHARA'S SAVIOR?!
H-HINOE! C-LISTERS ...
Hold on, Lord Natsume!
I'll drink this elixir and turn into an ogre for you!
gulp gulp gulp
gulp
SAKE
GANGING UP ON A BEAN SPROUT ?!
Fight fair!
YOU SHOULD BE ASHAMED !!
WHOA, STOP!
THANKS, BUT THINGS HAD FINALLY CALMED DOWN!
Ahh yum!
GRR
SAKE
HEH HEH
MR. NATSUME.
YOU HAVE MANY YOKAI WHO WILL COME TO YOUR AID, EVEN WITHOUT USING THE BOOK.

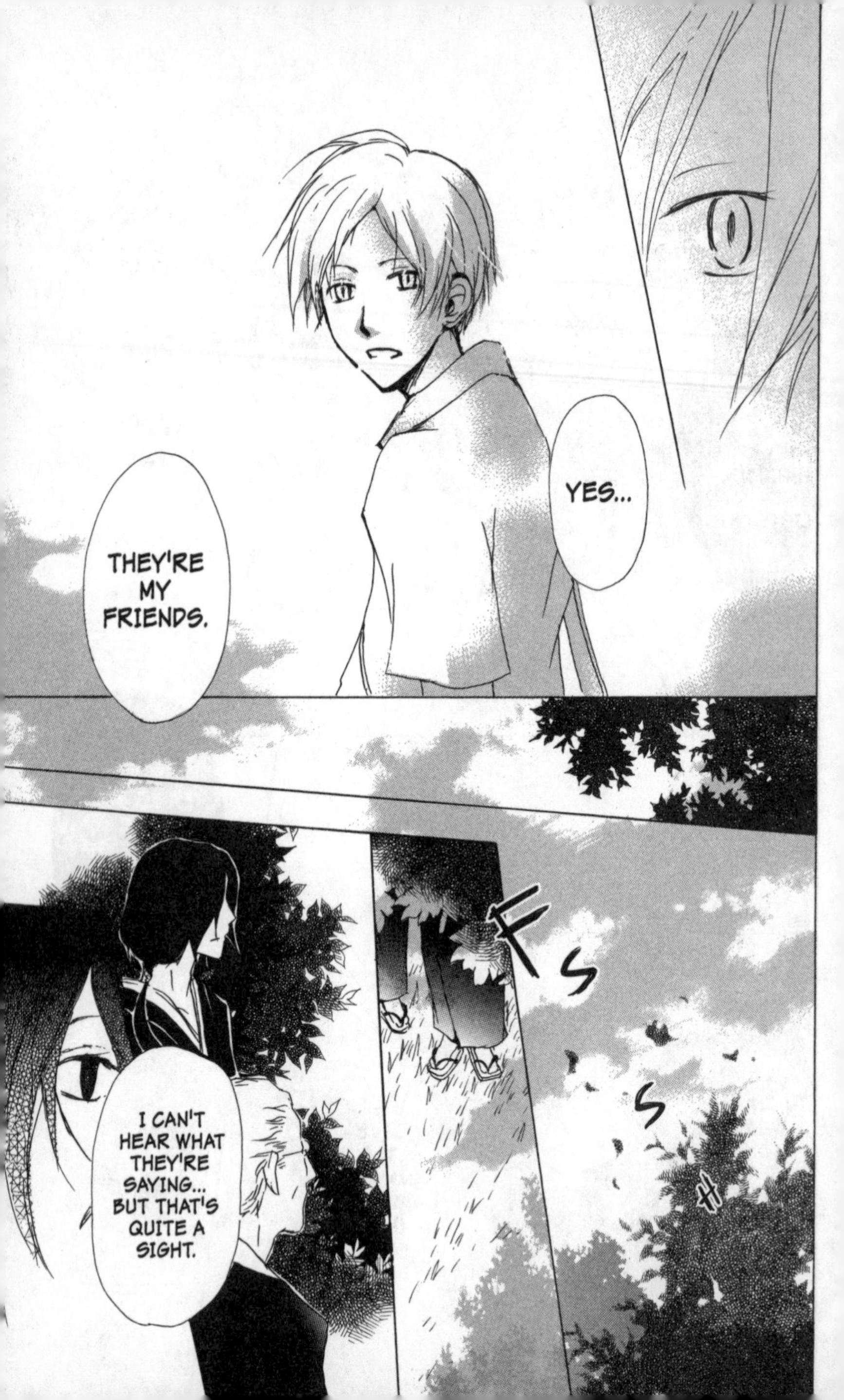
YES...
THEY'RE MY FRIENDS.
FSS
I CAN'T HEAR WHAT THEY'RE SAYING... BUT THAT'S QUITE A SIGHT.

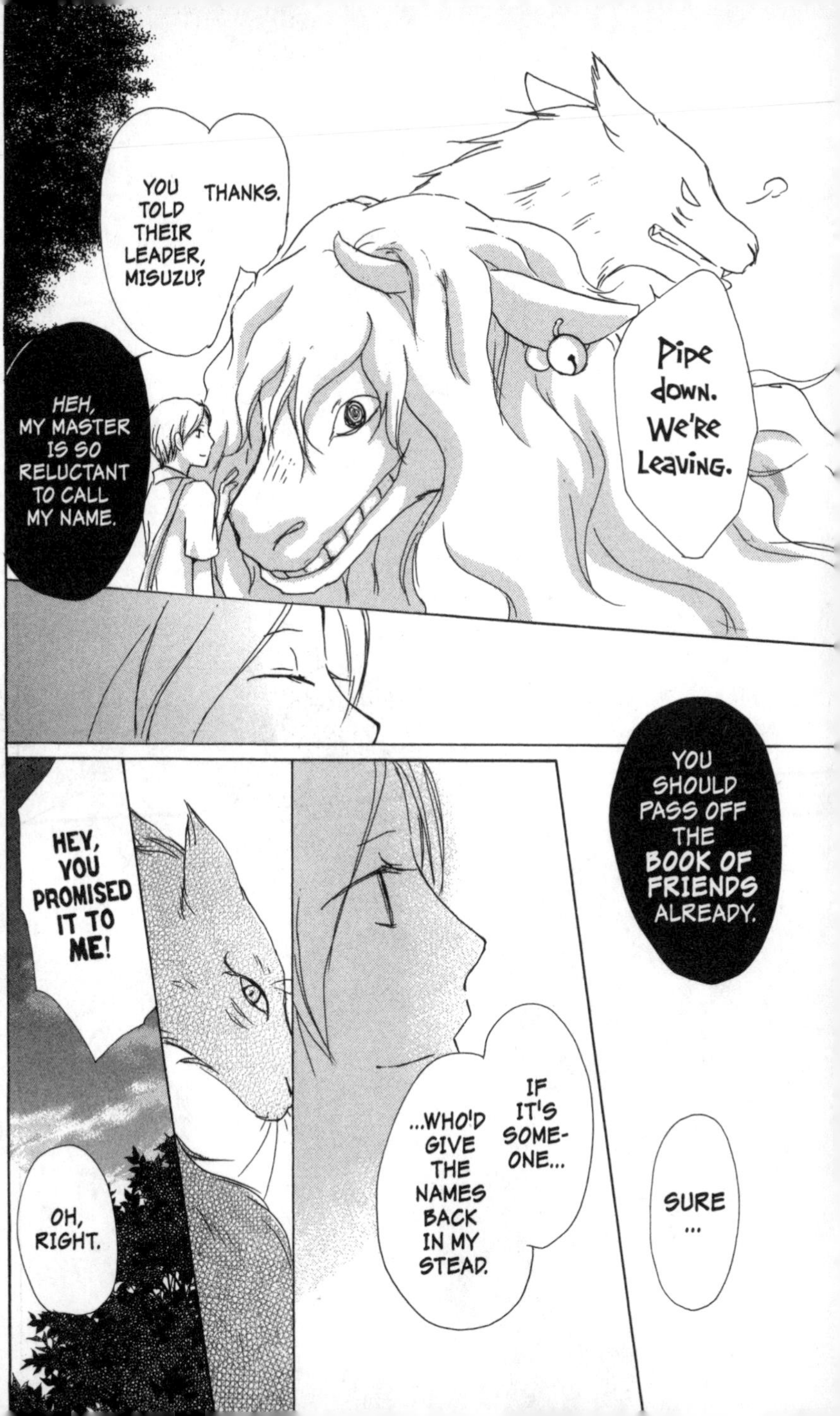
Pipe down. We're Leaving.
THANKS.
YOU TOLD THEIR LEADER, MISUZU?
HEH, MY MASTER IS SO RELUCTANT TO CALL MY NAME.
YOU SHOULD PASS OFF THE BOOK OF FRIENDS ALREADY.
SURE ...
IF IT'S SOME-ONE...
...WHO'D GIVE THE NAMES BACK IN MY STEAD.
HEY, YOU PROMISED IT TO ME!
OH, RIGHT.

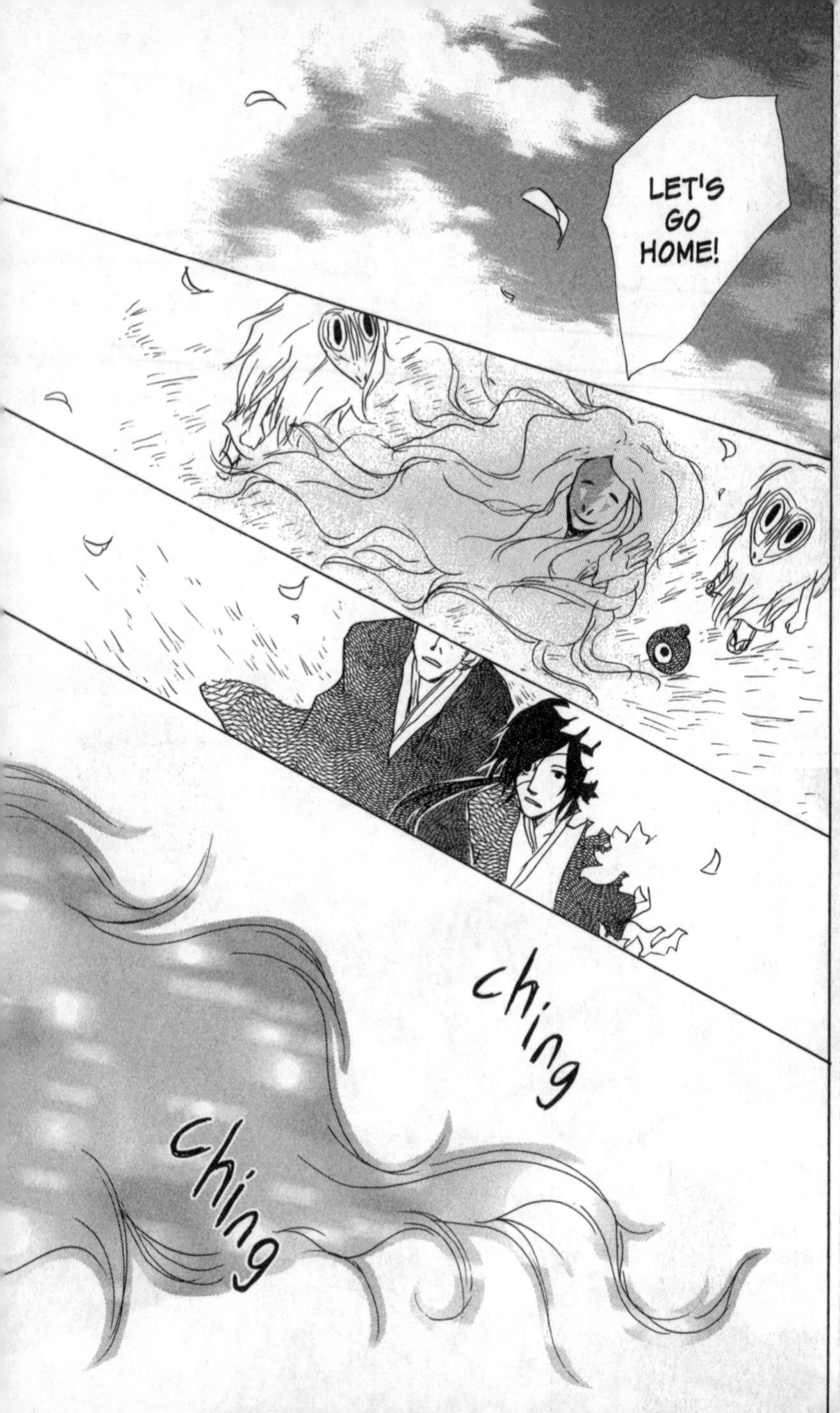
LET'S GO HOME!
ching
ching

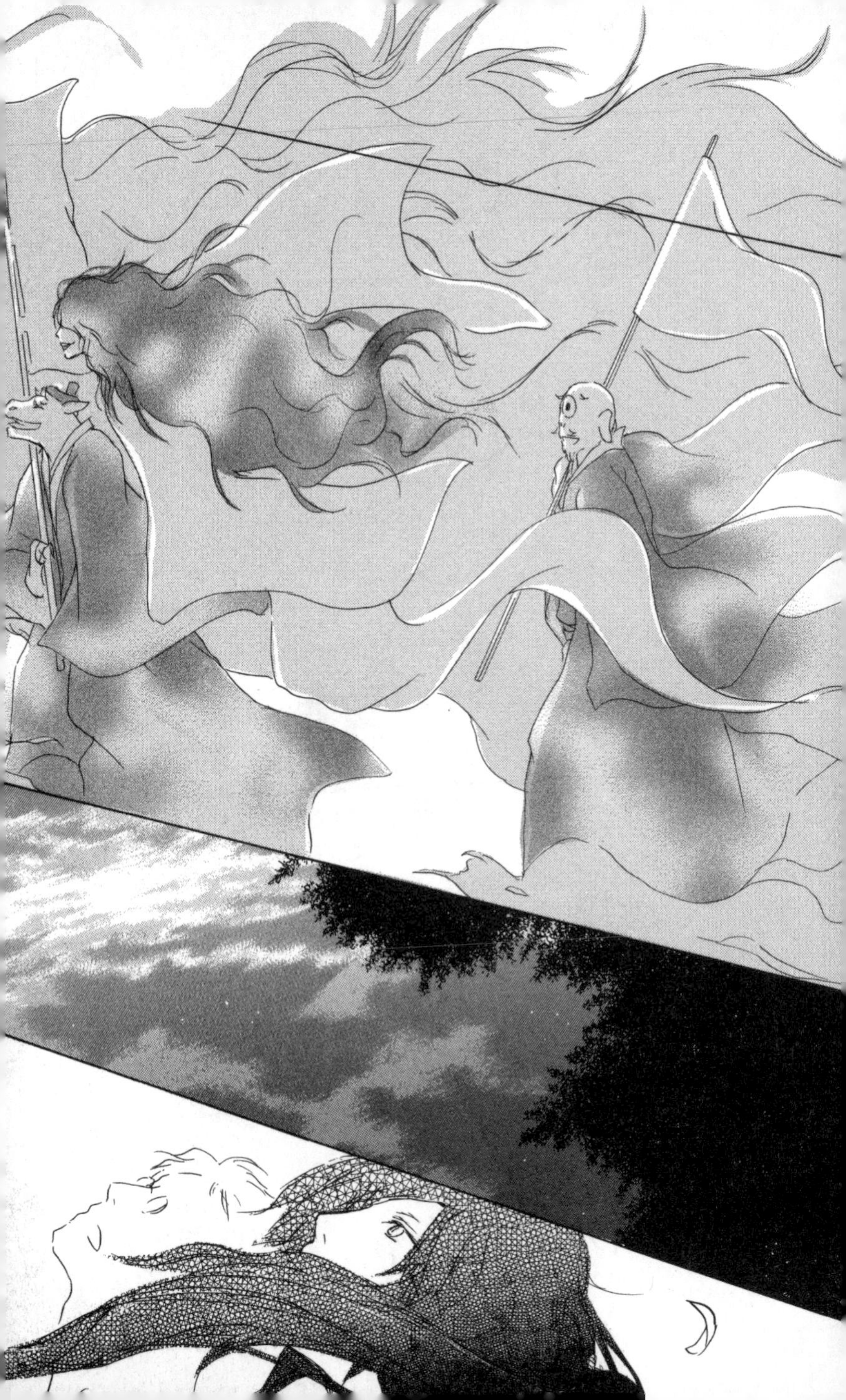

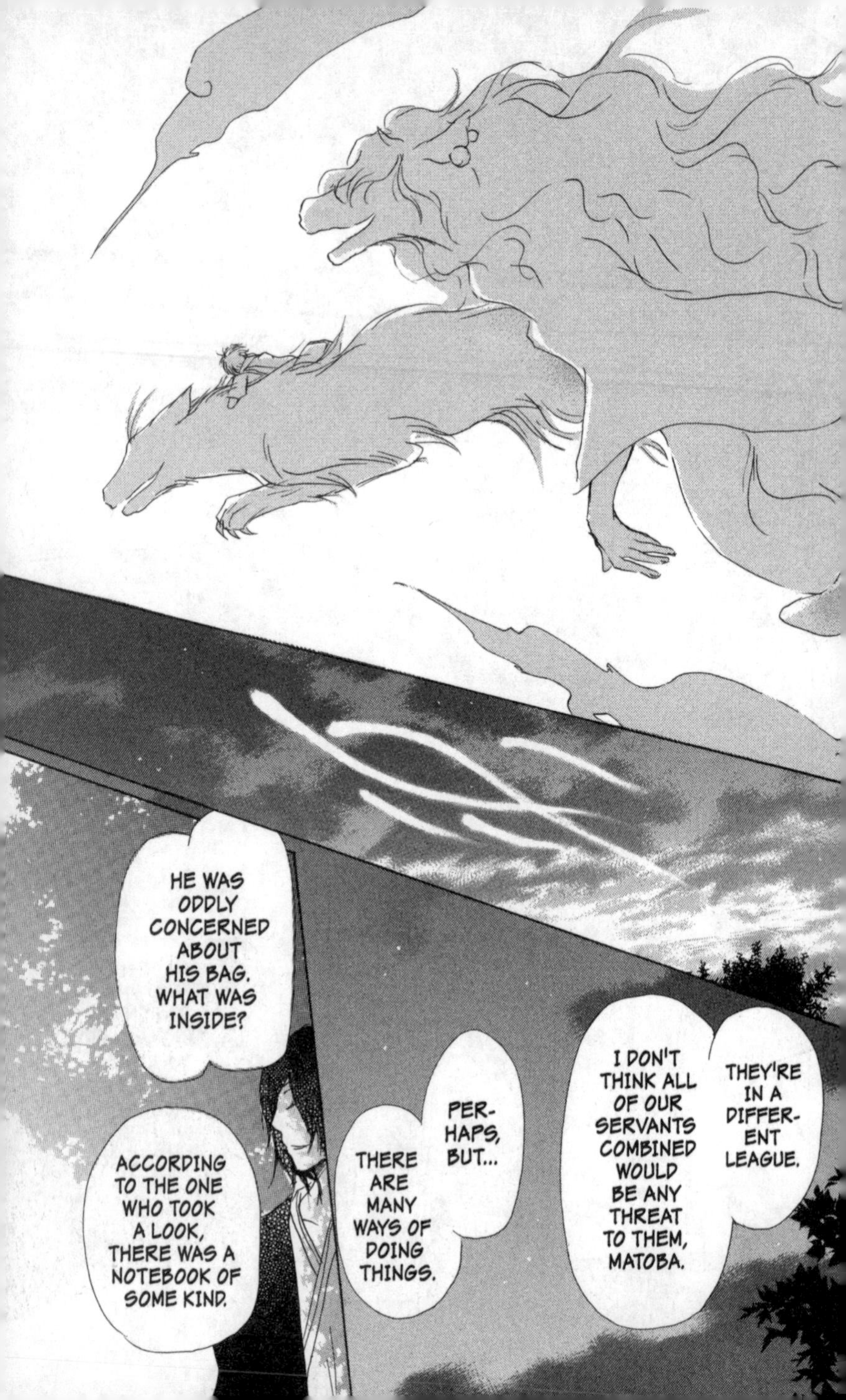
THEY'RE IN A DIFFER-ENT LEAGUE.
I DON'T THINK ALL OF OUR SERVANTS COMBINED WOULD BE ANY THREAT TO THEM, MATOBA.
PER-HAPS, BUT...
THERE ARE MANY WAYS OF DOING THINGS.
HE WAS ODDLY CONCERNED ABOUT HIS BAG. WHAT WAS INSIDE?
ACCORDING TO THE ONE WHO TOOK A LOOK, THERE WAS A NOTEBOOK OF SOME KIND.

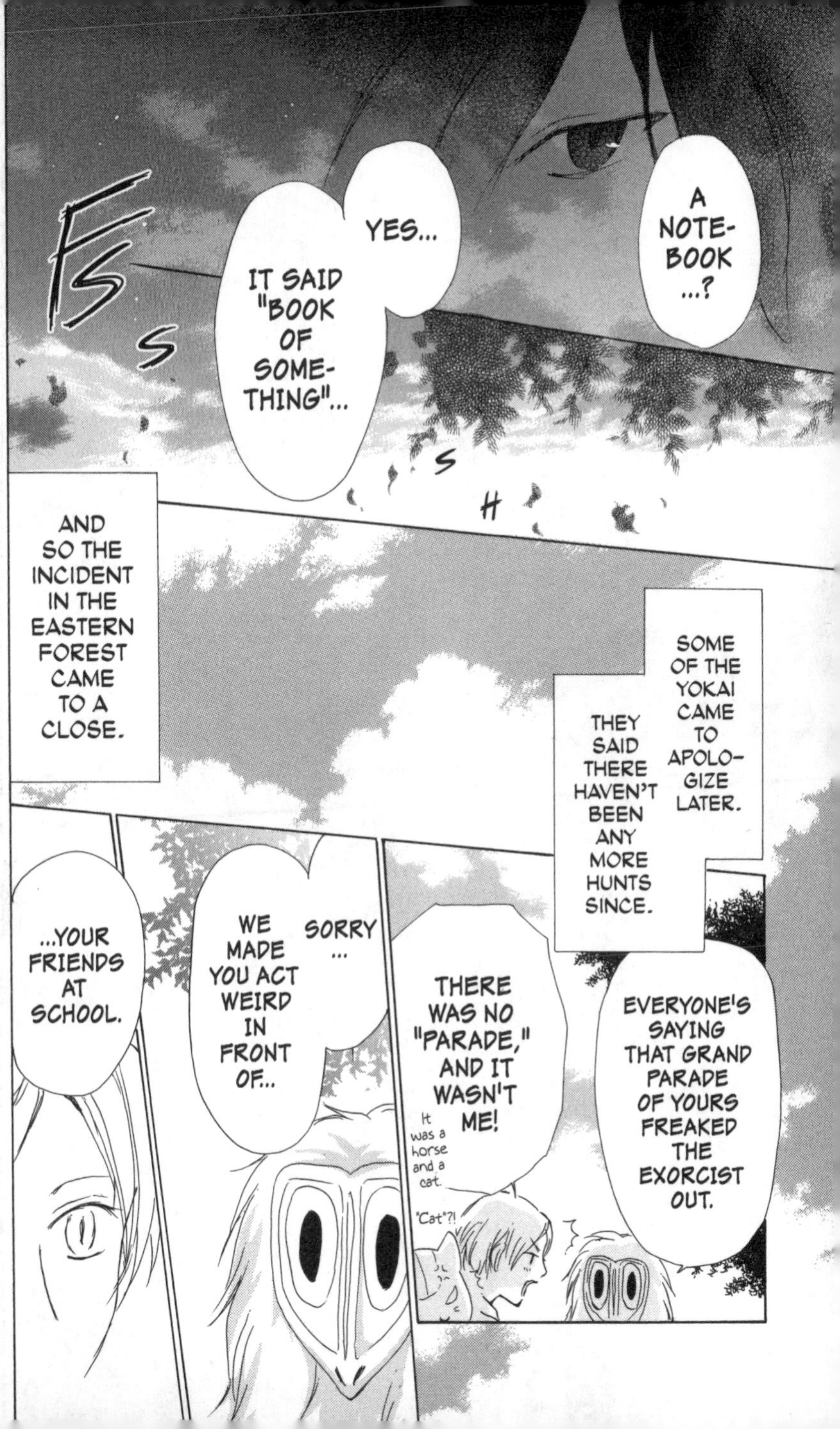

A NOTE-BOOK...?
YES...
IT SAID "BOOK OF SOME-THING"...
FSSSH
AND SO THE INCIDENT IN THE EASTERN FOREST CAME TO A CLOSE.
SOME OF THE YOKAI CAME TO APOLO-GIZE LATER.
THEY SAID THERE HAVEN'T BEEN ANY MORE HUNTS SINCE.
EVERYONE'S SAYING THAT GRAND PARADE OF YOURS FREAKED THE EXORCIST OUT.
THERE WAS NO "PARADE," AND IT WASN'T ME!
It was a horse and a cat.
"Cat"?!
SORRY...
WE MADE YOU ACT WEIRD IN FRONT OF...
...YOUR FRIENDS AT SCHOOL.

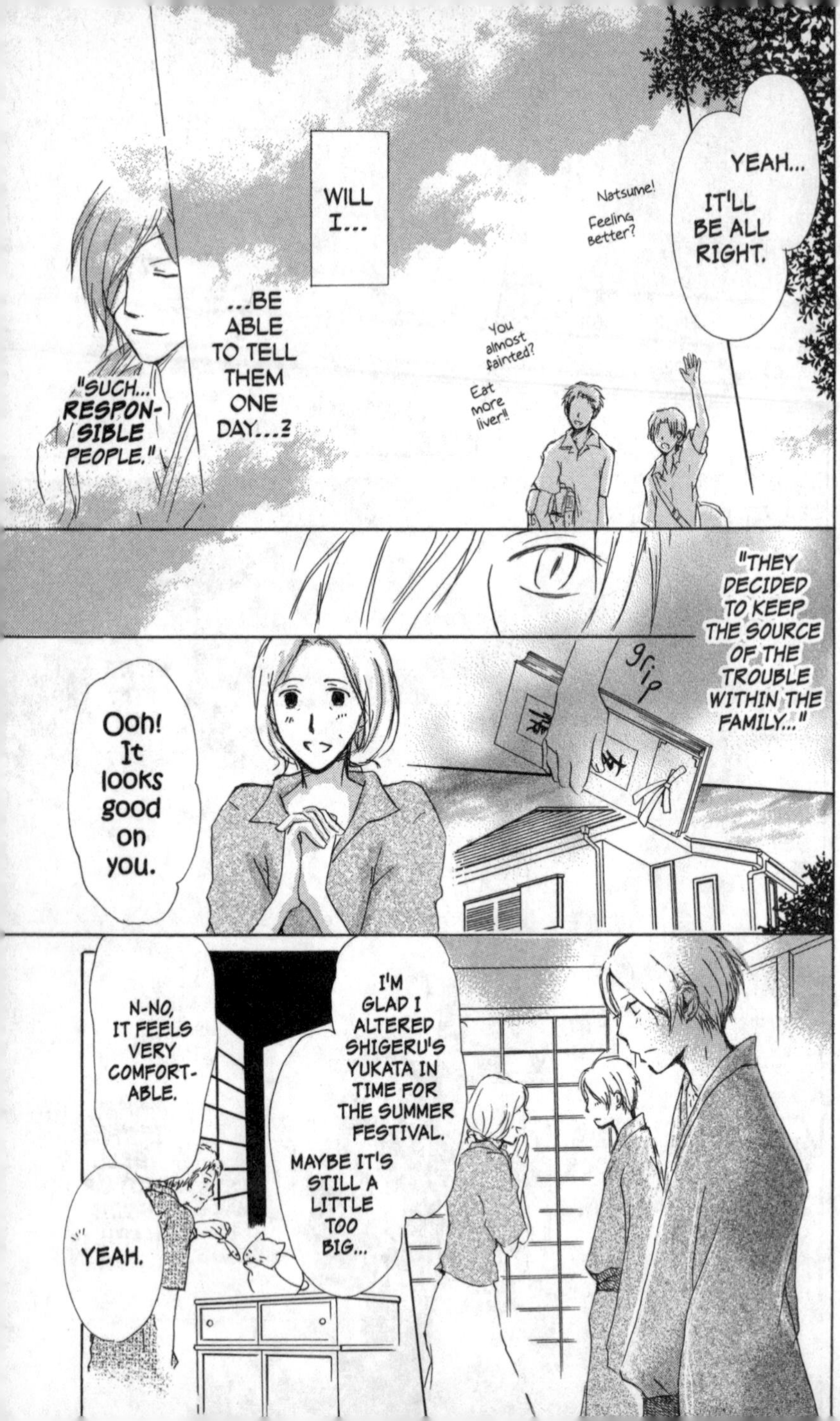

YEAH... IT'LL BE ALL RIGHT.
Natsume!
Feeling better?
You almost fainted?
Eat more liver!!
WILL I...
...BE ABLE TO TELL THEM ONE DAY...?
"SUCH... RESPONSIBLE PEOPLE."
"THEY DECIDED TO KEEP THE SOURCE OF THE TROUBLE WITHIN THE FAMILY..."
grip
Ooh! It looks good on you.
I'M GLAD I ALTERED SHIGERU'S YUKATA IN TIME FOR THE SUMMER FESTIVAL.
MAYBE IT'S STILL A LITTLE TOO BIG...
N-NO, IT FEELS VERY COMFORTABLE.
YEAH.

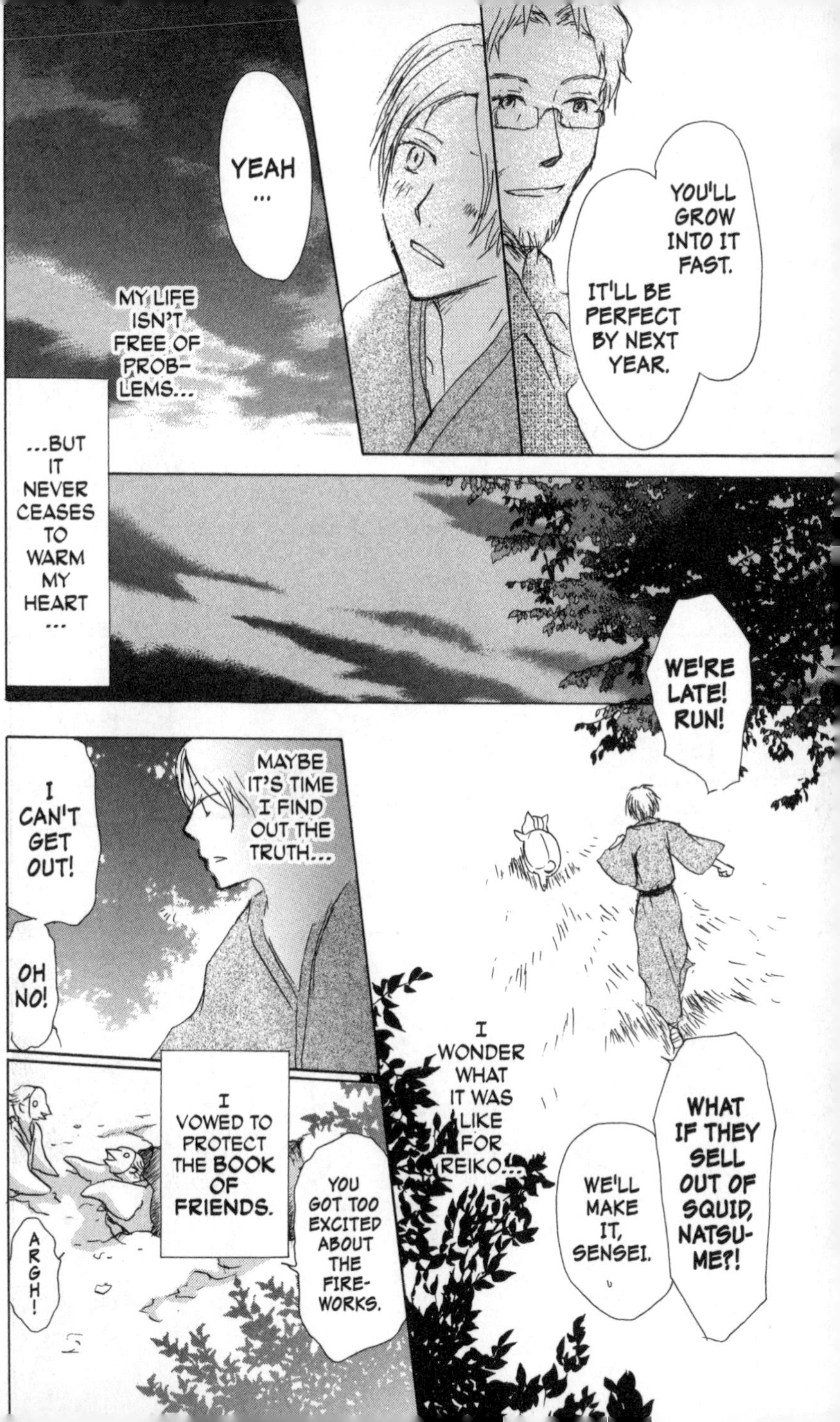
YOU'LL GROW INTO IT FAST. IT'LL BE PERFECT BY NEXT YEAR.
YEAH...
MY LIFE ISN'T FREE OF PROB-LEMS...
...BUT IT NEVER CEASES TO WARM MY HEART...
WE'RE LATE! RUN!
WHAT IF THEY SELL OUT OF SQUID, NATSU-ME?!
WE'LL MAKE IT, SENSEI.
I WONDER WHAT IT WAS LIKE FOR REIKO...
MAYBE IT'S TIME I FIND OUT THE TRUTH...
I CAN'T GET OUT!
OH NO!
I VOWED TO PROTECT THE BOOK OF FRIENDS.
YOU GOT TOO EXCITED ABOUT THE FIRE-WORKS.
ARGH!

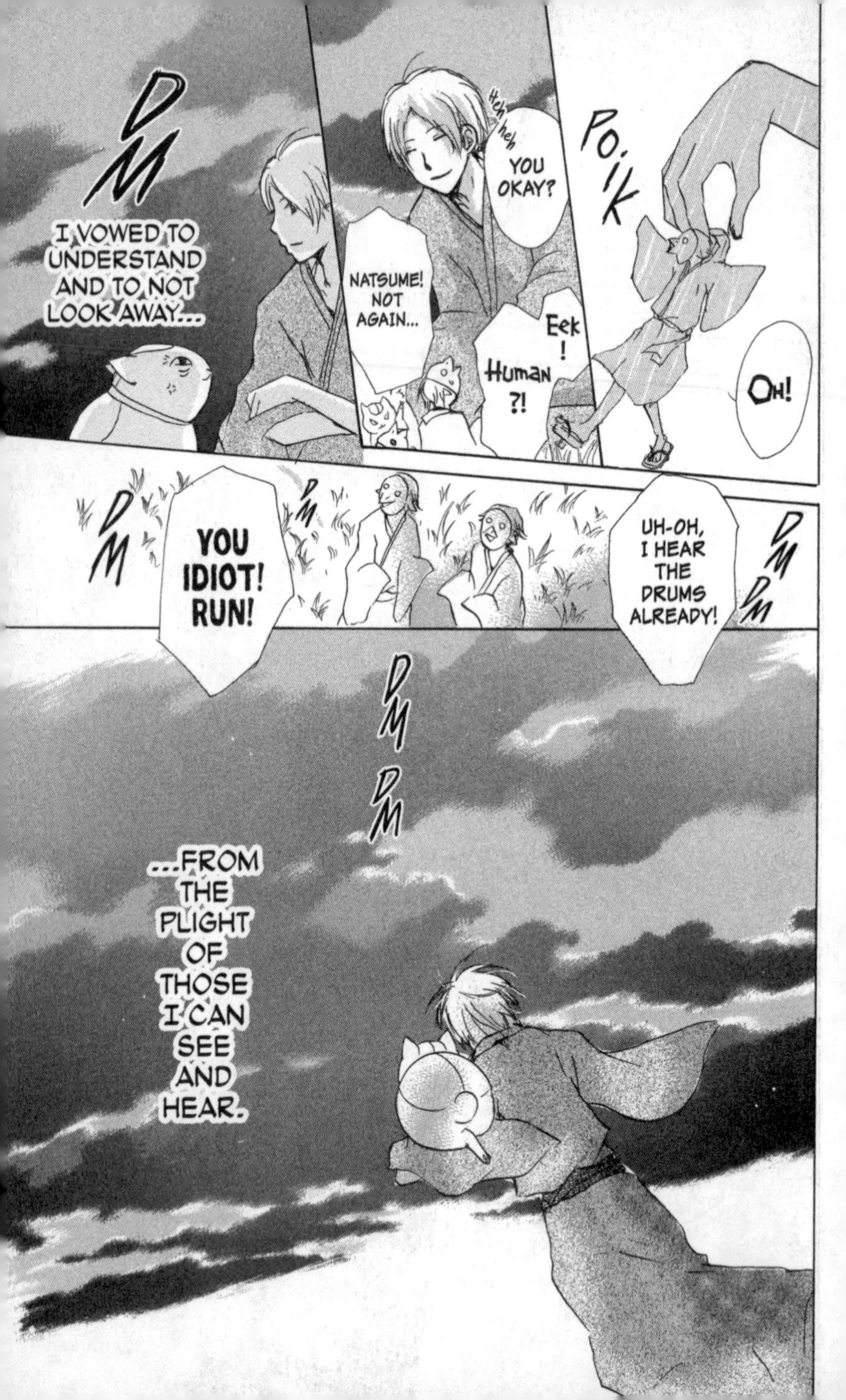
POIK
OH!
Heh heh
YOU OKAY?
NATSUME! NOT AGAIN...
Eek! Human?!
DM
I VOWED TO UNDERSTAND AND TO NOT LOOK AWAY...
DM DM
UH-OH, I HEAR THE DRUMS ALREADY!
DM
YOU IDIOT! RUN!
DM
DM DM
...FROM THE PLIGHT OF THOSE I CAN SEE AND HEAR.

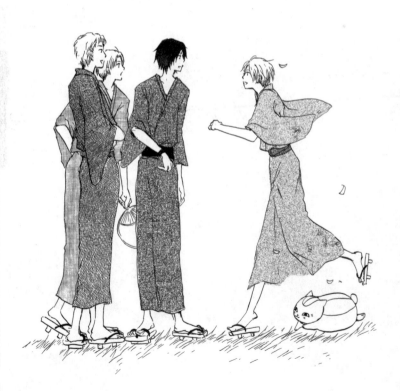

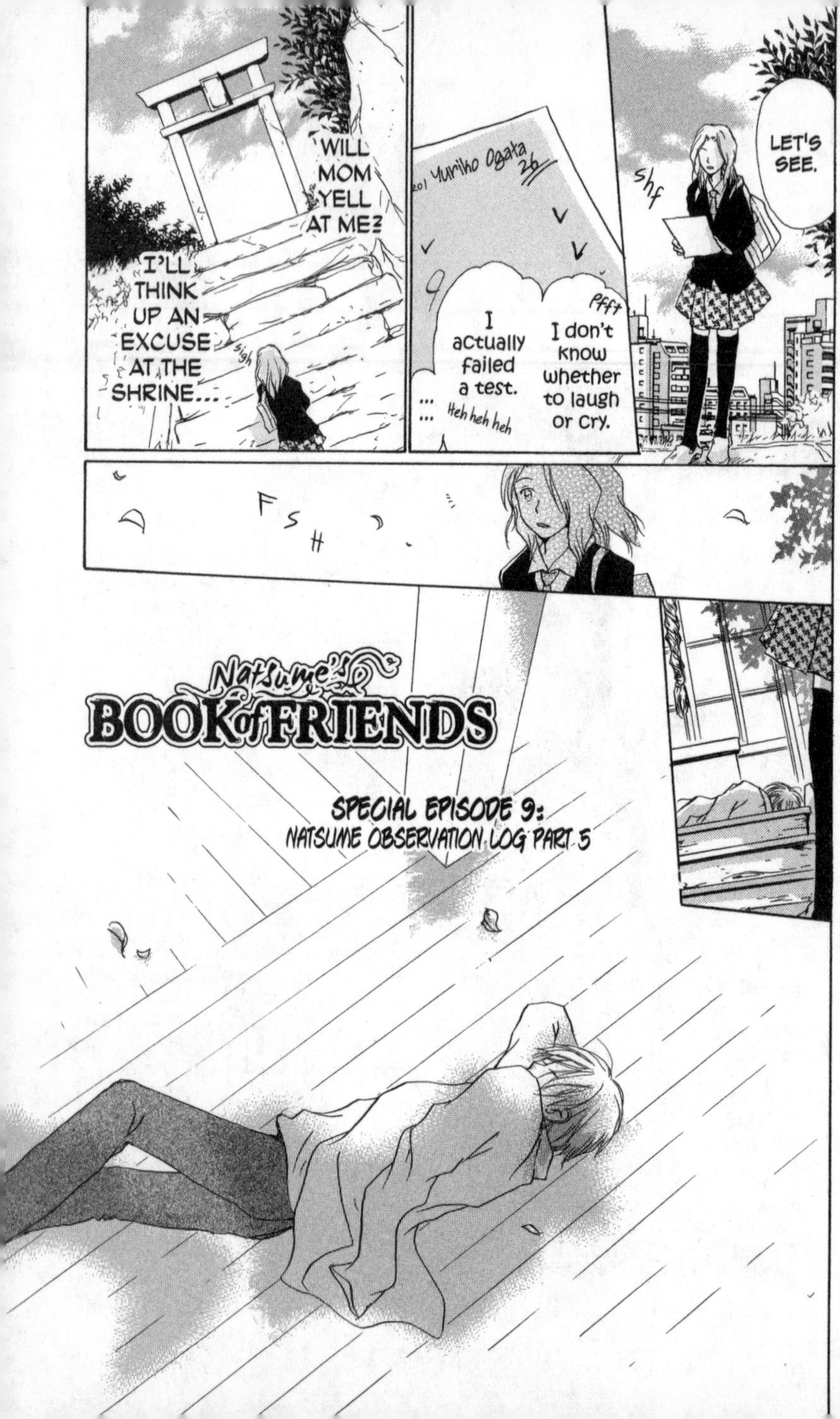
LET'S SEE.
shf
201 Yuriko Ogata 26
Pfft I don't know whether to laugh or cry.
I actually failed a test.
... ... Heh heh heh
WILL MOM YELL AT ME?
I'LL THINK UP AN EXCUSE AT THE SHRINE...
sigh
FSH
Natsume's BOOK of FRIENDS
SPECIAL EPISODE 9: NATSUME OBSERVATION LOG PART 5

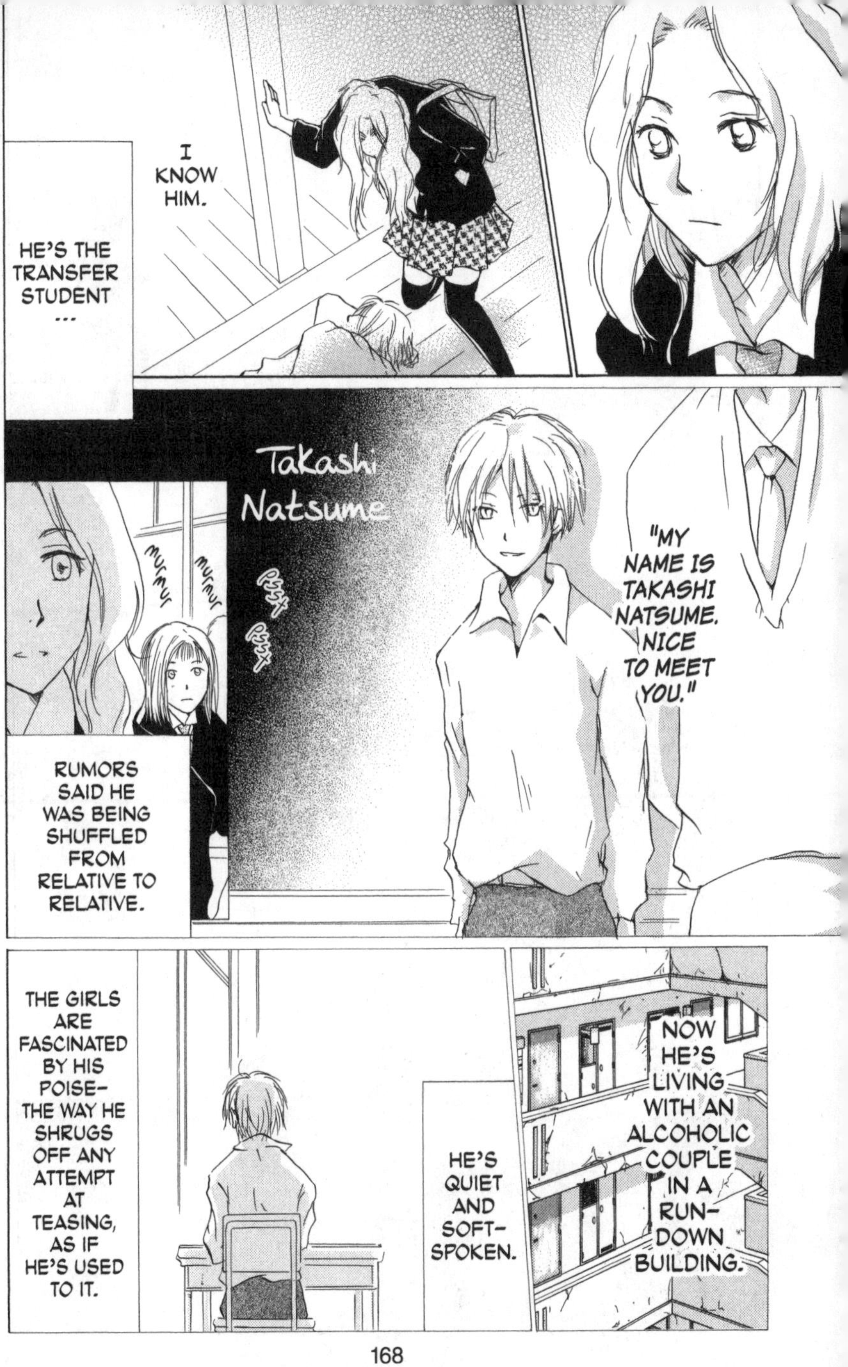
I KNOW HIM.
HE'S THE TRANSFER STUDENT ...
"MY NAME IS TAKASHI NATSUME. NICE TO MEET YOU."
Takashi Natsume
MURMUR
MURMUR
PSST PSST
RUMORS SAID HE WAS BEING SHUFFLED FROM RELATIVE TO RELATIVE.
NOW HE'S LIVING WITH AN ALCOHOLIC COUPLE IN A RUN-DOWN BUILDING.
HE'S QUIET AND SOFT-SPOKEN.
THE GIRLS ARE FASCINATED BY HIS POISE—THE WAY HE SHRUGS OFF ANY ATTEMPT AT TEASING, AS IF HE'S USED TO IT.

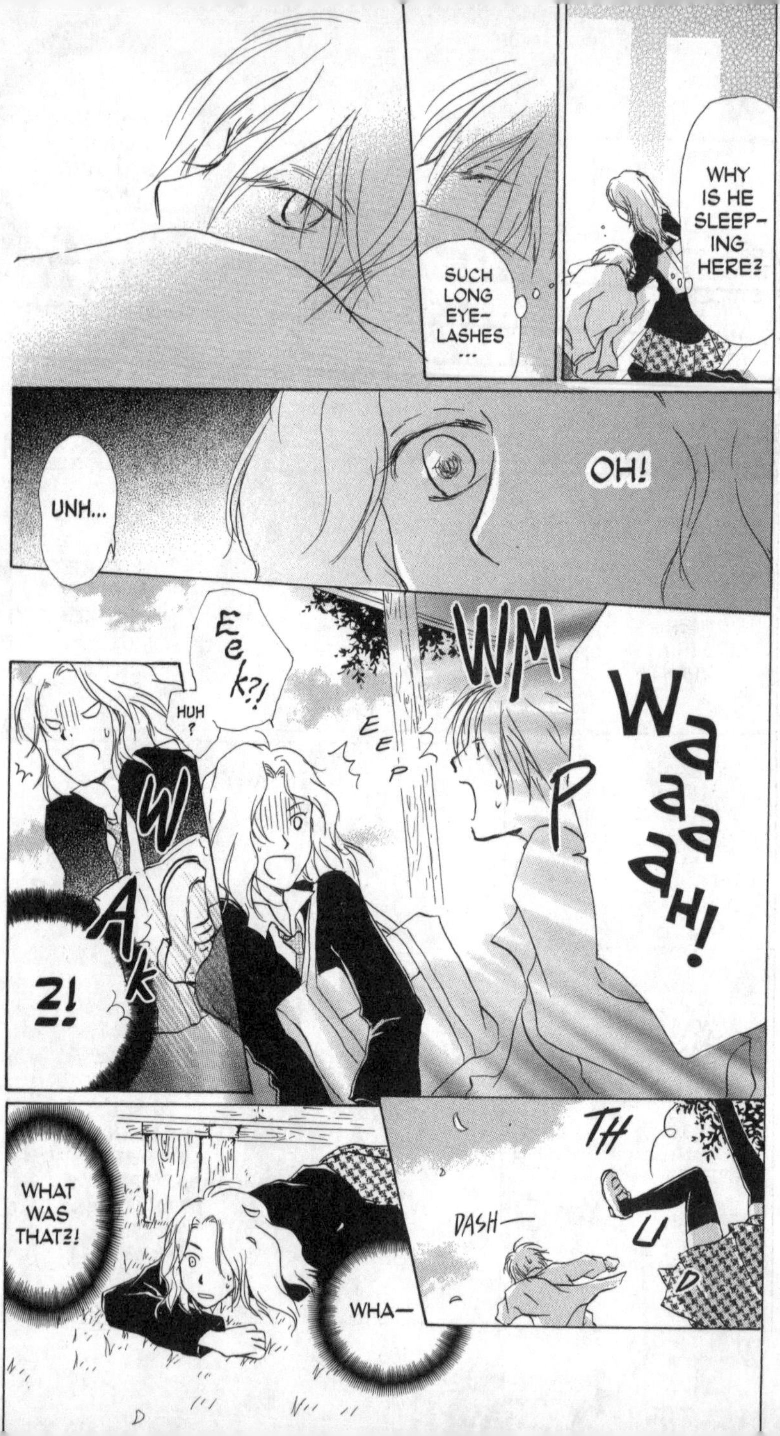
WHY IS HE SLEEPING HERE?
SUCH LONG EYELASHES...
OH!
UNH...
WMP
Waaaah!
Eek?!
EEP
HUH?
WAK?!
THUD
DASH—
WHAT WAS THAT?!
WHA—

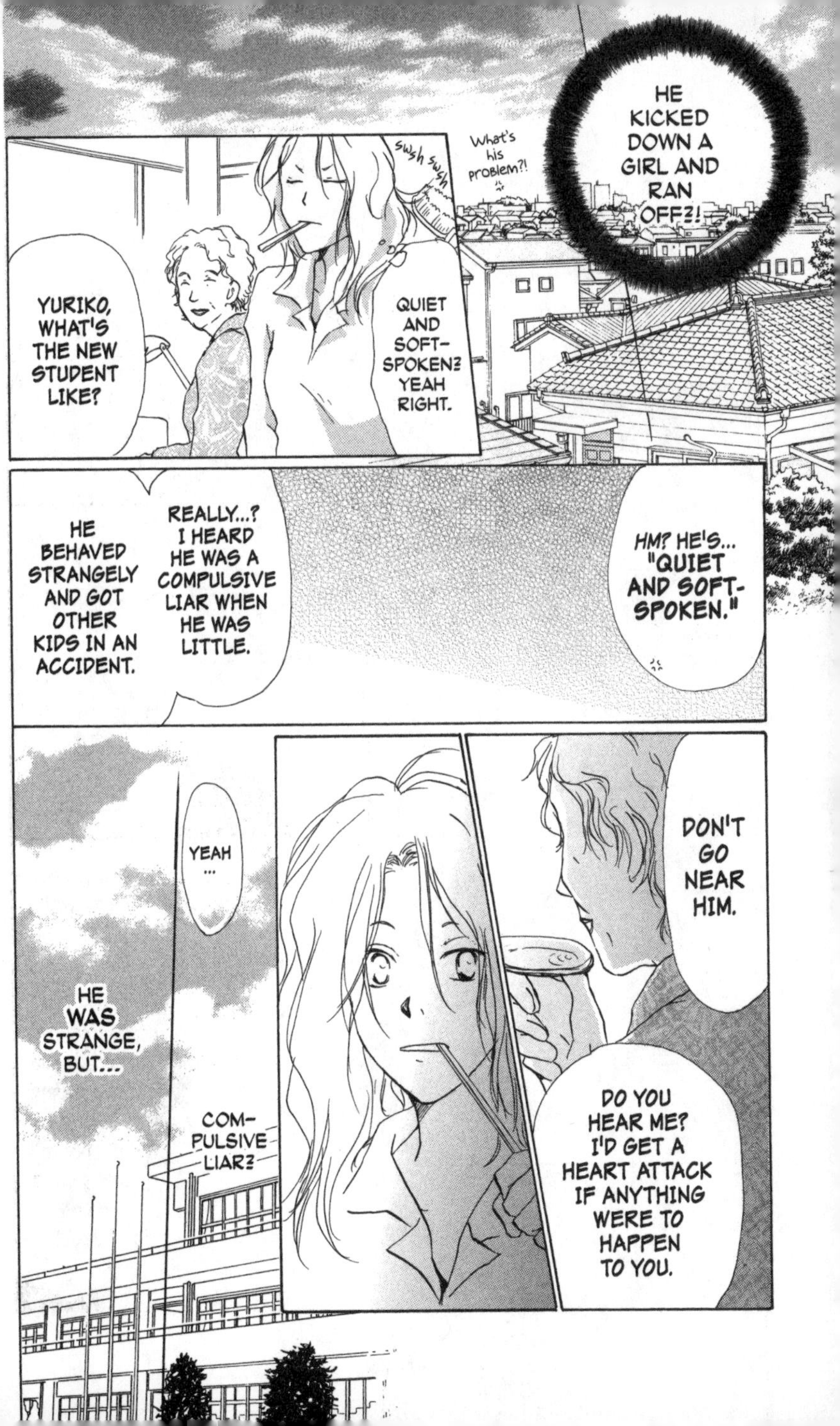
HE KICKED DOWN A GIRL AND RAN OFF?!
What's his problem?!
swsh swsh
QUIET AND SOFT-SPOKEN? YEAH RIGHT.
YURIKO, WHAT'S THE NEW STUDENT LIKE?
HM? HE'S... "QUIET AND SOFT-SPOKEN."
REALLY...? I HEARD HE WAS A COMPULSIVE LIAR WHEN HE WAS LITTLE.
HE BEHAVED STRANGELY AND GOT OTHER KIDS IN AN ACCIDENT.
DON'T GO NEAR HIM.
DO YOU HEAR ME? I'D GET A HEART ATTACK IF ANYTHING WERE TO HAPPEN TO YOU.
YEAH...
HE WAS STRANGE, BUT...
COMPULSIVE LIAR?

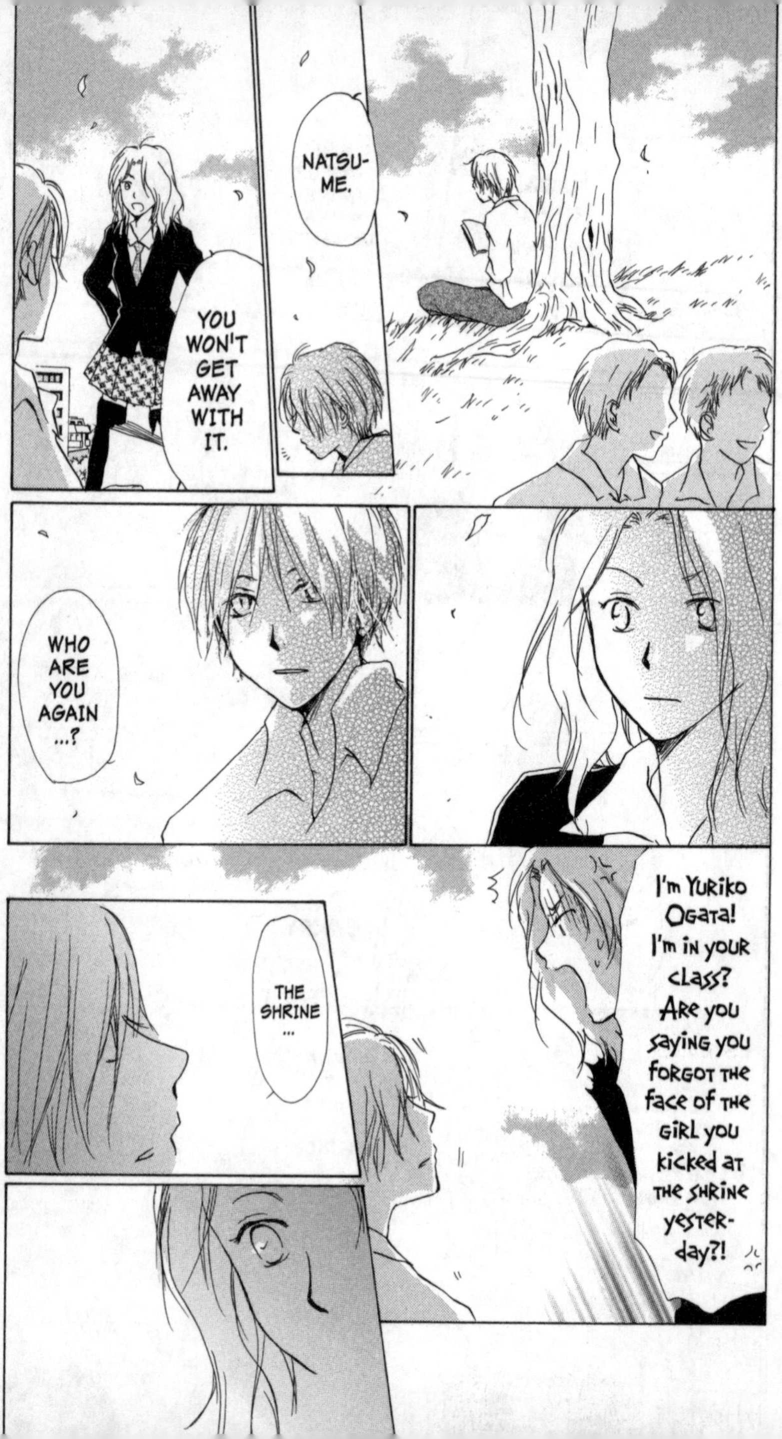
NATSU-ME.
YOU WON'T GET AWAY WITH IT.
WHO ARE YOU AGAIN ...?
I'm Yuriko Ogata! I'm in your class? Are you saying you forgot the face of the girl you kicked at the shrine yester-day?!
THE SHRINE ...

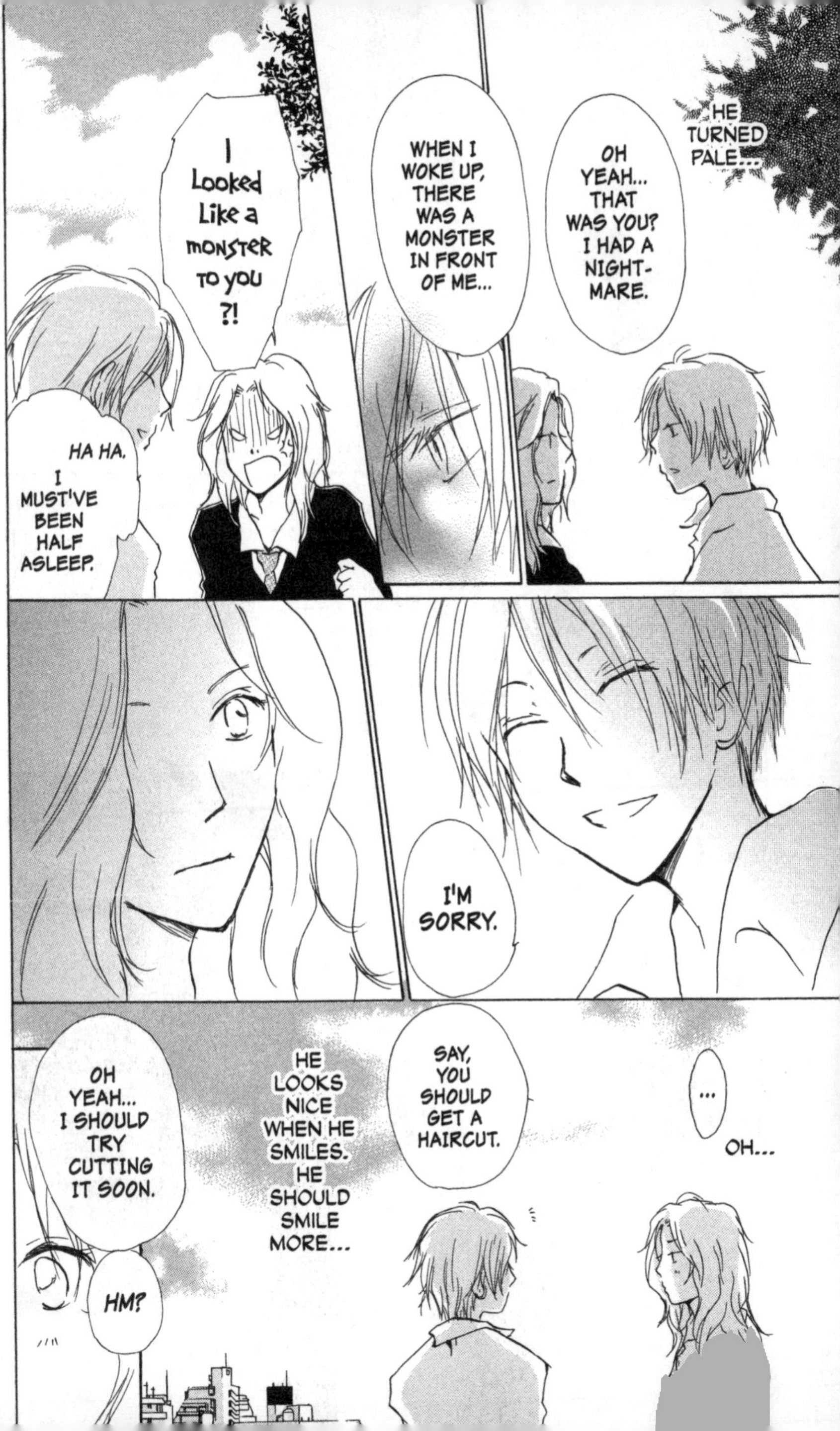

HE TURNED PALE...
OH YEAH... THAT WAS YOU? I HAD A NIGHT-MARE.
WHEN I WOKE UP, THERE WAS A MONSTER IN FRONT OF ME...
I Looked Like a monster to you ?!
HA HA. I MUST'VE BEEN HALF ASLEEP.
I'M SORRY.
...
OH...
SAY, YOU SHOULD GET A HAIRCUT.
HE LOOKS NICE WHEN HE SMILES. HE SHOULD SMILE MORE...
OH YEAH... I SHOULD TRY CUTTING IT SOON.
HM?

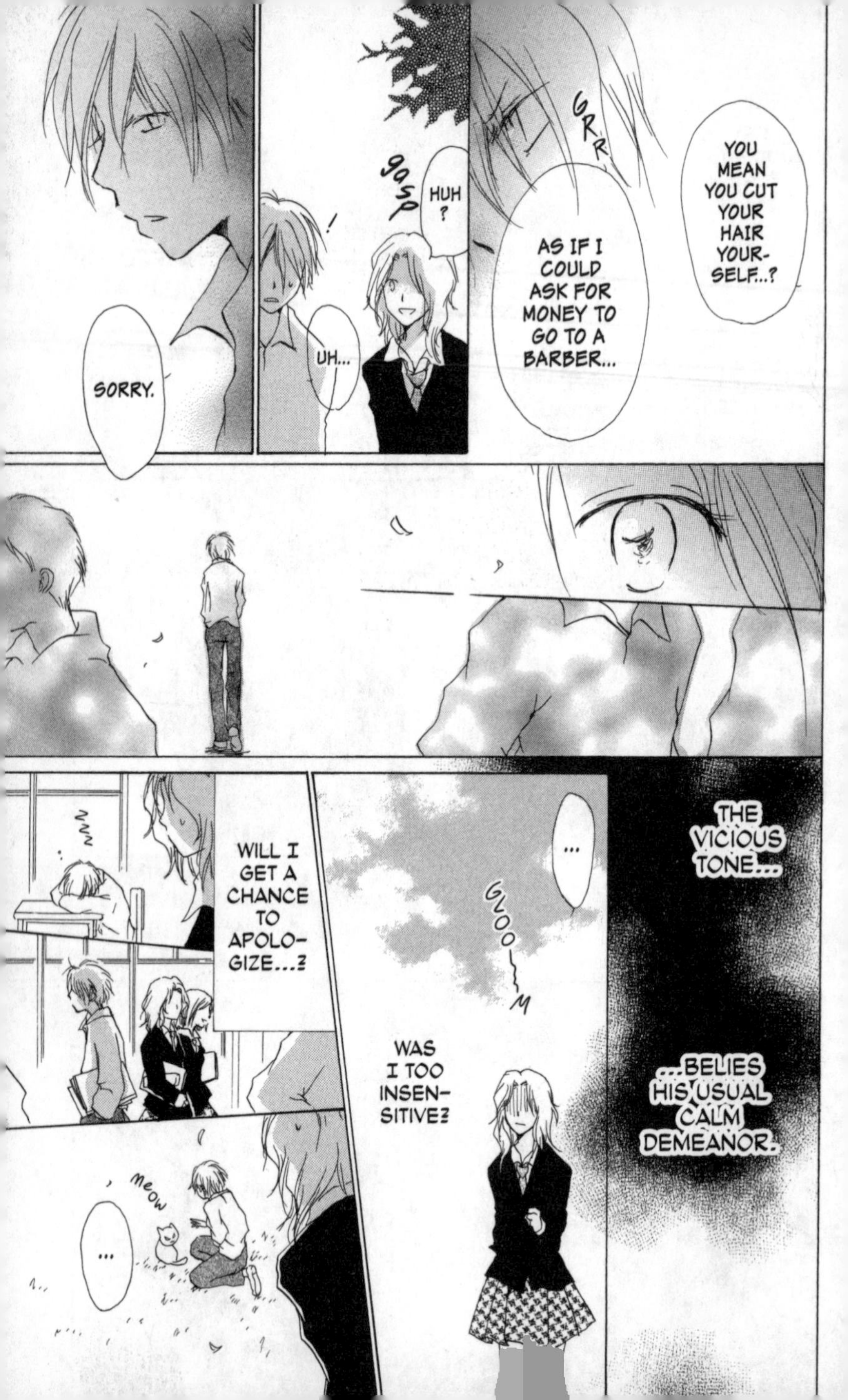
YOU MEAN YOU CUT YOUR HAIR YOURSELF...?
GRR
AS IF I COULD ASK FOR MONEY TO GO TO A BARBER...
HUH?
gasp
!
UH...
SORRY.
THE VICIOUS TONE...
...BELIES HIS USUAL CALM DEMEANOR.
...
GLOOM
WAS I TOO INSENSITIVE?
WILL I GET A CHANCE TO APOLOGIZE...?
ZZZ
meow
...

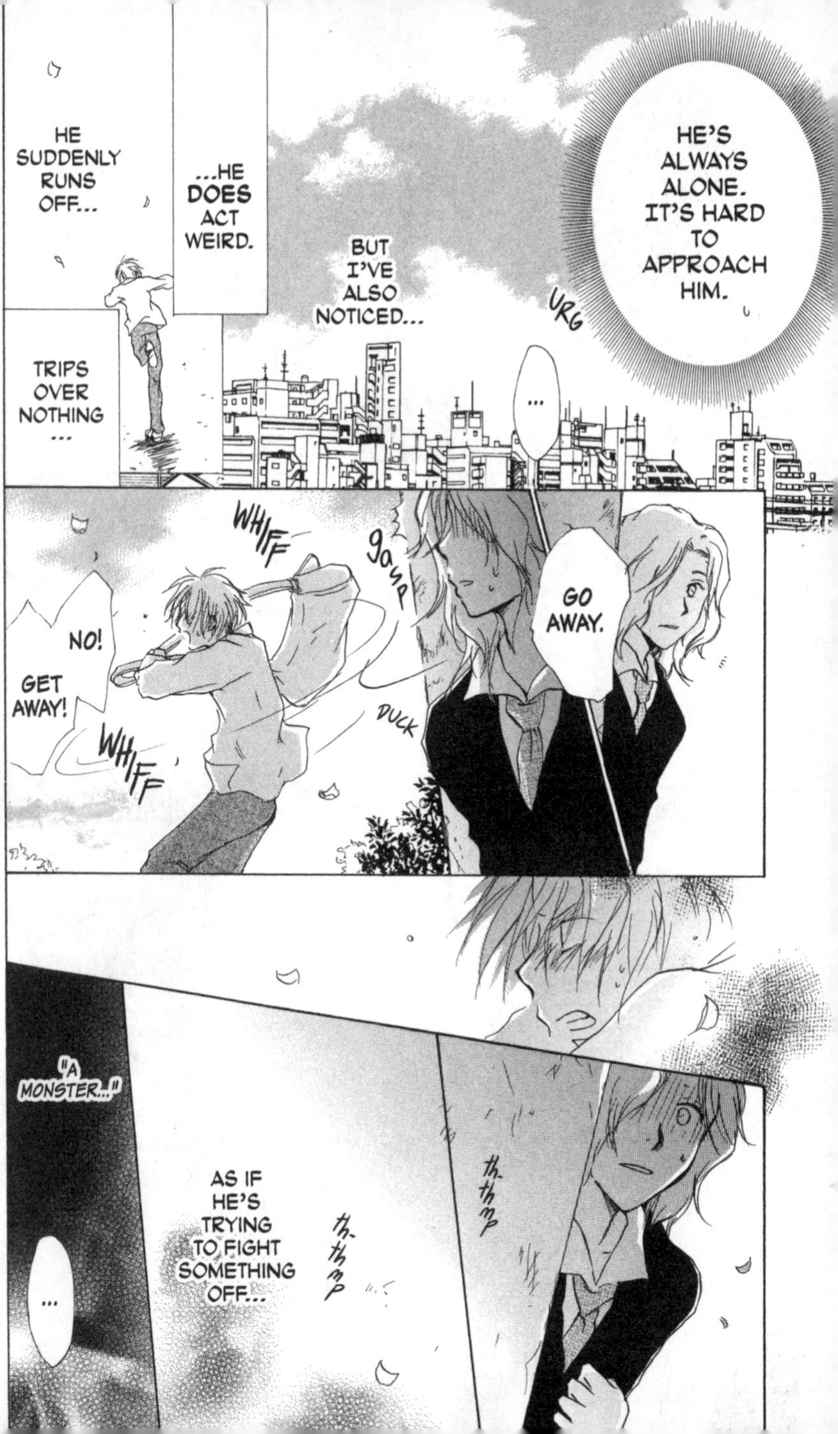
HE'S ALWAYS ALONE. IT'S HARD TO APPROACH HIM.
URG
...
BUT I'VE ALSO NOTICED...
...HE DOES ACT WEIRD.
HE SUDDENLY RUNS OFF...
TRIPS OVER NOTHING ...
GO AWAY.
gasp
WHIFF
DUCK
NO!
GET AWAY!
WHIFF
th-thmp
"A MONSTER..."
AS IF HE'S TRYING TO FIGHT SOMETHING OFF...
th-thmp
...

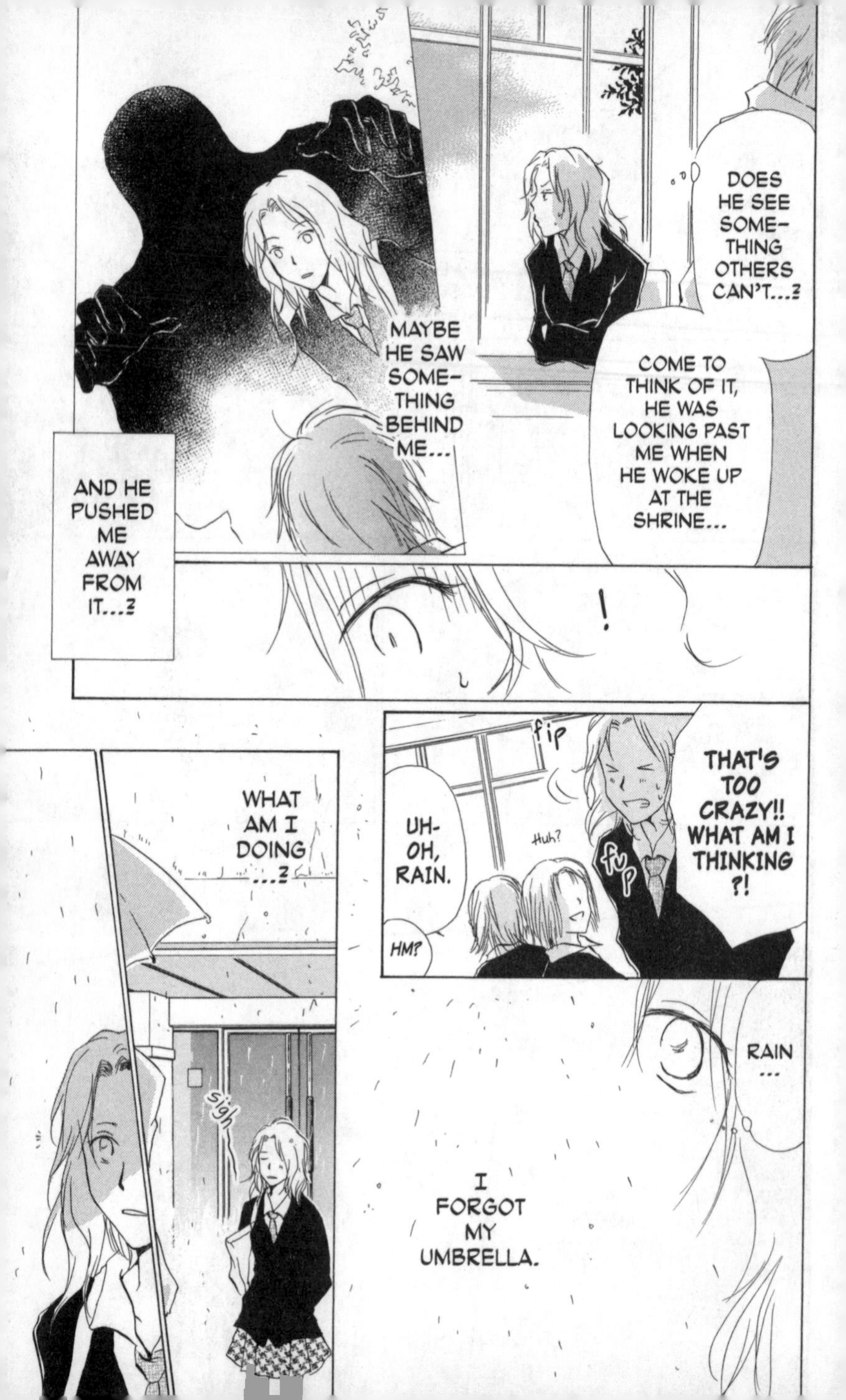
DOES HE SEE SOME-THING OTHERS CAN'T...?
COME TO THINK OF IT, HE WAS LOOKING PAST ME WHEN HE WOKE UP AT THE SHRINE...
MAYBE HE SAW SOME-THING BEHIND ME...
AND HE PUSHED ME AWAY FROM IT...?
!
fip
THAT'S TOO CRAZY!! WHAT AM I THINKING?!
fup
Huh?
UH-OH, RAIN.
HM?
RAIN...
I FORGOT MY UMBRELLA.
WHAT AM I DOING...?
sigh

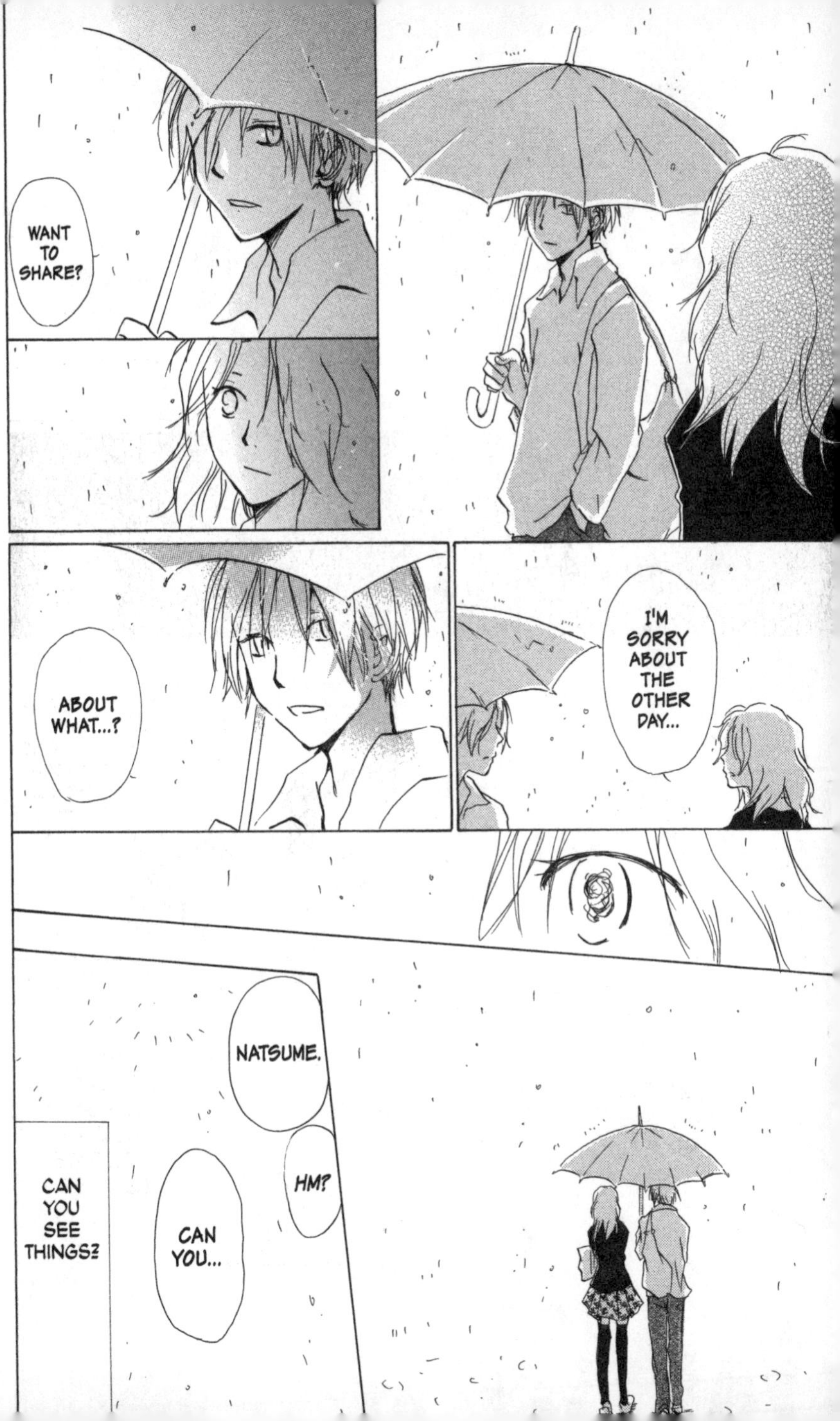
WANT TO SHARE?
I'M SORRY ABOUT THE OTHER DAY...
ABOUT WHAT...?
NATSUME.
HM?
CAN YOU...
CAN YOU SEE THINGS?

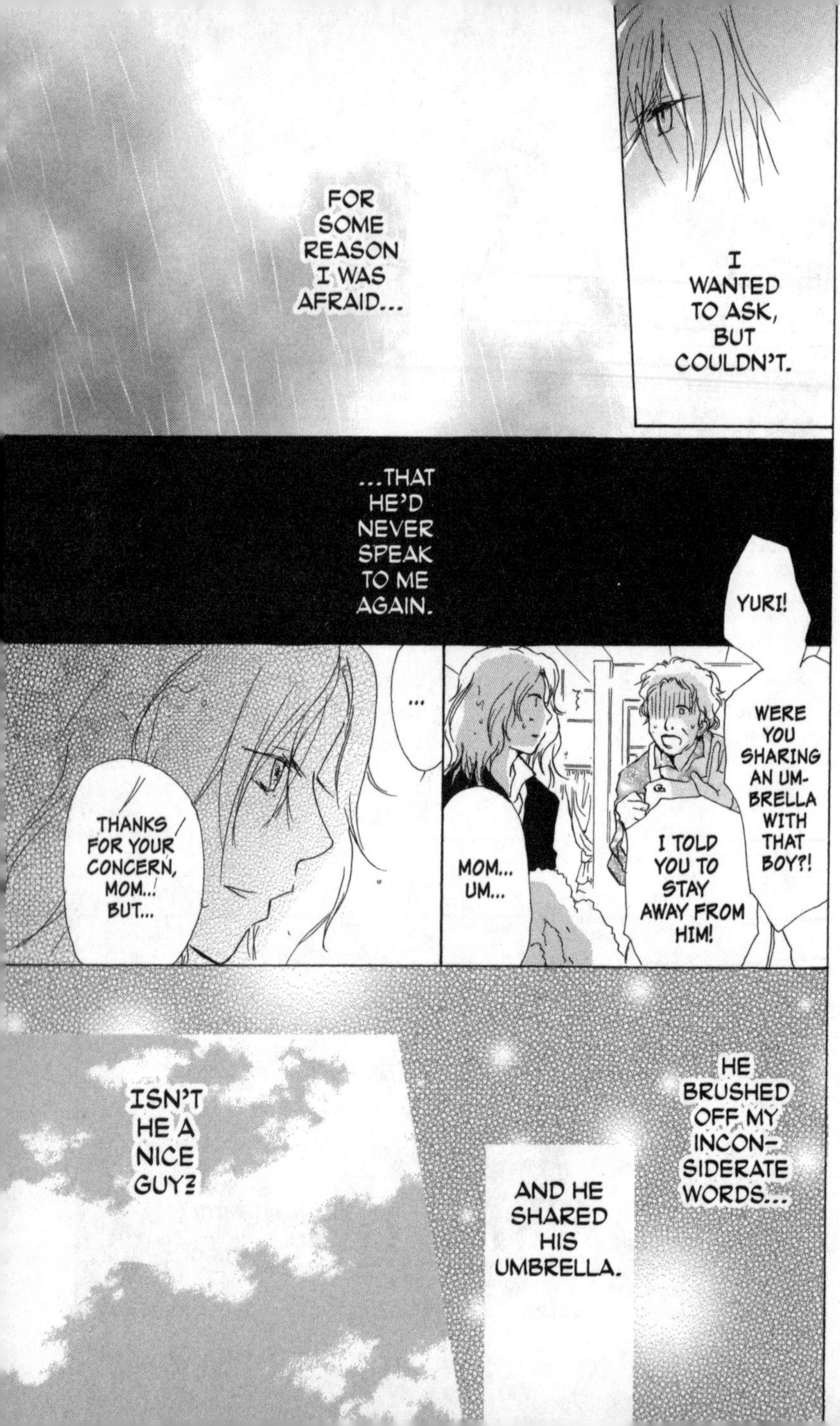
I WANTED TO ASK, BUT COULDN'T.
FOR SOME REASON I WAS AFRAID...
...THAT HE'D NEVER SPEAK TO ME AGAIN.
YURI!
WERE YOU SHARING AN UMBRELLA WITH THAT BOY?!
I TOLD YOU TO STAY AWAY FROM HIM!
MOM... UM...
...
THANKS FOR YOUR CONCERN, MOM... BUT...
HE BRUSHED OFF MY INCONSIDERATE WORDS...
AND HE SHARED HIS UMBRELLA.
ISN'T HE A NICE GUY?

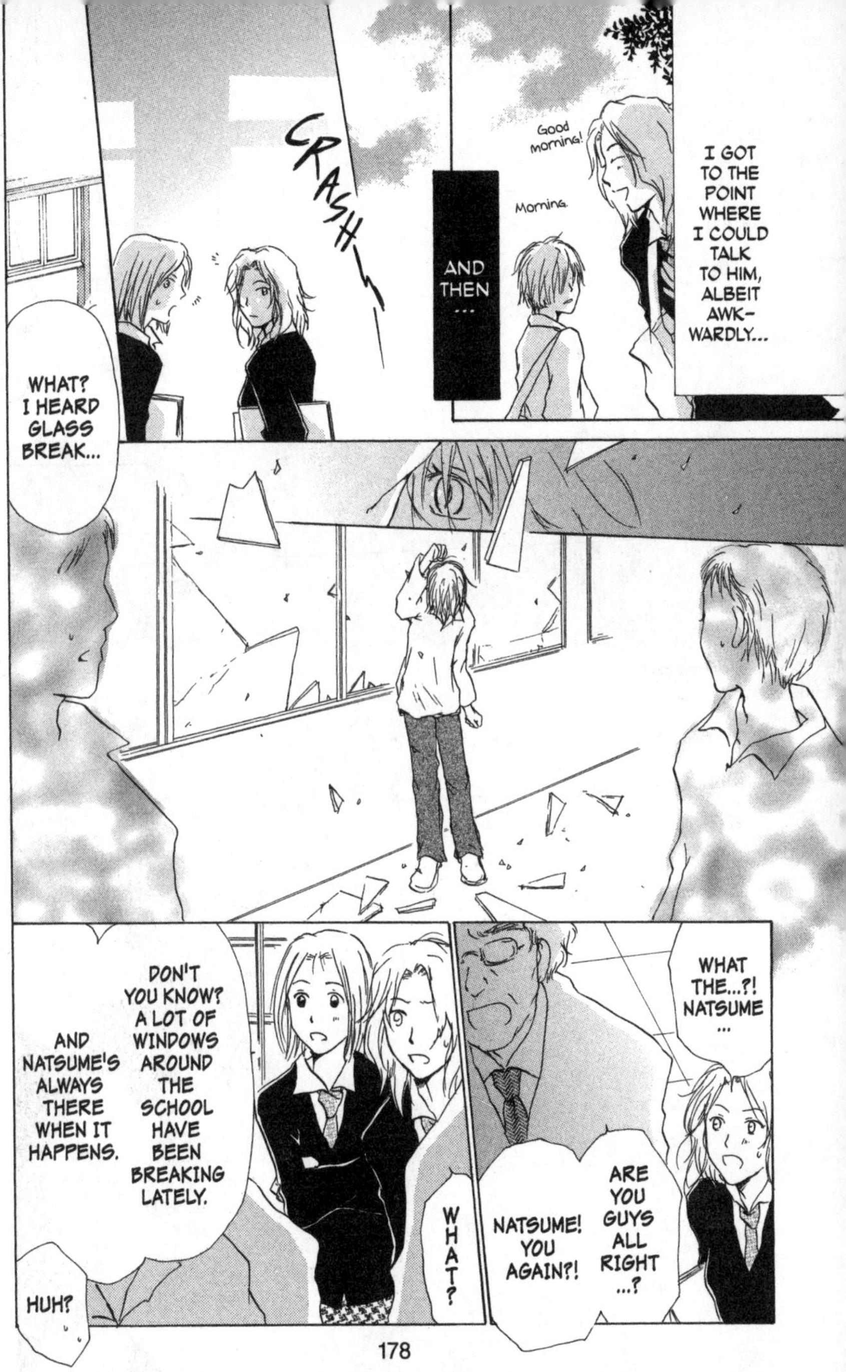
I GOT TO THE POINT WHERE I COULD TALK TO HIM, ALBEIT AWK-WARDLY...
Good morning!
Morning.
AND THEN...
CRASH
WHAT? I HEARD GLASS BREAK...
WHAT THE...?! NATSUME...
ARE YOU GUYS ALL RIGHT...?
NATSUME! YOU AGAIN?!
WHAT?
DON'T YOU KNOW? A LOT OF WINDOWS AROUND THE SCHOOL HAVE BEEN BREAKING LATELY.
AND NATSUME'S ALWAYS THERE WHEN IT HAPPENS.
HUH?

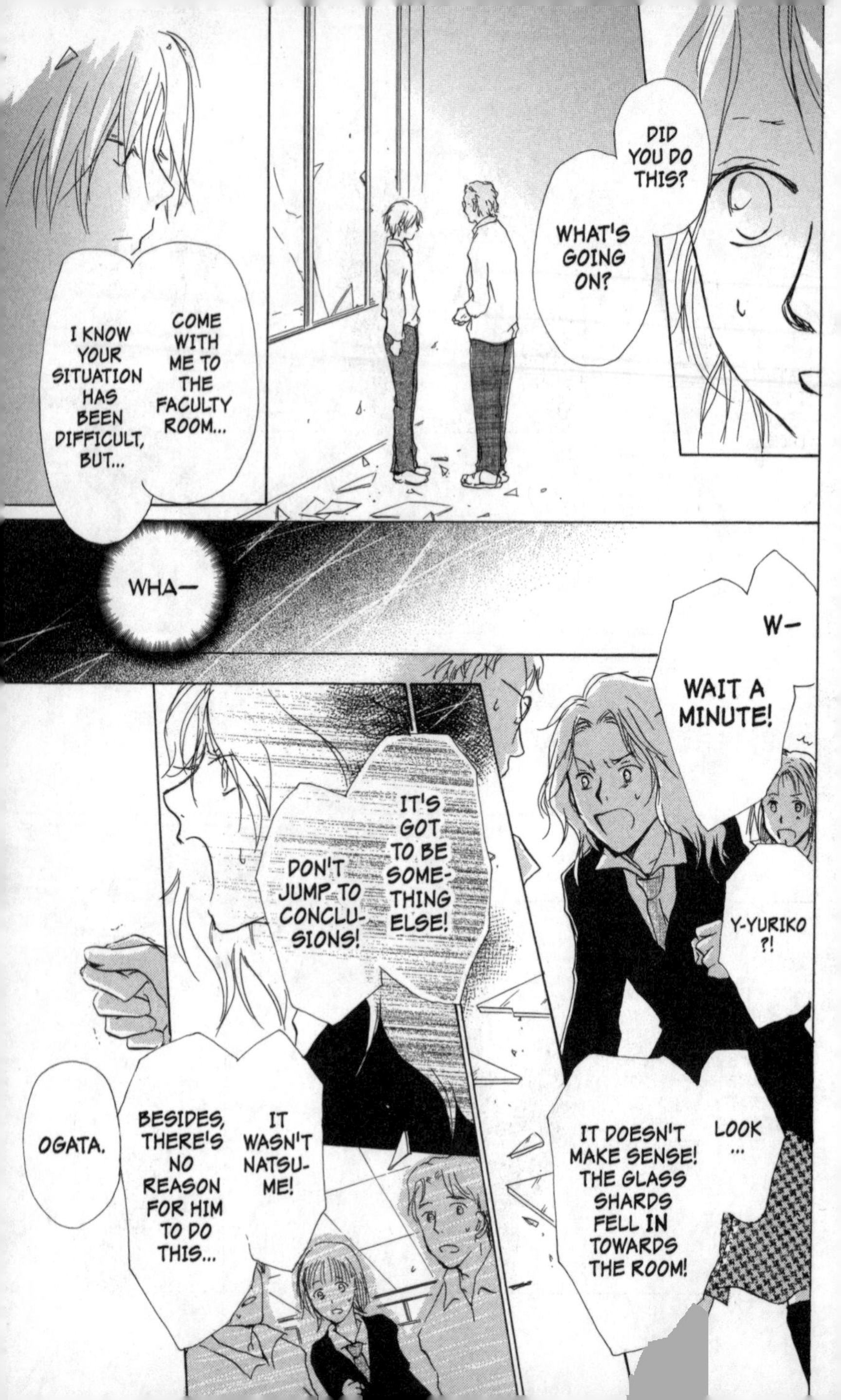

DID YOU DO THIS?
WHAT'S GOING ON?
COME WITH ME TO THE FACULTY ROOM...
I KNOW YOUR SITUATION HAS BEEN DIFFICULT, BUT...
WHA—
W—
WAIT A MINUTE!
Y-YURIKO?!
IT'S GOT TO BE SOME-THING ELSE!
DON'T JUMP TO CONCLU-SIONS!
LOOK...
IT DOESN'T MAKE SENSE! THE GLASS SHARDS FELL IN TOWARDS THE ROOM!
IT WASN'T NATSU-ME!
BESIDES, THERE'S NO REASON FOR HIM TO DO THIS...
OGATA.

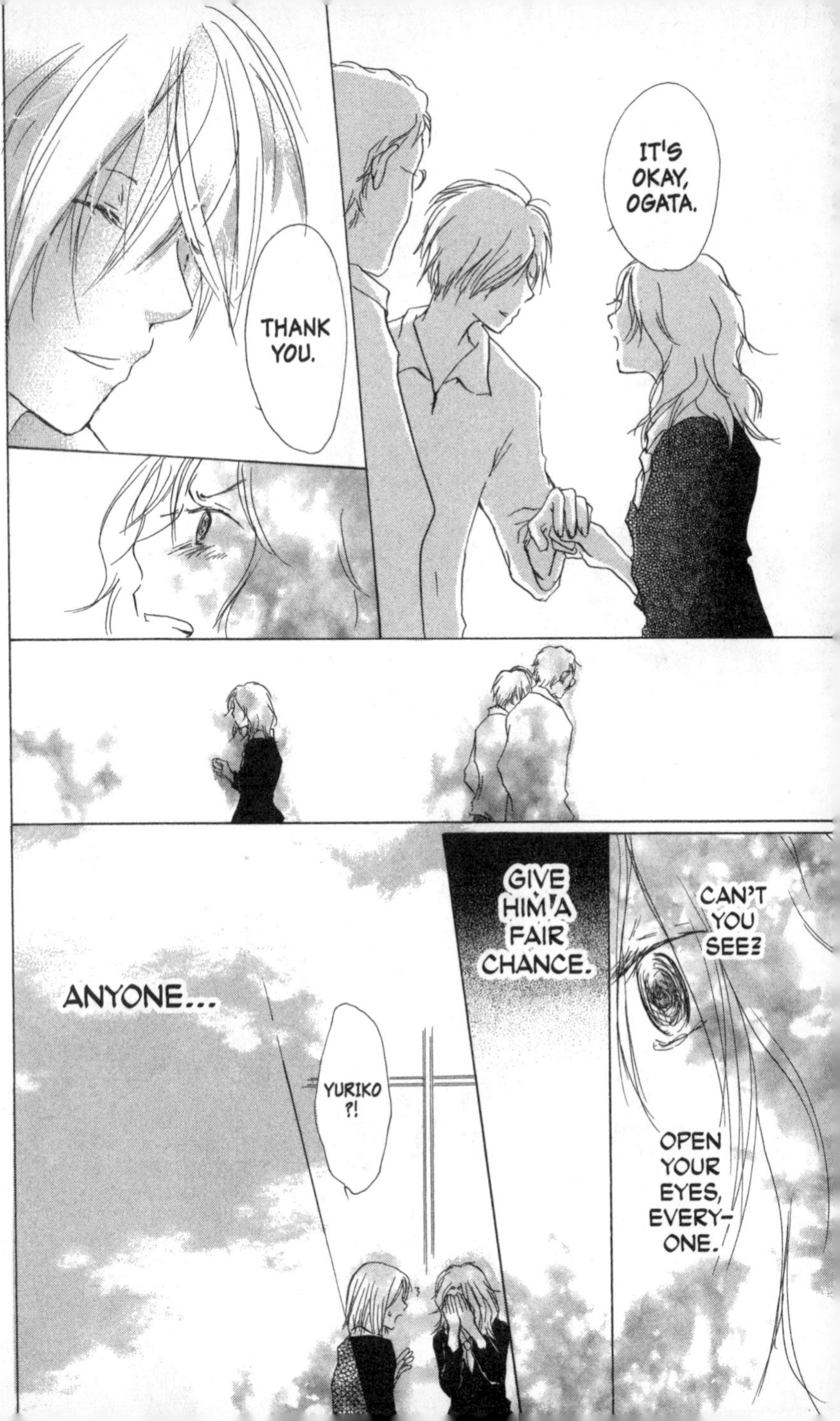
IT'S OKAY, OGATA.
THANK YOU.
CAN'T YOU SEE?
OPEN YOUR EYES, EVERYONE.
GIVE HIM A FAIR CHANCE.
ANYONE...
YURIKO?!

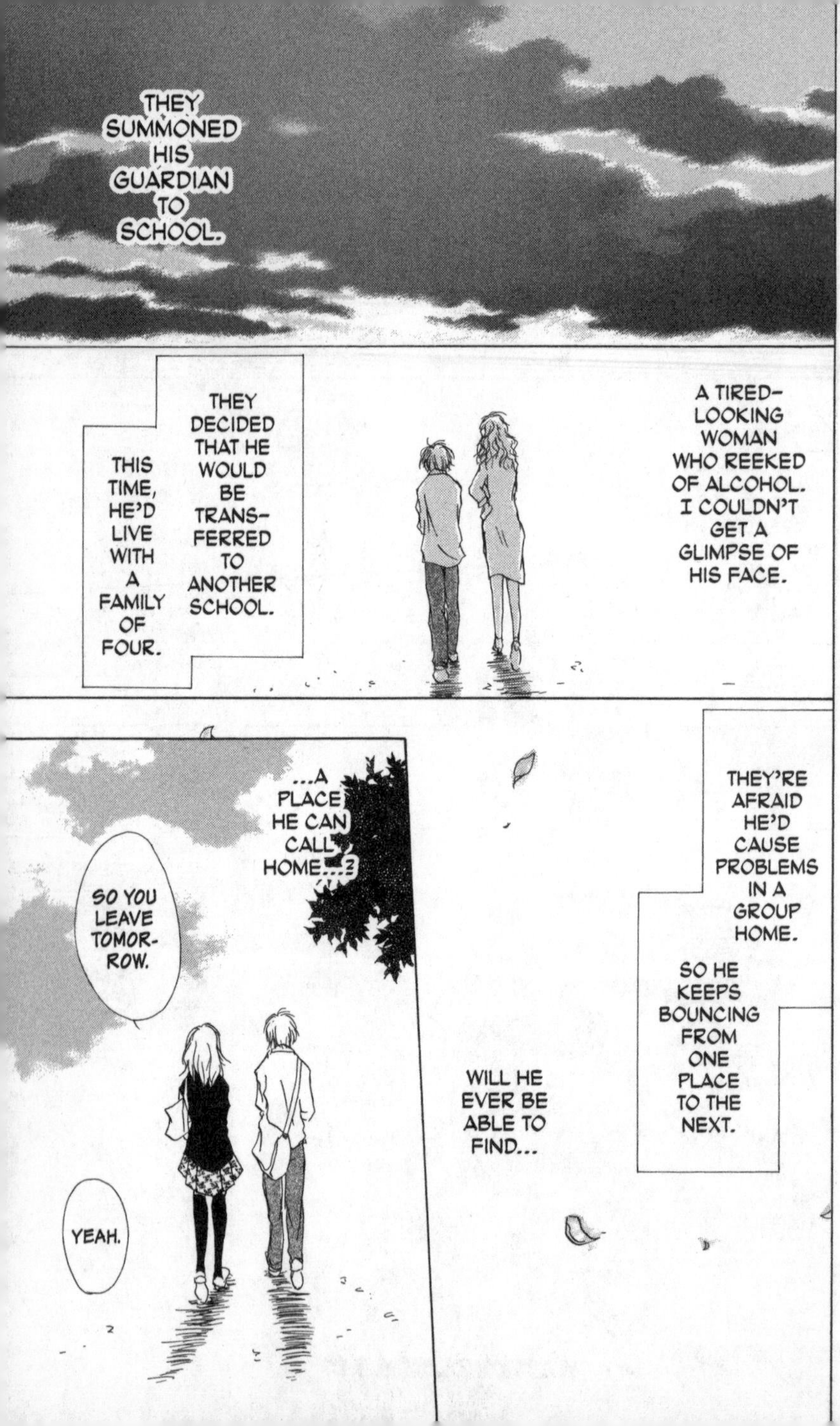
THEY SUMMONED HIS GUARDIAN TO SCHOOL.
A TIRED-LOOKING WOMAN WHO REEKED OF ALCOHOL. I COULDN'T GET A GLIMPSE OF HIS FACE.
THEY DECIDED THAT HE WOULD BE TRANSFERRED TO ANOTHER SCHOOL.
THIS TIME, HE'D LIVE WITH A FAMILY OF FOUR.
THEY'RE AFRAID HE'D CAUSE PROBLEMS IN A GROUP HOME.
SO HE KEEPS BOUNCING FROM ONE PLACE TO THE NEXT.
WILL HE EVER BE ABLE TO FIND...
...A PLACE HE CAN CALL HOME...?
SO YOU LEAVE TOMORROW.
YEAH.

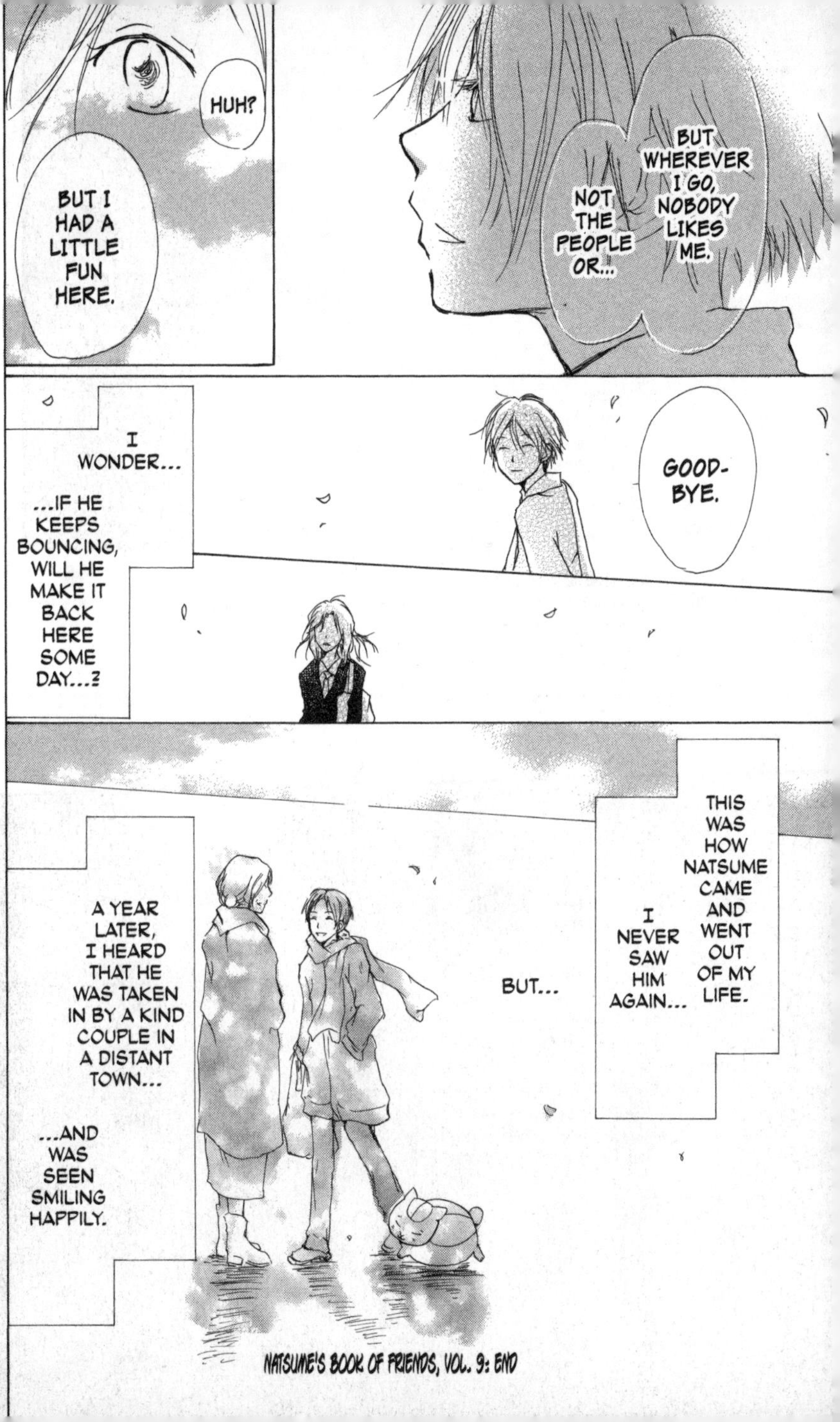
BUT WHEREVER I GO, NOBODY LIKES ME.
NOT THE PEOPLE OR...
HUH?
BUT I HAD A LITTLE FUN HERE.
GOOD-BYE.
I WONDER...
...IF HE KEEPS BOUNCING, WILL HE MAKE IT BACK HERE SOME DAY...?
THIS WAS HOW NATSUME CAME AND WENT OUT OF MY LIFE.
I NEVER SAW HIM AGAIN...
BUT...
A YEAR LATER, I HEARD THAT HE WAS TAKEN IN BY A KIND COUPLE IN A DISTANT TOWN...
...AND WAS SEEN SMILING HAPPILY.

NATSUME'S BOOK OF FRIENDS, VOL. 9: END

# AFTER-WORD

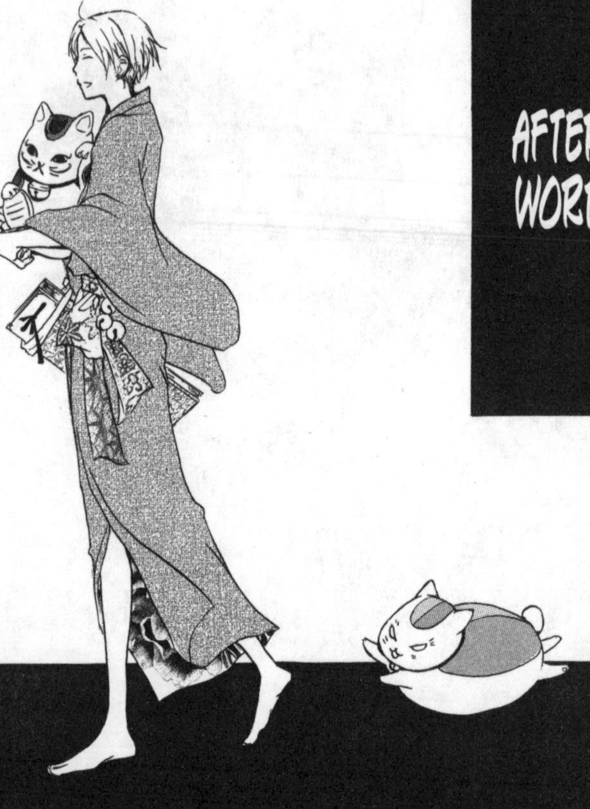

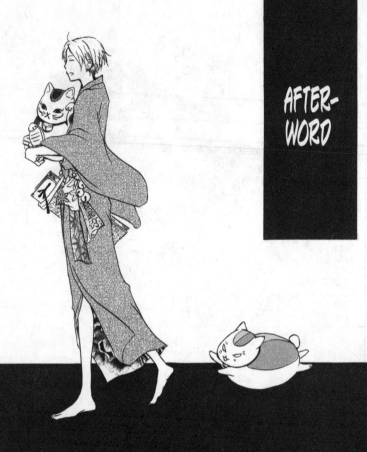

Thank you for reading. How did you like it? Please read this afterword at the end to avoid spoilers.

Natsume used to handle everything by himself because he didn't want to bother anyone, but now he's going to encounter some things beyond his ability. He kept avoiding the issue of relying on others, but I hope to give him the strength and the courage to face it.

And now, the afterword.

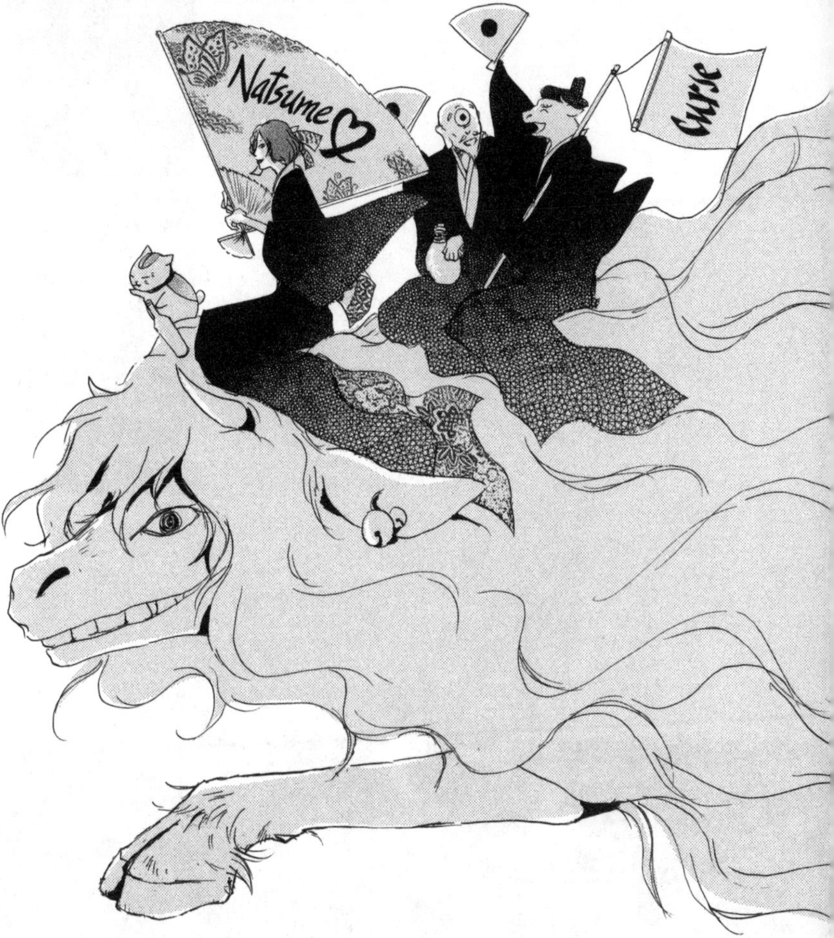
Natsume
Curse

## CHAPTERS 32, 33  Little One

I decided it was about time to draw something cute, and thought it would be fun to have an onslaught of fluffies. I feel lonely somehow when I draw Natsume and Nyanko Sensei alone together, which I hadn't experienced in a while. I only realized after I started the work how difficult it was to depict growing affection towards a creature that doesn't talk or even show any emotion. It was nerve-wracking. I also got to draw a two-page spread, so I had fun even though it was tough overall.

## CHAPTERS 34-36  The Eastern Forest

I suspect it's getting harder for Natsume to keep secrets. He doesn't particularly need to announce to people what he can see, but his dilemma is that the lies are snowballing. Still, it's a big deal for him that he has Taki and Tanuma, who are there to listen to the truth. This episode made Natsume even more leery of exorcists. But I think it'll get him to start thinking seriously about what to do with himself and about Reiko, about whom he assumed there wouldn't be anything nice to hear.

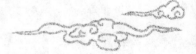

## SPECIAL EPISODE 9

It's been a while since I've done a story from a girl's perspective, and it was so much easier. This episode was published a while ago, before "A Place to Belong." But there were quite a few people who read "A Place to Belong" without having read this episode, who wrote in speculating the reason why his hair could be a little long. It made me really happy as a creator. I was happy yet nervous that people do notice the little details.

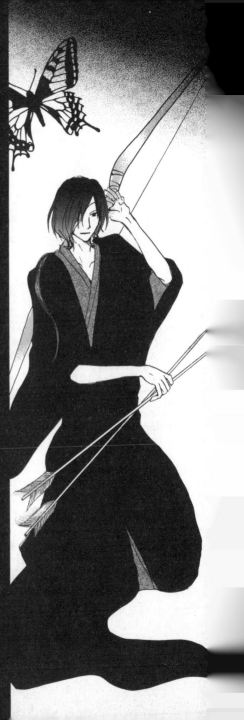

In the ninth volume, I focused on herds and groups. Like the fuzzballs, the clan of simian masks, Matoba and his people, Natsume and his pals, etc. Groups can be greatly helpful or a huge nuisance. Since Natsume likes to be a loner, I challenged him with things he'd prefer to avoid.

He sees the nuisance and the risks associated with relying on others, but I hope that these experiences will open his eyes and allow him to grow, and then maybe he and Nyanko Sensei can be more honest with how they feel towards each other.

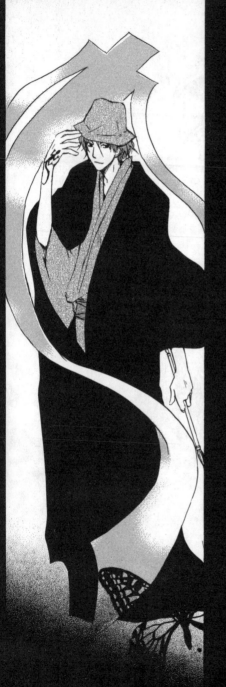

I enjoyed drawing a bit about Matoba. He has several titles. He's the organizer of the assembly of exorcists, so he's called "Chairman" during the meetings. He's the young head of the family from a regular human perspective, and known as the leader of his clan to yokai.

Natsume has been more relaxed lately, so it's very fun to draw something tense like this once in a while. I'd like to write thoroughly about exorcists some time when I have the opportunity.

Seeing Matoba and Natori side by side here, they're clearly eccentrics. I'm relieved that Natsume seems normal by comparison.

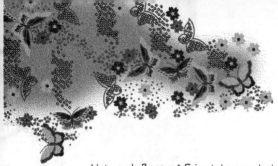

Natsume's Book of Friends has reached nine volumes. I'm savoring the experience and joys of developing characters over such a long period of time. I'm sure the people who have known me from my previous titles are amazed. I've received love and support from so many people, and I'm extremely grateful to everyone, including any new readers and people who have become fans through the lovingly created anime.

I'll keep drawing each episode with care.

Thank you again.

Nov. 2009

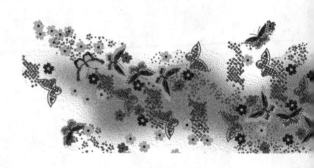

**Yuki Midorikawa**
**c/o Shojo Beat**
**Published by VIZ Media, LLC.**
**P.O. Box 77010**
**San Francicso, CA 94107**

My heroes:
Tamao Ohki
Chika
Mika
My sister
Mr. Sato
   Thank you.

AFTERWORD: END

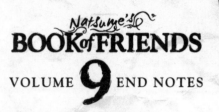
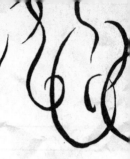

# Natsume's BOOK of FRIENDS

## VOLUME 9 END NOTES

**PAGE 72, PANEL 2:** *Festival*
Japanese festivals typically feature street stalls selling food, cheap souvenirs and toys, and booths of carnival games.

**PAGE 108, PANEL 5:** *Paulownia*
A fast-growing tree that produces lightweight, warp-resistant timber with a high ignition point, and is thus prized for making chests and furniture.

**PAGE 123, PANEL 5:** *Sweetfish*
A small fish related to smelt, aromatic when grilled and highly prized in Asia.

**PAGE 167, PANEL 2:** *Marks on paper*
On school tests in Japan, checkmarks are commonly used for wrong answers, and circles are used for right answers.

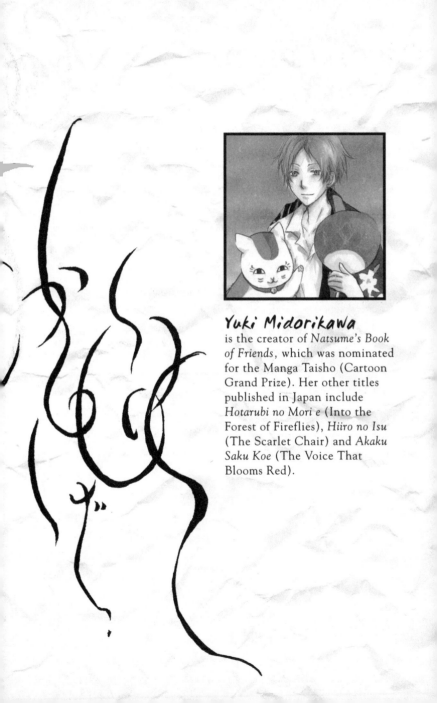

**Yuki Midorikawa**
is the creator of *Natsume's Book of Friends*, which was nominated for the Manga Taisho (Cartoon Grand Prize). Her other titles published in Japan include *Hotarubi no Mori e* (Into the Forest of Fireflies), *Hiiro no Isu* (The Scarlet Chair) and *Akaku Saku Koe* (The Voice That Blooms Red).

# NATSUME'S BOOK OF FRIENDS

Vol. 9
Shojo Beat Edition

STORY AND ART BY Yuki Midorikawa

Translation & Adaptation Lillian Olsen
Touch-up Art & Lettering Sabrina Heep
Design Fawn Lau
Editor Pancha Diaz

Natsume Yujincho by Yuki Midorikawa
© Yuki Midorikawa 2010
All rights reserved.
First published in Japan in 2010 by HAKUSENSHA, Inc., Tokyo.
English language translation rights arranged with HAKUSENSHA, Inc., Tokyo.

The stories, characters and incidents mentioned in this publication are entirely fictional.

Printed in Canada

Published by VIZ Media, LLC
P.O. Box 77010
San Francisco, CA 94107

10 9 8 7 6 5 4 3
First printing, October 2011
Third printing, October 2020

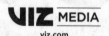

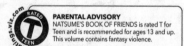

**PARENTAL ADVISORY**
NATSUME'S BOOK OF FRIENDS is rated T for Teen and is recommended for ages 13 and up. This volume contains fantasy violence.

# SURPRISE!

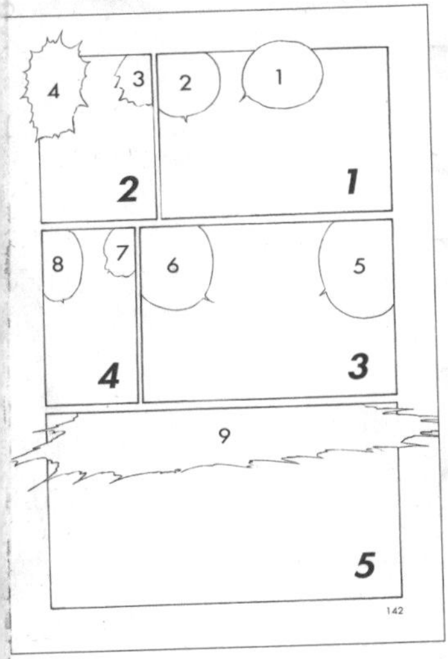
1
2
1
3
4
2
5
6
3
7
8
4
9
5
142

## You may be reading the wrong way!

It's true: In keeping with the original Japanese comic format, this book reads from right to left—so action, sound effects, and word balloons are completely reversed. This preserves the orientation of the original artwork—plus, it's fun! Check out the diagram shown here to get the hang of things, and then turn to the other side of the book to get started!

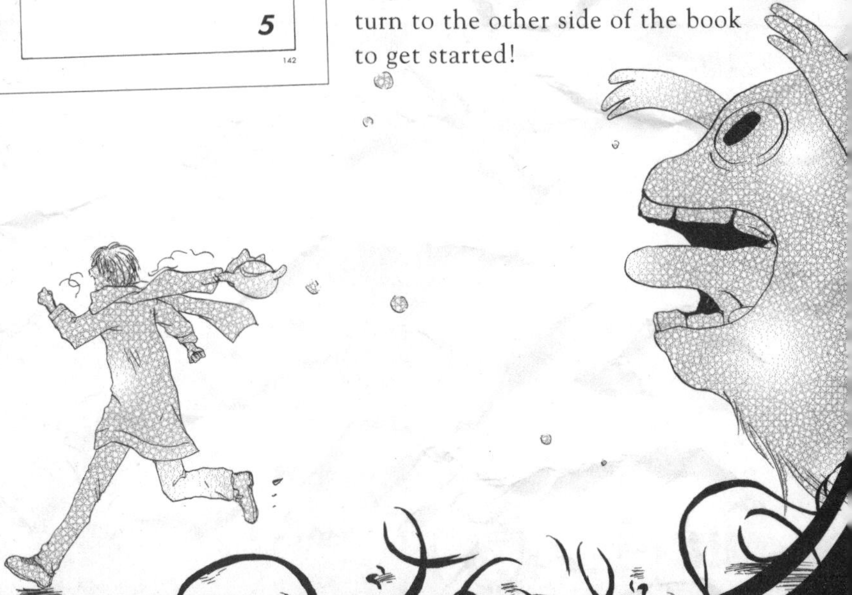

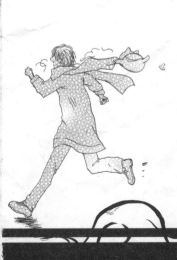